D1337251

Seven Years Old
in the
Home Environment

Publications from the Child Development Research Unit
University of Nottingham

Studies in Urban Childhood

Newson, John and Elizabeth, *Infant Care in an Urban Community* (George Allen & Unwin, 1963; Penguin Books, 1971)

Newson, John and Elizabeth, *Four Years Old in an Urban Community* (George Allen & Unwin, 1968; Penguin Books, 1970)

Hewett, Sheila, with John and Elizabeth Newson, *The Family and the Handicapped Child* (George Allen & Unwin, 1970)

Hewett, Sheila, *The Need for Long-Term Care: factors influencing the admission of children to hospitals for the subnormal, Occasional Paper 3* (IMMR, Butterworths, 1972)

Gregory, Susan, *The Deaf Child and his Family* (George Allen & Unwin, 1976)

Other publications

Cummings, Peter, *Education and the Severely Handicapped Child* (NSMHC, 1973)

Gillham, W. E. C. and Hesse, K. A., *The Nottingham Number Test* (University of London Press, 1974)

Gillham, W. E. C., *Teaching a Child to Read* (University of London Press, 1974)

Gillham, W. E. C. (ed.), *Psychology Today* (Hodder & Stoughton, 1975)

Gillham, W. E. C. (trans.), Vurpillot, E., *The Visual World of the Child* (George Allen & Unwin, 1976)

Newson, John and Matthews, M. L., *The Language of Basic Statistics* (Longman, 1971)

Seven Years Old
in the
Home Environment

John and Elizabeth Newson

Child Development Research Unit
University of Nottingham

London
George Allen & Unwin Ltd
Ruskin House   Museum Street

First published in 1976

© George Allen & Unwin Ltd, 1976

ISBN 0 04 136015 x

Printed in Great Britain
in 10 point Times Roman type
by Clarke, Doble & Brendon Ltd
Plymouth

Acknowledgements

The research programme of which the third stage is reported in this book was financed initially by generous grants from the Nuffield Foundation, and was subsequently supported, equally generously, by the Social Science Research Council. Our indebtedness to these bodies is great. In thanking them for recurrent kindnesses, we should also like to acknowledge our gratitude to the University of Nottingham, which has since given this research that measure of financial security which all long-term projects hope for and too few achieve.

In order to follow a large group of children through time, we are very dependent on the goodwill and co-operation of local authority departments, on whose efficient record-keeping we rely for sampling purposes and for tracing children who have moved. The City of Nottingham Health and Education Departments have actively given us their help over many years now; that we have come to expect their co-operation does not mean that we are less aware of our good fortune in having chosen to work in a city with a research-minded authority. Especial thanks are due to past and present Medical Officers of Health, Dr William Dodd and Dr Wilfrid Parry, and to past and present Directors of Education, Mr W. G. Jackson, Mr D. J. W. Sowell and Mr James Stone. To Mr B. O. Neep, Chief Education Welfare Officer, and his staff, we are particularly grateful for their unfailing kindness and friendliness on the many occasions when we have interrupted their work to check a new batch of addresses.

We probably demand far more than is reasonable of our interviewers: they not only have to maintain a very high level of interviewing skill, and code the results in rather complicated ways, but they are expected to contribute ideas, insights and expertise in long work sessions during the gestation of new interview schedules. If we seem to take their talents for granted, it must be because they offer them with such apparently effortless generosity; but we are endlessly appreciative of their efficiency as colleagues and of their niceness as friends. Our warmest thanks to Diane Barnes, Jean Crossland, Jean Jacobs, Dady Key and Margaret Rose. We have been equally fortunate in research assistants: Malcolm Fletcher had the backroom task of keeping abreast of the longitudinal data, and

Frances Canning looked at a sample of fatherless children for us. To both, our gratitude.

Seven hundred tape-recordings could result in a roomful of untranscribed tapes; that our interviews are condensed into only eight or nine fat books of typed quotations is due to the energy of our transcribers and typists, who finished listening to the last seven-year-old's mother just in time to start on the first of the eleven-year-olds. Thanks to them all, but particularly to Julia Hibbitt, Penelope Key and Beryl West; and to Jean Crossland, who once again transformed our tatty efforts into a meticulously typed book.

Two people ought really to have their names on the cover as coauthors. Our research colleagues Peter Barnes and Dady Key contribute, both creatively and in terms of organisation of data gathering and sheer hard work on data processing, to the success of this research programme. The personal commitment which they have brought to the project has given us incalculable support. Thanks are not quite appropriate from one half of a team to the other: we can only say that we have found working with them exciting and satisfying, and that we hope to prolong this collaboration for many years to come.

Although our own children say that they are now too old to be mentioned by name, we would still like to record our debt to them for giving us the practice to set beside the theory; and especially for teaching us about the total emotional involvement which is a part of the parental condition.

People occasionally comment that our books must be easy to write because the mothers contribute so many of the paragraphs. We must, however, claim considerable industry and effort in choosing amid so much vivid material; often we feel truly self-denying in leaving out some precisely pertinent illustration. Once again, the only possible dedication is to the families who allow us this privileged glimpse of their private lives.

Contents

Tables

The conventions observed in setting out these tables, together with the statistical procedures on which they are based, are explained on pages 21–24 and in Appendix II

Chapter 1

Orientation and Explanation

It is the function of Chapter 1 first to orient the reader to the viewpoint from which this research is undertaken; and secondly to make the ensuing chapters intelligible by explaining how our data has been collected, analysed and presented here.

This book and the volume that follows it[1] together represent the third stage of our long-term study of children growing up in a representative English midland city, Nottingham. We had every intention of writing one comparatively short book on the seven-year-old age-stage of development; when it came to it, we soon realised that the two linked worlds of home and school which our children were now inhabiting demanded two linked books. The links will in fact be very apparent: we have not attempted to keep school wholly out of this study, and even less in the second one have we concentrated on school to the exclusion of home, since we are deliberately concerned with the ways in which the child's formal educational experience is sustained or diminished by his home environment.

ORIENTATION

In this as in earlier studies, we have first of all concentrated upon looking at the process of child rearing through the eyes of ordinary mothers, and only then tried to put their perceptions into a broader social context. One of our primary aims has always been to draw attention to those aspects of child rearing which *parents themselves* take to be important. This attempt to achieve, at least on one level, a perspective as close as possible to those who are intimately and at first hand involved with bringing up their own children is not just a sociologically fashionable whim (though we are aware of our place in such a fashion); it stems from a theoretical outlook which has existential and phenomenological roots.

Many issues which define characteristic styles of child rearing only assume importance because of the cultural values which parents have learned to attach to them. Should babies be breast- or bottle-fed? Should they be offered food at predetermined times only, or reach for the nipple at their own sweet will? Should a toddler be expected to sleep with his mother, with sibs, with granny or alone? Should a nine-year-old girl be the casual playmate and companion of her brother, or should she be careful never to touch him, talk to him familiarly or sit on the same mat? and should he be encouraged to lend his possessions to his sister, or should he be strictly forbidden to do so?[2] Whether such issues are perceived as significant at all is something we need to know about a culture, before we can start to make statements about which way a particular issue is decided and by which subcultural groups. At the individual level, the degree to which parents perceive themselves to be behaving like everyone else, giving their statements an 'of course' quality, or whether they feel themselves to be out on a limb in relation to other parents, must necessarily colour the whole pattern of their child rearing.

Thus the view of reality to which children are called upon to react is one which is in large measure socially determined. It is delineated in terms of thoughts, feelings, beliefs and values supplied by people who are continuously involved in intimate interpersonal communication. From the beginning, parents offer their newborn child a framework of assumptions derived from social interaction with each other and with an assortment of human influences stretching back into their own babyhood. The sources of parental attitudes are obviously multiple and diverse, including as they do relatives, friends, neighbours, professional advisors, more distant 'experts' via the various media, and the observation of other parents like and unlike themselves.

The parental view of reality – the issues to which parents attach significance – must inevitably be partly focussed by their own upbringing: we can hardly help transmitting to our children the cultural beliefs which we ourselves have absorbed, or perhaps partly created, as a result of our early experiences. But the process of social learning by which young people acquire notions of how they will be expected to behave towards their own children does not cease at the moment when they take on parental responsibilities themselves. On the contrary, it is precisely at this point that additional social pressure, formal and informal, is directed towards young and inexperienced parents; and this pressure is explicitly intended to influence and change their attitudes towards children. Martha Wolfenstein has pointed out that 'American parents . . . . . do not expect to bring up their children in the way they were brought up, any more than they would want to . . . . . drive around in the family car of their childhood. They hope to bring up their children better than they were brought up themselves. For guidance in this undertaking they turn to the contemporary expert'.[3] In our own less expert-oriented society, this is still true: with the proviso that in child rearing all members of society regard themselves as experts, and claim the right to comment on the upbringing of the children of neighbours and friends. No parents can totally ignore such pressure: they may deliberately reject it, but its existence is a part of their social world which they cannot deny.

Moreover, children themselves – even in infancy – rapidly become an important element in the social equation. Each individual child has a unique human personality to be reckoned with, and loses no time in expressing wishes, intentions and feelings which parents can hardly ignore, though again they may choose to reject them. As reasoning and language develop, the child becomes a potent source of feedback to his parents on how their child-rearing practices compare with those of other parents: 'Jane's mother lets her stay up to watch *Come Dancing*'; 'John's mummy smacked him for taking his pants off'; 'Mary can't come and play on Sunday because she has to go to Sunday School'; 'Paul's Dad sent him to bed because he said a rude word'; 'Geoffrey has to save up his pocket money so as to have some spending money when he goes to the seaside'; '*Everyone's* allowed to ride a bike on main roads except me!'

Because of the intensity of the social interaction which takes place between young children and those who look after them, parents and children together continually redefine their own version of reality in terms of shared experiences to which by mutual consent they ascribe significance. In other words, it is characteristic of the human personality that it is mutable: that people change as a result of interacting socially one with another. It must be emphasised that this is true of parents as well as children: from the intermeshing of their lives, new or modified attitudes *for both* evolve. This means that in practice children socialise their parents as well as being socialised by them, in the beginning because their in-built sources of motivation are stronger than parents can foresee, and later because the more 'homegrown' core of their personality is given breadth and independence by experiences from outside the family. Socialisation must thus be recognised as a reciprocal social process, the outcome of which is that both parties change from what they might otherwise have become in a different social setting or in a different combination of individual temperaments. This is a view which most of us would readily accept as describing the dynamics of a prolonged marriage relationship: when people live together in close interpersonal contact, it is naturally assumed that mutual accommodation and adjustment will shift both personalities in directions which might have been otherwise with other partners. We are simply arguing that similar two-way processes occur between parents and children.

The theoretical implications of such a standpoint are, however, rather profound, because they compel us to question any simple model of one-way causal prediction in relation to child-rearing methods: the notion that the personality of a child is essentially determined by the way his parents have opted to treat him. Even when we can provide evidence of statistically significant associations in terms of group trends, the results must remain ambiguous and unamenable to simple cause/effect explanation. Do stubborn and wayward children get that way as a product of repressive discipline, or does stubbornness tend, in our culture, to call out a pattern of parental strictness which would not be evoked if the child were more placid and amenable by nature? Interpretations of correlations, even when statistically valid, may still only reflect our own particular cultural preconceptions: there are, after all, cultures where stubborn waywardness would be considered a special virtue, a trait to be deliberately nurtured in children, and where parents would be disappointed if it did *not* occur. The explanation of statistical association can only properly take place against a background of the cultural values and beliefs to which parents subscribe, coupled with the styles of life and work with which they may not be in total accord but which do in fact constrain them.

Thus in many ways the reader will find that we are far less interested in the actual snippets of behaviour which people perform, than in the frame of mind which brings them to the performance, how they justify what they do, and how they evaluate their intentions and the results. It is arguable that whether a child is physically or verbally chastised by his mother is of less moment to him than the spirit in which she does the chastising; and certainly we believe that mothers can more meaningfully be categorised by what they say about smacking than by how often they do it. Our most important use of behavioural snippets (and probably the most predictive) is in fact to regard them as straws in the wind which offer clues to how mothers *approach* the business of child rearing: so that, for instance, a mother's willingness to pin up or otherwise keep her child's drawings may have little significance as an incident on its own, but can be used with other behavioural indicators to tell us how far a general attitude of child-centredness informs her whole contribution to the relationship; similarly, the behavioural fact that a mother sometimes threatens her child with a policeman is of less importance than the attitude of mind which classes bamboozling as an appropriate technique for dealings with children.

It follows that it is not within our intentions or desires to provide, at the end of this research, recipes for child rearing. Obviously we hope that we are making some contribution to an understanding of the dynamics of the parent–child relationship, and that this will be helpful in giving insights to parents themselves; but we do not set out to prescribe behaviour as such. To quote Martha Wolfenstein again, 'Behaviour in adult–child relations is deeply rooted in strong and incompletely conscious feelings, not readily controllable by conscious good intentions'.[4]

Still less could we accept what has sometimes been suggested as the object of this kind of research: the devising of a set of optimal child-rearing strategies or controlling techniques designed to impose more effectively the will of one generation upon the members of the next, or to produce some particular kind of personality which somebody has decided is more acceptable than others. Although parents do attempt to control their children's behaviour (and indeed the development of their personalities) within limits, such an emphasis upon technique must ultimately be regarded as pathologically manipulative. Most of the parents in our study are concerned with techniques as such only as short-term expedients when they feel that the longer-term relationship in which ordinary communication takes place has momentarily broken down. In the longer-term perspective, their intentions are to provide a protected and positive social environment in which the child's autonomous personality development can take place. They respect, at least in theory, their children's right to move towards becoming effective adult members of society. They welcome signs that their children can exert social influence on other people as individuals in their own right. They hope that their children will become creative and independent. They expect to be changed by and to learn from their children. And if something goes wrong, they tend to accept at least some responsibility for falling short on what might well have been a far too complex assignment.

EXPLANATION

Basically, then, we have tried to paint a comprehensive and rounded picture of the seven-year-old growing up in this not a-typical English community in the second half of the twentieth century, and to explore the general feel of what it is like to be that child's mother. Obviously it was necessary for us to have some preconceived ideas of the kinds of questions we needed to ask; but the direction which the discussion took, and the emphasis which mothers placed upon different aspects of particular issues, were matters upon which we deliberately looked to our respondent to guide our thinking. This whole theme of the adoption of a *hypothesis-seeking* rather than *hypothesis-testing* approach is one which we have explored elsewhere;[5] rather than be repetitious, we refer the reader to that discussion. Similarly, the interviewing method as we have developed it has been described in general in our study of four-year-olds[6] and in detail in the 1976 paper just referred to; we do not propose to re-state here our reasons for choosing the strategies we have.

Briefly to set the study in context, it forms the third of a series in which we are following a sample of Nottingham children through childhood to the second generation. The children's mothers are interviewed at length in their own homes at what we consider to be focal points of development: around their children's first, fourth, seventh, eleventh and sixteenth birthdays. At any one age-stage, we have data on approximately 700 children;[7] losses are 'topped up' so that we can continue to make statistically useful statements on a cross-sectional basis at each stage. Eventually we shall be able to make longitudinal statements about a comparatively small group of children on whom we have data from one to sixteen years, and about much larger groups for whom our records start at four years or later and finish at sixteen or earlier. At sixteen the 'children' are themselves interviewed, separately from their mothers, and we hope to retrieve a proportion of them again at the birth of their first babies.

This longitudinal project was devised and undertaken quite independently of others concurrently in progress, but it is fortuitously very complementary to them: we have elsewhere discussed the longitudinal approach in relation to these various English studies.[8] Like them, the existence of a body of children on whom so much data was being collected has given rise to research involving subsamples of 'our' children.[9] In the Nottingham study, the class-stratified sample excluded three major groups: immigrants of less than ten years' standing, children with handicaps diagnosed by their first birthday and illegitimate children not legitimised by the first birthday. Comparative studies have now been completed or are in progress on all these groups.[10]

As before, we have had to cope with the basic technical problem of reconciling and blending different sorts of evidence to form an adequate perspective. On the qualitative side, we have verbatim transcripts of our tape-recorded interviews which show how the mothers received and interpreted our questions and what they actually said in response to wording that was expressly designed to provoke extended conversation. This in turn leads to quantitative evidence concerning the proportions of mothers whose answers fell into meaningfully different categories. To illustrate differences in attitude, we have again quoted extensively from transcripts; but we are obviously conscious that quotations can all too easily be selected so as to give credence to almost any theoretical generalisation. As a corrective, we need continually to refer back to the quantitative and statistical level of analysis. This enables us first to give an account of which things parents *typically* say and do in relation to seven-year-old children, and secondly to chart the variations in standpoint which characterise parents in different social circumstances.

From the earliest study, we were forced[11] to recognise the pervasive influence of social class as a determinant of different patterns of child rearing. We had been very ready to recognise other factors, such as the child's sex or his family position, as important; but at one and four years we could not identify either as a significant variable in relation to the questions we were asking. At seven, however, it quickly became clear that both sex and social class were operating at a high level of potency in the child's upbringing experience. We have therefore adopted a procedure for presenting our quantitative findings which allows us to observe the effects of sex and social class both separately and in combination.

Tables In an effort to make the statistical findings easy to follow, we have set out tables in a standard form which is followed, more or less consistently, throughout this volume. A typical example is shown below in illustration. These tables are normally used to show the percentage of mothers who answered some particular question in a defined way; but the method of presentation lends itself equally to the display of other information about the sample, such as, for example, the number of high scorers on some more sophisticated measure, derived from combining answers given to a group of questions which contribute towards a single theme: these combined measures we shall refer to as indices.

Specimen table   *Children who own more than ten books of their own, analysed on the basis of sex and social class*

	social class					summary		
	I&II	IIIwc	III man	IV	V	(middle class) I&II, IIIwc	(working class) IIIman, IV,V	overall popn.
	%	%	%	%	%	%	%	%
boys	98	70	48	43	28	85	45	56
girls	95	69	50	44	10	83	45	55
both	97	70	49	44	19	84	45	55

Significance: trend ↘ ****   m.class/w.class ***
(non-linear, p$=$0·06)
between sexes not significant, interaction class x sex n.s.

In the left-hand part of this table, the results are broken down in two ways, showing the percentages for five different social class groups and for boys and girls separately; the bottom line shows proportions for boys and girls combined. Social class is, as previously, ascribed according to the Registrar-General's classification,[12] with the modification that Classes I and II (upper and lower professional and managerial) are combined, while Class III is divided into white collar and manual workers; foremen in industry are included in the III white collar group, and class affiliation in any individual case is determined on the basis of whichever of the parents' occupations is higher in the class scale.

If the combined proportions for boys and girls increase or decrease consistently as a function of social class, this indicates a trend which can then be tested for statistical significance (see Appendix II).[13] The results of this trend test are indicated at the foot of the left-hand side of the table in terms of *direction* (upward from Class I to Class V ↗, or downward ↘) and of degree of significance (**** p $<0·001$; *** p $<0·01$; ** p $<0·02$; * p $<0·05$). The test used also allows us to say whether there is any evidence for non-linearity. In examining this half of the table, it is worth observing whether the boy/girl differences are consistently in the same direction throughout.

The right-hand part of the table first summarises the social class findings in terms of a broader comparison between middle-class children generally (Classes I and II, and III white collar) and working-class children generally (Classes III) manual (skilled), IV (semi-skilled) and V (unskilled)). It should be noted that our sample, while randomly drawn with respect to all other variables except the exclusions mentioned, is class-stratified: that is to say, it is weighted to include more of the low-frequency classes than would normally appear in a totally random sample.[14] In the summary table, the data is statistically treated to represent the proportions *which would occur in a fully random sample* (given the original exclusions), so that it now takes into account the fact that, for instance, most of the children in the working class belong to the skilled manual group. Similarly, the percentage figures given in the final column on the right provide a weighted estimate of what the proportions would be in a random cross-section of the overall population (again, given these exclusions).

The middle-class/working-class comparison is also tested for significance, and the result given at the foot of this section. The overall sex difference is tested on the basis of the difference shown in the 'overall population' column. The summary table is also used to provide evidence of any significant interaction between the two factors of class and sex. If, for instance, a sex difference is in one direction among working-class children but in the other direction or absent in middle-class children, this would be noted as a class/sex interaction of a given significance level (an example appears in Table 23).

Taking the specimen table for comment, we can see that, in the first place, there is a very marked downward trend in the proportions of children who own more than ten books as we move down the social scale. Proportions decrease at every level from 97% of children in the managerial and professional group (Class I & II) to a mere 19% in the unskilled manual group (Class V). There is also some suggestion that the drop is not evenly distributed through the whole scale, the difference between Class III manual and Class IV being much smaller than that between any other two class groups. This slight irregularity in the downward trend is confirmed by the test for non-linearity, which nearly, though not quite, reaches significance level. Except in Class V, sex differences are very small indeed, and their direction is not consistent from one class to the next; the overall sex difference is not significant. From the summary table, we can see a clearly significant difference on this variable between middle-class and working-class groups as a whole: scanning this table (which now minimises the effect of the Class v sex difference, since Class v makes up only 11% of the working class), there is obviously no sex difference between middle class and working class generally, and hence no class x sex interaction effect.

For future reference, it is perhaps worth noticing that in all these tables the size of sample is such that, broadly speaking, a difference between middle class and working class of 10% or more is likely to prove significant; while a difference of the order of 8% between boys and girls overall usually reaches significance.

Indices Every individual question contributes something to our understanding of the child-rearing process; but it is only when several related questions are considered together, and a pattern is seen to emerge from the responses, that the interpretation can be more confidently stated. We may do this simply by juxtaposing responses; a more useful method in some cases is to group different but related questions to provide an accumulation of evidence on a given theme for any given mother/child pair. An index is constructed by assigning scores to responses and summing these to give an individual child an overall score for that index. A potentially useful index is one which gives a reasonable spread of scores across the sample, and for the purposes of comparison it is desirable that the scatter of the scores should be similar. The index is operationally defined in terms of the questions that make it up; the label attached to it is an attempt to sum up this definition. Expressing the child's standing by this single figure allows for a more complex statistical treatment of the data, including the calculation of the degree of association between the various indices.

Indices of this sort, if they can be assumed to be valid as measurements which meaningfully distinguish individuals along a continuum, can be cross-correlated one with another and subjected to other forms of more detailed statistical analysis which are not generally possible on a head-counting or percentage-taking basis. There are, however, a number of problems which tend to arise when moving from the non-parametric domain towards methods where measurements on continua are deemed to be appropriate. First there is the question of deciding upon the rules which should be followed when attempting to put together separate pieces of information in order to arrive at a new dimension. The difficulty here is that there is no infallible and universally applicable set of statistical rules for arriving at forms of measurement which will turn out to be both meaningful and useful in promoting a deeper understanding of the theoretical questions at issue. In particular, we have yet to be convinced that procedures which rely on the selection of a few items from a larger pool on the criterion of maximising internal consistency between the chosen sub-set have any intrinsic merit. We are, in fact, inclined to the opinion that, in interpreting the answers given to the sorts of questions we are asking, the most prudent course may well be to rely most heavily upon a reasonably direct evaluation of the first-order data: namely, the proportions of mothers whose answers fall into categories which have been defined in everyday commonsense terms. In other words, the further we move from results which are directly and intuitively comprehensible, the less secure we ought to feel about the interpretations we are making.

In practice, therefore, what we have attempted to do in compiling our indices is to put together all those responses which seemed to us, *on the grounds of face validity*, to have some bearing on a more general underlying attitude or characteristic style of behaviour. The only serious technical considerations were that each index should, as far as possible, be based upon answers given to a variety of questions, preferably with a discernibly different specific content, and that each index should have a dispersion or scatter compatible with a score range of approximately ten points. In practice, this also generally resulted in a distribution of scores which was unimodal and approximately symmetrical, which makes it permissible to use conventional statistical methods when comparing means.

A further and related problem with continuous measures established in this way is to choose labels which adequately convey what is being measured. In particular there is a risk of reification: that the giving of a name to a constellation or pattern of answers may artificially establish in the mind of both investigator and reader a conceptual notion of greater salience and definition than is strictly justifiable in terms of the specific questions asked and the way the actual answers were coded. Simply the use of a quantitative scale of assessment is likely to suggest that it is possible, merely through a refinement of technique, to measure an abstract conceptual notion with the same accuracy and precision with which we measure the physical properties of real objects. It is a comfortable and rather dangerous human propensity to impose patterns on perceptions and then to manipulate the patterns as objects in their own right; to press the analogy, the organisation of a constellation of items into a plausible whole is not totally unlike learning to see a particular pattern of stars as a Great Bear or (alternatively!) a Plough.

Thus we invite the reader to scrutinise carefully the questions which any index comprises, together with the way in which they are scored, rather than to rely uncritically on a summarising label. These questions define the dimensions we use.

Other conventions   Finally, certain conventions which we have adopted in our reporting need to be re-stated.

All forenames and surnames used, both of members of the sample and of people to whom they refer, are of course pseudonyms. In the case of the 700 children, a name once ascribed is not used for anyone else in the sample: so that, for instance, 'Vicky' at seven is the same child as 'Vicky' at four and at one. We have found it necessary to duplicate sibs' names, though within families each sib retains its pseudonym through time. We have not usually thought it necessary to disguise names of places and shops, though we have done so with names of schools.

Occupations of fathers have been given with each quotation. We have not been altogether happy about describing individual women by the possibly diminishing term 'so-and-so's wife'. However, we have continued to do this because it in fact indicates their own status and life-style more economically than any other means available. Where the wife has a relevant or higher-status training or job, we have usually mentioned this in addition.

Some sharp-eyed readers may notice that certain children's fathers have changed their occupations; in these cases we have given the new occupation (and a new class affiliation if appropriate). Two fathers are now labelled 'student'; both are mature students, of course, one moving into psychology, the other into teaching. Occasionally a class tag only has been given, where from internal evidence the mother would otherwise be identifiable by friends or relatives.

It goes without saying that nothing has been added to quotations from transcripts; occasionally repetitiousness has been abridged, and in half-a-dozen cases the sentences have been re-ordered to avoid utter confusion on the reader's part. We have used a five-dot ellipsis (. . . . .) to denote an editorial omission and a three-dot one (. . .) to denote a tailing-off of speech.

The interview schedule which forms the core of the interview is given in full in Appendix I. It should be borne in mind that this schedule has been devised to be used by highly trained interviewers, and *not* as a straightforward questionnaire. While we do not object to its use in whole or in part by other research workers, we would also suggest that this should not be done without consulting the account of our interviewing method to which we have already referred.[15] In particular, we would explicitly condemn any use of the questions which contribute to our index scores in such a way as to derive such scores out of the context of the whole interview.

NOTES

1 John and Elizabeth Newson and Peter Barnes, *Perspectives on School at Seven Years Old.*

2 The taboo between brothers and sisters (in a much extended sense) is for instance reported in Margaret Mead, *Coming of Age in Samoa* (first published 1928), Penguin Books, Harmondsworth.

3 Martha Wolfenstein, Introduction to section on 'Child-rearing literature', in M. Mead and M. Wolfenstein, *Childhood in Contemporary Cultures*, University of Chicago Press, 1955.

4 Martha Wolfenstein, 'Implications of insight – I', in M. Mead and M. Wolfenstein, 1955. This valuable article raises many important issues for parents and professionals, and is by no means out of date.

5 John and Elizabeth Newson, 'Parental roles and social context', in M. Shipman (ed.), *The Organisation and Impact of Social Research: six original case studies in education and behavioural science*, Routledge & Kegan Paul, London, 1976.

6 John and Elizabeth Newson, *Four Years Old in an Urban Community*, Allen & Unwin, London, 1968; Penguin Books, Harmondsworth, 1970.

7 Details of the sample appear in Appendix II.

8 John and Elizabeth Newson and Peter Barnes, 'Longitudinal studies of children', in D. Pidgeon and D. Allen, *Measurement in Education*, BBC Publications, London, 1974.

9 Peter Barnes, 'Some factors associated with reading disability'; Audrey Fessler, 'The development of linguistic skills in primary school children'; Mary Croxen, 'The social adjustment of children': unpublished theses, University of Nottingham, 1974, 1966.

10 Sheila Hewett, *The Family and the Handicapped Child,* Allen & Unwin, London, 1970; Frances Canning, 'The socialisation of the child in the fatherless family', unpublished thesis, University of Nottingham, 1974; Heather Wood, 'Problems in the development and home-care of pre-school blind children', unpublished thesis, University of Nottingham, 1970; Susan Gregory, *The Deaf Child and his Family* (Allen & Unwin, London, forthcoming); J. S. Dosanjh and Angeline Grace, two comparative studies of Punjabi and Jamaican children in Nottingham (in progress).

11 'Forced' is the operative word in the context of that time. We have commented on the social problems of researchers on social class elsewhere (J. and E. Newson, in M. Shipman (ed.) 1976).

12 General Register Office, *Classification of Occupations*, HMSO, London, 1968.

13   P. Armitage, 'Tests for linear trends in proportions and frequencies', *Biometrics*, *11*, 1955, pp. 375–86.

14   A fully random sample of 700 would include 350 in Class III manual and only 56 in Class V; in order to make statements comparing class groups, we need at least 100 in each. To achieve this in a totally random sample, we would have to double our sample size and interview 600 Class III manual mothers unnecessarily.

15   J. and E. Newson, in M. Shipman (ed.), 1976.

Chapter 2

Spotlight on
Seven-Year-Olds

The 700 Nottingham children whom we last saw as four-year-olds have undergone the changes of three significant years. As we bring them once more into focus, the most obvious transformation is one of status: from a home-bound child whose autonomy was limited by the garden gate, or, at most, by the first street corner, to a school-child, inhabiting for the larger part of the day a world in which his mother has little part. At four we observed how much parents were motivated in their efforts towards socialisation by this impending change in the child's life-style: 'I don't want the teacher to think I've made her quite helpless'. At seven, a sense of change in the child himself is often made very explicit.

Laboratory technician's wife:
> She's changed such a lot since she's started school and been play-ing with other children, it wasn't until she started school that she got over her shyness. Well, now my sister says she just isn't the same girl, she's got a lot more confidence than before.

Shop manager's wife:
> She's improved immensely. She's not half as spoilt as she was. At one time I couldn't take her out without her saying "Can I have this, can I have that?" Now I can take her out and she never asks for a thing.

Postman's wife:
> I think she's a very kind little girl now. [Now? Do you mean she used not to be?] No, she was always the difficult one – exception-ally difficult, and she couldn't seem to sort herself out. She . . .

um . . . I think she found it difficult even to live with herself – she's got this quick temper – I think it's only now, since she's about six-and-a-half, that she's really . . . she's really . . . a nice little girl now. [Does this date from anything special, or has it gradually been happening?] Oh, well, I think it's gradual . . . [But you still sort of think of six-and-a-half as a kind of landmark?] Yes, yes – very much like that.

Postman's wife:

Well, I can't remember what I said, but now – he's ten times different – he's a typical "Just William" – he's the scruffiest, pigheaded, muckiest, lovable little chap you could ever . . . everybody thinks he's marvellous, and he is really. Everybody says "Your Geoffrey does make me laugh" – he's filthy – there's a football team of ten, and the goalkeeper's a filthy job, he'll volunteer for that – and he doesn't get just dirty, he gets absolutely . . .

What are the main changes that can be expected between four and seven? Physically speaking, the child's growth in height and weight is likely to have been steady but comparatively slow, from an average of 101 centimetres and 16·5 kilograms at four to 120 centimetres and 22·6 kilograms at seven. This is the period when the massive physical development of the first two years, having found its level, is consolidating, and growth is proceeding very evenly. It is also the period when boys and girls differ least from each other, both in height and weight (boys very slightly ahead) and in speed of growth. Girls will begin to move ahead in weight at about eight and in height at eleven, and remain in the lead until fourteen or so.[1]

From the point of view of intellectual ability, the four-year-old could be expected to cope reasonably well with simple analogies such as 'a brother is a boy; a sister is a . . . ?' or 'the sun shines during the day; the moon shines at . . . ?'; by seven he has progressed to 'the dog has hair; the bird has . . . ?'[2] At four he could identify the picture of one object among a group according to its function – 'Show me the one that we carry when it is raining'; 'show me the one that catches mice' – while at seven he can manage more abstract concepts such as 'In what way are wood and coal alike?' The four-year-old could give a simple answer to a question of social comprehension like 'Why do we have houses?', while the seven-year-old can deal with more complex problems such as 'What's the thing to do if another boy hits you without meaning to do it?' In general, these three years have seen a notable improvement in the child's ability to think and reason without the need of concrete or visual props: he can count, and manage very simple manipulations of numbers without painstakingly setting out little rows of buttons or pegs; better still, he has begun to make use of the symbols of letters and figures which will eventually be the key to any prospect of going on into the more abstract reaches of thought. His most important symbol, of course, as at four, is still the spoken word; and of these he has a collection at seven which has probably doubled since that time.[3]

Already at four, as we have seen, language was a potent factor in the relationship between the child and his mother. It could be used by her to delineate to the child the principles and values which informed her efforts to produce his 'good' behaviour, rationalising and justifying the demands she made on him; and it could be employed also to dramatise the consequences, real or imaginary, of his misdeeds and thus to magnify her power in his eyes and bring him under her control in the short term. Equally, the child's own active use of language was contributing, helpfully or otherwise, to the relationship: it could allow the child to make the mother a present, as it were, of his love for her ('He says he's got the bestest Mummy in the world – and tears run down my face!'); and it could make explicit his more negative feelings ('He's definitely more fond of his father, and he'll say "There are the two of you; I like one better than the other and it isn't *you!*" '), or point up very effectively his rejection of his mother's authority ('She said "Don't you smack me. I'm telling my Dad of you when he gets home. My Dad says you haven't got to hit me". You see – then she gets another one').

The development of so basic a tool for social relationships as language is likely to bring with it a development, for better or worse, of the relationship itself. 'I should say she's easier to handle now than she was when she was four', said a student teacher's wife; 'perhaps it's because we can reason with her, I don't know, but it's more or less that'. The chief negative characteristic of another little girl at four was her disconcerting habit of glowering at people from under her eyebrows as an expression of distrust: 'if you look up suddenly and find her doing it at you, it's quite a shock – oh, it's the most *penetrating* look, you know'. By seven the look was still there, but the child's contrariness was much more difficult to ignore: 'they all get on very well with each other, but June *does not* . . . . . she doesn't go after things in a way that makes you *want* to give in to her, if you know what I mean . . . . . I can sit and tell you about the nastiness,[4] but you've got to live with it to believe it, you know, it's so fantastic'. 'Roger's a child you either like him very much or you can't bear him at all, he just irritates you to death', said a clerical officer's wife, herself an SRN; 'I suppose really he talks to everyone as an adult and he's a child and it's a bit upsetting. He's intelligent, but he's very *wearing* with it'. That last sentence could be ruefully echoed by a number of parents, pride and exhaustion fighting for precedence.

Warehouse manager and his wife:
  [Father:] Howard's got this idea that whatever you tell him, nothing can be done without an argument, there's got to be . . . [Mother:] . . . the why and the wherefore, and [Father:] he convinces you in the end that the thing you're talking about is rubbish; and if you really get mad and shout at him, he still has to have the last word every time, doesn't he? [Mother:] It really is a problem. [F:] He has to have the last word, no matter *what* you've done to him. [M:] It bothers me, it *does*. [F:] If you hit him unconscious . . . [M:] not that we do . . . [F:] . . . not that we do – if we did do, and he was just going down, he'd *still* be saying something to you – he's got to have the last word. [M:] It bothers me – it really does – why is he such a *definite* personality? I mean, the other children – mind you, they can be naughty at times and stubborn at times, but they haven't got this *strong* sort of personality where they have to say no and no and no . . . [F:] You say things to your children, and let's face it, parents *aren't* always right, you say wrong things to your children, and children accept it because you're their mother or their father, and they say yes like pudding: well he doesn't want to *do* this; he wants to argue it out, and quite honestly sometimes he *is* right, in a lot of things, and he's got the intelligence to *think* that he's right, and he'll point out to you where you're wrong; where most children, they look upon their parents as sort of a god, their father or mother can do no wrong, they're perfect, but not him – "No, no, no, *no!*" – and this is why we think that he's going to be . . . if he puts this all to good use, he'll be Prime Minister.

Although the child has much greater scope now for making his presence felt, both within the family and in other social groups outside, it is one of the most striking characteristics of seven-year-olds that they are also very much more able to restrain their spontaneous impulses. This stems largely from a greatly increased awareness of self, combined with a more subtle and sensitive capacity for social empathy. At four the child was still very much the prisoner of his own egocentricity; now, conscious of himself as a participant in social interchange, he is also able (at least to some useful extent) to see himself as others see him, to anticipate the reactions of other people to himself, and to modify what he does, what he says, and even his form of words and tone of voice, accordingly. Tact and discretion become meaningful concepts in his behavioural repertoire. He is becoming more aware of, and concerned about, what other people will think of him, both adults and children.

Sometimes this will mean that, although he has a greater ability to communicate, the child does in fact communicate less, being inhibited in advance by the anticipated response, or simply choosing to keep private some area of feeling. Now, when he is upset, he often manages not to cry; when he is worried or frightened, he may hide the fact from the casual onlooker; filled with delight, he may assume a cool nonchalance instead of literally jumping for joy as he would have done earlier. Most seven-year-olds are at least able to contain or delay for a while the expression of emotion, even though the outburst may only be postponed until they reach the sanctuary of home or familiar arms.

This discrimination between the kind of behaviour which the child can allow himself in public, as it were, and the more spontaneous letting-go which is saved for the family circle, is one aspect of his increased social sensitivity. It is in fact an extension of the principle which we saw already beginning to operate at four in relation to temper tantrums[5] (and which of course continues into adulthood): that one's most uncontrolled, disruptive, superficially 'worst' behaviour is reserved for those who love one best, who will not be too permanently offended at being used as a sounding-board for unrestrained emotion, and upon whose forgiveness one can afford to rely. In many more everyday ways, however, the seven-year-old shows an appreciation of the differences in 'social distance' between himself and the various people with whom he comes in contact. In the ordinary course of events he will notice that there are some people with whom his mother seems careful to be formal and polite, even deferential; others with whom she chats and gossips, but still retains a degree of restraint; others again before whom she will show anger, grief and pain. He will hear conventional remarks made to an outsider which are afterwards disowned in family privacy, and respect expressed in the presence of authority

B

which is later negated by words of scorn. Thus the child learns a code of social conduct which teaches that different behaviours are considered appropriate in different social situations, and that, as a corollary, his interpretation of other people's behaviour towards him may need to take into account the context of their action in social terms.

This seems a very complex and subtle piece of social learning; and, set down in this manner, it may also seem sad that, in an age when we pay lip-service to directness and honesty in human relationships, we should also deliberately cultivate a degree of social inhibition in children as young as seven. This in effect is what socialisation is about, however: that a child should progress beyond the single-minded egocentricity of the baby, and begin to acknowledge and become sensitive to the demands and expectations of others. In the process of socialisation, parents usually manage to tolerate a great deal of disruptive and defiant behaviour *so long as it takes place in privacy*; what they appear to be asking of the child from four onward is in fact discretion: a sense of time and place. The forebodings as to whether the child might 'show them up' or 'let them down' in public, which we noted at four, have at seven developed into an assumption that the child should by now be trustworthy in this respect; thus the mother may be used to nagging or shouting at the child to get things done at home, but in the doctor's surgery or the headteacher's office she will expect a lift of her eyebrow to be heeded, in recognition of altered circumstances for both of them. Similarly, parents will expect the seven-year-old to understand that the 'how' of communication can in practice be as important as the 'what', in the sense that a cross or petulant voice can prevent people listening. When June's mother says 'She doesn't go after things in a way that makes you *want* to give it to her, if you know what I mean', she is consciously describing a real social handicap in June; Clare's mother says 'I sometimes have to remind her to tidy up her voice and her face a bit' – and, in another context, 'If she wants [her sister] to do a particular thing, I try and show her that there are other ways than pressurising'. Jeremy's mother acts out the lesson for him: 'It happens rarely that he will give me orders: you know, "Get me this, give me that"; and I just pretend not to hear, and he says "I told you to do so-and-so", and I still pretend not to hear; and if he insists, then I say "When you talk to me in that tone, I just go deaf, I don't hear" '.

Obviously one cannot expect perfect diplomacy from a seven-year-old, nor would most parents wish for the deviousness which this might imply. The importance of a subtle sensitivity to social expectations, which we have called 'social empathy', can be appreciated when one considers the intractable problem presented when it is absent, as in the autistic child. In the ordinary seven-year-old, parents are still likely to experience moments when the child seems immune to social pressures, perhaps under the counter-inducement of some strongly conflicting desire or emotion; if these occasions are frequent, they can seem very difficult to cope with, for a failure of social empathy strikes at the heart of the socialisation process. In a sense, a pact which the child has made with the mother has been broken. Compare these two children, for instance: the girl receives and understands a complicated message from her mother without a word being spoken; the boy has (in his mother's own opinion) had his sensitivity blunted by her over-reliance on smacks, so that now he waits for this cruder message.

Lace hand's wife:
   Last Sunday I wasn't feeling very well and I asked her to wash up for me, you know, and she turned round and she said "I'm not doing them", she says, "it isn't my job". Well, it's the first time she's ever said that to me. Well I was really, you know, hurt, and I just looked at her; and she just sat there and looked at my face, and she said "Ooh, I'm sorry", and she did it.

Machine operator's wife:
   I think what it is, you know, he's had so many little smacks to *get* him to do things that now he doesn't even hear you if you just *tell* him to do things; I mean he's much worse for that than what he was, he used to take *some* notice of you – but now – you can tell him till you're blue in the face, he just seems to have to have that little smack to go with it, you know.

The nub of socialisation is that the mother should, one way or another, succeed in communicating to the child what behaviour is acceptable and what is not; and this demands at least a minimal receptivity in the child. When it is blatantly obvious that the child has opted out of the communication, inevitably the mother feels at a loss. A postal worker's wife, who knows herself to be desperately lacking in confidence in her dealings with her children, is undermined further by Dawn's habit of grinning and laughing whenever she is rebuked: 'You can't seem as if you can get to her – make her understand'. 'I try and explain to him why he's wrong', says a lorry driver's wife, 'and he'll listen to me, and I know very well he's not taking the blindest bit of notice of me . . . you think you've got through to him, and you haven't, and he *frustrates* me'. We saw at four that basically smacking could be seen as an attempt to get through to the child; and at seven mothers are still more concerned with smacking as a message rather than as a punishment: 'She howls and stamps and shrieks, "It's not fair", and on and on', says a jointer's wife, 'yet she'd do the same thing again an hour after, she couldn't care tuppence'. A teacher's wife, who has never smacked a great deal, expresses the development in the subtlety of the message: 'At one time I could smack Penelope, and she'd say "Well, you haven't hurt me" and it wouldn't make any difference, but now if I do it she's most hurt, her *feelings* are hurt, and so her reactions are different'. An unusually explicit example of a broken pact is described by the mother of Roger, who is 'intelligent, but very *wearing* with it'; here the child's burning impulse to tease his brother *now* is paramount over his own future self-interest, but the incident does in fact crystallise a lack of social empathy which is a fundamental problem for this little boy.

> Last night he stayed up to watch *The Man from U.N.C.L.E.* – which he's been *longing* to see, and we've not allowed him to stay up that late. Now, you see – Edward [3] won't go to bed without Roger, so I said "Shall we have a trick night tonight?" So Roger puts his pyjamas on, on top of all his clothes, and goes to bed with Edward, and then Edward goes to sleep and Roger comes down and takes off his pyjamas; and that was all right last night, that was fine. Well now – now this is how Roger's mind works – they were coming back from school, with me, and Roger says: "You know last night, when you went to bed, Edward, I put my pyjamas on top of my clothes, and I saw *The Man from U.N.C.L.E.*, and you didn't know, hah hah HAH!" And Edward turned round and said "He didn't, did he, Cherry?", and Cherry [11] had the presence of mind to say "No, he's telling you a fib, Edward". Now can you make a child out, like that? – and yet he wants to do the same thing again next week!

'He doesn't conform to the normal, average child in behaviour . . .'
In the foregoing paragraphs, we have tried to indicate the major areas of change to be expected between four and seven years; but it is a truism that there is no such thing as an average child, and this chapter would be extremely misleading if it attempted to focus

upon one composite image of a seven-year-old. At every age, even
at one day, temperamental differences can be very easily discerned;[6]
socialisation does little to iron out these differences, indeed sometimes it appears to highlight and consolidate them. Even within
families, although we did not specifically ask questions about how
siblings differed, the point was continually made, and to a degree
which does not seem explicable by simple reference to the child's sex
or ordinal position. Sometimes the difference was expressed in terms
of the mother's relationship with the child – 'Marion and I are
mostly in step, but Rachel and I are out of step, I don't know
why' – but inevitably, since mothers find themselves adapting beyond
their own expectations to meet their children's personalities,[7] such
differences will be reflected in the ways they evolve for dealing with
the individual child. For example, on the question of 'undesirable'
friendships, one mother said that with her other children she would
actively discourage friendships of which she disapproved, whereas
in Harold's case she would ignore them because 'his personality is
such that he will never ever be really friendly with anybody for
long, so it's always going to be a short-term thing'; especially
frequently, smacking was instanced as a response which seemed
appropriate to one child's temperament but not to another's. Some
mothers almost felt that we were wasting our time with the child
we had selected – 'She's quite easy to manage, unlike her brother; I
believe I mentioned before when you came that I wish you were
doing her brother instead!' – and it is clear that certain children
demand a disproportionate share of their mothers' thought and
energy. Inevitably, too, the child's disposition affects the family
atmosphere.

Building worker's wife:
  She isn't unmanageable, but she is a difficult child to handle,
  definitely. I won't say I'm doing it the right way, probably I'm
  not, but *I* find it difficult . . . she doesn't fit, you see, and the
  others do – we have our problems with all of them, naturally, you
  do, but as I say they all *fit in* – they all have their little awkward
  moments, but more or less they will go with the crowd; but June
  won't, she's a complete individual, you know. I know it's better
  for *her* to be an individual – she will probably be the one to stand
  on her own feet later on, er, perhaps get the furthest, I don't
  know – but at the moment she is a problem. As I said before, she
  was always a good baby, and beautiful as a little one, but now
  the problems are arising with her, definitely . . . the look on her

face when she comes home's enough to say "I'm home – look out for squalls"!

It seems useful at this point, then, to try and give some idea of the *range* of personality types with which we are here concerned. Later we shall be looking at these divisions of personality in a more systematic way; but for the moment an impressionistic patchwork will be enough – an assembly of individuals such as any junior-school teacher might find herself facing in class on the first day of term. The quotations which are starred were given in answer to the question 'How would you describe him now to someone who didn't know him at all?' Veronica, Guy and Barbara might all be described as children who like to keep things moving around them; all of them thrive on action, and create their own much of the time.

* Salesman's wife:
Well, I should say Veronica's typically a bomb from when she wakes up till she goes to bed. I mean, a bomb does describe her, although she doesn't have *one* explosion, she keeps *on*; she's very very inquiring – you don't get any relaxation when she's with you, you know, that's why when she's gone to bed you want to . . . er . . . I mean, when she's at school, well, you can relax I know, but I *miss* her – I miss her terribly, and if she had to stay for a meal at school it would be a very long day. And although she comes home and I wonder, good gracious, what's going to happen at dinner-time, I'd *rather* her come home. It's a funny feeling, that is, but I mean – sometimes she comes in and she doesn't wait, honestly, doesn't wait to get through the door, "Mummy", she says, and she's always so happy to see you – she's absolutely full of life – I think she enjoys every minute she lives, honestly I do.

Business executive's wife:
He's that type of child, not aggressive, but a born leader. It's just that he's got a terrific personality, you know, he's got a pleasant way of doing it, he doesn't appear to be bossing [other children], but my husband says, you know, "Honestly, listen to him!" You know, he gets around them all the time, but he's got a very pleasant way of doing it, he's very, er, cute with it, you know. He's constantly going to parties on Saturdays, he's *extremely* popular at school. He's a born leader, he likes to be organising.

Miner's wife:

She takes an interest in everything, Barbara does. She was writing about the miners last week, all sorts of things, and then she was writing about your car. She wanted to know all about how many gallons it used, its number, all sorts of things. She tells me all about it, you know, if there's a play at school – mind you, she's a bit *too* enthusiastic if there's a play. She came home one day, and she insisted that I had to make some wings for the Fairy Queen and some witches' hats. I said "Well, I ain't really got time", we was decorating, I said "When d'you want them?" – "Oh, tomorrow". I said "I *can't*, are you forced to have them, Barbara?" – "Oh yes, I got to". Well, I said I'd get the material and make them. Well, I was in such a state, so I ring up the headteacher, and I said "When exactly do you want these hats for, I could do 'em towards the end of the week". "What hats?" she said. I told her. "Oh", she says, "she's far too enthusiastic, Mrs Riley, don't you dare make anything, all the children make their own", she said; "If she comes any more tales like that, I know how busy you are, with her enthusiastic ways, just let me know, I'll tell you what you really need". 'Cause Barbara always tells me she needs twice what she really does, so she can do better than anyone else in the school. "I know what it is, she's awfully enthusiastic, Mrs Riley, and she lets it run away with her, she's got to be the boss of everything". I know she's ever so bossy.

These three often involve their parents in their busy lives; a few, however, are busy in a way that as far as possible is meant to exclude parents.

* Labourer's wife:

Well, I can't actually say he's bad. He's a bit nerve-racking . . . . . he's been a bit of a rogue in his time, you know – all accidents. He's had some bangs on his head, you know. I've had him lost – run over – ooh, *stitches!* – he's had more stitches than he's had hot dinners, I think. A lad and a half, he is! . . . . . I had to take him into a police station one day to more or less frighten him, to quieten him down a bit. You know Bath Street Park? Well, it's a long way from here, well that's where I found him one day. I'd told him three times – "*Stop here*" – really pronounced my words to him; I says "You are *not* to go on that park". *That's* as much notice as he took; he was there. When he seen me, he went flying round the other side, and I went like a ninny round the other side to catch him. I thought to myself "You bogger!" Police station – I don't think he knew it *were* one till I got him in. He didn't take a bit of notice what the policeman was saying to him. Wayne's that sort of boy that more or less runs his own life, you know – he's "I'll do what I want, damn what *you* say I've got to do".

Other children are not so much headstrong and wild as negativistic. 'He objects in principle and then considers the matter', says a research worker's wife; but there are some children whose parents would think themselves lucky if they reached the stage of considering. These are children who find life a battle, the world constitutionally against them, and we have already met a few of them: Howard who may yet be Prime Minister, June who doesn't fit in, Roger who sabotaged his own chances of staying up to see *The Man from U.N.C.L.E.* These children are not to be confused with the larger group of cheerfully aggressive extroverts (like Stanley, who 'comes in nice as pie . . . . . but after his dinner he's always spoiling for a fight'); they tend to be intelligent, argumentative, to have feelings of persecution and to be exhaustingly persistent in opposition, since they usually manage to find some principle on which to base their obstinacy. They do not seem to enjoy the battles particularly, however, and often one has a sense of a compulsive resistance. They are different in a very significant way from children like Wayne (above) who 'more or less runs his own life': Wayne will do his best to avoid being caught, and his policy is to keep out of the way of adults, whereas these negativistic children often seem deliberately to provoke and prolong a clash. Roger's mother, when we asked about the child's desire for company, said perceptively, 'Roger must have someone there, if not to play with just to antagonise'; and that does seem to be a real need for this group.

* Roger's mother again:
> Well, I don't know how to describe him really. He's very unusual – he doesn't conform to the normal, average child in behaviour . . . very demanding . . . the whole house is upset by his presence [laughed] – his personality rules the house when he's at home – but his headmistress says he's withdrawn at school, withdrawn and sensitive and nervous, and we can't make this out at all . . . . . Roger can just fall out with you by a look; I mean, I can just say "Hello, dear – have you got on all right at school?" and he'll say "Oh, you're on to me again are you!" or

"Never mind about that!" He's very egocentric and he's got persecution mania – I mean, if he trips over something he'll say somebody put it there on purpose . . . . . No matter how much you say to him you shouldn't do that, *"Why* shouldn't I?" But he's very loving and very sensitive to you, and he *knows* he's so wearing at times, and he's frightened nobody likes him, I know that; he's *so* wearing, with Roger every day's a shock – I can't explain him – I don't think he's an average child, do you?

Baker's wife:
There's certain things I don't understand in Richard's mind. When we're going out, he'll say he doesn't want to go, and yet really he *wants* to go, things like that. He's got a strange quirk there – he says he doesn't want his meal, and yet you know he will eat it. It seems as though he wants to be obstinate, to be awkward. Don't think it's for attention, he gets plenty of that. I just don't get it, about this streak, it's very hard to explain, isn't it? Just a queer streak. If we offered him a party, he doesn't want a party; doesn't want to go anywhere exciting, but he does really, but he *says* he doesn't. He objects. [It seems important to him to object?] Evidently it is, he does it that often, you know. We don't particularly talk him round, we have to *make* him do things, you see – if you talked to Richard all the time, you'd never get anywhere. It is awkward – obstruculous – that's the only word for it.[8]

* Locomotive driver's wife:
I should say he's very lovable – very affectionate – *very* bad-tempered: he's a complete mix-up, you know, he's got this tremendous affection and desire to do things for people and help them, and then he's got this temper and wanting his own way all the time. [He was a very determined little boy when he was four, wasn't he?] Yes, we keep saying it's a sort of passing phase, but unfortunately the phase is not passing [laughed] – he's seven now, and it's still fighting all the way with him. He'll have the last word – no matter what's going to happen to him, he's still got to have that last word, it's a constant battle with him . . . . . People who don't know him think he's very self-confident – he's a chatterbox, he's got that lively look about him – but underneath he's timorous and holding back. He doesn't have all that much self-confidence really – it's all outward.

It is very evident that the negativistic children are also highly complex personalities, which makes them still more baffling to their parents. June's mother kept returning to what she called June's 'dual personality'.

* Well, actually there's two sides to her: away from home, at school, at my mother's, at my sister's, she's a charming child – does everything for everybody, you know, gets on with people – she's marvellous; but at home she's an *absolute terror* at the moment – nasty – can't get on with anyone – she won't do anything unless you're paying her for it . . . . . I say to the teachers "How do you get on with June? Do you find her nasty with the other children?" – "Oh no, June is a *charming* child". You know, it puzzles me – it does, honestly – whether it's just her way of showing off I don't know; but as I say, there's two absolutely different Junes.

However, there are many children who are complex without being at all negativistic; amenable, comparatively 'easy' children who to the casual eye are uncomplicated creatures, but whose mothers are aware of special vulnerabilities and of hidden currents beneath the calm surface.

* Student's wife:
He's a physical sort of person, he likes lots of space and to be able to throw himself about. He's very responsible, he can be trusted; he's very co-operative as a child. The only sort of difficulty at the moment in looking after James is that he's not terribly resourceful . . . . . He's deceptive in one respect; he appears very placid, but in fact he's the kind of person who gets very upset *inside* himself, and unless you know him you don't realise this. Outwardly he appears very lethargic and not very quick to respond to things.

* Bleacher's wife:
She's a comic – she's a nice little thing, if she were somebody else's I'd say she was a nice little girl; she's not shy . . . . . She's not hard to manage at all; but she's a child that you're never quite sure what she's thinking. She has this way which I think is something *I* had as a child, if anything upsets her or she doesn't want it, she'll shut it off – she has this attitude "Oh well, never mind, Mum, don't let's talk about it, eh, Mum?" She can do this shutting off, and you think to yourself, Oh Edwina, you are a bit hard-hearted, doesn't it upset you, don't you care? – and yet

maybe a week after she'll sort of bring this thing up, and she's thought deeply about it really, but she's not shown it at that particular time.

As one might expect, most children have their good and their bad moments, like the little girl in the nursery rhyme: 'When she was good, she was very very good, but when she was bad she was horrid'. A student teacher said of his daughter 'If you'd asked us this morning – the very devil! But tonight she's as different again'. 'Some days she'll be as good as gold', said a presser's wife, 'and others, she *won't* do as she's told – you can shout, and hit her and one thing and another, and she just won't. I think it's the way she gets up in the morning, same as everyone else!' There are some, however, who seem to be particularly amenable and easy to cope with, problem-free children of a sunny disposition who seem to co-operate naturally in their own socialisation. These are not the ones who have been disciplined *out* of rebellion, but children to whom rebellion has never seemed relevant. One of the things which their parents often find especially pleasant about them is their capacity for appreciation of things and people.

Teacher's wife:
Mark's a very affectionate child; very happy, jolly – a *gentle* child . . . . . He's great company – a little chatterbox – I like to hear him talking. I like his interest in people – he's very very fond of people – I think it's a nice side to his nature that he's so fond of people. And of course he's got this wonderful feeling that everyone likes *him* – he'd be very surprised if he thought anybody didn't like him; that comes partly from the feeling that he likes everybody. And if you criticise anybody, suppose you say "Oh, what an awful frock so-and-so had on", he'll say "Yes, but she's a very nice *person*".

Cold food packer's wife:
It wouldn't matter what you did for Nicholas, he appreciates everything – if you knitted him a sweater he'd be thrilled – ever such an appreciative child, he really is, and you love to do things for him. Every little thing he appreciates – even if you've just got him a nice tea ready, you know.

Class v mother:
I've often said to him, you know, "Clear the table for me and I'll give you threepence"; he's cleared it, and then he's looked at me

and said "It's all right, Mum, keep the threepence". He's often done that. I think he feels a little bit responsible for me with me being like this [invalid]; I don't think it's right to make them feel *too* responsible for me, sort of thing, but he really enjoys doing things – he really enjoys it.

Clerk's wife:
She's so sensitive to people's feelings – if you have an off day or something like that, she can sense it, she can know how to cheer anybody up. She can go to her grandparents and she'll say "Oh Nana, those covers *do* look nice", and you wouldn't think she'd notice anything like that; but she can be very diplomatic and she can make you feel a million dollars, she can really. She really has a beautiful nature like that, it's nice, she can really make you feel marvellous.

Labourer's wife:
That child, he's never got on my nerves once, not once; he sits there, he finds his own interests – Batman – he don't come pester-me for this and that. If he's asked me for some money and I say "No, you can't have none today", he'll look at me – he'll say to me "Can't you afford it?" – and I'll say "I'll give you something on Friday", and then he'll say "All right, Mum"; whereas the others, they just sort of pester and pester – keep asking and asking – but Sandy not, he's really a good child – I've never known one like him.

Since we are concerned here mainly with the mother's view of the child, the descriptions we get will obviously be weighted by her degree of involvement in particular areas of his life. She is likely to be aware of his response to his brothers and sisters, his father and the neighbourhood children, for instance; but she has much less access to information on how he copes with peer group or adult relationships at school, and must rely on circumstantial evidence like 'constantly going to parties on Saturdays', or upon straight-forward report from teachers or children, some of which will conflict with her own impressions – 'his headmistress says he's withdrawn at school', ' "Oh no, June is a *charming* child" '. There are some regions of behaviour, however, in which she will probably be especially conscious of the child as an individual, and nowhere so much as where her own role as comforter and protector is invoked. Because our society places a certain value on courage and the stiff upper lip, fears and worries, even when they are engendered in the school situation, are often concealed from teachers and other adults, however potentially sympathetic, and saved up for mother. She is the person who is most likely to realise that the child has anxieties, and she usually recognises as her responsibility the task of comforting him and building up his confidence. Her acceptance of this responsibility will make her sensitive to small signs which may not be explicit at all: 'I think he does worry, and yet he's the type of kiddy that sort of shrugs it off', said a window cleaner's wife – 'he's a child that *makes out* he's bold, and yet he's not as bold as what he thinks he is'. In general, our impression has been that mothers are on the whole rather subtle assessors of their children's anxieties at this age, though they often confess themselves at a loss when it comes to dealing with them. Later we shall look more closely at the special worries of seven-year-olds; at this point, it will be enough to identify another personality group, those for whom anxiety is a way of life, the immediate response to situations presenting the smallest degree of challenge.

Presser's wife:
She's a worrier – what you'd call a whittler. Now in school, if the teacher says "Put your hand up if you can't do a thing", well she concentrates very well but she worries. She *is* a worrier. If she forgets anything for school . . . now take her plimsolls. The other day she came from school and the children who haven't got plimsolls, or they've worn out, have to get a pair or they have to write a letter to school. Well I went straight up the next day to get her some because she worried about it. I *said* I was going to get it, but she wouldn't *believe* me, till I'd actually got them. I know the teacher won't shout at her, you know. It's just that *she* thinks she'll get shouted at. It's silly really, but I have to go out and I have to buy it for her. She don't actually *demand* it, but she likes to get it that day the teacher asks her. She's a little whittler and worrier.

School caretaker's wife:
He'll sit and worry about it, and I'll say "Now what's the matter?" – "I don't know" – "Well, talk about it, you've only got to talk about it and it goes away, you see". 'Cause he used to have a habit of coming in and starting to look sorrowful and weepy like this, and I'd say "Well, you've only got to talk about it and you'll find the answer, and then you won't worry, so let's *have* the

worry"; and usually now he tells you what it is that's bothering him – if it's something he can't do at school we'll have it out and reassure him before he goes . . . . . In these last holidays his teacher got married, teacher's got a different name, you see, so – "Oh, I've forgotten what to call her!" I said "Just call her Miss Simms", or whatever her name was. "But it's not, is it?" So then we said "Well, *somebody*'ll know her name"; and the little girl that lives across here, she's in her class, but she couldn't remember her name either, but she said "Well, Peter so-and-so answers the register first, so I'll have to listen what *he* calls her". But he was really worried, so I said "Well, I think everybody will call her Miss Simms, and she'll say 'I'm married now and my name is Mrs whatever-it-is' ". Well, we're all right now we know it's Mrs Morris, but on that Monday morning it was dreadful.

Hosiery trimmer's wife:
New things bother him an awful lot. During the winter I bought him a duffle coat. Well, now that the weather's better he still insists that he goes to school in this duffle coat; he doesn't like *change*, and when he went into one class from another it took him an awful long while to settle down. He's a little bit like his Daddy like that, his Dad's the sort of feller he's worked for the same firm for years, and change frightens him I think. Kevin would tend to be a little bit that way himself. He don't want nothing new. It upsets his routine, you see.

There are also a few children who are known to have certain anxieties, but who by seven have erected considerable defences even against those nearest to them and make it a matter of pride not to seem 'bothered'. Superficially these tend to be independent, rather self-willed children, whose parents do not find them easy to manage, and they are less communicative than the negativistic group. Often, like the child who follows, they were themselves already a source of anxiety to their mothers at four; by seven the lack of communication becomes more marked, perhaps because more is expected.

*Machine operator's wife:
She's very deep; oh, *very* deep; you've got to go a long way to fetch the *love* out of her, you know what I mean? She's *got* plenty – but on the surface you'd think she was a very *hard* little girl, you know. Mind you, I think it's jealousy more than anything, I always have done, you know. [She was jealous when she was

four, wasn't she?] Yes, and it's still there, you know; and why, I *don't* know – I mean it's just *there*, she ought to have been an only child, you know . . . . . Like I say, she's very deep; often something's gone off, like at school, and to *us*, *nothing's* gone off, we've had no inkling; and gradually it will all come out *later* that she's been worried about it – and that worries *me*, it does really.

*'She's a progressive, she **wants** to learn different things. . .'*
The widening horizons of the seven-year-old present to the investigator a range of relevant topics rather different from those which concerned us at four. Certain issues remain important, although within a changed context; questions of the mother's subjective evaluation of the child and his behaviour, her expression of affection towards him and his towards her, her sanctions concerning the things he may or may not do or say, her willingness to communicate with him in words and to be truthful to him, her use of punishment of various kinds, and the image of their mutual relationship which she tries to convey to him in democratic or authoritarian terms. Some topics which were intensely relevant at four for considerable numbers of children have now receded into the past: fantasy playmates, bedtime rituals, toilet training, mealtime difficulties, dummy-sucking habits and dependence upon transitional objects (cuddly blankets and the like) – all these tend to be memories only for the seven-year-old's mother, bitter or sweetly nostalgic as the case may be. Where there persists a problem – the child still wetting the bed or retaining food fads – there is the feeling now that it is not so much a live issue as a dull ache; objectively a problem that persists until seven must be presumed more serious, but in practical terms the heat must go out of any battle over three or four years, and a degree of resignation sets in.

Some of the topics which we discussed at length at the four-year-old stage are of equal interest at seven, yet have radically changed in character during the three intervening years. Independence is an example. At four, the concept of independence referred mainly to self-help in terms of dressing, undressing and coping with the lavatory; in addition, we asked about clearing up toys, playing without demanding attention and making small purchases unaided. For the more mobile seven-year-old, independence is a much broader concept. Tidying-up becomes a rather more urgent issue, and is extended to other small jobs in the house, sometimes including responsibility for other children or for animals; some of the children clearly take

pleasure in 'looking after' the rest of the family, and a few receive
recognition of their usefulness in a very material form.

Structural cleaner's wife:
He'll get up in the morning without any of us knowing and he'll
make a fire and he'll mash a cup of tea and make toast and bring
it to bed to us, and he'll wake us up and bring dishes of porridge
for the children. He doesn't do it every day, just when he feels
like it. We praise him, you see, and make him feel very proud of it
– but I'm terrified all the while of him on the stove and with the
fire.

Lorry driver's wife:
He gets a shilling a week extra because he brings in the coal. His
father gives him that, and then he gets threepence extra 'cause
he gets my husband's football coupon and then takes it back to the
shop with the money. He does little jobs like that.

Financial independence is another aspect of this topic. Not many
four-year-olds receive a regular allowance of money, except sometimes (almost in fun) to bring them into parity with older brothers
and sisters; they are much more likely to be given occasional little
presents or sweets during a shopping expedition. At seven, however,
while few of the children draw regular wages as such, many can
earn the odd new penny[9] or two if they wish to, and almost all can
count on a basic sum of pocket money, sometimes calculated on a
complicated incentive system.

University lecturer's wife:
Well, we have just installed a new system by which he gets a
pound a month, and out of this he has to finance all his bus fares
– he has the choice of walking [to school] or going by bus, and
if he walks he keeps the money; and he has to finance his own
sweets and so on. [How much are the bus fares?] Twopence – if
he bussed the maximum four journeys it would work out at eight-
pence [per day]. But they get this money now holidays or school,
illness or not illness . . . his brother *always* walks, he would go
on hands and knees rather than take a bus. (See also p. 240 below).

The spending of his own money once more involves the child in
independent action, and the frequent encouragement to 'save up for
something worth having' may, once he has amassed 25 new pence

or so, attract him further afield than the nearest sweetshop. The question of how far the child is allowed to go on his own is a real issue at this age; in contrast with four-year-olds, who on the whole prefer not to stray out of sight of home, seven-year-olds have many interests which tempt them to the next street and beyond, with the adventurousness to follow such temptations. The fact that they go to and from school each day familiarises them with short journeys, and widens the circle of children they know by sight, who in turn act as lures away from their own territory. At the same time, most children of seven are not yet considered by their mothers to be absolutely trustworthy in negotiating really busy roads, still less in knowing how to cope with the 'strange men' who lurk at the back of every mother's mind. Thus the child's broadening range is none the less hedged about by rules and sanctions which are comparatively firmly enforced – 'my biggest rule'; 'I've dinned it into them that I must know where they are'; 'She knows she can't go beyond Nuthall Road'.

Machine operator's wife:
> She goes to the shops for me, but I might just as well do my own errands, because I'm hanging over my front gate all the while she's gone, looking to see if she's on the way back . . . . . [You're in a nice position here, aren't you, having the park so close?] Well, in a way it's nice; on the other hand, *because* it's so close, they think they can go in there on their own – they don't want me to come with them – but it's really no help to me, I could just as well spend the time taking them out, because all the while they're in there I'm hanging over the railings at the top, or else standing against my bedroom window to see if they're all right; you see you never know, do you?

Wayne, whose mother chased him round the park and finally took him to the police 'to quieten him down a bit', spends his pocket money in the amusement arcade – 'on the one-armed bandits more than likely – that's another place he shoots off to, and I don't like him going. Damned nuisance they are'. Wayne's mother never knows where he is – 'You just have to sit and wait till you see him' – and Wayne himself stands out as an exception among seven-year-olds in that he is totally unamenable to the restrictions of movement which the great majority resign themselves to accepting for a while yet.

The fact that the child can range a little further afield immediately means that he now has far more opportunity to choose his own friends. We saw at four that pre-school children, especially in working-class families, are on the whole limited to playmates who live within sight of home; beyond this, they are dependent upon their mothers to take them visiting – not an easy context in which to make real friendships. Many children at four were isolated from their peers for accidental geographical reasons. The seven-year-old, on the other hand, has at the very least about thirty to forty children among whom to choose at school. However, opportunity for choice involves a corollary: submission to other people's choices. Thus the child might at four have been friendly or unsociable without this being particularly remarked upon, and his *popularity* would hardly have been a real issue: at seven his capacity for mixing is regarded as an important talent, and an indifference to other children is a source of worry. One mother says that she is 'a bit unhappy because Alison is so much of a loner', although Alison herself is not unhappy: 'she doesn't care about other children – even if they didn't exist, it wouldn't bother her – it's *her* choice, very much so'. For probably a majority of children, however, to have friends will already be important for its implication that one has indeed been chosen by others: the child begins to be aware of his popularity rating (not in so many words, obviously), and this becomes just one of those 'reflected appraisals' which, as Harry Stack Sullivan once said, make up the self and give the child an idea of his own identity. When Roger's mother says 'He's frightened nobody likes him', she is referring to a complaint which every mother will take seriously, for it is indeed a damaging fear. In essence, then, while the child has for most of his life been capable of friendliness, he is now becoming much more conscious of the *process* of friendship.

Implicit in companionship between children is also, at this age, the continuing problem of quarrels. There is a very heavy overlap here between four and seven, in that many of the basic preoccupations of mothers seem much the same: how to get the timid child to stand up for itself, how to prevent the tougher ones fighting too much. Many of the statements made could have come straight from the four-year-old interviews.

Maintenance man's wife:
Well, I don't interfere really, because I've found that if you do, you get into trouble with the mothers, and while you're falling out with the mothers the children are making up, so that's another hard lesson I've learned. I would never fall out with other children, I'd let them sort it out themselves.

Engineer's wife:

[Do you ever tell him what he should do in his quarrels, or help him to manage them in any way?] Well, yes, I told him don't stand there and let the children hit him. I told him he's got to hit them back, and if he don't, I shall hit *him*. He seems to make excuses for not hitting the other child back.

Teacher's wife:

I should just tell him to come away. I'd never tell him to hit back – and this is quite interesting, in that I said to Vivian [brother aged eighteen] once – we were discussing this subject one teatime, and I said to Vivian "Well, I'd never tell him to hit back", and he said "No. I know you wouldn't, and you never did to *me*. And I'd got to find that out for myself". Now Vivian, of course, is also a very gentle type of person, and the situation arose more with Vivian – there were more boys around who fought. And I would never dream of telling Vivian to hit back, any more than I do with Mark. But Vivian thinks it's quite wrong, he thinks it's just silliness, because he says Mark will have to find out for himself at school that you jolly well have to or you go under, you see. He thinks that I should tell Mark, if the situation arose, to hit back. But I know I shouldn't – "I should go away and leave it – he'll come round later", or "You'll both be feeling better later". But I can *see* Vivian's point of view, but I could do nothing about it, myself.

On the other hand, there are three simple yet significant developments which change the nature of quarrelling at seven. The first is that the sheer size of the children make them much more formidable adversaries at this age, so that one is immediately struck, in reading through the transcripts, by the number of relatively serious injuries mentioned.[10] According to circumstance and attitude, this factor may make the mother either more careful in her supervision or more complacent in her knowledge that her child can look after himself.

University teacher's wife:

The only trouble we have is that Charles has what I call his continental temper – he has got this terrific temper which is in the family, and when this flares up he's very physically strong, and we have had occasion when if he had the yard-broom in his hand he'd just knock the child with this broomstick. *Because* he's strong,

I had to be a bit fierce about this – um – because he doesn't mean any harm, once the situation has been dealt with there's no rancour or unpleasantness or anything like this – he's stronger than is *convenient*, if he's got a shovel or a thing like that around. [Do you interfere usually?] Yes I do, because I know he is very strong, and he has occasionally hit other children. [Would you interfere if he didn't have this "continental temper"?] I would *hover* [laughed], and if things seemed to be taking a dangerous turn I would interfere.

Lorry driver's wife:
Well, there's one boy in particular in Sharon's class, and last summer he used to get Sharon round the throat. And one or two times she's come in and she's been really breathless, and in fact many times I thought he would probably strangle her in temper; and I said to her one day, I said "If you make Don cry the next time he gets you like that", I said, "I'll give you a shilling". I did. I said "If you can't hit him, kick him as hard as you can and he won't do it again". You know, this particular day she'd been out and she'd been in a big quarrel, and I said "We'll have no more of your tales, you can stick up for yourself, I just don't want to know" – and I shoved her out of the front door. Anyway – she came tearing round the back door – "Mummy, mummy, I made him cry, I made him cry", she says, "you come and see, you come and see". So of course we had to go out the front door, and there he was hobbling down the street, he was holding his leg. So I says "You've kicked him". So he says "Yes, I have kicked him", she says, "look what he's done to my neck again!" – and he really did mark her neck terrible; and after that he hasn't been so bad with her. But his mother told her off for kicking him and making a lump on his leg, but I said "You tell Don that when he stops getting Sharon round the throat, Sharon will stop kicking him on his legs". 'Cause I'm the sort of person that I can tell anybody off, 'cause I came from a rough area where I lived as a child, 'cause we really got it when we was kids, I mean sticking up for ourselves, and so I've taught Sharon – you've got to sort your differences out yourselves. But I've always said "Don't you hit first, but if anybody hits you, then you hit back, don't sort of be put on" – when boys have been a bit rough, "Kick 'em", you know, "get your own back someways", you know.

Window cleaner's wife:
He came home with a beautiful black eye, and I was raving mad

because his eye did really look bad – you know, it really worried me – I thought it had caught his eye inside. Course, I got that mad, and all of a sudden he said "You see my eye, you ought to see the other guy's face!" – and that was that!

The second development is the pleasure which some children take in bullying, together with a certain cunning which can keep it secret long enough for the victim's life to be made a misery. We do not suggest that a large proportion of seven-year-olds are bullies; but we collected a number of examples (mainly from the victims' point of view, naturally), and it may be noticed that both Sharon's tormentor (above) and Vicky Lievesley's (below) are in the child's class at school.

Railwayman's wife:
She was frightened to death of this lad – well, lad, he's only a little boy, same age as Vicky. Well, I went to this kid's party, and his mother says "Go and play in the front room" – and – "We'll put the tape-recorder on!" Anyway, when she played it back, this boy was saying to our Vicky: "If you don't shut up, Lievesley, we'll beat yer up". He didn't know the tape-recorder was on, you see. Well then – I thought "Perhaps *that's* at the bottom of it" – because she hadn't been eating, she didn't want to go to school, she went ever so thin, she was nasty-tempered and irritable; so I says, "Vicky, does Malcolm say that often?" "Yes, Mummy", she says, "but don't tell him, will you, because", she says, "I've had to stop in the toilet at playtime for three weeks" – because he'd been, you know, frightening her. Vicky's really a tell-tale, you see, and she'd told the teacher this boy had broken her pencil, and he's had it in for her for ages. "I'll get my gang on you, Lievesley!" he was saying. "Oh, please don't, Malcolm", she'd say. "Well", I said, "I'm not going to have you stopping in the stinking toilets", and I went to the headmistress and we got to the bottom of it and we changed her school. And this boy's mother and me was two big friends, you see; well, we still are, really, but we're not so friendly as we *was*.

The third development, which is clearly of lasting and increasing importance, is the improvement in language, not only as a tool for communication generally, but as a weapon in the armoury of children's warfare. However much parents may deplore their children's acquisition of an abusive vocabulary, it is certainly true that such useful words as 'beast', 'big-ears' and 'boss-eyed twit', or the taunting phrases of scorn like 'mardy mardy *mus*tard',[11] can offer a very effective safety-valve in a quarrel that would otherwise be fought out with fists and feet. By seven, children have not yet reached the ultra-sophisticated use of sarcasm, veiled invective or the barbed compliment which can eventually make it unnecessary for them ever to lift a finger in the prosecution of their aggression; but many of them, especially girls, are becoming adept at verbalising their quarrels and at using threats of withdrawal – 'All right, I'm not playing with you any more, you're not my friend'. In addition, of course, because the seven-year-old is very much a sociable animal while the four-year-old is barely so, threats of this kind now have real force.

This brings us back once again to what we see as the central change between four and seven: the growth of social empathy which is part and parcel of the child's development into a social creature inhabiting not one social context but several. No longer can he see himself merely as the centre of a family group from which he makes little forays into a wider world. Now he not only makes contact with other worlds but belongs to them in his own right. Once, as he recognised that his parents could be different from those of other children, he learned to identify with them, gaining prestige with the boast '*My* daddy can drive at a hundred miles an hour!' Now he identifies with two or more groups at once: '*We* went to Mablethorpe on Sunday', he says to his teacher, and '*We've* been making a collage of a space-landing', he tells his mother (or, a frequent example: 'If I'm trying to teach him something, and I know perfectly well it's right – "Oh, that's not how we do it at school", he says'). At the same time, his peers are no longer just companionable bodies with whom to play in geographical proximity but psychological separation: now in playing they can each become vital members of an integrated communal game, every child holding a key role, so that the whole group is clearly greater than the sum of its parts and the withdrawal of one child can spoil the action completely. Here again the child is evolving one more social group with which to identify – a shifting and changing group as yet, perhaps, as its fickle members create and abandon loyalties to suit expedience and mood ('You're not coming to my party, then, is she, Susan?'), but one which can be seen by the child to exist, and to confer status on its members and shame upon those who are excluded. The beginnings of real loyalty and obligation can be detected in some of these peer group relationships.

Bus cleaner's wife:

He's a little chap that, you know, if he sees anybody that hasn't got anybody, he'll go to them, you see – he's one for going for all the little odds and ends, you know what I mean? He's very funny that way. Now I've had three or four little dark children come, and he's sat in our house crying, because some of the lads have been on to them at school and called them "blacky negroes" and owt like that; and he's sat there crying for them, and he's palled up with them, you know, and played with them, till they've got used to it and carried on on their own, and then he'd play with somebody *else* that needed it.

School is the context which crystallises the child's transformation into a social creature, which formalises his experience of the peer group and of outside adult authority, and which presents a new set of demands which may be totally alien to the expectations of home but which are too powerful for the child to reject altogether. 'No man ever looks at the world with pristine eyes', wrote Ruth Benedict: 'He sees it *edited* by a definite set of customs and institutions and ways of thinking'.[12] If the home is the medium through which the child acquires his first understanding of the world, the second edition is the school's; and the place of the teacher in helping the child to dovetail the two versions successfully is crucial. Both parents and teachers can walk a knife-edge in keeping the child's loyalties to both groups intact.

Cotton winder's wife:

He likes her, but he hasn't idolised her the same as Jimmy used to idolise her – there was nobody like Jimmy's teacher, and Tony's got the same one but he's not that much fussy. I think this one, she pampers them, you know, she speaks to them *down*, as children. Well, Tony don't like to be that, he's your equal, and me and Grandma we talk to him like we talk to a grown-up man, you know; but this teacher is a children's teacher, and Tony is resenting it, he don't like to be treated like that at school, you know. I think if she asked him "Well, what do you think of that, Tony?" – you know, asked him for his opinion – he'd appreciate her more; but she doesn't, she'll say "*I* think this" and "*I* think that". She don't give him a chance to say what *he* thinks, and he likes everybody to know what he thinks, you see!

Student psychologist's wife (herself in similar training):

Oh, my word, she's absolutely gospel, it's sickening! He comes home and makes statements she's made. Of course, *she's* right, and in fact if we think or say or suggest anything different, we – oh dear! – we're terribly criticised. He thinks we're foolish. He accepts every word that comes out of her mouth. I sometimes wonder if she realises the extent of her influence . . . . . Generally the conversation starts from a categorical statement from James which is his teaching repeated; and then we say, well, not everyone would necessarily agree with that, *we* don't, but not to worry about it. The conversation generally goes along these lines. Teacher hands out a great many categorical statements about God and the world and the course of relations between the two; and, while we don't want – er – to cause a serious conflict in his mind in the sense that the two people who have the most authority in his life apparently don't appear to agree, at the same time – um – we feel that there is perhaps a case to be made for making statements less categorical so that there remains an open question; and at school it isn't put across as an open question at all, and this is perhaps one thing about school that we don't care for too much.

Probably teachers are often not aware of how much time parents can spend smoothing over small misunderstandings that loom large to the child, or polishing up the teacher's image when she herself has acted thoughtlessly.

Lorry driver's wife:

Sharon made a mistake in her copy-book – she was painting some stilts, and it said "Paint the stilts yellow", and she painted them black, and she was terrified to go to school, and she came home and she cried. She really takes pride in her work, you know, that's what would upset her, because she'd done it wrong, and trying to rub it out made it worse. She didn't want to go back to school knowing she'd done all this mess, you see, in this new book. So I says, "I'm not having this carry-on", I said, "I'm going down there", I said, "I doubt if you'll get a smack for doing it wrong". So I went in to see the teacher when she came in, I said "I can't understand why she's so upset". So she said "Oh Sharon, why ever should you make your mother think that you're afraid?" We got it all ironed out in the finish, we all learn from our own mistakes.

Chemical worker's wife:
It was that the teacher shouted at her, and I don't think she did *really*, it was just she was that type of teacher. [What did you say to her about that?] Oh, we had to persuade her that she didn't really mean it. When she shouted, she was only telling her what to do, and it was her *way* of telling them. It's very hard to explain to a child, isn't it?

By moving directly from the four-year-old to the seven-year-old, we have, of course, denied ourselves the opportunity of watching the child making the initial adjustment from home to school. That this can be a very demanding and sometimes traumatic adjustment is clear from the number of mothers who, without being asked a direct question about it, harked back to that period. At four, only 11% spent even as much as one morning a week at playgroup or nursery, and the mothers of only 5% were in full-time work; so that, for the great majority, school at five would have been their first experience of *having* to stay away from their mothers and under the jurisdiction of someone else on anything more than an occasional basis. Obviously there will be some children who simply miss their mothers and who find it difficult to cope with the knowledge that the separation will last several hours; others can adjust to the fact of separation, but find some particular aspect of school distressing. Many seem to have been overwhelmed by numbers, and the sheer noise and bustle of living in a busy community; not all five-year-olds can be given the gentle introduction to school that Edwin's teacher was able to provide.

Labourer's wife:
He was terrible when he first started school, but of course he had to go. He used to say he liked the school, but *he didn't like the end of part one*. Meaning playtime! He was just lost, you see. Ooh, we had a terrible time with him, but this headmistress was marvellous. Ooh, it was pitiful, you know, I never thought I'd have one of mine like that – he used to say "I'll try not to cry, but it's coming, it's coming!" – because he was really trying, and it was really pathetic, you know, and yet he'd wanted to go to school that much. Ooh – he didn't eat a thing for a fortnight, and the headmistress said she thought he'd be better off in smaller surroundings. He was moved to the annexe, and it's much smaller there, only two classrooms, it's like a village school on its own, and from that day he was a different child. He just took to it

straight away, and now he won't have time off at all, really, you wouldn't think it was the same child. But that headmistress was really wonderful with him.

Other children find the idea of doing things as a group very discordant with their previous experience, and may, if they are strong-minded enough, resist assimilation for a long time. Ross, a cost accountant's son, 'went on strike for three months'.

> He sat with his arms folded and would not do anything, and the teacher, this one particular day, she said "Come along, Ross, I want you to come for P.E." He said "What's that?" She said, "Well, it's a sort of exercise". So he said "I'm not coming", he said, "I've quite sufficient exercise walking up and down to school"; and she said to me "I had to walk out because I wanted to laugh, and I daren't let him see me laugh, but he wouldn't come"; and for three months he never did a thing – she couldn't do a thing with him at all, he just sat at the desk and refused to move. I felt dreadful about it. . .

It must be remembered that parents are uniquely able to take the individuality of the child into account in the way they treat him, and characteristically do so (as we saw repeatedly at the four-year-old stage); at school, not only is it less possible for the teacher to make special allowances for the individual – both because she may not even know his foibles and because she has others to consider – but, over and above this, school education intentionally sets out to teach group co-operation, and to show that sometimes individuals must be prepared for the sake of expedience to accept a group pattern of behaviour rather than making an issue out of every personal preference. It is easy to see how an intelligent child who has been allowed some responsibility for decision making can find this frustrating.

University teacher's wife:
> When he first went to school he was a very awkward little child, he took a very independent attitude and would only do things which he agreed with. He took a very strong line about this. He objected to answering the register because he considered it would be quicker and more efficient if the teacher just looked up; and I felt he'd *got* to conform in this way. . .

While it was not feasible for us to make a study of the total sample between five and six years, we felt that this period of settling down at school should not be lost to us altogether. Seventy-nine of the children were therefore the subjects of an investigation at school which linked certain factors in their personality and upbringing at four with their adjustment to their first year at primary school. The results of this study by Mary Croxen are available in thesis form.[13]

The school situation at seven is somewhat different. At the time of the interview, according to the date of their birthday, some of the children had just moved up into the junior school while others were still at infants' school. For many of those who were now 'juniors', the move had meant a change of schools;[14] for others, infant and junior departments formed an integrated school under one headteacher, but the move at seven would still be referred to as 'going up into the juniors'. For all the children, then, a conscious change in school status was either recently achieved or imminent.

The fifth, seventh and eleventh birthdays, for children who attend state schools in England, may all be considered as 'rites of passage' because of their significance in terms of scholastic status. Although the fifth and the eleventh produce the most obvious changes in the child's daily life, the seventh can in some ways involve greater, if more subtle, changes in pressures and expectations. This is because the two years in infant school are known (if not accepted by all parents) to be a time for the 'play way' in education. Hence the infant school child is expected to be literally playing himself into the learning process, and even those mothers who would prefer the use of semi-formal methods are more concerned at this age that the child should adjust happily to school as a whole. By seven, however, the honeymoon period is very definitely felt, by both parents and teachers, to be over; infant teachers begin to tell the children 'You'll have to try a bit harder than this in the juniors, you know!', and parents start taking a critical look at their children's progress by the only measuring-rod they have – the ability to read. When the child's achievement does not reach the standard they have in mind, anxieties begin to stir; for those with grammar school aspirations, it is now that they begin to wonder about their child's chances.[15]

Machine operator's wife:

It's *not* a good school. I think they take far too long over teaching them to read; I mean, they're just playing right up to the

juniors. I had a word with the headmistress about it, I said "Don't
you think she should be able to read by now? All this playing
about isn't doing her any good". But she said "Well, it's the new
education, my dear – it's not like it was in *your* day!" Well, I'm
a *nit* – I *hated* school – but I'm sure I could read at that age, and
when I think that Carolyn might be a worse nit than *I* am. . . !
I mean, now the headmistress showed me a piece of embroidery;
she said "Now a child's done that, and this is what our methods
do – every child has its own good points, and our methods *bring
out* that good point". Well, that frightened me all the more – I
thought, what's the good of it if the only thing they can do is *sew*?
I mean, I know she didn't mean it like that, but . . . If I could
afford it, I'd send mine to a private school – I would, they do get
them reading there. There was a little boy when we were on
holiday, he was only five and he was reading all the names off all
the vans that went past, I mean he *really could read*; and I felt
ashamed to think that Carolyn was seven and couldn't.

Thus, even if the question of 11+ selection is not yet broached at
all, the child starting his junior school years is likely to feel, and
probably to be told explicitly, that the time has come when he is
supposed to be settling down to hard work. Julian was missing the
motherliness of his previous teacher, and his mother commented:
'I think what it is, these are apt to be less friendly – they're more
teacherified than the infants teachers'. Perhaps this partly reflects the
fact that the basic skills of reading and writing can be acquired via
many different routes according to the child's choice, whereas the
techniques which will be needed by the time the child leaves the
junior school have to be passed on in a more deliberately pedagogic
fashion. It seems fairly inevitable that the pace will be stepped up at
this stage, for both teachers and taught. Whether the child accedes to
expectation is, of course, another matter; but certainly parents often
notice a sudden alteration in the child's feeling about school which
seems to mirror in various ways the heightened pressures upon
him.

Departmental manager's wife:
His main thought is to do well and get all the team points he can,
and that's a little incentive, I suppose, they get when they're in the
junior school. He's just moved from the infants to the juniors,
and here they get team points, and he's absolutely furious if he's
earned six points and the little boy next door, he's also in the same

group, he loses six – he thinks it's *his* six – and that sort of thing really makes him wild.

Structural cleaner's wife:

We have these pretend headaches and aches and pains when it's school in a morning – his legs'll ache, or his back's aching. The other day he said as he went through the gate a spell came over him and he said "Stuart, you don't like school – don't go". He actually *said* that, he told me, and I said "Yes, and the next spell is coming over you if you don't get to school!" He really dreads school – when they were in the infants, instead of learning them, they let them play all day at this school, and now he's in the juniors . . . . . he hadn't had that training, and they've got men teachers, you see, and he's been threatened if they're late they have the strap – he goes out the house about 8.30 in the morning so that he isn't late.

Scientific officer's wife:

He suddenly seems to have grown up very quickly. Going into the juniors and talking about it beforehand altered him quite a lot – he certainly seems to have emerged from being a – a – primary state to juniors all at once – been very sudden.

For those children who are reading fluently by seven, the already widened horizons of their age-group are extended immeasurably further. The addicts stand out. 'If she's getting dressed', says a clerk's wife, 'You're on to her, "Aren't you dressed yet?" and you look around and she's got a book hidden somewhere and she keeps going and having a sly look at it. If she's got a book in her hand, you might as well talk to a brick wall, she's unconscious if she's got a book". Alex reads 'everything on sauce bottles and vinegar bottles – everything that's written'; Oliver races his parents for the evening paper. Gerry is teetering on the edge of 'real' reading, but for him the battle is clearly already won.

G.P.O. engineer's wife:

He's got one book that we particularly had to buy him because they read it at school and he was really thrilled with it – the teacher, I think she must have read so much every day or every time she got the book out; and the day that they finished the book, he came home in tears because the book had finished, it was *The Hobbit*; and it's rather an advanced book really, but *I* started reading it with him because he was so thrilled over this book.

Mrs Chatham gave him the title so we could order it from Sisson and Parker's, and we did have to get him this book, I think the story's really made an impression on him, he's sort of got to *possess* the book.

Children who are beginning to look at newspapers are likely to be becoming aware of events far beyond their own everyday world; it must be remembered that a passive exposure to television news programmes will have been available to most children for as long as they can remember. Some of them take a serious if occasional interest in particularly dramatic or disastrous occurrences, especially where other children are involved: two such events which continually recurred as topics of curiosity and fear were the Moors murders and the Aberfan disaster. The scale of such tragedies can bring the child to ask for himself the questions which have puzzled mankind for hundreds of years. Julian is absent-minded and 'lives in a dream-world', emerging sometimes to baffle his mother, a lorry driver's wife: 'He said "Mummy, you know God is supposed to love everybody – well, why does he let people be murdered?" Well, I mean how can you answer things like that? I said "Well, the devil makes people bad – the devil is responsible for evil". He said "Yes, Mummy, but God is stronger than the devil, why does he *let* him do it?" You're lost. I said "It's man commits murder, Julian, you can't blame God for everything that happens" '. 'She asks some comical questions, but some of them I should say are eye-opening', said a supervisor's wife. Mary's mother, another lorry driver's wife, tried to answer 'as best she could' but found her 'wanting to know the most difficult questions – she was on about who was the first people on earth and who made them, and who made God and who was God's mummy, and who made *her*'; the most recent of her questions had been 'How does Jesus get down to do his shopping?'

There is nothing illogical about such a question – nor even especially naïve, given the context of the other statements about Jesus which are commonly made by adults to children; but it is very characteristic of the intelligent seven-year-old to combine an apparent social sophistication and a comparatively mature problem-solving ability with great lacunae of ignorance and misconception. Teachers know that children of this age can experience real difficulty with such elementary concepts as the addition of two-figure numbers, telling the time, or even the sequence of the days of the week or months of the year.[16] Anyone who takes the trouble to map a child's conceptual limits more thoroughly will soon discover quite staggering gaps in what adults take to be basic understanding – gaps which are often only discerned when the child is caught in some bizarre mistake. For instance, even the child of a close-knit extended family may have a very imperfect comprehension of the relation of kinship which exists between people he knows extremely well: he may know both auntie and grandpa as people he sees every week, yet be baffled when asked who auntie's daddy is. In this kind of problem, he is not helped by the fact that his estimates of people's ages are likely to be wildly inaccurate and inconsistent; many a mother, fishing for details of her child's new teacher, has learned that 'she's nice and jolly and about fifty', only to be faced on Open Day by a bright-eyed girl not long out of her teens.

In quasi-scientific matters, the child's ignorance may be still more profound. One intelligent little girl told us in all seriousness that if she took her mother's umbrella and 'jumped off the gatepost with it on the right sort of sunny windy day' she would fly up into the air like Mary Poppins. When we asked her if she had ever tried this, she said she was scared to – not that she might fall, but because she 'might come down in a foreign country'. Another seven-year-old, with a measured I.Q. of 157, was asked 'If you stood *here* and the sun was over *there*, where would your shadow be?; she stood up and contorted herself in an effort to see her heels, saying 'Shadows are always behind you, aren't they?' – and, taking a pencil, proceeded to draw a picture of herself with shadow, the shadow's head growing out of her heels. A similar experiment, when a class of seven-year-olds was asked to 'draw a man and his dog, and put in the sun and the shadows', produced a rich collection of pictures in which every possible drawable solution to the problem was represented. The child considered brightest in the class, a surgeon's daughter, queried 'Do dogs *have* shadows?' and was told to make up her own mind; she decided they did not. For this child, shadows were clearly a phenomenon immanent in the individual (like a soul), rather than a product of his relation to the light source.[17]

'The age of seven years, which coincides with the real start of formal education', writes Piaget, 'marks a decisive turning-point in mental development'.[18] Piaget's studies have amply demonstrated that children of this age still have difficulty in reasoning things out logically from first principles, even though in the field of concrete action they are well able to solve intricate problems of method and causality. What is more, partly because of their school experience, they are beginning to realise that in the realm of abstract thinking it is quite easy for their reasoning to lead to conclusions which practical experiment shows to be false or nonsensical. At the same time, they begin to understand that reasoning can be a very powerful tool: at school it is apparent that those who can use reason command respect, and that to succeed it is no longer enough to be 'good' – one also needs to be clever. School thus makes ever increasing demands upon their reasoning ability at a time when they know that they dare not yet trust their intellectual judgement too far: the seven-year-old has his intellectual limitations, but because of his increased social consciousness he is also acutely *aware* that he has them.

Children's fears and worries at seven are often the result of a heightened ability to imagine disasters in terrifying detail (disasters now including situations of social contretemps), combined with a naïveté which prevents the child knowing when imagination has taken him beyond the bounds of reason and plausibility. The mother of another little girl said that her daughter was at once afraid and fascinated by the sight of a man with an artificial leg. Because the child continued to seem disturbed about it, her mother decided to talk the matter out with her, when it emerged that what really worried her was the thought that, if the man took his leg off to have a bath, the bath-water would somehow get up inside him. At the same time, we must remember that the fears that we call 'superstitions' characteristically arise from a causal connection being inferred between two coincident happenings, and that such fears are not confined to children: compare the two following quotations.

It upset her when we lost the boy – he had leukaemia – she's had her nerves to contend with since we lost him – she tends to worry a bit more than she did last time I saw you . . . . . asking questions about *why* he died; and is *she* going to die when she's seven, which is when he died. She's nearly seven, in a fortnight, and I think it's at the back of her mind and she's afraid of approaching seven.

. . . always talking about dying, and what happened to her when she was dead. I feel this might have had something to do with me, I don't know. It's a silly thing, but – er – my mother died when she was thirty-five, and her mother died when she was thirty-five, and it was a sort of thing that stuck in my mind, that I might be the third. Silly superstition, you know, and I wondered whether I'd passed it on to her in any way – I've never said anything to her, I've not said anything to anyone about it, but I wondered . . .

Seven also seems to be a fertile age for the enjoyable traditional superstitions which pass from one child to another by word of mouth – 'Step on a crack and you'll break your back' – and it can of course be argued that some of the misconceptions and errors that abound at this stage are built into the child by the way in which our culture bombards him with a 'blooming buzzing confusion' of fairy-tale and documentary, religious belief and folk lore, scientific fact and science fiction. In a world peopled by Gentle Jesus and Santa Claus, angels and astronauts, witches who turn princes into frogs and 'spare parts' surgeons who turn bits of one person into another, one can hardly wonder if the child finds it difficult to pick its way between the probable and the impossible – nor laugh at the little boy whose dearest wish, expressed most seriously, was to 'get a heart transplant for his teddy-bear'. Over and above these considerations, however, it seems inevitable that children at this stage of intellectual development should be highly prone to a kind of conceptual indigestion which only time will cure.

We headed this section with a mother's comment, 'She's a progressive, she *wants* to learn things'. The growing-up aspect of the seven-year-old is something which can give parents a great sense of satisfaction. For some, the child is emerging from earlier problems: 'It's like a cloud going away from me, because I was so worried about him and I can see him altering so much'; others appreciate 'just the fact that she is growing up and that we can talk to her . . . . . more of an *adult* in the house, someone you can have a little conversation with, without thinking she's a baby'. Asked 'Now that James is seven, what is it about him that gives you most pleasure?' a student psychologist's wife replied:

This is the most difficult question – to put one's finger on a concrete thing and say, This is it. I don't know – it's a sort of combination of feeling that he's sort of growing fast, developing fast and being a *person*; and however sort of angry and frustrated I get with the sort of person he is sometimes – and I do quite often – there is no doubt about it that he is a very *real* person, and he's kind, and generous, and that underneath what is sometimes a rather rough, rugged exterior, there is a very very sort of sentimental kind of heart, you know. I have a feeling he is a terribly nice person, he's a very lovable character; and I also have a feeling that I've had a very little to do with it, and therefore it's even more delightful and surprising.

'Progressive' seems to sum up the essential quality rather well.

c

NOTES

1   J. M. Tanner, R. H. Whitehouse and M. Takaishi, 'Standards from birth to maturity for height, weight, height velocity, and weight velocity: British children, 1965', *Arch. Dis. in Childhood, 41*, 1966.

2   These problems, and those that follow, are all items from the Binet test: Lewis Terman and M. A. Merrill, *Stanford-Binet Intelligence Scale*, 3rd revision, Harrap, London, 1961.

3   M. Smith, *Vocabulary in Young Children*, Iowa Studies in Child Welfare, Iowa, 1962.

4   'Nastiness' = bad-temperedness, Nottingham usage.

5   See especially pp. 452–3, J. and E. Newson, 1968 (Pelican edn. pp. 481–2).

6   Differences in 'sensory sensitivity', for example, found by Korner, 'have major implications for how [infants] will experience the world around them, how much stimulation they require, and how much stimulation they can take'. A. Korner, 'Individual differences at birth: implications for early experience and later development', *Amer. J. Orthopsychiat., 41* (4), 1971.

7   J. and E. Newson, 1968, see index under *adaptation of parent to child*.

8   At four, Richard's 'obstruculousness' was centred upon his habit of soiling, and this problem dominated the relationship (see J. and E. Newson, 1968, pp. 325–6, Pelican edn. pp. 346–7).

9   Since the fieldwork for this study was completed before decimalisation, references in the quotations will be in terms of the old coinage; in the text, the decimal system is used.

10 T. C. N. Gibbens has made the point that 'murder by children is surprisingly uncommon, considering the violence of their resentments, jealousies and hostilities'. Review of *The Case of Mary Bell, New Society*, 22, no. 522, 1972.

11 – chanted, of course, to the well-known tune

– an alternative lyric is '*I* know a *se*cret!'

12 Ruth Benedict, *Patterns of Culture*, Routledge & Kegan Paul, London, 1935.

13 The full report can be referred to on application to the University of Nottingham Library: Mary Croxen, 'Social adjustment of children', unpublished thesis, University of Nottingham, 1966.

14 At the time of the fieldwork, Nottingham had 15 infant schools functioning separately, 26 on the same site as their junior school but with a separate headteacher, and 19 integrated infant-and-junior schools under one headteacher.

15 Until September 1973 Nottingham had one comprehensive school only: a boys' school situated on a Corporation housing estate and drawing its intake exclusively from the estate.

16 The Stanford-Binet Intelligence Scale (L. Terman and M. A. Merrill,

1961) expects an understanding of the sequence of days of the week at eight years.

17 We are indebted for this study to Christine Farrington, and also to Nigel Blagg who carried out a further investigation of this and related concepts (unpublished student projects, University of Nottingham).

18 Jean Piaget, *Six Psychological Studies*, University of London Press, 1968.

Chapter 3

Out and About

Although the seven-year-old's contact with the world outside his family is steadily increasing, and although his membership of outside social groups already claims a considerable proportion of his time and energy, most children of this age are not so adventurous that they will willingly cut themselves off from home and familiar things for more than a very few hours at a time. They may relish new experiences, and even seek them, but, on the whole, their serenity depends upon the new situation retaining some element of the familiar – or, failing this, at least an early and defined time limit. It is probably true to say that the majority of seven-year-olds will not enjoy visiting strange places unless they are in the company of people they already know well and have learned to trust, and that, conversely, they tolerate new people best when they are on their own home ground. It follows that when both people and surroundings are unfamiliar the child is likely to feel insecure and ill at ease, if not positively unhappy, even if the occasion is supposed to be a pleasurable one. There are, of course, fairly large individual differences in the readiness with which seven-year-olds adapt to change of this kind, and we shall be exploring these temperamental variations further in Chapter 11. Our point of departure here is that the home base – not just the house itself, but its immediate surroundings, the people, animals and artefacts it contains, and the well-worn ritual of the daily round associated with it – provides a comfortable framework within which the child can be spontaneous and feel free to cope with new ideas and experiences at his own pace; separated from the home base, he is also cut off from his frame of reference, and this may initially have a disorienting and disturbing effect.[1]

Labourer's wife:
  One thing I wish is that she could get out of this being shy,

because when you take her anywhere . . . Now last week we happened to call at my husband's brother's; well, I think we stopped about half-an-hour, and I don't think she opened her mouth, and it seems as though it makes you feel a bit uncomfortable . . . . . It makes you feel as though you're saying "Say hello, then – say hello!" – it makes you feel a bit uncomfortable yourself. Yet when we left his brother's I said "Well, aren't you going to give him a kiss?" – and she went straight up to him and gave him a kiss, and yet she'd never spoken all the while we were there.

Policeman's wife:
She's never stayed the night away. We took her once to stay with a friend of hers, and when we got her there she wouldn't stay, she had to come back with me. She was going for a week, but she didn't stay a night.

Tobacco worker's wife:
[. . . is he bothered by what he isn't used to?] Well, he was bothered when we moved up here. He broke his heart when he left his old school and all his friends, and he just wouldn't settle. He wouldn't sort of accept the new school or new friends, you know, he wouldn't go out of here for about three months. It was a bad time – last November – it was the winter, you know, not like the weather now, but it did take him longer than I thought; because he knew we'd *got* to leave, and he was quite looking forward to it. 'Course, then when the time came, he didn't want to.

Company director's wife:
[Does he go to his friends' houses?] Well, that's it, he won't go. I've managed to get him to two parties this year, I think, but he's refused to go. He's very sort of anti-party, er . . . you see, he's terribly conservative about food, it may sound peculiar, but he loathes any kind of fancy food, he wants plain bread and butter. I say "What did you have to eat?" – "Crisps, sausages and orange squash". So I said "Well, that's all right, I mean it'll keep you going", but he said "I feel so silly not eating the other things, but I don't like them". [He doesn't just go and play in their gardens?] He hasn't been, but I think he might go, but only so long as he knows he doesn't have to stay for tea. I think he's afraid of looking silly.

'Staying at home, that's the best outing he can suggest', said another mother glumly; but, although she described her son's preferences as 'a bit deadly', a certain limitation on adventurousness is very generally regarded as an advantage. The few mothers with fearless children who will go anywhere and speak to anyone are considered, by themselves and by other mothers, to have something of a problem on their hands. In fact, as soon as the child walks unaccompanied down a city street, his mother is faced with one of the central dilemmas of bringing up a child in modern urban society. She wants him to be outgoing and receptive, both socially and intellectually, and these characteristics can be encouraged without any check when he is at home and when he is in school – that is, while he is under adult supervision. It is *between* home and school that the difficulty arises, and here mothers become consciously ambivalent about the friendliness or independence which in other ways they value. The two big hazards that worry them are traffic and 'strangers'. These potential dangers have in common that they are only likely to occur if the mother is not present. Consequently, the mother has the option of preventing them by deliberately cutting down to the minimum the time the child spends out of her sight; alternatively, or (more likely) in addition, she will try as best she can to arm him with admonitions intended to protect him in her absence.

'If the weather's fine I don't have any trouble . . .'

In trying to discover how far mothers attempt to control their children's movements outside the home, it seemed important first of all to know to what extent the children themselves preferred to be out of the house. At this point we were interested not so much in the question of wandering, but in the mere choice between indoors and outdoors. We assumed, apparently correctly, that this might be at least partly a matter of temperament, and therefore we included our first question on this topic among the ten questions on the child's general personality (Questions 6–15)[2] which are introduced by the query 'How would you describe him now to someone who didn't know him at all?'

We asked, very simply: 'Would you call him an indoor child or an outdoor child?' and the question was a good one in the sense that this dimension of personality was readily recognised as meaningful by mothers and answers were given without difficulty. Seventy-five per cent of all children were in fact placed unambiguously in one category or the other, the other 25% being regarded as 'a bit of both' or 'either way, depending on what the weather's like'.

Our tabular presentation of the data in this book is explained on pages 21–4 above. The first table given below is fairly typical of the patterns into which our data tends to fall at this age-stage, in that clear breaks are seen both between social classes and between sexes.

Sixty per cent of children overall are described as outdoor children, but this rises to 71% in Class v and drops to 44% in Class i and ii. The difference between working class and middle class generally is significant (64% against 48%), though it is confused by the fact that, in Class iiiwc, boys align themselves with working-class children while girls are indistinguishable from Class i and ii. Overall, more boys than girls are said to be outdoor (67% against 52%), but the differences between the sexes are much less at the top and bottom ends of the class scale: comparing both sex and class trends, one might say that the professional-class male group is behaving girlishly whereas the unskilled manual-class female group is behaving boyishly. It is necessary to keep in mind the contribution of these two groups when interpreting the summary tables.

Table 1   *Children described unambiguously as 'outdoor children'*

| | social class | | | | | summary | | |
	I&II	IIIwc	III man	IV	V	I&II IIIwc	IIIman, IV,V	overall popn.
	%	%	%	%	%	%	%	%
boys	46	63	70	75	75	54	72	67
girls	42	41	57	48	67	41	56	52
both	44	52	64	62	71	48	64	60

Significance: trend ↗ ****   m.class/w.class ****
                                between sexes ****

However, when we come to look at the group described as indoor children (Table 2), the pattern of class and sex differences disappears almost completely. The reverse of the patterns shown by the outdoor children is absorbed into the middle category of those who vary or are both indoor and outdoor, and the indoor children (15% of the total) can be seen as a group of individualists showing no significant alignment with sex or social class.

How is this data to be interpreted? In the first place, with 60% of all children described unambiguously as outdoor children (25% as 'varies'), it would appear that there are a number of pressures tending in this direction for children generally. Although many parents value a child's enjoyment of his own indoor pursuits, very few would want this to be an *exclusive* enjoyment. At this age,

Table 2 *Children described unambiguously as 'indoor children'*

| | social class | | | | | summary | | |
	I&III	IIIwc	III man	IV	V	I&II, IIIwc	IIIman, IV, V	overall popn.
	%	%	%	%	%	%	%	%
boys	16	19	13	1	7	17	10	12
girls	20	18	13	29	18	19	17	17
both	18	19	13	15	13	18	14	15

Significance: trend n.s.   m.class/w.class n.s.
                   between sexes p = approx. 0·07

peaceable activities outside in good weather are seldom interrupted simply for the sake of bringing the child indoors; there has to be a reason such as a meal or visitors. On the other hand, there is an assumption that to be outdoors is in itself good for the child, and he may well be urged outside just to 'get some air in his lungs' or 'so as not to waste the sunshine'. It is interesting that there does not seem to be a derogatory phrase for outside activity to parallel Kipling's 'frowst with a book by the fire'.

In terms of the actual activities available to children indoors and out, it is not easy to make a case for outside being so much more attractive generally. Footballs, bicycles and other children seem the main draws; but these may be equalled indoors by television, reading and drawing, and the various indoor pleasures such as Lego-type constructional sets, dolls and toy soldiers, board games and collections, which we shall be looking at later. However, it is certainly true that the more obviously 'educational' activities tend to take place indoors; and active encouragement of these may well contribute to the 52% of middle-class children (compared with 36% working-class) who are either partly or wholly 'indoor' children.

A further class weighting is given by the material circumstances of the family, which we noted at four as being relevant to how far the child was likely to be physically 'off out' among the peer group or retained within the family circle. Descending the social scale, the accommodation dwindles while the family size increases, so that the mother is less able to tolerate children playing indoors and it quite simply becomes necessary to regard the street as overspill space. Furthermore, as one moves up the scale, the child is much more likely to have some place in the house which belongs to him, where he can keep his own things (see pp. 129–35 below); this immediately means that indoor play is both more positively encouraged and more inherently attractive for the child further up the class scale.

It is difficult to separate parental pressures and child preferences, but there would seem to be a general parental approval and child acceptance of outdoor play, which is coupled with a class-correlated pressure for indoor activities *as well* rather than instead; girls are more inclined to spend some of their playtime indoors, and probably (taking into account other findings in this chapter) have greater pressure put on them to do so. The exclusively indoor children are different, however. The fact that the sex/class patterns break down in their case seems to indicate that they are in fact *resisters* of the pressure for outdoor play, and that they in a sense choose to be as they are for temperamental reasons, defying cultural and subcultural expectation in the process.

If one looks a little more closely at the group of indoor children, further patterns emerge. Family size in itself is not a pre-disposing factor, but family position is, in that the first- and second-born are rather more likely than later-born children to be described as 'indoor' (significant at the 0·05 level). Thus it does not appear that the older children are pushed out to make room for the younger ones, but that the older ones, if they make the demand to stay in, have a better chance of carrying their point: possibly they acquire the habit of being indoors while there is still enough space, and are then more difficult to dislodge, so that when the pressure builds up it is younger siblings who are pushed out. As one might expect, indoor children are much less likely to play 'often' with other children outside the family (0·001 level); their frequency of playing with their own siblings is no different from that of children who play outdoors.

In terms of temperament, indoor boys, but not indoor girls, are more likely than other children to be described as at least somewhat 'shy' (Question 10; p $<0·01$) and indoor children of both sexes are more inclined to be 'worriers' (Question 11; p $<0·01$). There is *no* correlation between an 'indoor' preference and ease of management (Question 7), either placidity or 'temperament' (Question 6), or compliance/negativism; in other words, these children are not a particularly acquiescent group just because they choose to stay in. Indoor children *are* more capable of sitting still (p $<0·001$) – or perhaps those who cannot sit still are not tolerated as indoor children; they are also more likely to be capable of reading silently without mouthing (a measure of reading efficiency), social class being held constant. This last finding is one small part of an intricate pattern of circumstances surrounding reading ability which will be examined in detail elsewhere,[3] and which has far-reaching implications for the child's later attainment and opportunities.

'The garden's so nice, there isn't any point in them playing in the street'
'They've got to be able to rove about a bit now they're older'
To be an 'outside' child does not necessarily involve playing in the street (unless one lives in a high-rise flat, which does not apply to our seven-year-olds).[4] Almost without exception, the housing occupied by these children has access at least to a traffic-free terrace yard; council houses on estates all have enclosed gardens, and so do the suburban owner-occupied houses. Thus we were interested to know whether children used the street as anything more than a route to school or shop, since it was clear that some choice existed. The terrace yards are usually very small, but even in the suburbs the children often prefer to play in the street, partly because there are more interesting things there, including other children, and partly because an extended paved area offers more satisfying opportunities for cycling, skipping, hopscotch and marbles, and even doll's pram promenading.

Lorry driver's wife:
> If she's on her own, she gets her bike out and swizzes round the close – she had stabilisers on, but we took 'em off, and she's as daffy as anything. She don't like standing on her head, though. Her friends all stand on their heads, and she can't bear that. "Well", I says, "you're dizzy enough standing on your feet!"

Production worker's wife:
> Bernice'll generally take my broom and the little girl next door and the one over the road – they'll spend half-an-hour up and down on their broomsticks, pretending they're horses.

Coal driver's mate's wife:
> He goes off collecting things on the building sites – he goes with my sister's boy – where they're demolishing the houses. He takes a hammer with him. He's never in.

Building labourer's wife:
> Well, it's outside on the front [pavement], there's a family next door now, and they're always playing while the daylight – they usually have half-an-hour in here till they get on our nerves

and then shoo them out; well, if they all come in there's five. I chuck some of them outside and leave the quiet ones in till they decide to go out and skip – this Chinese skipping.

The question we asked, in the context of a discussion on 'things he does on his own', was 'Does he play or roam around in the street at all?' We were looking simply for the basic fact that this was within the child's normal range of activities, and not trying to gauge how much of his time he spent there: so that the children whose mothers answered 'Yes' ranged from 'half-an-hour on their broomsticks' to 'just comes in when he's hungry'. The results are given in Table 3. Seventy-four per cent of all children do use the street as a play place, varying significantly from 65% at the top of the social class scale to 83% at the bottom. Obviously one would expect a social class difference, if only on the basis of accommodation; what is interesting here is that a majority of middle-class children, almost all of whom have gardens, choose and are allowed to play in the street at least some of the time.

Table 3 *Children who 'play or roam around in the street'*

	social class					summary		
	I&II	IIIwc	III man	IV	V	I&II, IIIwc	IIIman, IV,V	overall popn.
	%	%	%	%	%	%	%	%
boys	75	78	83	75	89	76	82	81
girls	54	59	70	73	77	56	71	67
both	65	68	76	74	83	66	77	74

Significance: trend ↗ ****   m.class/w.class ***
                    between sexes ****

The potential danger attached to playing in residential streets will of course vary from one road to another; but overall it can be said that the central working-class roads tend to be more dangerous places, as measured by the actual accidents occurring in them, than middle-class and partly middle-class areas (suburban and estate).[5] They are narrower, so that traffic is more difficult to see and avoid, and they are more often used by heavy vehicles as routes to and from factories and warehouses. Working-class mothers very often express their worries about the dangers of playing out on the street, even within sight of home, but few of them prevent their children from playing out: these two, who do, know themselves to be exceptions.[6]

Caretaker's wife:

> If he wanted to go out we'd draw the line, I'd say 'Well, you won't be able to go round the corner so I'd sooner you stay where you are'; because they're all on this road here, they go out at eighteen months running round the streets, and they're dirty, they'll be sitting in the gutter playing mudpies, and I don't think it's necessary. But round here they don't seem to realise; once I fetched in a child that had got out of the gate, and this woman said to me "Oh, blimey, molly-coddled!" – and *he* was three. "Well", I said, "if you think that of a three-year-old and think it's molly-coddling him, *yes*".

Bricklayer's wife:

> [Only allowed out briefly under her supervision] Mind you, I don't know whether I'm doing the right thing or not, my husband says I'm not but it's just . . . well, he got hit by a car once on Hartley Road [busy, but not a major road], and I've always that fear, you know what I mean. My husband disagrees, he says I must give them confidence, you know, but it's just that my nerves aren't very well. I let them cross here at the toffee shop [very quiet road], but I smack them if they go near Hartley Road, they get smacks, because I'm afraid of it and I shouldn't like to go through it all again of them having an accident. But my husband disagrees there, you must give them confidence, you must let them cross, but no, I don't think so. They're young yet. I win there.

Middle-class mothers, on the other hand, do not often worry about the traffic in their own road; they mostly let the child play outside the garden if he wishes because they feel the local road is safe enough, whereas working-class mothers are less happy about safety but more constrained by circumstance. It is of interest that the middle-class mother below, who lives in a working-class street, does *not* feel she has any choice, and keeps her child in; the street is a busy main road, and unaccompanied children can always be seen on it.

Shopkeeper's wife:

> Well, I suppose in a built-up district like this he couldn't fail really to be an indoor child . . . . . He's delighted when he can go

fishing or to Wollaton Park or go away for a day or anything like that; but I mean, around here, apart from playing in the streets, look how busy – it's a main road, you see, and I couldn't possibly allow him to be playing on a main road, so I suppose circumstances have made him indoor; it isn't that he wants to be – if he could, he probably would be more outdoor.

Once the child is playing out in the street at all, the question arises as to how far he may go. He may have to traverse several streets and a busy road on the journey to school; is he allowed to do so in the course of his play? Does his mother expect to keep a check on him at all times, so that she always knows just where to find him? Once he has told her his destination, may he go as far as he likes, or are there definite boundaries – and do those boundaries allow for the crossing of main roads? What happens if he has express permission to go to a friend's, and the friend wants to move on to a third child's house? What about the time between leaving school and reaching home? – does he have to report home first before playing out, and is there in fact someone there to report to – or does his mother fetch him herself from school? All of these questions are important in deciding how far children of this age are autonomous in their spare time, and how far their mothers retain control of their movements.

The relevant questions follow; it will be seen that they are not all asked consecutively, and their contexts can be found in the schedule (Appendix I).

17. What about when he comes out of school in the afternoon? Do you fetch him usually?
 (*If NO*) Does he come straight home, or does he play out or go somewhere else before coming home? (*Prompt if necessary*):
 Do you have any rules about coming straight home?
 Are you usually here when he gets back from school?
18. When he gets home, what does he do with his free time until bedtime?
35. Does he see his friends in the weekend?
36. Do they come and play at your house?
37. Does he go to theirs?
78. Does he play or roam around in the street at all?
79. Does he go to the shops on his own?
80. Do you trust him now to cross busy roads on his own?
81. Can you always find him when you want him?

82. Do you have any problem over his wandering off so that you don't know where he is?
83. Do you have any rules about telling you where he's going before he goes out?
84. Have you any rules about how far he can go on his own?
85. Does he ever go to a park or recreation ground by himself?

Coming home from school is not, strictly speaking, the same as playing out in the street; but since it offers a great many opportunities for becoming so, it demands attention here. To start with those children who do not have the chance to wander off on the way home, we can look at those who are met at school by a parent. These can be seen in Table 4.

Table 4   *Children who are fetched from school*

	social class						summary	
	I&II	IIIwc	III man	IV	V	I&II, IIIwc	IIIman, IV,V	overall popn.
	%	%	%	%	%	%	%	%
boys	22	21	13	7	16	21	12	15
girls	45	20	29	28	26	34	29	30
both	34	21	21	18	21	27	21	22

Significance: trend $\searrow$ ***   m.class/w.class $p < 0.08$
                    between sexes ****

There is not much evidence of a steady social class trend here; instead, there is a very clear break between Class I and II and all the rest. Partly this difference can be explained by the greater availability of private cars in this class to transport children to school, together with a larger number of wives who are able to drive and who may organise themselves into group rotas for the ferrying of their children. Beyond this, Class I and II children are likely to have slightly greater distances to travel, not just because their housing areas are less densely populated, but also because their parents are less willing to accept as a matter of course the nearest school to their home; 12% of Class I and II children attend private schools (2% over all classes), when nearness is not necessarily a predisposing factor in choice of school; in addition, others succeed in finding places at certain primary schools of high reputation in preference to the one designated for their locality.[7] However, considerations of need do not seem to account for the whole of the difference, some of which must be attributed to Class I and II parents' protective (or controlling, or over-protective – choose your epithet) attitude to their children. It should be added that some children think it beneath their dignity to be collected; one boy thought it made him look ridiculous, and a girl told her mother with some asperity, 'You needn't fetch me, I'm quite compident!' At the same time, if class attitudes differ, the prevailing class composition of the school is likely to affect whether parents waiting at the gate are considered normal or 'ridiculous'.

Of more interest than the class difference, however, is the salient disparity between the treatment of boys and of girls in this matter. Apart from an anomalous result in Class IIIwc, a consistently larger number of girls is escorted from school to the extent of a ratio of 2 : 1 in a random sample.[8]

'Once he's been at home, I know he's there and he's safe'
However, the great majority of all seven-year-olds (78%) make their own way home from school; and, although we said earlier that walking home is not the same as playing out, the extent to which it is not is very much a measure of mothers' determination that it should not become so. Ninety-two per cent (including those who fetch the child themselves) make it an unbendable rule that the child should report home first, even if he just 'pokes his head round the door, changes his shoes, and we don't see him till it's dark sometimes'. An assortment of quotations will give an idea of the unanimity of opinion.

College lecturer:
I fetch him three out of five days a week, and the others he comes home alone. He comes to the house always, to the gate, but it sometimes takes a long time, sometimes it takes him twenty minutes for a ten-minute walk, but this is because he is slow. He must go immediately out to play, he gets out his bike and off to some friend's house, or fetch them round here. I am emphatic that he comes here before going anywhere else.

Miner's wife:
No, if she's going to her friend's, it's only round the corner, she'll tell me. Once or twice – there was a girl you know and she'd call in there before she got home, and I shouted at her once or twice if she hadn't been home. Oh, she must come home first. I don't mind where she's gone, but she must come home first and tell me she's going.

Cycle worker's wife:
He doesn't go anywhere else before coming home, because he
knows what he gets if he does, but sometimes it's, um, a little bit
later than it ought to be; mind you, it's only roughly – it might be
a matter of ten to fifteen minutes at the longest – 'cause they'll
play just coming down the roads.

Lorry driver's wife:
I've drummed that into him ever since they've been tiny.

Children who do not conform to this rule can expect trouble.

Nylon winder's wife:
He comes home with his sister, the one who's ten. He plays about
sometimes, sometimes I have to go out looking for him. He plays
on those factory slags . . . . . I always tell them they must come
straight home first, being as there's been a lot of things in the
paper; come straight home first and then they play out afterwards.
But he doesn't do it, only if his sister is with him to see that he
does. [So what do you say if he's late?] I keep him in.

Company director's wife:
[any problem . . . ?] Mainly that he went somewhere after school
without telling me, and there was quite a kerfuffle; and, er, I sort
of put it to him, how would *he* feel if he came home and found
me not here and didn't know where I was – and, um, it seemed
to have quite the desired effect.

Jointer's wife:
If you'd come on Friday, I could have told you something about
seven-year-olds then! I was about ready to murder her, I was
nearly throwing her out of the house. Dinner-time – instead of
coming home the way she's *supposed* to come, which is down
Bathley Street, she went all the way round Wilford Crescent with
one of her friends, and down and round in a circle, you see. Well,
I was out looking for her the front way and her Dad was looking
the back way, when she walked in. Well, the thing is she *knows*
which way she's supposed to come and she'd just defied us. That's
what made me mad. But she doesn't care. So she got walloped.
So then it was screams and yells and kicks – the lot. Temper! So
she said she wasn't going back to school in the afternoon. So I
said to my mother "Just look after baby while I whip her into
school", and we went up that road – well, I've never been up it so

fast in my life! And in she went, with a smacked bottom to help her on her way. She was a real pitiful sight, with tears rolling down her cheeks and two girls going in each side of her! "Ooh", they said, "your Cheryl's crying!" "Yes", I said, "and well she might!"

Once again, however, in the 11% of cases where either no rule exists or it is habitually broken, the child in question is more than twice as likely to be a boy than a girl; and this last point is further corroborated by looking at the 5% of children who, having come home on their own, have to let themselves into the house or otherwise wait around for an adult to arrive. No seven-year-old was reported as having to wait more than half-an-hour on his own other than occasionally, although mothers who regularly have this difficulty often rely on neighbours, relatives or older siblings to fill the home-coming gap. The number of children coming home to a completely empty house is not large in Nottingham at this age, but for boys the overall figure is 7%, whereas for girls it is less than 3% (significance level: $p < 0.05$). Class differences are not significant. Although it is easy for arrangements of this kind to go wrong, mothers do seem to show a good deal of concern that their children should be happily catered for during the family homecoming period.

Part-time hospital ancillary worker:
Someone was sort of looking after him just for half-an-hour, and then I couldn't rely on them, so he started letting himself in – which I didn't like, so I used to ring him up from the hospital – have a word with him; so really he was waiting anticipating the call for about ten minutes, and I used to talk to him for about five, and then it was almost time for Philip [brother aged ten] to come home, so it wasn't long, but I didn't like doing it, and I don't think he was keen on me doing it either. Since then, my husband's got here for 3.30, he's on holiday, and I should get mornings by the time they go back. I don't think he likes it – at first I thought, oh, he thinks he's big that he can open the back door – and of course there were a lot of rules and regulations – but he started to cry about two to three weeks ago, "I don't like coming in by myself", and he's never said it before.

'It's a functional thing if one knows where a member of the family is ...'
When the child is around the home base, either in the evenings or

during week-ends and holidays, there are two main strategies used
by the mother in supervising his movements: to insist on his giving
her notice before any sortie, and to set boundaries. Like reporting
back after school, the first is widely demanded, though the rate of
failure seems rather higher – perhaps because children returning
from school have the motivation of tiredness and hunger to help
them obey.

Teacher's wife:

I'm very firm about that. He didn't use to do it last year, but
when he suddenly realised that by coming and saying "I'm going
to John's", I wasn't going to say "Oh no you can't" – now he
knows that I will just say "Right!", he comes always. And if he's
playing at John's and he's going on to Michael's, he comes and
says "I'm just going to Michael's", and I say "Right" – so now I
really do know where he is.

Student's wife:

We got a lot of this wandering off and not saying where she was
going. She would say where she was going and that child
wouldn't be in, and she'd wander on, so we had to put our foot
down with a firm hand and say "Come and tell us, if they're not
in, where you're going", and she does now – more or less!

Cabinet maker's wife:

I've got a very little rule here, I like them to come and ask if
they can go to a certain home; but sometimes he just doddles off
and doesn't bother to ask, and I think, where on earth has he
gone? But he'll be back and say "Well, I've been to so-and-so's
house". I'll say "Why didn't you come and ask Mummy first,
I've been anxious about you". He'll say "I'm sorry".

Architect's wife:

Well, I've sort of made this a rule of the whole family, that it's a
functional thing if one knows where a member of the family is. It's
not a question of "Where are you going?" – it's more "It's useful
if I know where you are".

Lorry driver's wife:

He tells me he's going somewhere – if he comes in and says "Can
I go out?", I say "Yes, and where are you going?" He says "Oh,
I'm going to play with Martin". Well, half-an-hour later I may
go and get him, and it's "Oh, well, he left here, Mrs Matthews,
and I reckon he's gone so-and-so". Well, instead of coming to

tell me he's gone so-and-so, he just shoots off. I mostly know just about where he is, but you can't always find him.

The percentages of mothers having a 'giving notice' rule are shown in Table 5. We have only included here those who impose a firm rule; those who are merely hopeful that the child will tell them, but do not try to enforce this, are omitted from these figures. Class differences show no consistent trend, but Class v mothers are some-

Table 5 *Mothers who have a firm rule that child should give notice of his destination before going anywhere*

| | social class | | | | | summary | | |
	I&II	IIIwc	III man	IV	V	I&II, IIIwc	IIIman, IV,V	overall popn.
	%	%	%	%	%	%	%	%
boys	72	70	70	64	65	71	68	69
girls	83	81	89	80	67	82	85	84
both	78	75	80	72	66	77	76	77

Significance: trend n.s.   m.class/w.class   n.s.
          between sexes   ****

what less likely than the rest to have any rule: however, they still show a clear majority for giving notice. Once more, supervision of girls is significantly greater than that of boys.

The question of boundaries was also investigated in terms of the existence of 'rules', on the basis of whether the mother had laid down a precise geographical limit to the child's wanderings, whether she made an *ad hoc* decision in each case or had a rather vague idea of his limits which might not even be known to the child, or whether she simply left it to his own adventurousness. We did not attempt to measure the child's area of movement, because to be useful this complicated assessment would then have had to be weighted by traffic density and other neighbourhood factors, and the whole operation seemed over-particularised for our purposes; information on this topic is in any case being collected by other workers in Nottingham.[9] Sixty-two per cent of mothers overall laid down exact geographical boundaries; class and sex differences were not significant, and perhaps this suggests that the rule of 'how far' is in fact largely determined by the individual area and the hazards it contains. Obviously these hazards will include busy roads and other kinds of

accident black spots such as canals, railway embankments and
derelict buildings; but parks and recreation grounds, intended for
children's use, are often also forbidden territory for seven-year-olds,
as we shall see shortly.

The range of permitted distances can be gauged from the illustrations below; although we did not compile figures on how far children
were allowed to go, it can be said that the first and last mothers of
the group that follows are very unusual in the lines they take. It may
be of interest that at four the last child was especially valued for
being 'sensible' and 'a *boy* – not a sissy-type child'.

Bricklayer's wife [same as on page 76] – back street off medium-busy
road:
> [Does he play or roam around in the street at all?] No – no. I
> never let him out more than five minutes, that's when I'm scrub-
> bing the front, you know.

Warehouse manager's wife – suburban roads, both moderately
quiet:
> Well, we don't allow him to go anywhere, you see. His Grandma,
> she lives in the next road, at right angles to this – she's probably,
> as the crow flies, fifty yards away, and we don't let him do *that*,
> because he's got the bottom of the road to cross, and there are
> people who go round here at a tremendous rate.

Cycle worker's wife – non-traffic terrace, moderately quiet street:
> I tell him, I say "Don't go out of the street, Philip". If I go to
> the top of the yard and he's not in sight, I'll probably find him
> with his little friends down the terrace here.

Nylon winder's wife – quiet back street off very busy main road:
> There's a woman up the street, and she comes here for the kiddies
> to do errands, you see. And she got ever so nasty with me last
> week because I wouldn't let Stanley go, 'cause he was the only one
> in. And I says, "No", I says, "I don't care what you say, I'm *not*
> letting Stanley go. He's never crossed that road for *me* unless
> someone's with him".

Metal polisher's wife – medium-busy road:
> During the summer he went on the Forest [common land, ten
> minutes' walk] a couple of times, and it was about two hours
> before we found him. Mostly when the circus comes in – he gets
> to watch it come in. I mean, I always say I'll take him, but he
> couldn't wait until I was ready, you know, so he goes off with

other friends, of course. [And do you mind that?] Yes, I do, I'm
cross with him actually. [Does it often happen?] Yes, it used to,
but I put my foot down and said he couldn't go out if he didn't
tell me where he was going. Well, now he tells me where he is or
where he's going to be, so he has improved on that one.

Caretaker's wife – medium-busy road through small council estate:
So long as I know where he's going. He went up to town to get
me a Mothering Sunday present – right into town, to the Co-op
[far side of City centre] – well, I didn't know where he'd gone,
and that really worried me till he got back. [If he wanted to go
again, would you let him?] Oh yes, so long as I *knew* he was
going, I'd let him. [And if he wanted to go further on his own –
to Radford or Bulwell, say? (Bulwell is furthest limit of city on
opposite side from mother)] Oh yes – so long as he told me.

On the whole, children of this age seem to accept boundaries
with reasonably good grace; perhaps their mothers are for the most
part able to stretch the limits at an even pace with the child's own
growing adventurousness and dependability. There can in fact be
something reassuring and secure in the existence of boundaries
within which the child can feel safe from the more dangerous world
outside, and many children not only are content with the familiar
ground but turn away from the opportunity to break out, as if this
would violate the established order of things. 'I did suggest one day
last week that he should cross Perry Road [a comparatively quiet
main road] to go to the shops', said a teacher's wife, 'and he said
"Oh, but I don't cross Perry Road" '. However, a minority of
mothers (12% overall) found that they could not manage to keep
track of their children as they would like to; they 'often' could not
find the child when they wanted him, and for some of them the
child's propensity for 'wandering off' presented a real problem
(Table 6).

Rigger's mate's wife:
He plays on the street. Always missing. We've got to look for him
every night. [. . . any problem . . . ?] Yes, because he can go miles
away without ever telling you where he's going – he will, often.
The other night they were looking for him, yes, at ten past nine,
and I *said* to him "If you'd just *told* me where you were going,
because I can come straight away and get you when I need you".
But we were looking for him at ten past nine – he was up at
Bilborough [neighbouring council estate].

Coal driver's wife:

About five weeks ago he had the urge to wander away from home; we've found him down Trent Bridge; up Arnold [opposite ends of the City]. We've had the police four or five times, but as I say, he hasn't done it for about three or four weeks now . . . oh, it was a nightmare. Quarter past ten when the police caught him last month at Trent Bridge.

Electrician's wife:

He has gone off on his own, yes, he's taken himself off to my mother-in-law's, that's two miles away at Bramcote Hills, you know. Yes, she rang up one day and said "Someone wants to speak to you" – he'd walked all the way. [Had you been worried?] No, I thought he was with his friend actually – he'd gone out to call for his friend and he ended up at my mother-in-law's two miles away. [Has he done it again?] Yes, he did it the week after, so – my husband fetched him home the first time – so the second time he said "Well, I'm not fetching him, he can walk home and

Table 6 *Children who 'often' cannot be found when wanted, including those who present a 'wandering off' problem*

| | social class | | | | | summary | | |
	I&II	*IIIwc*	*III man*	*IV*	*V*	*I&II, IIIwc*	*IIIman, IV,V*	*overall popn.*
	%	%	%	%	%	%	%	%
boys	13	12	16	28	25	13	20	18
girls	5	4	7	4	10	4	7	6
both	9	8	12	16	17	8	13	12

Significance: trend ↗ *** m.class/w.class n.s.
between sexes ****

then he'll think twice about it". It was a *bigger* worry to me, because he didn't roll home until 6.45 p.m. In fact my husband had to go out looking for him – it was a bigger worry, I can assure you, I'd got the police at the door. Oh, we were all out to search. It was a bigger worry to let him come home on his own than to have fetched him, I can tell you; but he came in with a bunch of flowers and not a care in the world, you know. Course, they don't understand, do they, what a worry it is – but he came home with a bunch of flowers, and that was that.

Although the differences between classes are not large, the over-all trend in proportions is consistent enough to be significant, and shows an increase in wanderers and persistently unfindable children as we descend the class scale. A further class consideration of relevance to wandering should be mentioned in this context: we cannot quantify it, but it does emerge when reading through the verbatim transcripts. This is, that the middle-class and upper-working-class mothers are by circumstance better able to cope with the immediate practical problem of a wandering child. Further down the social scale, for one thing, the mother is more likely to be physically tied by a number of younger children; a driver's mate's wife with three younger than Winnie, who had 'had the police out all over Nottingham', said that it was very difficult: 'I can't run about after them all the time – she takes advantage a little bit, because she knows I can't get out'. A labourer's wife agreed; with four children, she said, 'They don't take much notice of you if you have that many, 'cause they know you can't run after them'. On top of this is the question of the use of amenities which are not available to lower-working-class mothers. Further up the class scale, stories of wandering are sprinkled with casual mentions of such con-veniences; in the last quotation, the child phoned home from his grandmother's, and was later collected by car (the first time), and similar examples are the norm: 'I said "Phone through to Daddy and tell him Gerald isn't in" '; 'My husband gets in the car and does a round tour'; 'The lady next door went riding round looking for him'. Whether this factor makes any difference to the incidence of wandering is hard to say, since it could work either way; we merely wish to remind the reader once again that, in practical terms, the impact of an experience may itself vary between class groups.

The sex difference shown in Table 6 is clear and unmistakable: three times as many boys as girls are 'often' unfindable. It is again, of course, difficult to separate the girls' preferences (traditionally supposed to be home-centred) from the demands made upon them; the kinds of play preferred by girls (discussed in Chapter 5) would support the theory that girls do not want to wander anyway, but certainly much more pressure is also put upon them to stay within call. In addition, in the stories about boys' escapades there is often a kind of reluctant pride in the child's rugged independence[10] which can hardly fail to be imparted to the child, and which is not evident in accounts of mothers' anxieties about girls' wanderings. The next mother has been 'harassed stiff' about her son, yet basic-ally she feels he will always come through unscathed; the one who follows her has been far more worried by her daughter (led astray by an eight-year-old boy!), even though she too has never failed to turn up in the end.

Labourer's wife:
[. . . any problem . . . ?] Oh yes, many a time. Sometimes when he goes out he's gone for about three hours and I'm worrying where he's gone to; but he's one of them sort of boys, he can go but he'll always come back. I mean, the other day he went – about what time would it be, half past nine, quarter to ten? – and he didn't come back till dinner-time, and I was harassed stiff, but he came polling in as if nowt had happened – "Is me dinner ready?"

Miner's wife:
A boy across there, he's about eighteen months older than her . . . . . he had a big influence on her, she did what *he* said. And on top of that he was a wanderer, and he was encouraging her to wander too. It was a nightmare, she was *always* missing. In the finish, he took her into town on the bus! Well, that was it, her Dad gave her a good hiding for that, and we told her she wasn't to play with him any more.

'You read in the papers of such awful things happening . . .'
With a majority of 88% of children who can easily, or with a very small expenditure of effort, be found when wanted, the picture begins to emerge of the seven-year-old as basically a territorial animal whose terrain is limited not so much by physical boundaries as by familiarity and habit, backed up by certain fairly explicit rules which are laid down by his mother and designed to promote a healthy fear of the dangers he may meet if he strays too far. We have seen that 62% of mothers set defined boundaries, 77% have firm rules that the child must tell them his destination before going anywhere (and report back as often as he changes his mind), and 92% expect the child to report home after school, as his first priority. In other words, children of this age are supposed to keep within their habitual territorial limits, and if they venture outside them special precautions are usually thought necessary; a child may be given permission to go shopping with a trustworthy elder sibling, or the mother may feel that there is safety in numbers, and allow the child to go with a group of his peers to the park, recreation ground or Saturday afternoon cinema, when he would not be allowed there

on his own. The basic rule, however, is that the mother (or occasionally some other responsible adult) should know just what is going
on, and that the child himself should understand that a framework
exists out of which it is unwise, and possibly dangerous, to be
tempted.

Salesman's wife:
[Do you have any rules about telling you where she's going before
she goes out?] Oh yes – in fact she recites it all to me now. She'll
come in and say, "I'm going to the park, Mam". I'll say, "Well
remember . . ."
"I know – *take nothing of anybody,*
Don't speak to anybody,
And if you go with friends, come back with them."
I'll say, "All right, as long as you know". "All right, Mother."

Although the fear of harm or danger to the child has been
implicit in the whole issue of supervision of children's movements,
we have not yet discussed directly the specific perils which cause
such anxiety. The four main possibilities in an urban environment
seem to be getting lost, non-traffic accidents, traffic accidents and
sexual molestation.

The first we can discount, as it does not seem to worry mothers
at this age: or rather, they can trust their children to wander only
within their capabilities of finding the way back. In this, children
of seven differ from four-year-olds, who are both more heedless of
the long-term pattern of their actions and less able to rectify the
situation by seeking help verbally and putting verbal advice into
practice.

Non-traffic accidents seem very specific to the individual locality,
the dangerous situations available in it and the child's own play-
preferences. In the Meadows area, parents worry about the river;
people living near the canal know it to be a potential danger, and
a number of children have in the past been injured while climbing
on factory roofs. One boy in our sample has been rescued from
the steep face of the Castle Rock; but even recreation grounds, with
their heavy-duty swings and see-saws, can be a source of broken
teeth, cut eyes and the like, especially if older and rougher children
play there. On the whole, mothers do their best to identify the
special dangers of their neighbourhood and warn the children about
these specifically; though as many of us know, looking back on our
own childhoods, the really dangerous activity could have been one

which never occurred to our mothers, and of which they remained happily unaware.

Traffic accidents and molestation have two things in common: they can happen at any time when the child is on his own outside home ground, and their prevention entails curbing two qualities which parents otherwise like to encourage – adventurousness and friendliness. In addition, any parent who reads the local paper (and the *Nottingham Evening Post* is estimated by its circulation office to reach about 80% of households) will be reminded rather frequently that such things do happen, and to children in neighbourhoods which they themselves know well. The special significance of a local paper is that it reports relatively minor accidents in detail, as well as fatalities, and that it also gives generous coverage to suspicious incidents, as well as those where a child is actually physically molested; and when the place of the occurrence is only a bus-ride away, every mother must feel some involvement. A few children in our sample have already experienced such incidents, either themselves or through siblings: June's younger brother has been seriously disabled after being knocked down by a bus near his home; Stanley's ten-year-old sister was the victim of attempted rape on the waste ground at the end of the street (convicted case); Roy was in hospital for three days with concussion after being hit by a car outside his house; Patricia's sister is receiving psychiatric treatment for school phobia after being chased by a man on her way home. These experiences, even if vicarious, do not leave children untouched.

Scaffolder's wife:

> She always comes straight home – they all do, I've always drilled that into them. She seems to have got the message. 'Cause the oldest girl, she went to Colwick Woods once, and a man got hold of her, but she had the sense to bite his hand – he put his hand over her mouth and she bit it; and he let her go, you see. But it frightened her and frightened the others too, because they knew about it.

From the parents' standpoint, there is no obvious solution to the traffic hazard. The planner's dream of a complete separation of pedestrians and motor vehicles[11] is unlikely, at the present rate of progress, to attain reality for most children in the next two or three generations. Road safety programmes try to instil a list of do's and don'ts, enlisting the child's natural motives of self-preservation, but often meet with only modified success because the child who fully obeys instructions (such as 'wait till the road is clear') may never get across some roads at all; unfortunately, the skills involved in road-crossing are so complex, and the situations to be met so variable, that rules for dealing with them can only over-simplify the issue. At some stage, however, the child has to be allowed to face the problem on his own, and to learn from first-hand experience how to choose his tactics safely in the negotiation of busy roads.

To decide just when a child is ready to cross major roads alone is not at all an easy matter. In some cases, the child's own caution prevents him from attempting it, even when his parents think him sensible enough to be allowed to try, and the wise strategy might indeed be simply to wait until the child both wants to cope alone and demonstrates (perhaps clandestinely) that he is able to do so. More than one of these mothers had learned only after the event that this stage had been reached: 'He *has* crossed Mansfield Road, but unknown to me, actually; my mother-in-law was at the crossing, but he didn't see her . . . . . I nearly went up to the ceiling before I opened my mouth to say a word, I was so agitated . . . . . I *would* trust him to go now, but I'd be very worried'. In other cases, however, the child appears all too blasé about the dangers involved, and the mother's main anxiety is that his confidence is not matched by his skill, and that he might in the event be fearless to the point of being foolhardy.

Designer's wife:

[Do you trust him now to cross busy roads on his own?] If you'd asked me this two months ago, I'd have said yes; but we had an experience the other week where he wasn't as alert as I'd have believed him to have been, and he did avoid quite a nasty accident, actually. He . . . he just forgot that time, so I wouldn't know, with a busy road, to be perfectly honest – I wouldn't be very happy about a busy road, no.

Baker's wife:

Well, I do, but I must say that there's always that fear in my mind about Richard. He doesn't seem like Paul [sibling], you know, I feel frightened all the time he's out. Paul I could trust, oh, from a very early age; Richard just seems that little bit . . . I don't know . . . [Father:] A bit more harebrained, you know. [Mother:] Yes, we seem to be more frightened about him. Why, I can't explain. He's quite a sensible kiddy, I don't know why

I feel that way, but, um . . . [Would you let him go across South-church Drive (main road through council estate)?] Well, I should let him go up there, but not where the main shops, Woolworth's, are, not yet. [Because it's a long way, or the traffic is bad?] I don't really know . . . he's quite a sensible kiddy . . . [Father:] He's not quite so stable. [Mother:] He's not as stable as Paul, that's definite. [Father:] I've taken him round once or twice on his bike, you know, and he's . . . as regards looking right and left, things like that, he seems to forget occasionally, you know . . .

Once again, therefore, as with other issues, the mother will tend to act partly in accordance with her own capacity for calm ('I *could* trust her, but it's my own mind, you know') and partly according to the temperament of the child in question. However, because parents know that even capable children are sometimes impulsive, that even careful motorists are sometimes momentarily distracted, and that heavy traffic and children are poor mixers anyway, there is likely to be a period for every parent when the child is trusted as an act of faith which must be taken sooner or later, but at the expense of a good deal of worry.

Building worker's wife:
Yes, I do trust her . . . er . . . I got a bit frightened after Brendan's accident [sibling, leg amputation]; you know, I still drum it into them; but I think, while the road's there, they've *got* to be trusted – they *have* to cross the road to get to school, so I just keep my fingers crossed and hope for the best.

Wholesaler's wife:
Of course, he doesn't go into town alone or anything like that, but he's quite capable of crossing busy roads, and he realises that there are dangers. There was an accident a little while ago involving a child who lives just round here; and of course immediately there was a rush that night to fetch the children out of school; but I said "No – I've *told* you what you must do, you *know* what you must do, and if I *come* for you and you run away from me, I can't do anything about it – you're responsible for yourself now". And I think – of course, there *are* always accidents – but he *is* responsible enough if he thinks, so I let him go on his own. Mind you . . . I was looking out of the bedroom window to see him come down the road that night!

Commercial traveller's wife:
> I'm *not* very happy, you know, but I feel that he knows the consequences of taking any risks.

At this age, 40% of children overall are trusted to cross busy roads on their own. There is no significant sex difference, which probably reflects the wording of the question in terms of trust rather than the child's actual activities: observation of children's road-crossing behaviour suggests that girls tend to be less 'heedless' than boys,[12] which may well be recognised by parents, thus reducing the sex differences shown elsewhere in this chapter. Class differences are not very obvious, but there is a slight suggestion of a class trend ($p \backsimeq 0.06$) when the boys are looked at on their own: boys are more likely to be trusted to cross busy roads as one descends the social scale (36% in Class I and II increases steadily to 53% in Class V).

The 60% who do *not* trust their children to this extent know, however, that they are only putting off the evil hour, and that sooner or later they will have to expose their children to this kind of risk. In the end, it is only through such exposure, and perhaps by experiencing fear as a result of heedlessness or misjudgement, that children learn to be reasonably reliable in coping with busy roads.

Parental fears that their children will be molested by strangers[13] are an equally live issue, and the anxiety applies to boys as well as girls – although for girls, of course, the dangers of sexual assault tend to be taken particularly seriously. The exact nature of the danger will not, however, be made clear to the child, but referred to in terms of 'harm', 'hurt', 'take you away'. Nearly all children are warned explicitly never to go off with a 'strange man', never to accept lifts from strangers and not to take sweets offered by people they do not know. This lesson is also reinforced by headteachers in assembly and by the police, who visit primary schools and warn children in much the same terms, particularly when any suspicious behaviour has been reported locally. Through the medium of television, the child will also become aware of the more monstrous cases of child abduction and murder; some children are very disturbed by such reports.

Builder's labourer's wife:
> Sometimes she's a bit scared when she hears on TV about those little girls having been picked up – or such as the Moors murders – and we try, like, not to let her take too much notice of them.

And her Daddy'll say "Oh, well . . ." and try to put her off –
"Well, that was a long while ago" – but she's pretty intelligent –
she knows – she hears at school, a bad man was after a little girl,
or something like that. She wants all the details. It does trouble
her, yes.

Again, the dilemma can be seen: the mother *needs* a modicum of
fear in her child in order to protect it, but does not want it distressed.
She also wishes it to be friendly, but not so friendly as to lay itself
open to abuse; to be straightforward and trusting, but not to trust
dangerously.

Building worker's wife:
[What about new people? Is she shy?] Oh no, quite the reverse,
especially with men – she frightens me at times. You know, if any
men come here we don't know – the milkman, you know how
often they change about – she's all round them – women as well,
but mostly men; and she'll talk to anybody in the street, "Hullo",
she'll say. She frightens me at times, because you have to be so
careful; because there's been two or three little incidents up here
of children being abducted and taken on to those fields and that
– it does really frighten you. I *insist* that she comes straight home
and that I know where she is. She will speak and react to anyone.

Warehouse manager's wife:
Well, we drill this into him so much, trying to, you know, show
him examples as well, anything you read in the papers or you
see on TV – you know, "Look what happened to that boy, he got
attacked here or he got run over there". He understands.

Bus driver's wife:
You know, you read in the papers of such awful things happening,
about children, you know, being run off with and everything;
well, every night I say to her "Has anybody spoke to you or
anything like that?" and she says "No", and I says "Well, don't
you ever speak to anybody while you're at school" [*sic*]. I always
warn her never to take sweets off anybody or anything like that –
that's the only worry I've got about her – otherwise she's a very
good child, and she's always dead on 4.15, and I know where she
is if I ever want her when she's out playing.

Labourer's wife:
He'd probably go with them if anyone offered to take him. I
mean, even a stranger he'd go with – I've tried to drill it into him

not to talk to men or anything, but he don't seem to take any notice of you . . . . . One night he came in with a two-shilling piece in his hand. It appears some man had given it to him – God knows where he'd been. I couldn't fathom out – I've never found out where he went . . . . . Nowt bothers Wayne.

Machinist's wife:
I think he would be easily led – that is the reason I go up to school to fetch him. I think he'd take a person at their word.

Obviously one solution to the problem can be to prolong super-vision, and supervision may well be prolonged for this reason, as we can see from the last statement; the intensification of this fear where girls are concerned is certainly a major factor in the finding that twice as many girls as boys are escorted from school. Once more, however, this solution is only a temporary one, and there will come a time when the child has to be allowed much greater freedom and independence of movement, like it or not. Thus, when we return to these families at the eleven-year-old stage, when the child moves on to secondary school and inevitably takes a giant stride further out of the home orbit, we shall find the topic still very much alive.

'Mine seems to be the place where they all accumulate . . .'
One way of ensuring that the child will remain contentedly within call, and yet have the social contact he needs and which so often tempts him away, is to offer a welcome to his friends.

Craftsman's wife (manager in her own business):
They nearly always play here, I think because there's a junked-up garden and a full-up shed – I think we are about the most easy-going of them. So you see we get them all. It suits me fine, because I can keep my eye on Simon without him being tied without friends, sort of thing; so it works very well.

Here again, a certain ambivalence often makes itself felt; the con-venience of knowing where one's own child is can be marred by the chagrin of seeing house and garden reduced to a shambles twice as quickly as the residents could manage unaided. If the children visit each other turn and turn about, mothers can happily shift responsibility one to another; but where one child's house is too often preferred, his mother is likely to reflect upon her neighbours' houses, remaining tidy while her own becomes stickily lived-in, and to suspect that she has the worst of the bargain: 'it makes me a bit cross sometimes when I think about it'. Two opposing views:

Metal polisher's wife:
His friend comes here to play, but he doesn't go to his friend's house, because *his* mother doesn't allow him to play inside. I'm afraid that's one-sided. [That's rather sad, isn't it?] It is really; you know, she's just one of those types who won't have them inside, I don't know why. The little boy goes out in the morning, and if he goes back before his lunch, he's in trouble; one of those types.

Dry cleaner's wife:
Harry [friend] don't like to come here, because I make him do as he's told, you see. I mean, I not let him jump on my furniture, and knock my home about, where I think he *can* at his own home – although they've got a nice home; but I think his Mam lets him jump around on the furniture too much. Well, it takes a lot of working for, don't it, and therefore you don't want it banging about, you see. Jimmy's made to come off the furniture – I mean, he'll get on that arm or he'll get on this arm when he's, you know, took away with the horses on the television, and he's riding, but we make him get off, you see.

In the course of discussing the child's friendships (Questions 32–45), we asked about friends whom he might see in the weekend (to separate off the question of school friends), followed by the question 'Do they come and play at your house?' Replies were categorised into three groups, according to whether another child or children played at the house most weeks, only sometimes, or not at all. The results for the two outside categories are given in Table 7. In the category 'Friends play at child's house *most weeks*', the main class difference occurs between Class I and II and the rest (72% against 57%, significant at the 0·001 level). In the category of 'Friends come to play *not at all*', the overall class difference is clearer: in the unskilled and semi-skilled families, one fifth of these children do not have friends to the house, whereas this proportion drops to less than a tenth in the middle class generally, and to less than a twentieth in Class I and II. The class differences in this category are highly significant. With regard to sex differences, these can be seen (significant at the 0·01 level) in the '*most weeks*' category: girls are more likely than boys to have their friends in

Table 7 *Frequency with which child's friend(s) come to play at his house*

	social class					summary		
	I&II	IIIwc	III man	IV	V	I&II, IIIwc	IIIman, IV,V	overall popn.
	%	%	%	%	%	%	%	%
a. 'most weeks'								
boys	68	54	48	47	54	62	49	52
girls	75	63	67	53	59	69	63	65
both	72	59	57	50	57	65	56	58

Significance: trend ↘ ****   m.class/w.class **

between sexes ***

b. 'not at all'								
boys	3	5	21	23	19	4	21	17
girls	5	12	9	15	26	8	12	11
both	4	9	15	19	22	6	17	14

Significance: trend ↗ ****   m.class/w.class ****

between sexes n.s.

sex x class interaction **

frequently. In the category of children who have their friends to play *'not at all'*, however, the sex difference does not reach significance, and this is because it is cancelled out by an interesting sex-by-class interaction: in the middle class the trend reverses, and rather fewer boys than girls have *no friends* in (interaction significant at 0·02). A possible reason for this may be a group of middle-class mothers who want their children under their eye, preferably without an invasion of other children, but who feel that they have to allow boys' friends in to provide amusement, whereas for girls they are more able to offer amusement themselves in the form of domestic activities. We would not want to make too much of this point, however, especially as the figures in the middle class refer to a very small minority (6%).

The fact that middle-class mothers have on the whole more space available would seem to make this result predictable: the inclusion of neighbours' children as well as one's own could make already overcrowded conditions intolerable. The point that they also tend to have more valuable possessions, and might therefore be

D

considered more vulnerable to damage, is balanced by their being
better able to replace them; it may be remembered that, at four,
Class I and II mothers were less restrictive than other classes on
the question of children making a mess and using furniture for their
play.[14] On reading the actual replies mothers give, however, the
impression is that in *every* class visiting children are seen as a
mixed blessing, but that the further one moves down the social scale,
the more likely the mother is to forbid entry on this account: 'I
never allow them in', says a labourer's wife, and a bus cleaner's
wife explains, 'Well, I have had three or four of them in, but I
find that they go too mad when they get together, so I've stopped
it'. Further up the scale, on the other hand, the mother will grumble
but permit *within certain controls*. These statements also convey
a sense of the middle-class mother having a more formal idea of her
supervision responsibilities towards children playing at her house.

Research chemist's wife:
   This problem of play – inviting children and so on, it did become
   a problem the week before she had her birthday. She brought
   two children home – I was cross about it – mostly because I was
   busy dressmaking and so on; it does depend on whether *I* feel
   outgoing or not, which is hardly fair on her, but . . . oh, I was
   raving, and – "I *wish* you wouldn't bring anybody home", and
   she said "Well, I did ask their Mummies", and I said "Well,
   suppose I wanted to go out, what would you do then?" I *am*
   finding this difficult with Eleanor; but I think – you know – I'm
   sure Gill will find it easier, and by the time Beth's gone through
   it and Jenny's gone through it, I shall have accepted this [younger
   siblings]. I don't like her bringing people home without having
   asked; on the other hand, the arrangements you have to go to
   with the mother to see if it's all right on the 'phone, it's terrible,
   you see . . .

Warehouse manager's wife:
   There has been one particular lad, and he's very wild, and every
   time he came here he'd get up on top of the garage roof and I'd
   have a fit. [Father:] Because he could soon damage the other
   children – not so much what he's going to do to ours – but if
   they have an accident in our yard, as I say to the wife, if he falls
   off the roof and breaks a leg – what's his father going to think?
   Because if ours was doing the same, we'd be going hairless, you
   know, if he'd been on someone else's roof.

Company director's wife:

Most weeks – I wouldn't say most *days*; if it's fine and they come, I don't mind a bit. I've got a sort of room they can come in and out, sort of, down here, and they keep a lot of toys there, you know, and they dress up; but if it's pouring with rain, they come in for about half-an-hour and then they go home, because you can't cope with them throwing things around inside.

'. . . *not so much that I don't trust her – it's for my own peace of mind . . .*'

We can now go on to draw together the various findings described in this chapter and to find a common thread among them. We propose to do this in terms of what we shall call the 'chaperonage factor': the extent to which children in their ordinary everyday experience come under the supervision of their parents (or a

Table 8   *An index of chaperonage*

Based on	Situation	Criterion	Score
Q17	Coming out of school	Fetched	2
		Comes straight home (or straight to arranged place)	1
		Plays out first	0
Q17	Rule re 'straight home'	M has this rule	1
		No rule	0
Q17	Adult at home on child's return	Yes	1
		No	0
Q36	Childs friends come to play at his house	Yes	1
		No	0
Q78	Child plays in street	Yes	0
		No	1
Q81 and Q82	Child can be found when wanted; child presents wandering problem	Always findable	3
		Sometimes not	2
		Often not	1
		Real problem	0
Q83	Rules re telling M where he is going	Yes, definite	2
		Would like, not enforced	1
		No rules	0
Q84	Rules re how far he may go	M has a rule	1
		No rules	0
Q85	N's expeditions on own (park, recreation ground, swimming bath, pictures, library prompted)	None	1
		Any	0

Score range: 0–13

parental delegate), either by remaining within the immediate parental orbit, or by acceding to certain conditions (in particular, staying within boundaries and keeping the parent precisely informed) when they move beyond that orbit.

It is possible to devise an index of chaperonage for each child, based upon a scoring system for the questions already discussed, with one addition. This scoring system is set out in Table 8. The addition comes from Question 85: 'Does he ever go to a park or recreation ground by himself? (prompt:) swimming bath alone? pictures alone? anywhere else?' (including library from Question 123 if child goes there alone).

Using this index, theoretically a range of chaperonage scores from 0 to 13 is possible; the actual range obtained is 0 to 11. Analysing the data as usual by class and sex, and taking means of scores from each class/sex group, the results appearing in Table 9 emerge. The most unambiguous finding is the difference between sexes, which is significant at the 0·001 level. Between middle and working classes there is a difference which reaches significance at 0·05, but when one looks at class groups individually a class trend can be seen which is significant at the 0·01 level.

These results confirm beyond any reasonable doubt that by the age of seven, and in a whole variety of ways, the daily experience of little boys in terms of where they are allowed to go, how they spend their time and to what extent they are kept under adult surveillance is already markedly different from that of little girls.[15] The factors underlying this divergence are complex and probably reflect an interaction between innate temperamental differences and social pressures. Many studies can be cited[16] to show that whereas boys tend generally to be thrusting, aggressive, active and thing-

Table 9   *Children's mean scores on the chaperonage factor*

| | social class | | | | | | summary | | |
	I&II	IIIwc	III man	IV	V		I&II, IIIwc	IIIman, IV,V	overall popn.
	%	%	%	%	%		%	%	%
boys	9·6	9·2	9·1	8·6	8·4		9·4	8·9	9·0
girls	10·6	10·3	10·3	10·0	9·2		10·5	10·1	10·2
both	10·1	9·7	9·7	9·3	8·7		9·9	9·5	9·6

Significance: trend ↓ ***   m.class/w.class   *
                between sexes ****

oriented from an early age, girls on the whole tend to be more nurturant, amenable, sedentary and person-oriented. It seems doubtful that basic constitutional factors are unimportant in the aetiology of such sex differences; but in practice it is extremely difficult to isolate biological determinants from socio-cultural influences, which may also be shown to be operating even before the child himself is born. In other words, there are clearly defined differences in the way parents think of, feel about and act towards their children which depend upon whether the child is a boy or a girl; and, if this was difficult for us to show at four, it must be remembered that at that age supervision is almost total anyway.

English parents in a contemporary urban setting are not alone in placing a certain emphasis upon what might be called 'the chaperonage of females'. Among human societies all over the world and throughout recorded time, it has been a fairly universal cultural preoccupation to place restrictions upon the geographical mobility of women and girls, and, in particular, to limit the possibility of chance encounters between dependent daughters and adult male strangers. The evidence we have discussed clearly indicates that in our own culture, too, the chaperonage factor exerts an important influence upon the daily life experience of girls as compared with boys even by the tender age of seven, ensuring that girls lead a more sheltered and protected existence. This in itself is of interest: but the implications are of greater consequence, since children who are kept under closer and more continuous surveillance must inevitably *come under consistently greater pressure towards conformity with adult standards and values*.

Over and above the sex difference, it is clear from our analysis that the chaperonage factor discriminates between the different social class groups, so that a descent of the scale involves a falling-off of adult supervision. We have elsewhere sought explanations for similar differences in terms of certain class-related variables such as family size or living conditions: we have suggested, for instance, that children in large families will be difficult to contain in a small house, and that mothers of such families will not have the time to make continual checks on the whereabouts of their seven-year-olds. Using these same scores, it was not, however, possible to demonstrate any consistent differences between large families (four or more children) and smaller families, either within the sample as a whole or within separate class groups. Again, one might suppose that in the more densely populated 'Central' areas, where the houses often have shared backyards opening directly on to the street, and where private gardens are few and very small, the children might wander off more frequently. However, if class is held constant, the results indicate no real differences between the 'Estate' and 'Other' districts in terms of chaperonage. There was some indication (not quite significant) that 'Central' district children differed from the rest, but in fact the direction of the difference suggests that children in these more dangerous streets are, if anything, kept under closer supervision, class for class, than children elsewhere. In practice more lower-working-class families live in central districts; thus the implication of these results where class is held constant is that, if *residential district* were held constant, class differences overall would be still greater. It must be concluded, therefore, that the social class difference in surveillance and chaperonage is in fact due more to a difference in basic attitudes than to the circumstances in which families are constrained to live.

It will be seen that, in a sense, the reverse of chaperonage is independence: that is, the factors which we have been considering all appear to be related to how far a child has developed skills of self-reliance and can be expected to look after himself when he is out and about on his own. However, we prefer for the moment not to discuss the findings in these terms, for the reason that further analysis shows independence to be complicated by the context in which it takes place and the nature of the situational demands made upon the child. For instance, in the preceding discussion we have met children who have learned to stand on their own feet in the company of their peers, finding their amusement out on the street, and fighting their own battles as the need arises; however, there are other kinds of independence which may be no less important in the total socialisation process. The child who can deal politely with a stranger at the door, who can answer the telephone and take a message efficiently, who can behave acceptably in a café or at the theatre, and who can be confidently requested to tidy up his playthings before visitors arrive is also demonstrably self-reliant in the sense that he can be trusted to behave in a responsible and 'grown-up' manner. Inevitably, therefore, the question of chaperonage will recur in many guises as we look more closely at the circumstances and considerations which shape patterns of behaviour in seven-year-old children.

NOTES

1 Obviously the home can itself be inhibiting and stultifying, and moving out of its ambience could be liberating in the long term. But this book

is about seven-year-olds, and we are concerned with what is possible and probable in the context of this developmental stage.

2 See interview schedule, Appendix I, p. 409.

3 J. and E. Newson and P. Barnes, *Perspectives on School at Seven Years Old*.

4 As in the preceding study, the sample can be divided into three roughly equal groups with regard to the type of residential district: 'Central', the older working-class districts within about a mile radius from the City centre; 'Estate', referring to three major council housing complexes; and 'Suburban', which includes scattered small groupings of council houses together with suburban areas generally. Tower block flats are not included, as none was occupied by our children at seven.

5 Notified road accidents to pedestrian children under fourteen during the period 1969–73 inclusive numbered 1,087 in our 'central' area, compared with 390 in the 'suburban' area and 264 in the 'estate' area (62%, 22% and 15% respectively) (personal communication from A. Routledge and R. Repetto-Wright, Child Accident Research Unit, University of of Nottingham).

6 Both these mothers in fact moved to middle-class areas a year or two later.

7 This has in fact led to protests in the City by parents living near favoured schools who felt that their children were being squeezed out by children from neighbouring districts.

8 This greater supervision of girls is reflected in the road accident rates for this age-group, although there is some evidence that boys compound their unsupervised state by being also temperamentally less cautious. The ratio of boys' accidents to girls' accidents at seven is in fact 2:1.

9 C. I. Howarth, D. A. Routledge and R. Repetto-Wright: 'An analysis of road accidents involving child pedestrians', *Ergonomics*, 1974; 'The exposure of young children to accident risks as pedestrians', *Ergonomics*, 1975; 'A comparison of interviews and observation to obtain measures of children's exposure to risk as pedestrians', *Ergonomics*, 1975.

10 See also the caretaker's wife on page 85 and the electrician's wife on page 86.

11 See, for instance, Paul Ritter, *Planning for Man and Motor*, Pergamon, London, 1964.

12 'Heedless' here defined in terms of 'not looking'; 'running'; and observer's judgement of the act—all these show a sex difference. C .I. Howarth, D. A. Routledge and R. Repetto-Wright, 1974.

13 It is interesting that it always seems to be 'strangers' against whom children are warned. Gibbens and Prince, investigating a random sample of 82 cases of sexual molestation, found that a complete stranger was involved in only 32% of cases. 36% were neighbours or 'family friends', and in 21% of cases the child's father or stepfather was the molestor. T. C. N. Gibbens and Joyce Prince, 'Child victims of sex offences', paper published by the Institute for the Study and Treatment of Delinquency, London, 1963.

14 J. and E. Newson, 1968, pp. 153–9 (Pelican edn. pp. 160–9).

15 Because the means of these scores cluster in a range of 8·4–10·6, readers who are unused to interpreting statistical data may feel that the differences are not very great. They are of a similar order, in fact, to

the differences in height between men and women, which most people would agree is a 'marked difference'.

16   For instance, see W. C. McGrew, 'Aspects of social development in nursery school children with emphasis on introduction to the group', in N. Blurton Jones (ed.), *Ethological Studies of Child Behaviour,* Cambridge University Press, 1972. A useful summary of sex differences in a variety of behaviour areas is given in Eleanor Maccoby (ed.), *The Development of Sex Differences,* Tavistock, London, 1967.

Chapter 4

Playthings and Pastimes

This chapter and the next could equally well have been titled 'The What and How of Children's Play': for in them we are concerned first with the specific occupations in which the child engages and the toys and materials which are the tools of his play; and secondly with the more general question of the ways in which children play, the tendencies which may emerge in certain groups to favour a particular style of play, and the significance which can be seen in such tendencies for the child's total development at this stage.

When mothers are asked to describe the home-based activities of their children, their accounts at seven characteristically show a notable verbal difference from those which they gave when the child was only four: at seven they are expressed in the third person singular, whereas at four the first person plural was very much in evidence. Looking back to the four-year-old stage, we find 66% of mothers at that time actively participating in their children's play *on the level of the child himself*, quite apart from those who help him in more 'educational' pursuits; and the quotations we gave then[1] showed clearly the degree to which the mother could be drawn into the child's play: 'Cowboys . . . . . I have to hide behind the settee and they come riding round it . . . '; 'we get all these pillows off the settee here . . . we all have to get on and go for a ride'; 'I'm the patient, or the baby, or the little girl's aunt'; 'we have to fight, and I'm the Sheriff of Nottingham and he's Robin Hood'; 'we go on a rocket . . . when the spin drier's on for the noise . . .'; 'Oh, we have a jolly time!' By seven, however, this quality of involvement is very rare, and the mother has withdrawn to the role of onlooker only.

Student teacher's wife (herself a teacher):
    Fantasy; dressing-up; house. [Father:] Farm, with Martin.

[Mother:] Yes, well, that's Martin; but with the other children it will be some form of imaginative play. [Father:] *Energetic* imaginative play. [Mother:] *Energetic* imaginative play! [Does she build things or make things at all?] Those are the things that she does when she's alone and has to amuse herself. [Father:] That Lego[2] comes out very much in the morning. At the weekend when we stay in bed late, Antonia will build with Lego. [Mother:] But not with other children – this is on her own. She goes up and down [on her bike] with them if they've got their bicycles. [Father:] I was just thinking, building with other children – what about the house they have out in the grass? [Mother:] Building with junk stuff. They construct dens and houses. [Is this part of an imaginative game?] Yes.

Tobacco worker's wife:
He won't stay at one thing, you know; he's got a tool set of his own, and he likes to make things, and he gets everything out; and whereas one child will sit all morning, he'll have ten minutes – he sort of crams three or four things into one hour, you know – move about from one thing to another.

Business executive's wife:
He's invariably getting this big sketch block out . . . er . . . he plays a lot with cars . . . um . . . he has a huge railway layout. Now the railway didn't go down very well at all, it did too much for itself; it went by itself and he had nothing to do but stand there. That for Guy isn't good enough, he's creative, he likes to be making things, doing the work himself, he doesn't like things to be doing it for him. So I'm afraid he stripped the whole table. It's a huge table with a centre piece that you can stand up, and has grass and fields all around; and he bought the garden set, I think, with everything in. That occupies a whole corner, he makes all the flowers and things, and then he builds up a whole farm of the 'Britains' things, that's in another corner, and he spends a lot of time with that . . .

Postal worker's wife:
He'll play Monopoly for hours by himself – any game on his own; even if it needs two or three players, he'll play two or three players by himself. He had that Monopoly until I thought it was monopolising *him*!

Pipe inspector's wife:
Ooh! I don't know what they play. I think they play hide-and-seek. They play certain games but I don't go out to see.

This change is probably due to a number of factors. Physically the child is not so much under his mother's eye, in that he is trusted on the street for much of his free time; intellectually, he has a greater capacity for concentration and more ability to busy himself without help; socially, he is more likely to find companionship among his peers instead of from his mother, and better able to cope, one way or another, with the ups and downs of sociable play. In practice, then, seven-year-olds are more or less content to be left to their own devices, and, within the limits of the chaperonage factor, will generally take their friends off to play somewhere out of the way of the adults, whose presence may indeed be seen as a hindrance even though the activities contemplated are perfectly legal. Often this means that parents are only let into the secret of what the particular game is all about when a serious difference of opinion drives some of the children to seek adult intervention.

Inevitably, this disengagement of the mother has the effect that parents of seven-year-olds will vary much more in their awareness of the children's activities: the first and the last of the group of quotations just given show different degrees of interest in the minutiae of the child's play. Despite this difficulty, we still found it possible to build up a picture of the children's play interests by asking a number of rather specific questions about special enthusiasms, hobbies, collections and toys most used, as well as more general questions about activities taking place at certain times of day or week. The main relevant questions were as follows; their context can be seen by referring to the interview schedule in Appendix I.

16. We should like to know something now about what sort of things N likes doing when he's not at school. What about in the morning? Does he have any time to himself between waking up and leaving for school? (*If any*): What does he usually do in that time? How does he amuse himself?
18. When he gets home, what does he do with his free time until bedtime?
19. Some children seem to spend a great deal of time doing one or two special things, like reading or drawing or making models. Has N a special hobby of this sort?
20. Has he any (other) special toy or game that takes up a lot of his time?
21. Has he anything he collects, or anything that he gradually adds to? (*If bought*): Does he spend his own money on this?

30. Now that N is at school, does he have enough time to do all the things he wants to do at home?

31. What about days when there's no school? What does he do with his time mostly? (*Include those occupations which child has on any average weekend, and prompt 'inside?' or 'outside?' as necessary*)

46. What sort of games does N mostly play with other children? (*Place in order of his preference; prompt all if necessary*)

.... *Rough and tumble*

.... *Construction*

.... *Imaginative games*

47. Does he ever have play-acting games *when he's on his own* – either being someone himself or making up a story with dolls or toy animals or puppets?

The answers involving specific games, toys and activities were not easy to code in any formal way or to analyse quantitatively. Although one can ask what a child likes doing best, or how he spends his time before breakfast, it is difficult to gauge phrases like 'he's football-mad' or 'comics, that's what she likes more than owt' in terms of hours of occupation, let alone the intensity or the persistence of the interest. A child like Guy in the third quotation above, for instance, shows an integrated and consistent pattern of play interests (heavily backed up by his parents – see the further quotation on page 126) which contrasts markedly with the activities of 'flitting' children and bored children, and must inevitably hold significance for his total intellectual development. We have tried to explore such differences between children both in terms of temperament ('Is he a busy sort of child, or does he easily get bored?') and under the heading of educational home activities parallel to school (companion volume to this). At this stage of the discussion, however, we will be looking at play activities in terms of popularity as measured (rather crudely) by a simple count of how many parents mentioned particular interests.

It should also be borne in mind that the questions themselves mention certain activities, either in the main body of the question or as explanatory prompts, so that there is a little contamination here. It is difficult to know how to deal with this problem; one would prefer never to use examples, but they do sometimes seem necessary in order to direct the mother's attention to the precise area of investigation. In general, prompting of an activity may inflate the number of mentions it receives (though use of phrases like 'a great deal of time' (Question 19) cuts down purely 'frivolous' mentions); conversely, however, the negative answer acquires greater force if prompts are used. Also, failure to prompt can result in artificially *de*flated figures if the item is marginal to the subject under discussion: for instance, bicycles were not specifically asked about, and it was found at a late stage that prompting them after Question 19 produced significantly more mentions. Many mothers were, quite understandably, not counting them as 'toys . . . that take up a lot of his time'; thus cycling had to come out in answers to a 'what does he do with his time' question, and the figure was a good deal smaller than it might have been.

Eventually, then, we built up a very general impression of the activities and toys which appeared most popular at seven; and it seems useful to discuss these in terms of indoor and outdoor play, games which are played according to rules, and commercial toys of special appeal. Collections form a category of their own.

'. . . *up to an hour upstairs . . . pottering about and doing things . . .*'
The indoor pursuit most frequently mentioned is drawing; and if we add to this 'crayonning' or 'colouring' and 'painting', it is quite clear that graphic self-expression, even if occasionally confined to cheap painting-books for colouring, is a major preoccupation for children in this age-group. We can be reasonably confident that this is so, because at a later stage in the interview we also asked the direct question 'Does he do any drawing or painting at home?' The answers given were coded into three categories: 'most days', 'sometimes' and 'not much'. Table 10 shows how strikingly popular this activity is: 91% draw or paint reasonably often, and 40% 'most days'. There is no consistent sex difference, but analysis by class shows a significant trend (0·01 level) for children who seldom draw to increase in number as we descend the social scale. Even so, the most noteworthy fact in this table is the popularity of drawing at every class level.

Pencils and crayons are, of course, among the more obvious materials which can be given to children when they are bored and ask for 'something to do'; they are also cheap and readily available at any corner shop. It is probable, too, that the advent of felt-tipped and fibre-tipped pens, especially since they have moved from the art-shop to the newsagent's, where they can be bought singly for a few pence, have given a fresh impetus to children's desire to draw: good clear colours go a long way to make up for poor quality paper or an uncertain line, and, hopefully, protract the golden age

Table 10 *Frequency of drawing or painting at home*

	social class					summary		
	I&II	IIIwc	III man	IV	V	I&II IIIwc	IIIman, IV,V	overall popn.
	%	%	%	%	%	%	%	%
'most days'								
boys	47	41	39	28	35	44	36	39
girls	46	45	36	43	49	46	39	41
both	47	43	38	36	42	45	38	40
'not much'								
boys	9	5	10	14	12	7	11	10
girls	2	4	10	9	18	3	11	9
both	5	5	10	11	15	5	11	9

Significance on 'not much' data: trend ↗ ***   m.class/w.class **
between sexes n.s.

of artistic creativity.[3] One should not assume, however, that children who draw at home are necessarily being as creative as all that; sometimes the motive seems more a desire to put one's own signature on record, an ego-statement as it were, like a dog using a lamp-post. The first of the children below seems to be in something of a rut.

Accountant's wife:
Max has two things that he draws, and those are: boats and planes flying above them; or just planes.

Dancing instructor's wife:
He sticks some up – if he thinks they're good ones he sticks them up on his wall, but they're all the same type of thing: bombs falling out of aeroplanes, and ships being torpedoed, and guns firing. Well, the teacher at school says they're very . . . they've got plenty of *action*; but as I say, it bothers me a bit. But you wouldn't really call him artistic.

Insurance agent's wife:
She likes to go to Granny's, but we have to take her books, crayons and her desk with her, and I have to load them up in the car.

Electrician's wife:

Drawing – he's always drawing. He's drawn since, ooh, since he was three, and he always *could* draw – oh yes, he could draw a train ever so good when he was three. I always wish I'd kept some of his drawings because they were *so* good – army scenes – tanks and soldiers, just little soldiers, not big men, but ever so good; it's amazing, really, for a three-year-old; and that's what made me think, oh, he'll get on quicker at school as he's got the ability to draw. But he hasn't – he seemed to stop dead once he got to school – now he's just starting again.

Labourer's wife:

She did do, but I've threw the paints away. She'll paint and she'll get it all over the other parts, you know; it's with them slap-dashing it at school.

A second major interest is 'reading': a blanket term which no doubt includes a good deal of looking at picture-books, magazines and comics without understanding the written text properly. There turn out to be many comic addicts, in particular, who cannot actually read words at all. 'Real' reading is discussed more fully in the 'school' volume; here we are simply concerned with the child's interest in sitting over reading material. For 37% of boys and 51% of girls, reading is named as a 'special hobby', rising to 63% among middle-class girls; both sex and class differences are significant (at the 0·001 and 0·01 levels respectively). As with drawing, we have an additional source of information later in the interview where, after establishing a measure of the child's reading ability, we asked (Question 121) 'Does he read/look at books[4] much at home?' As the data from this question is also a matter of interest rather than ability, we include it here, in Table 11. Obviously the figures cover a larger group of children than those for whom reading is a 'special hobby'; and since 'much' is a relative term, partially dependent upon parents' expectations, this can only be a fairly crude assessment of which children include reading or pre-reading among their home activities. A safeguard is, however, that any class difference we may find will be underestimated rather than inflated: i.e. if middle-class parents expect more reading, they are more likely to say 'no, not much' for the borderline child, and *vice versa*. The same is true for sex differences in so far as people have a stereotype of girls being more studious and boys more harum-scarum.

Despite these reasons for the figures given in Table 11 being muted, as it were, the differences found are highly significant between

Table 11   *Children who read/look at books[5] 'much' at home*

| | social class | | | | | summary | | |
	I&II	IIIwc	III man	IV	V	I&II, IIIwc	IIIman, IV,V	overall popn.
	%	%	%	%	%	%	%	%
boys	84	79	66	59	60	82	64	69
girls	91	86	84	77	72	88	81	83
both	87	82	75	68	66	85	72	76

Significance: trend ↘ ****   m.class/w.class ****
                    between sexes ****

both classes and sexes, so that the effect of being a middle-class girl
as opposed to a working-class boy is very marked indeed.

Shopkeeper's wife:
  Ooh, she can read anything, she takes the Bible to bed sometimes
  and reads out of that; and I say to her "You can't understand
  that – you can't read some of the words" – "Oh well, I skip some
  of those". *Tiny* print. She can read anything. She loves books,
  she's got dozens. All her pocket money goes on books.

Student teacher (wife also a teacher):
  Occasionally I've caught her sitting with the dictionary, looking
  at the dictionary; she may ask what a word means, and we tell
  her, and then she'll go and look at it possibly in the dictionary,
  and interest herself in other words. [She's a browser, in fact?]
  Oh, yes.

Businessman's wife (herself a teacher):
  He doesn't really ask a lot of questions: I think he finds, now he
  can read, you know, he can read so much he doesn't ask. I mean,
  he'll pick up the evening paper and start on it at night – it's a
  battle who's to get there first.

Labourer's wife:
  I buy the comics for myself, I like to read the *Dianne*, the *Bunty*
  and the *Judy*, and she's always reading them; and especially them
  thriller comics, and she likes to read *them* and all.

Lorry driver's wife:
  She doesn't really, not at home. She'll just sit and bzzzz all the
  pages over, and then she'll put it down, you know; she doesn't
  seem very enthusiastic about it.

Warper's wife:
He has all the comics – fifteen a week.

Cycle assembler's wife:
Oh yes, he's *got* books. I bet there's four upstairs. He had three at Christmas, and he's not gone through them at all yet. He's not been interested in them at all. He doesn't have a comic; though his brother has comics regularly. He's just the opposite for reading. It never occurs to him to slip through a comic.

Handyman's wife:
I've never seen Arnold pick up a book.

Writing also features prominently as a home interest. One might expect that, in contrast to reading, this activity would imply a fair degree of understanding of the meaning of written words; however, this is not necessarily found to be so upon inquiry. Quite a large group of children seem to enjoy the mechanical act of writing, and spend much of their time copying words which they cannot in fact read. Thus even those for whom writing is a 'special hobby' may not in fact be writing down their own thoughts, but often merely lists of words. Here again, we returned to the subject later in the interview, asking (at Question 136) 'Does he do any writing for his own pleasure?' and following up with further questions to find out what kind of writing this was; so that again we can present data in terms of the *act* of writing (i.e. the child's general interest) at this point, and elsewhere look at the degree of sophistication with which his literacy was being put into practice. The data obtained in answer to the question 'Does he do any writing for his own pleasure?' is given in Table 12; the answers have been divided under three headings: 'a lot', 'occasionally' and 'none at all', and the two extreme categories are shown here. Compulsory 'thank you' letters are discounted as writing for pleasure. Both groups show marked class and sex differences, significant at the 0·001 level; especially noteworthy is the effect of being a middle-class girl (48% write 'a lot', compared with 21% of middle-class boys and working-class girls, and 15% of working-class boys) – while to be a professional/managerial-class girl gives a 65% chance of writing 'a lot'.

Miner's wife:
He writes about anything, but he writes just as he speaks. He writes 'pencil' – PENSUL. I can read it. He left me a note Saturday

night, on the front door. It said "Look on the dresser" – well, I knew it said "Look on the dresser" – and he wrote a note something about some tins, but I couldn't figure that out. [Does he ever write letters to people?] Yes – they don't get sent. I think they could read them, but he never finishes, he never sends them. He'll say "Dear John, I am not coming to your birthday party" – things like that. [Has he ever written a letter that got sent?] Yes, 'cause he sent me a letter when I was away. It didn't say much. He likes it if it isn't too long. If I copy it all out into writing, such a lot of writing, he won't finish it. He likes copying stories out of books, even though he doesn't know what it all says. He loves copying.

Table 12 *Children who write at home for their own pleasure*

	social class					summary		
	I&II	IIIwc	III man	IV	V	I&II, IIIwc	IIIman, IV,V	overall popn.
	%	%	%	%	%	%	%	%
a. 'A lot'								
boys	26	16	15	21	5	21	15	17
girls	65	31	18	27	31	48	21	29
both	45	23	17	24	18	35	18	23

Significance: trend ↓ ***   m.class/w.class ****
between sexes ****

b. 'Not at all'								
boys	39	35	48	42	43	37	46	44
girls	13	24	36	34	26	18	35	30
both	26	30	42	38	34	28	41	37

Significance: trend n.s.   m.class/w.class ***
between sexes ****

Executive's wife:
A thing he's been doing recently is organising a little club for himself and his friends. He does that before he goes to school; on his own, he comes and asks if he can get up a little earlier, and gets on with it – makes the lists and marks the paper and sets the room.

Optician's wife:
Oh, she writes quite a lot. She writes stories, and she writes letters to her Grandfather and her aunts in Scotland. Usually newsy letters – what you don't want them to know!

Coalman's wife:
Yes, every night they go and get a threepenny writing book and scribble in it.

Company director's wife:
No, well it's with a gun at his head to make him do any at all.

Other indoor 'special hobbies' are less well documented, not having been further probed. The next most popular activities overall are model-making, and sewing, knitting or making dolls' clothes, very much polarised by sex. Not a single boy was said to sew, while among girls this varied by class from a third of the group at the top of the social scale to just over a twentieth at the bottom. Knitting as a hobby was also a girls-only occupation, apart from two lonely male stalwarts in Class I and II; 15% among middle-class girls reduced to 3% in Class V. Making models was a special interest of 19% of boys, but only 4% of girls; often father was a prime mover in the model-making projects (chiefly intricate plastic aircraft, ships, cars, buildings or knights in armour, made up from bought kits and glue: these are obtainable quite cheaply in terms of cost for hours of occupation, and are available in an enormous range from Woolworth's, toy shops and newsagents). Models of this kind are often displayed in the sitting-room, and sometimes form the basis of extensive collections. Constructions involving the child's own creative ideas were comparatively rarely reported, perhaps because the results served a fleeting purpose for the child's play but were not display pieces. As in drawing, seven is a crisis age for creativity in the sense that the child's capacity for self-criticism may easily overtake his skills, and discourage him from the consistent effort which would bring his ability up to his own expectations.

GPO engineer's wife:
He'll come in from school and he gets a marvellous idea of making something, and you *know* that it won't come . . . you know what I mean? I let him do it, and he gets a bit . . . you know . . . if it won't come out exactly as he wants it to come out – he tends to lose interest. If he's making anything – he's got some

marvellous *ideas*, like, but they've all got to happen ever so quickly . . .

Miner's wife:
He does draw, but he likes to make things. Fantastic things – imaginary things. Daleks – anything – you know, robots, ships, anything like that, and he's made Indian hats. Only the other day he had a bit of corrugated cardboard, and I just watched him, and he got a piece of string in the cardboard, he'd got some plastic scissors; and when he'd finished it, it just looked to me just like an ordinary . . . just folded it round, sort of thing . . . but to him it was one of those things the Indians keep their arrows in.

Prison officer's wife:
She loves getting the glue out and playing with ordinary ink.

Labourer's wife:
He's *got* a lot of toys . . . as I see it, he doesn't play with toys much at all. He seems as though – if he's got a few sticks and a nail . . . . .

'Cutting-out' and making scrapbooks is a preferred occupation for about a tenth of the children, and shows no significant difference between the sexes, nor any class difference. 'Doing sums' is a hobby for about one in twenty children. The only other indoor activities (as opposed to special toys) which were mentioned more than very occasionally were cooking (not confined to girls) and listening to records.

All these popular pastimes can be thought of as a continuation of interests which are also encouraged at school: thus the majority of preferred indoor activities might broadly be described as educational. It follows that the child who chooses to spend a high proportion of his time on indoor hobbies is quite likely to be pursuing 'educational' kinds of interests to an above-average extent: which is in line with the finding mentioned briefly in the last chapter, that 'indoor children' tend in fact to be better readers.

'He comes in when he's hungry . . .'
Despite the traffic hazard, the single most popular outdoor activity, in terms of the number of times it was mentioned, is riding around on a bicycle, even though bicycles were not specifically asked about. Almost half the middle-class children are said to spend a lot of

time on their bikes, or on the more limited and rarer scooter; among working-class children, the figure drops to a little less than a third, but is still unrivalled as top activity, even by football, except among Class v boys.[6]

In view of parents' worries about traffic, it is doubtful whether many of these children are using their bicycles to travel far afield (from interviewing at the next stage of the study, it is clear that few do even at eleven years); and it seems likely that the main purpose of having a bike at seven is not in fact to travel from one place to another at all. More often, it seems, bikes are used simply for the joy and exhilaration of riding for its own sake – 'just swizzing round the close' – the machine serving as an extension of the child's own body to propel him on something faster and more exciting than feet, and offering an opportunity both for perfecting a new set of skills and for savouring the accompanying sensations of finely gauged balance and rapid movement through air. Much of the time, therefore, the children just go out for a little ride, 'biking up and down the crescent' or round the block, not intending to go anywhere special, nor even particularly looking for other children to play with; though an audience is always welcome, and one bike out is likely to attract others.

Swings, both in public parks and in private gardens, are also popular, and these again are a device through which the child extends his bodily prowess and perfects interesting movement patterns and sensations – for which reason they remain the basic piece of playground equipment right through this age and beyond, especially for girls.

Interest in sand and water play – except perhaps at the seaside, where the scale on which the materials are provided renews the old pleasure – seems to be a good deal less intense now than at four years; but playing with a ball, again with the accent on new skills, is next in popularity to bicycles as far as boys are concerned. Ball games are in fact liked by both sexes, though girls leave them to take fourth place; but the two sexes play differently, girls favouring those bouncing games in which the skill consists in one person keeping the ball in continuous motion, often to the rhythm of a counting jingle,[7] or in performing prescribed contortions of the body in relation to the moving ball, while boys prefer football or cricket. Football is more popular than cricket, perhaps partly because the season is longer; but there is more to it than that, in that footballers outnumber cricketers in the middle class by two to one, but in the working class by about five to one.

For girls, the second favourite outside activity is skipping, followed by roller-skating. Skipping, like ball-bouncing, can be competitive or solitary, and is performed within a traditional series of rhymes and chants to which the actions are closely fitted. There are a number of variants on skipping which develop the proportions of crazes from time to time and then settle back into rarity: notably 'Chinese skipping'. In this the rope is weighted at one end and formed into a loop at the other, the loop lies loosely round the ankle, and by a series of hops from one foot to the other and a circular motion of the body, the rope is swung in a circle to its full length with the looped foot as axis, and the skill lies in keeping the rope swinging while avoiding its scything action with the other leg. There is also a 'skipping hoop' available, which at the time of writing has not caught on in any numbers: though the popularity of the 'hula hoop' craze some years ago (where the hoop had to be kept spinning around the body by gyrations of the hips) is attested by the number of wrenched parental backs at that time. Hoops hardly gained a mention during the period of the survey, however. These crazes seem to come and go, but basic skipping remains much the same through generations, and even the jingles persist almost unchanged.[8]

'Making dens' and 'digging' or 'gardening' were the only other specifically outdoor activities spontaneously mentioned in any numbers. Den-making, of course, is often an adjunct to games of cowboys and Indians, secret societies, 'house' or 'doctors', which we shall be discussing shortly; but boys, in particular, seem to derive a special pleasure from building rough shelters and digging large holes as occupations in their own right without necessarily having any special end in view.

As happy as we once, to kneel and draw
The chalky ring, and knuckle down at taw;
To pitch the ball into the grounded hat
Or drive it devious with a dext'rous pat . . .
Cowper, *Tirocinium*

Apart from the more conventional rule-based games such as football and cricket, and the skipping and ball-bouncing games already touched on, a number of other outdoor games played by rules were mentioned: hide and seek, hopscotch, tag and queeny-queeny, for instance. What is remarkable about these games is not their occurrence but their rarity in the transcripts; we thought at first that perhaps mothers were simply not sufficiently knowledgeable about the details of games in current favour, but eventually we came to the conclusion that an additional factor was operating: that these are games which are essentially playground rather than neighbourhood or garden games, and that there is in fact a very big difference between home and school with regard to the games which are considered appropriate in the two environments. Thus the games collected by the Opies in 'street and playground' may in fact have much less relevance to the garden or backyard, or even to the less populated streets, than one might expect.[9] Our own junior-school daughter could think of a long list of games which she and her friends played in the school playground, and another long list of games played out of school; but she could not think of one which was played both in and out of school, even though the 'best friend' with whom she played incessantly at home was also her constant companion at school.

Perhaps for similar reasons, the other traditional playground occupations – marbles, conkers, flick-cards, whip-and-top,[10] and the ancient game of fivestones, jacks, dibs or alleygobs – were only very rarely mentioned as games in the home context. Where these did come up, it was usually in answer to our question on whether the child collected anything. To tap the full richness of children's interest and inventiveness, it does seem necessary either to question the children themselves or to observe their behaviour systematically and perhaps unobtrusively. It was not, however, within the scope of this study to break into the private world of the child as the Opies have done so successfully: their own documentation on this particular aspect of childhood is so detailed that there would be little point in repeating it here for one locality. The absence of these games in mothers' reports simply underlines two points which are of some interest: first, that school and home behaviour are two quite different areas of study (an observation which we have already made and which will recur); secondly, a belief which we share with the Opies, that there exist whole tracts of childhood experience from which adults are quite deliberately shut out: a process of exclusion which accompanies a deepening consciousness of self, coupled with a growing identification with the peer group, and which appears to gather momentum around the age of seven with which we are here concerned.

To an extent, children's play interests will inevitably be influenced by the toys which are available via ordinary commercial sources. Occasionally, devoted parents may go to the trouble of making special toys for their children – toys made by parents in our sample

to meet a special need of the child included a marble-run, a peri-
scope, a play-house, a box-cart, stilts, a dolls' house, and enough
dolls' clothes and dolls' bedding to stock a dolls' draper's – and once
in a while some precious family heirloom like a Victorian rocking-
horse or a model yacht will be handed down to the next generation;
but in an industrialised society, for the majority of children, most
of the while, the word 'toy' has now come to mean an object made
on a factory production line. Often they will be marketed with the
support of national advertising campaigns on television or in
magazines and comics: with the result that the nineteenth-century
exploitation of children as producers has been replaced in the late
twentieth century by a more subtle commercial exploitation of
children as consumers. In so far as one accepts that children are
peculiarly vulnerable as compared with other groups, this has rightly
become a focus of serious concern.[11] We have to acknowledge,
however, that commercial toys play a significant part in children's
development.

Parents are likely to know a good deal about the toys their
children have and whether they are played with, because in the first
place they have either bought the toys themselves or had to make
sure that the children have properly thanked the donors; in the
second place, they are actively involved in keeping them tidy or in
persuading the children to do so; and, thirdly, the gap between their
own expenditure on a toy and the return in terms of the child's
enjoyment of it is often a sore point. 'We've bought them tape-
recorders', says Rita's mother, 'they've got transistor radios to take
upstairs in the bedroom, they've got the desk and that – but they
don't seem to bother with them'; and Valerie's mother complains:
'I bought her a typewriter; but these things [i.e. interests] don't last'.

Building worker's wife:
   We bought her a lovely shop – she was shop mad, so we bought
   her a really good one – a big one – there was a counter and scales,
   everything. *That* was a nine days' wonder – she hasn't looked at
   it for three or four months, really.

Greengrocer's wife:
   Actually he's got a big train set, but he's not awfully bothered, he
   doesn't seem ever so bothered. It's a wind-up one, it's quite a
   good one really, but he doesn't seem ever so bothered, so we don't
   worry him about it – well, it's no use forcing him on it, it's there
   if he wants it.

Loco fireman's wife:

> He *likes* toys, we *buy* him toys, but he doesn't seem to PLAY with toys very much, you know; as I say, he's got a lot of these little cars – always seeing them in the shops, you know, and he'll have them on birthdays and that, but then he hasn't bothered with them any more – he's really better with some old boxes and things.

Rule-controlled games which are played indoors are also more amenable to observation, because these are games in which parents' participation is much more welcome. Board games, for instance, were mentioned as a frequent occupation for about 10% of children: snakes and ladders and Ludo retain their appeal for this age-group, and Monopoly is the most popular of the commercial board games. Chess, dominoes, tiddlywinks, draughts, bingo and card games received only occasional mentions; once again, it must be remembered that the questions as asked referred to the child's usual day-to-day occupations in his spare time, so that failure to mention does not mean that the game is outside the child's experience. The unifying factor in these games is that they involve a formal rule structure by which the players must abide if the game is to be played successfully; also most of them call for some degree of sustained concentration and the ability to count and keep the score, even if the child is playing alone.

Pipe fitter's wife:

> She's learned *herself* to count, to tell you the truth – she's had the Ludo or snakes and ladders. She'll throw the dice, and she's just like lightning with the adding the numbers up – she's really quick at it – my eldest daughter can't add up half as fast as what she can. I think it's only by playing with herself – because she's had a lot of time off school with her asthma, and she'll sit while I'm doing the work with this Ludo game, and she'll play for hours with it – 'cause I keep her on the settee when she's not well.

Furthermore, if the child wants to play to win (and winning usually seems important to the seven-year-old), such games may demand an ability to devise a forward-looking strategy, or perhaps to cheat with aplomb. They also need a certain amount of social co-operation, or at least social know-how, if the game is to be carried through to the end.

Of other commercially produced games, the only type which

received frequent mention was jigsaw puzzles, which are played with often by between 10 and 15% of children overall.

Jigsaw puzzles and the board and card games are of interest as a group in that they are indoor, sedentary pastimes which require some degree of concentration and mental effort; from this point of view, it is noteworthy that they are mentioned more than twice as often for middle-class boys as for working-class boys, and almost twice as often for working-class girls as for working-class boys. There is an interaction between class and sex, however, in that middle-class boys are significantly *more* likely than middle-class girls to play this type of game often. An element in this finding may be that competitive games of all kinds appeal more strongly to boys than to girls, and because middle-class boys spend more time than working-class boys in indoor activities, they tend to find an outlet in this particular way.

Among commercial toys as opposed to games, toy cars come first, claiming a good deal of the time of about 30% of boys (all classes), but no girls at all; train sets, though much rarer, are also an exclusively male preserve. Lego is also very popular, played with often by 35% of middle-class boys and 15% of working-class boys. Lego has in common with jigsaws and board games that it is sedentary and demands concentration, and it is interesting that a similar class difference is found in a constructional game. It is also liked by a few girls (5%). The Lego firm has since produced a line in matching dolls'-house furniture as an accessory, and this may well expand the female market. Although a little over 10% of middle-class boys play with Meccano, only a handful of working-class boys do, and no girls; possibly Meccano now depends heavily on its sentimental appeal for fathers who played with it in their own youth, which would at once impose a more rigid class restriction.

Dolls and their accessories – dolls'-houses, furniture, clothes and prams – were the major preoccupation for about 65% of girls, with no class loading; one or two boys played with soft animals, but otherwise the only doll to break the sex barrier was Action Man. This phenomenon has been a deliberate attempt to interest boys in the lucrative market represented by the various doll-and-accessories series originating in the United States and typified by 'Sindy' doll. An earlier male doll, 'Sindy's boy-friend, Paul', was too cissy to appeal to anyone but the feminine owners of Sindy. Action Man began as an all-American fighting man in full military uniform, supported by accessory packs for different kinds of warfare, with an arsenal of weapons including twee little hand grenades!

His commercial success was somewhat marred by the squeamish-
ness of liberal professional-class parents, and later developments
attempted to overcome this by the inclusion of kits for romantic
civilian roles such as polar explorer, mountaineer, skin diver, astronaut and so on. At the time of the survey, however, this development had not caught on sufficiently for Action Man to occupy more
than 3% of boys frequently, and no girls were mentioned, though
they might well enjoy the little camping outfits and sleeping-bags
with which he is now equipped. Small plastic soldiers, cowboys and
Indians, battle equipment and all the impedimenta of space travel,
the successors to the lead soldiers which have now become col-
lectors' pieces, were a good deal more popular with boys than
Action Man – probably because they do in fact give greater scope
for real action.

Dancing instructor's wife:
> He's very fond of model soldiers and – um – all sorts of warfare,
> I'm afraid . . . he'll play guns quite happily on his own, setting
> them all up, and having battles and things like that. It's always
> something with spears or guns or something; other children may
> be painting and drawing, but he's always fighting battles and
> explosions and things. It bothers me a little, that does sometimes.

The special interest of both dolls and toy soldiers is that they are
a potent medium for role-playing and fantasy play; and these we
shall turn to in the next chapter.

We should not move on from this discussion of the materials
of children's play without mentioning the 'junk' materials with
which children occupy themselves in the hope that some useful or
satisfying object will result from their labours. Scissors and paper,
wire, flex, batteries and bulbs, broken clocks and radios, wood and
nails, old boxes and tins, planks, bits of cardboard, staples, cotton-
reels, squeezy bottles and egg-boxes, as well as conventional sewing
materials, were all mentioned as being preferred 'toys' for some
children. Doubtless some of this enthusiasm comes from the teachers,
whose inventiveness in producing something out of nothing is an
admired feature of primary school open days; certainly, also, the
BBC children's programme *Blue Peter* has inspired hundreds of
children to transform household waste into dragons and moon-
scapes – sometimes to the horror of inadequate parents, pressed to
take over the advisory role when *Blue Peter*'s Valerie Singleton has
faded out of vision.

'You name it, Simon collects it . . .'

The following are *some* of the things collected by children in our sample: silver paper, acorns, matchboxes, string, buttons, tins, nuts and bolts, stones, conkers, tickets, boxes, religious texts, cigarette cartons, toffee papers, make-up, matchsticks, free gifts, 'rubbish', bottle-tops, nails, cheese-boxes, handbags, handkerchiefs, pens and pencils, plastic gardens, jigsaws, gollywogs, caterpillars, car numbers, marbles, model planes, soft toy animals, leaves, coins, chemistry set equipment, records, Meccano, costume dolls, dolls' clothes, books, little cars, feathers, money, Action Man sets, comics, jewellery, magazine pictures, scraps, beermats, dolls'-house furniture, labels, postcards, ornaments, railway accessories, drawings, badges, fir-cones, tea cards, Lego parts, stamps, soldiers, marbles, bubble-gum cards, bricks, cactuses, footballers [*sic*], sweets, insects, Premium bonds, Scalectrix accessories, shells, 'anything that's weird or ghastly', and pictures of Cliff Richard.

The reader may remember that, when these children were four, the mother's desire to stem the rising tide of the child's possessions by throwing out those she considered superfluous, opposed by the child's attachment to his own 'junk', was a potent source of conflict for many, and recognised as a real dilemma by most. By seven the dilemma remains, modified to some extent by the fact that the child himself is rather more selective in what he collects. There are still a few magpies, however, like Mark, whose father says he 'checks the dustbins twice a week to see we haven't thrown anything away'; but even among these, one should distinguish between those who collect a great many *categories* of things – like the first two children below – and those who, like the third and fourth, will add to their hoard anything portable, simply for the joy of possession.

Teacher's wife:

> He collects everything he can – he's an absolute squirrel! Tea cards he collects and puts in a book, but otherwise *any*thing – from empty cartons to big boxes – buttons – anything; plus cars, which he will buy himself sometimes . . . He's very very careful – almost *too* careful; he's rather the way I am. He doesn't *use* things; he looks at them, and lines them up, and looks at them, and then puts them away in boxes – which is *so* like me!

Self-employed craftsman's wife:

> He collects anything he can lay his hands on: matchboxes – conkers – pieces of string; er . . . cigarette cards – bottle-tops –

badges: you name it, Simon collects it! If you look under his bed, you can't see for boxes.

Nylon winder's wife:
At night when I see that his trousers are clean and ready for next morning, you see, I mostly sort out his pockets, and he's got stones in, bits of string, all the things he picks up in the street – they're mostly all full of rammel,[12] you know! But nothing *special*.

Railwayman's wife:
She collects *everything* if I let her! She does, really and truly. In that box there – it's like a bomb had hit it when I come home at night-time.

The collection of special categories of objects does, of course, involve a certain amount of persistence, if only of one particular interest over time, and there is a wide scatter in this characteristic at seven. Obviously, the degree to which the parents encourage and back up the child's enthusiasm must influence his staying power; but this is not the whole story. 'Do you know, we've tried *all* ways to get him interested in a hobby, because I think it's a good thing myself', said a foreman's wife; 'but no, he's *not* bothered'. The first mother below is also supportive and encouraging, without much result.

Loco fireman's wife:
He has got a little book that he collects tea coupons a lady in the street gives him; but he's very full of enthusiasm for a thing to start with, but I'm afraid it sort of peters out – you know, it doesn't last very long. He gets these wild enthusiasms, you know, he's going to do marvels, but it doesn't last, he goes on to something else – he's not really a collector for long.

Labourer's wife:
No – no – he isn't anything like that. He's very *changeable* you see; he's for one thing, he concentrates all his time on it for a day or two, then he's completely forgotten it. [Does he add bits to his train set?] Not unless my husband buys it.

Auto-electrician's wife:
Pauline's collecting these doll's dresses and things for her Sindy, and sometimes we'll see an outfit that she really wants, and I know that she's been saving up for quite a while but just can't make it; then we do put a bit on to [what she's saved].

University teacher's wife:

> Charles collects stones – he wants to be an archaeologist or a geologist, and he collects any stone of interesting shape, size or colour; and now he's making drawers for a little museum upstairs, and he spent some of his birthday money on archaeological tools – hammer and chisel, and all that.

Charles's initial interest is given every opportunity to develop by being treated with a certain professional respect by museum-minded parents; Guy, a business executive's son (the 'born leader' of page 38), sweeps his parents along with him – the impetus comes from the child, but his parents are actively responsive to his demands:

> He went mad keen on churches, we had to go everywhere to churches – that was the summer before last. Oh, everywhere, we went in the most fusty old churchyards and weird places. The gentleman up the hill is a photographer for the *Guardian Journal*, and he had a terrific amount of photographs he'd taken of churches, hundreds of them, and he gave them all to Guy, so we've got those along with everything else upstairs. Then last year it was farms, absolutely mad keen on farming. All summer long we were racing round finding farms . . . until it wore off about the end of September. I don't know what it'll be this year!

The incidence of collections is shown in Table 13. The most striking apparent difference is between boys and girls: 80% of boys overall, compared with 66% of girls, collect things. When one looks at *what* is collected by the different sexes, however, this difference

Table 13   *Children who have specific collections*

	social class					summary		
	I&II	IIIwc	III man	IV	V	I&II, IIIwc	IIIman, IV,V	overall popn.
	%	%	%	%	%	%	%	%
boys	85	81	81	78	74	83	80	80
girls	79	72	65	60	46	76	62	66
both	82	77	73	69	60	79	71	73

Significance: trend ↘ ****   m.class/w.class **
                    between sexes ****

seems to be partly an artefact, and should not be made too much of. The outstanding collector's items for boys are the picture-cards included in packets of tea and in packs of bubble-gum, which is frequently bought more for the card than for the gum itself: these are either stuck in albums or, less often, used for playing flick-cards, and they also have some currency value as 'swaps'. Only a few girls collect picture-cards; and one of our daughters points out that the content of the cards is for the most part of interest to boys only, being series on footballers, war incidents, Batman, Thunderbirds and space travel – 'unfit for human consumption', as a sweetshop-owning mother suggested, referring to the cards, not the bubble-gum. Certainly some of these series are excessively bloodthirsty, and positively disliked by girls. Picture-cards are closely followed for popularity among boys by Lego parts and small model cars.

The only comparable feminine collections are dolls and their accessories; and here we have a difficulty in that a child might, like Pauline above, spend all her pocket money on dolls and have enough to be considered a 'collection' if they were mere objects like cars or Lego, yet the child's regard for each doll as an individual might prevent her mother classifying this as a collection. As the reluctant grandparents of about thirty dolls belonging to one of our children, we are conscious that we might well not have mentioned them in answer to the 'collections' question, any more than one would say of a large family that the mother collects children. 'Costume dolls' are another matter, of course, in that they are chosen and valued for their clothes rather than their personalities, which tend to be vacuous; and dolls' accessories are certainly regarded as collections. Here one comes to another point, however, that minimises the sex difference shown in the table: that picture-cards, small cars and Lego tend to be a good deal cheaper, unit for unit, than dolls' things (apart from dolls'-house fittings, a less expensive[13] but more specialist group), and are therefore much more likely to be acquired in sufficient numbers to constitute a collection in the mother's eyes. In particular, this may contribute heavily to the notable drop in girls' collections in Class v.

If one extracts the figures for these four major items, there is a fairly even spread of the less common collections across the sex barrier. Stamp collecting, for example, is fairly popular with children of both sexes. Girls tend to collect ornaments and jewellery, but this is balanced by boys collecting badges and insignia. Both sexes seem to enjoy collecting shells, stones and other natural history items such as leaves, flowers and insects, and both are equally ready to seize upon the left-overs of the consumer society – empty containers, labels, tickets, postal advertisements, coupons and old magazines.

The class differences are not excessively large, but they are very consistent, and the trend (more collections as one ascends the social scale) is highly significant. Apart from the low figure for Class v girls already commented on, this does not seem accountable in terms of money available: working-class families on the whole are heavy spenders on toys, and certainly working-class children have more money in their own pockets than middle-class children (see Table 25, page 237). The differences are not great enough to bear much theoretical analysis, especially as we are dealing with majority figures in every class; the fact that they are there, however, may be one more facet of the middle-class ethic of long-term satisfactions which is discussed in Chapter 7. Collecting is essentially an occupation involving rather longer-term aims than the amusement of the moment.

'I think a child has a bit of security if he has things of his own'
'I think it makes them selfish, don't you?'
The functions of toys in the development of the child are many and various, and we have discussed them at length elsewhere;[14] but not least among them is one which has little to do with the child's actual play activities, but consists in the sheer satisfaction of the knowledge of ownership. A child's personal possessions, including first of all his name and his memories, but extending to the material objects that he can touch and hold and know to be his, establish him in his own identity and confirm him as a person in his own right. There are still institutions where the very clothes of the children are communally owned because it is considered too much trouble to allow each child its own, and where the bedtime teddies, that most intimate possession, are doled out haphazardly to any crying child from an impersonal ward stock-box. We are beginning to realise now what damage can be done to children in such environments by conditions which so diminish their private image of their own individuality.

To a much lesser degree (lesser because parents and siblings are themselves a kind of possession), children living in their own families can be at risk of a similar deprivation. 'There isn't really room for her to collect anything', said a scaffolder's wife bringing up seven children in a small terraced house with a shared backyard: 'If she collected anything, the others would have a go at it and spread them around. The other girl, she tries to save things, but you know the others have a play with them, and she don't get them back, and she gives up'. At four, we examined children's property rights in terms of their mothers' willingness to give or throw things away in the child's despite;[15] at seven we were interested in the mothers' attitudes to rights of private property as between siblings, and we also wanted to discover how far the children of a family were catered for in terms of play-space and storage-space which was recognised as such, and which thus offered the child certain personal territorial rights even if partly shared with siblings. Obviously these factors are also relevant to the discussion of chaperonage with which we were occupied in the last chapter, in that children's inclination to spend a lot of their time at home and under supervision will depend partly upon the facilities which their parents are able to provide for their play and the extent to which they can be contented and busy indoors.

The questions with which we explored this topic were these:

22. (*If any siblings*): Some parents like children to have their own special toys, and some think that all the toys should belong to the whole family. How do you feel about that?

23. Do the children (does N) have a special place of their (his) own where they (he) can keep their (his) own things? (*specify*) (*If a general room, ask*): Do they keep things in their bedroom?

24. Does N play there a lot? (*prompt if necessary*): Which room does he mostly play in?

Looking first at the provision of storage space, the most popular place for keeping toys was the child's own bedroom (85% of all children, girls and boys). As at four years, finding a place for the child's increasing possessions seemed a problem, and a common solution was to put them in cardboard grocery boxes under the bed. Sex and class differences were negligible, with the exception that Class v children were less likely than others to keep toys in the bedroom (64%); this is probably because, with larger families and less adequate accommodation, these children's bedrooms are likely to be more cramped and crowded, with little room for anything other than the beds themselves. If one divides families into large (four or more children) and small, 76% of children in large families keep toys in the bedroom, whereas 92% in small families do so.[16]

From the mother's point of view, storage space is needed for the sake of tidiness; from the child's, its main function is to emphasise his ownership and to protect his possessions from marauding siblings.

E

The need for such protection was often recognised as a problem, and some mothers took considerable trouble to provide it. Jeffrey's mother, a manager's wife, indicating the overflowing toybox in the living-room, said 'That's all Gillian's toys; we've got another box with a lock on it where Jefferey can keep his things, right separate; because of course she's at the age of destruction [2] and he'd have no toys at all if she was allowed to get at them'. Rodney, a sales representative's child, had adopted for himself a more drastic solution: 'All the good ones that he possesses, he takes them to his Nana's with him because the others break them'. Other 'special places' are private by convention or the mother's fiat, rather than through locks or distance: Rex, a builder's son, has 'an old sideboard upstairs, re-stained with new handles'; Duncan and his brothers, an advertising manager's children, have 'an old display unit in three shelves, and each shelf is divided into three, and so each child has one portion of each shelf'; Beryl, the daughter of an electrician, can use her parents' wardrobe for 'real private things'; and Karen, a miner's child, has got 'three – there's a cupboard there, and she's took over me dressing-table upstairs, that's hers, so she reckons, *and* a front-room cupboard'.

On the whole, siblings have physical access to each other's possessions, subject to rules which the mother may try to set out about sharing and borrowing. The erection of such a rule system (and worse, its enforcement) presents parents with a dilemma: they want their children to be generous, and they also want them to respect the property rights of others. In fact, a strict mutual regard for the sanctity of property rights offers an ideal opportunity for owners to show voluntary generosity, and so can have an important function in the mother's socialisation scheme. In theory, it seems a simple case of 'do as you would be done by'; in practice, as usual, things are more difficult.

Student psychologist's wife (herself in similar training):
Well, this is a great source of trouble, we're always having to sort this out. What they get at Christmas rather establishes ownership . . . . . if the other one wants to use it, we say, Well, ask. When the request is refused, this is when the trouble starts. I would never force them to let the other use a toy that had arrived in their stocking, but it's difficult to know what to do, and I think if there's trouble, there's trouble. [Would it be true to say of any toy, "*This* toy belongs to *you*, and this to *you*"?] Yes, for most of them. There have been times when [my husband] has brought

home something and says "This is for everyone"; and we've
found *that* causes so much trouble, we try not to do this now.

Scientific research worker's wife:
  I don't get asked. "What's mine is *mine*, it's not yours!" and it's
  only by a trading process that we exchange toys, you see. "I lend
  you my car and you lend me . . .", that sort of business. *Sometimes* they will play together and pool their toys, make a big
  model on the floor; but in general it's "That's *mine*, and you
  can't have it!"

Commercial traveller's wife:
  Well, I find it absolutely impossible to keep a thing separate from
  one in turn. I wouldn't encourage it, in any case. I know that –
  really and truly – it must be nice. I can't remember back to my
  own childhood; course, being a girl, I didn't have the same problem that boys have all together, but – um – I find it impossible,
  and I say to them "Well, if you want to keep your own special
  one, then you must hide it away." They're old enough to realise.

Communal ownership might seem a solution to the dilemma, again
in theory, and we wondered whether in fact some mothers would
prefer that all toys were jointly owned. Obviously, most mothers
want their children to share on a temporary basis, and care was
taken to ensure that the mother was referring to actual ownership
rather than mere communal play. Their answers to this question fall
into three groups: those who preferred communal ownership, those
who thought each child should have his own so that any one toy
could be recognised as belonging to a particular child, and those who
considered a combination of joint and private ownership the most
satisfactory. Illustrations of these three points of view are given
below, and Table 14 shows the incidence of mothers' belief in com·
munal ownership.

Private ownership:

Bricklayer's wife:
  I think it's nice for them to have their own toys really; I mean,
  I like *my* things, I wouldn't like to think anyone was going to
  share *my* things. I think it should be the same for them.

Furniture machinist's wife:
  Well, I think a child should have its own toys. They have a strict
  understanding. I think a child has a bit of security if he has things

of his own. She's encouraged to be generous. I'm not saying she
should be *possessive*.

Miner's wife:
> I think they should have their own special toys but they should be
> taught to lend their toys. They must respect each other's belong-
> ings. He's taught what belongs to Alison, and if she says he can
> have it, that's all right. But he mustn't ask *me* for what is
> Alison's. He must ask her.

Building foreman's wife:
> Well, I'll tell you the way *I* feel about it: I like them each to
> have their own, because they fight such a lot about them, you
> know. I think it gives you more peace if they each have their
> own toys, that's my feeling.

Some private, some communal:

Representative's wife:
> I feel if it's a big toy like, well, Ralph's got a racing car and
> train set, well I say he ought to share it with the younger one;
> but the little things he can have to himself.

Professional engineer's wife:
> Well, they have their own special ones, but after a while some
> toys like Lego and skipping ropes and tricycles, they all seem to
> be shared. But the books, dolls and cars and that are their own.

Communal ownership:

Casual car repairer's wife:
> I like 'em to mix, because I mean if a child has his own toys – a
> special toy – well, what's worse than a greedy child? Another
> child comes along – "I want it" – which is only natural if they're
> playing outside; and the child that it belongs to is going to start
> and cry, scream and play up; well, what toys they've got, they
> share among them. I mean with the younger one it is a bit difficult;
> but I've always brought them up to that. I don't keep a special
> thing, even if they've had something bought special for them, like.
> He'll perhaps keep it for a week to start, but then everybody else'd
> have it.

Disabled labourer's wife:
> I think they should share and share alike, I don't think they

should have anything that just belongs to one person, I mean I think it makes them selfish, don't you?

Unemployed labourer's wife (nine children):
Oh no, I think they all ought to play with one another's. Well, I mean with a family like ours, I mean they have to, don't they? You can't just buy one and tell him to keep it to himself. To tell you the truth, they don't have toys long enough to keep them, only Alec and Michael [two youngest].

Table 14   *Mothers believing that all toys should be communally owned*

| | social class | | | | | | summary | | |
	I&II	IIIwc	III man	IV	V		I&II, IIIwc	IIIman, IV,V	overall popn.
	%	%	%	%	%		%	%	%
boys	9	14	17	28	23		11	20	18
girls	5	9	14	7	21		7	13	12
both	7	12	16	18	22		9	17	15

Significance: trend ↗ ****   m.class/w.class **
                              between sexes *

Overall, 15% of mothers think toys should be jointly owned. The social class difference – more mothers inclining to communal ownership as we descend the social scale – is consistent and highly significant. Although girls seem consistently more likely than boys to be allowed proprietary rights, the difference barely reaches significance. Among the remaining 85% who preferred a system of private property, 50% thought *all* the toys should belong to individual children and 35% that some toys should be communal.

Although bedrooms are the preferred place for storage of toys, this is not to say that they are much used for play: while 85% keep their possessions in their bedroom, only 27% overall use it as a regular play-space. However, there are interesting class differences in this: 41% of Class I and II children play in their bedrooms, compared with 27% for Class III (white collar and manual combined) and 17% for semi-skilled and unskilled families. Sex differences are not significant. Boys and girls are combined in Table 15, which also shows class differences in the proportions of families who have a special place in the house allotted to the children for their play; this includes playrooms, bedrooms regarded as play-places, and a small group of 2% who set aside a corner in the living-room where the child can keep *and leave out* his toys. Here again, the social classes fall into a similar pattern, and sex differences are not significant.[17]

There seem to be two reasons for the class differences in use of the bedroom for play. One is clearly a question of income and housing standards: a well-lit and properly heated bedroom with a warm floor surface is obviously a more inviting place for a child to spend his time in, and many households cannot afford to heat more than one room. Also, if several children are sleeping in one room, there simply will not be enough space for play, other than *on* the beds – and we saw at four that working-class mothers are not usually very happy about children using beds for playing on, even at that age.

Table 15   *Indoor play-space*

	I&II	IIIwc	III man	IV	V	overall popn.
social class						
	%	%	%	%	%	%
bed/playroom	41	28	27	16	18	27
special play-place (including above)	63	39	39	27	27	40

Significance: trend (bed/playroom) ↘ **** (special place) ↘ ****

In these conditions, there is little choice: 'he has to play in here [general family living-room], 'cause there ain't nowhere else *to* play, is there?' as a labourer's wife said. Over and above this, however, we detected a feeling among a number of mothers of families below Class II that the bedroom is somehow not a *proper* place for the child to play in regularly. Mrs Bailey, the miner's wife whose daughter had taken over her mother's dressing-table for her possessions, said that Karen had 'tried' to play in her own bedroom – 'but I've shouted at her'. An electrician's wife said 'I don't like them messing about upstairs – I much prefer them to be down here, you know, where I can keep an eye on them'.

Thus, although many mothers would like their child to have a place which he can call his own and in which he can be private, and although the wish for such facilities is often a reason for moving house, there is a small group of mothers (not found in Class I and II) who somewhat distrust the child's desire for privacy, and who actively prevent his attempts at finding it. This view is put by the bleacher's wife below. The first mother is bringing up seven children in a council house, and space is naturally very tight; the second and third are in precisely equivalent conditions to each other (each has one boy and one girl in a three-bedroomed house), but their attitudes on privacy are very different.

Building worker's wife:
I do keep the front room as a playroom, but of course, they have to share it; I haven't got it furnished at all, not properly. They do go and play in there if the weather's wet; or if they want to, as I say, they can go into their own bedroom if they want complete privacy – but there again, June and Heather share, which makes it rather awkward. If I could give them all a room of their own, I would do.

Auto electrician's wife:
Oh yes; it's not very big, but it is a place where she can go, and she can shut the door and do what she pleases.

Bleacher's wife:
With having the outhouse out here, they'll go in there, but – um – there is . . . I don't know . . . I suppose it's me . . . but I'm not all that keen on that, because the little girl a few doors up, you know . . . well, I think *all* children . . . I don't really recall . . . I've tried to think about it, that, you know, how they become inquisitive about their own body and that; and I did hear that she was in the outhouse up the road with this little girl; and then they was in mine one day, and they'd shut the door, and I always say "Now you leave the door *open*"; and I don't really like that, I *have* spoke, they know all about that sort of thing and that; and I've always said, if a little boy does this to you, does this and that and the other; and she *knows* that – and yet, on the other hand, I don't want to make it so that she wouldn't *dare* – say if the doctor said "Well, take your clothes off, Edwina", I don't want her to get so that she'd throw a fit because she had to; some do, don't they? I don't want her to be ashamed, to think her body's something she's got to hide; but on the other hand I say "It's *yours*, Edwina, and you must look after it and keep it nice and sweet" and all that sort of thing; and yet I know children *do* go through these little things. And so I'm not all that keen on having them upstairs on their own.

Briefly to summarise the findings of this section, it appears that there are fairly wide class differences in the actual provision for children's privacy both of ownership and of play-space. In particular, the professional/managerial class separate off from the rest in their ability and wish to provide a special play-space for the children, even if this is simply the child's bedroom arranged in such a way that play is possible and expected. The great majority of parents overall think that children should have possessions of their own, but the Class v child is three times more likely than the Class i and ii child to have his property rights submerged into communal ownership. The small but significant class trend on children's private collections fits consistently into a picture which emerges from the whole of the material presented in this chapter: that, as one ascends the social scale, one finds a more facilitating environment for such activities as drawing, painting, reading and the following of special interests generally, and that this facilitating environment consists both in the encouraging attitudes of parents towards such pursuits and in the congenial material setting for the fostering of 'educational' activities which, further up the scale, parents are more able and more concerned to provide. Thus, at the upper end of the scale, children's play is more likely to be regarded as intrinsically valuable and interesting, of educational importance to the child, and worthy of respect because it is a medium for his creativity. Further down the scale, play is seen more as an amusement, a 'childish' occupation which may or may not keep the child out of mischief; when he is indoors, in particular, the emphasis tends to be on *not* being a nuisance and *not* making a mess, so that creative activities which do make a mess are often vetoed at an early stage, and it sometimes appears that (indoors) passive, inactive behaviour which does not disrupt is considered especially virtuous. One might in fact go further, and suggest that at the lower end of the class scale parents expect the child to prosecute the busy and active part of his life *outside* the home, and then come in to relax; whereas at the upper end he is expected to 'let off steam' physically for relaxation outside, and then come in and get on with something more serious and creative. Inactivity indoors for the middle-class child is not immediately acceptable.

Teacher's wife (herself a research assistant):
He isn't a busy sort of child all the time, but he's not bored; he *likes* to do nothing at all. He's very very happy to sit down, usually with his thumb in, and do nothing: that is when he's completely contented and relaxed and happy, and he'll spend ten minutes many a time doing nothing – which, for a long time, Louise [adolescent sister] and I couldn't understand, and we used

to say "Why don't you find something to *do*? Go and get a book
or something!" Until suddenly, about six months ago, it suddenly
dawned on me that I mustn't say that, he *loves* sitting doing
nothing – that it wasn't boredom at all, for him.

In part, of course, if this suggestion is true, such expectations
reflect the work styles of professional versus manual workers in
particular: professionals normally expect their work to overflow
into their evenings, and often do their most concentrated or creative
work out of office hours, whereas manual workers' need for
inactivity is the more pressing because more physical. In our discussion of the four-year-old, we made the assertion that 'within any
society, the range of available occupations, work-roles and work-
habits, income and demands upon income, standards of nutrition
and housing, educational possibilities, and the geographical environment all interact in more or less subtle ways to evolve the customs
and beliefs, attitudes and fashions, which make up what has aptly
been called the web of culture; and the individual family's place in
these systems, whether objectively or subjectively assessed, can be
ignored neither by the members of that family nor by anyone who
tries to understand its internal relationships'. As these children grow
older, such factors become more clearly discernible in the lives they
lead now, and shape with increasing pressure the adults they will
become.

NOTES

1   J. and E. Newson, 1968, pp. 167–9 (Pelican edn. pp. 176–7).
2   Basically consisting of small interlocking bricks in ABS plastic, Lego now
    includes a multitude of accessories in the form of motors, wheels,
    windows, lighting units, graphics, etc., etc., and has captured the
    imaginations and the market that once belonged to Meccano.
3   After examining 24,000 entries in the *Observer* 'Paint Mummy' child-
    ren's competition in 1965, and a further 15,000 painted 'Daddies' the
    following year, we came to the conclusion that seven is a crisis age
    for the child as artist. Until this age, the child is spontaneous and
    unselfconscious in his productions, combining colour and line in a
    haphazard harmony, and achieving highly decorative effects partly
    because he is not burdened by considerations of reproductive exactness.
    At about seven, often a stultifying inhibition descends as the child
    consciously begins to strive for a representationalism which will gain
    him kudos with his friends. Perhaps this is one part of the work ethos
    attached to 'going up to the juniors'! At all events, while some
    children emerge from this slough with the confidence of new-found
    skills, others seem despondently to abandon their artistic life soon after

seven. John and Elizabeth Newson, Notes to exhibition, *The Innocent Eye*, British Association for the Advancement of Science Annual Meeting, Nottingham, 1966; also Elizabeth Newson, *The Innocent Eye*, illustrated audiotape, Medical Recording Service Foundation, Chelmsford, Essex, 1972.

4 Comics count.

5 Comics count.

6 A major industry in Nottingham is bicycle manufacture, and new cut-price bicycles are easily come by.

7 Many counting jingles for ball games will be found in Iona and Peter Opie, *The Lore and Language of Schoolchildren*, Oxford University Press, 1959.

8 The two following, and others, current in Nottingham playgrounds today, were used by one of the authors in Liverpool in 1936.

> I know a black man,
> He's double-jointed
> Gave me a kiss
> And left me disappointed.
> How many kisses did he give you?
> One, two, three, four, etc.

> I am a Girl Guide dressed in blue
> These are the actions I must do
> Bow to the king
> Curtsey to the queen
> And turn away from the boys in green.

9 The Opies themselves make the point that aggressive gang games are highly popular in the school playground but hardly seen 'in the street or the wasteland'. Iona and Peter Opie, *Children's Games in Street and Playground*, Oxford University Press, 1969, pp. 13–14.

10 Although the traditional wood and leather whip and top are still obtainable in Nottingham for a few pence, things are not what they were; in the early 'fifties, primary teachers in the whip and top season (spring term) crossed the playground at their peril, whips flailing ankles from all sides.

11 Ron Goulart, *The Assault on Childhood*, Gollancz, London, 1970. We would not wish to imply that these two kinds of exploitation are equally harmful; as we have suggested elsewhere, consideration for the finer points of children's mental health is a civilised luxury which our society can regard as a priority only because it has been comparatively successful in solving the basic problems of children's physical survival (John and Elizabeth Newson, 'Cultural aspects of child rearing in the English-speaking world', in M. P. M. Richards (ed.), *The Integration of a Child into a Social World*, Cambridge University Press, 1974).

12 Rammel = rubbish, Nottingham usage.

13 As we go to press, this situation has been changed by the import from Sweden of extremely expensive (and also extremely popular) dolls'-house accessories.

14 John and Elizabeth Newson (ed.), study in preparation. Papers available from authors.

15 J. and E. Newson, 1968, pp. 139–50 (Pelican edn. pp. 145–57).

16 One's own bed, or at least one's own permanent place in a big bed, might seem to be the most basic 'personal space'; perhaps because of this, poorer mothers often do not like discussing sleeping arrangements, and we drew the line at this intrusion. For this reason, we unfortunately have no data on whether children have their own bed or half-bed.

17 The numbers at the lower end of the scale may in fact seem surprisingly high. Many of these 'playrooms', however, are simply unfurnished rooms, sometimes erstwhile front parlours, which have been abandoned by the family for living in and turned over to the children; often they are repositories for all the family junk. Useful enough in summer, they can be extremely unwelcoming in winter, since they are seldom heated and often not cleaned.

Chapter 5

The Constraints
of Reality

In the last chapter, we were concerned with the materials chosen
by children for their play; in this one we shall look at the ways in
which they play and the kinds of activities with which they prefer to
fill their free time. In particular, we shall examine in detail the
place of fantasy in the seven-year-old's life, and the degree to which
reality now intrudes upon, and even supplants, the imaginative
element.

Having asked a number of rather specific questions about the
child's play activities before school-time, after school, in the weekend and so on, and having also some information on special hobbies,
toys and collections, we attempted to structure the emerging picture
of the child's free play by asking his mother to place in *his* preference order the child's choice of activities when playing with other
children. For convenience, we divided possible activities into three
categories: rough and tumble play, constructional play and imaginative play.[1] 'Rough and tumble' included climbing, kicking a ball
around, riding about on bikes and scooters, wrestling and puppy-
play, and big-muscle activity generally.

Unemployed labourer's wife:
He likes throwing and footballing. More throwing than anything.

Builder's wife:
With others he likes striding walls. It's a game – if one falls they
tip one another and they're out, and they have to wait on the
others. Striding walls.

'Constructional play' was explained as 'building things and making
things', and included both large projects such as dens and wigwams

and more table-based constructions such as Lego, Meccano or cutting-out and modelling.

Maintenance worker's wife:
He's not interested in toys, he likes to make things. He can always find something to do, even if it's only with a cardboard box.

University teacher's wife (re untidiness, in a child whose main outdoor activity was making dens):
A lot of this is obscured by *indoor* den-making – you go into his room and think it's ghastly and terrible, but actually it's meant to *be* something; and this makes it very difficult to tidy up sometimes, because something *we* think should be tidied away into a cupboard is a radio receiver or something like that – he wants it that way.

Teacher's wife:
Sellotape is the greatest love of his life, and he uses it for all conceivable things – if he can involve Sellotape in something, he will.

Imaginative play, in the context of 'play with other children', tended to be essentially role-playing games – school, hospital, 'house', cowboys and Indians, Batman and Robin and so on. To count for this category, the game had to involve a definite progression of action: a story or episode had to be acted out. At the time of the fieldwork, many little boys spent hours on end wearing Batman cloaks and rushing around shouting 'Pow!' and 'Batman!'; and it is a perennial amusement for owners of guns[2] to leap about shooting each other in a rather inconsequential manner: these activities were categorised as 'rough and tumble' rather than imaginative. Obviously it was not always easy to be sure whether the individual child's games met our criterion of having a developing plot (however simple), and we had to trust to mothers' estimates of this. Some were more sure of their answers than others; most gave reasonably firm replies, but they might still be wrong. To the extent that they were being asked to produce evidence on which to base their judgement, they were more likely to have been wrong in not having noticed imaginative games that *were* going on than in thinking imaginative play was occurring when it was not. Thus the parents who take less notice anyway are likely to report the least preference for imaginative play. However, the kind of imaginative activity most easily missed is the private fantasy game which excludes both mothers *and other children*, and this we were not concerned with here, having specified activities involving the child with others.

University teacher's wife:
> They have endless games of house and school – serial stories, really, they go on for days on the same theme. They set out their room as a schoolroom and every doll has a desk of some sort, about fifteen or more, and they all have exercise books and drawing books. Every doll has its own personality, of course, and the girls each have their own names and personalities as teachers – the school seems a bit rigid and bossy, actually. Their brother is a bit above this sort of thing, but even he gets drawn in from time to time – comes and gives the school-children a lecture or takes them on an educational visit!

Lorry driver's wife:
> He usually plays Batman or something. I'm afraid it's all Batman, apart from his cards and Thunderbirds – he pinches about every scarf I own, I think, and they're covered in holes. [When he plays Batman, does there seem to be a story to it, or is it just rushing about for the excitement of it?] Oh no, there's a story. They sort of sit down and work it all out first. It's usually what's been on TV the week before.

Labourer's wife:
> He'll get his postman things out, he's made all sort of letters and a bag, and he's got a hat, and they'll play postman for a while . . .

Foreman's wife:
> They'll all be Thunderbirds, you know, calling each other – they call each other on the intercom – they'll send each other on missions to the wicket-pitch. Julia next door – she's got a veil – he's the rescuer, oh dear! She finishes up as a beautiful princess in her wedding veil, waiting to be rescued.

Builder's wife:
> Cowboys – they have to get dressed up. Cowboy suits, and my scarves round their face. I think it's this television. He puts a nylon stocking round his face, you know, it's this TV you know, he's seen *The Invisible Man*. Have you seen it? Well, since then he's beginning to put things round his face now. I think the telly's really more to do with it, you know, what with cowboys and one

thing and another. There's always a robbery, always has to be a robbery.

It is clear from some of these accounts that television has a strong influence on the role-playing games played by groups of children, particularly, perhaps, for little boys; and we did wonder whether stories taken straight from 'what's been on TV the week before' should be disallowed as an imaginative game. However, in practice this seemed too fine a point to investigate with any certainty, and we decided to include games of television origin provided they met the plot criterion – especially as it was evident that a game based upon last week's programme would often be elaborated past recognition by the inspiration of the children and by the coming to hand of such opportune accessories as Julia's wedding veil.[3]

Table 16 shows the preferences and the least preferred activities for boys and girls in different social class groups. The overall high or low ratings of the three kinds of activities are not of particular interest, since they are partly determined by the specification of the question: one would not expect, for example, constructional games to rate very highly as 'games he mostly plays with other children', since by nature they lend themselves mainly to solitary play. Thus the noteworthy patterns in this table are those which show differences of preference between classes and between sexes.

The most interesting sex difference, perhaps, is that for a fifth of the boys, but for well under a tenth of the girls, imaginative play is put last (significant at the 0·001 level). Class differences are evident in the figures for all types of play. 'Rough and tumble' play is placed last for about a quarter of middle-class boys but only 8% of working-class boys (difference significant at the 0·001 level); and girls show a rather similar pattern, but with the break coming between professional/managerial and white-collar families. For half the Class I and II boys, and more than two-thirds of the other boys, constructional play is put last (significant at the 0·001 level); it comes last for two-thirds of Class I and II girls and more than four-fifths of other girls (significant at the 0·02 level). Imaginative play is popular for middle-class children generally, taking first place for half the boys and almost three-quarters of the girls; but it decreases significantly for working-class children p <0·001), even though it is still a majority first choice for working-class girls, declining more dramatically for working-class boys. All these results, in fact, combine to give a picture of a working-class child whose play interests and activities as shown in the company of other children are well

Table 16   *Preferred modes of play with other children*

	social class					summary		
	I&II	IIIwc	III man	IV	V	I&II, IIIwc	IIIman, IV,V	overall popn.
	%	%	%	%	%	%	%	%
'Rough and tumble' placed first								
boys	41	43	58	63	60	42	59	55
girls	22	31	34	39	39	26	36	33
'Rough and tumble' placed last								
boys	25	21	8	8	8	23	8	12
girls	27	14	11	13	5	21	10	13
'Constructional' placed first								
boys	8	5	7	6	8	7	7	7
girls	1	0	2	5	3	1	3	2
'Constructional' placed last								
boys	52	67	71	66	64	59	69	67
girls	67	80	84	77	89	73	83	80
'Imaginative, role-playing' placed first								
boys	51	52	35	31	32	52	34	38
girls	77	69	64	56	58	73	62	65
'Imaginative, role-playing' placed last								
boys	22	12	20	25	27	18	22	21
girls	6	6	5	11	5	6	6	6

adapted to coping with the social demands of a large peer group in a relatively unstructured setting – the city street or the mêlée of the school playground, for example; while the middle class child is more likely to feel at home in smaller groups with more closely defined aims. In this sense it can be said that the middle-class child, especially if he comes from Class I and II, is in his interests and inclinations the better adapted for the demands of the classroom, whereas the working-class child is the more suited to playground life. This conclusion is reinforced by other data still to be presented, as well as by what has already been said on the chaperonage factor, and it has obvious implications for the relative effectiveness of school education.

One cannot ignore, of course, the fact that the play-preferences given are at one remove from the child in that they show the situation *as the mother sees it*, and may thus be contaminated by her own attitudes as to what kind of play is acceptable or 'natural' or 'right' for a given sex in a given cultural setting. This proviso is always implicit in the method used here for obtaining data, and we can only continue to draw attention to it; while reminding the reader again that the mother's attitude, if it rubs off on her answer to us, is also one of the cultural pressures which rub off on the child and determine his ultimate total situation, in which we are chiefly interested. Thus, for instance, it is possible that Class v mothers underestimate the true incidence of imaginative play in their boys, and, if so, this may be because they think that imagination is morally questionable and perhaps effeminate, whereas rough and tumble play is suitably aggressive for their stereotype of a 'normal healthy boy': yet if all these hypotheses are true, the admittedly contaminated results are still of interest in indicating differences of attitude to play distinguishing the social classes which will exert a significant effect on behaviour via the encouragement or discouragement of specific kinds of play for the individual child.

Thus it does not seem reasonable to dismiss such a clear-cut and consistent pattern of results, showing differences of this magnitude, as being 'simply' due to a response-bias reflecting differences in attitudes of parents which are not paralleled by differences in the real behaviour of the children themselves; and the sex divergence is as meaningful as the social class trend. Looking beyond the bare categories to the transcripts themselves, it is clear that not only are girls more drawn to imaginative play anyway, but their play differs from the dramatic play of boys in style and nature, both in relation to the play objects with which it is concerned, and with regard to the adult behaviour which it rehearses.

The use of dolls, which on the whole are intended to approximate to real babies and real children, must immediately make it easier for girls to project their own feelings wholeheartedly on to their play objects; and it is also noticeable that girls make more use of *each other*, and of younger children, as vital elements in their imaginative play. There is, of course, no intrinsic reason why boys should not play imaginative sequential games based upon their own preferred play objects such as cars, trains and toy soldiers; indeed, many of them do, on their own, but these toys are more difficult to incorporate into group play with a coherent theme, because it is less easy to endow them with defined personality traits which can be properly appreciated by all the participating children.

Girls' play tends to mirror fairly closely the role behaviour of those adult women who are constantly available to the children's observation in their daily lives: which means that it is concerned with looking after babies, keeping house, shopping, taking children to the doctor, perhaps going on holiday *en famille*, and so on – all of which activities are very close to the real-life preoccupations of their own mothers, *even where their own mother is at work*. The only career behaviour which children have ample opportunity to observe at first hand is teaching, almost invariably a woman's job in the immediate experience of children of this age; and 'school' is in fact a favourite game for girls. Doctor and nurse games might be more often played, but they are deliberately discouraged by many mothers who recognise that they are frequently used as a medium for sexual exploration which rather few are willing to accept.

While the roles of mother and teacher are familiar to the child, and easily identified with by girls, the work-roles of men are not so amenable to observation, taking place as they do at a distance from the child. Probably for this reason, boys of this age seldom base their dramatic play on ordinary masculine work roles (other than soldiers, of whom there are almost none in our sample of fathers); in contrast with that of girls, the imaginative play of boys appears to draw much more heavily upon fiction. Frequently they adopt the heroic roles which they see portrayed in television serials or comics, or which they know to be very far removed from their own enviroment (astronaut or cowboy); and this immediately means that boys are likely to feel less surely identified with their imaginative episodes, and to recognise them more readily as mere make-believe, unconnected with the real daily lives of ordinary men like their own fathers. Of course, boys can and do incorporate a little romantic fantasy into more orthodox games such as cricket and football, by identifying with the star of their choice whenever they are in control of the ball; but the actual course of a real rule-bound game will generally tend to interfere with the coherence of whatever fantasy theme they attempt to sustain as the game is played through.

The differences in the kinds of roles and plots chosen by boys and by girls have implications for the organisational dynamics of the group game. The use which girls make of each other and of younger children, which we noted above, is partly possible because the family-based situations which they enact tend to offer a greater number of satisfying and complementary roles. Boys' fantasies, on the other hand, tend to be more clear-cut in terms of goodies and baddies, leader and led, and are therefore less satisfactory for those participants who do not achieve a star part: this means that their imaginative group play calls for certain organisational skills in the peer group leader, who must be able to ensure that all the children are getting enough out of the game to want to go on play- ing. Where none of the group has the subtlety in handling relation- ships or the panache to carry the others with him, the game may well break down into mere rough and tumble; what was intended to be a fully plotted Batman adventure comes to grief on the basic point of who is to be Batman, and deteriorates into five little Bat- men rushing to and fro shouting 'Pow!' at each other. In essence, boys' imaginative games tend to consist of a series of climaxes, the thrills and terrors leading up to a final dénouement; whereas girls play out the traditional phrase 'and they lived happily ever after', in which the fantasy is sustained on a lower key but, by definition, without a time limit.

The quite striking polarisation of children's play-preferences according to the sex of the child, as shown in both this and the previous chapter, can hardly be regarded as a novel finding; and it is of interest to us principally because it was not so dramatically noticeable at the pre-school stage. This is not simply, or even mainly, that the difference is *created* in the children by social pres- sures between four and seven years: much of the apparent change during these years must be due to the fact that four-year-olds are a good deal less autonomous than seven-year-olds, and have very much less opportunity, in their more sheltered environment, to carry through their preferences into their behaviour; nor have they reached a stage in their development of co-operative group play where the differences which we have noted at seven would be so obvious. In addition, the much more dependent, clinging behaviour of the four-year-old generally would tend to mask sex differences somewhat.

Sexual polarisation in interests does seem to represent a cultur- ally universal phenomenon which is not at all easy to explain in purely environmental terms, as learned behaviour entirely deriving from the child's adoption of a member of the same sex as an appro- priate model. In Derek Wright's commonsense words, 'it seems in- conceivable that the many structural and functional [sex] differences will not have some behavioural consequences. But it is probable that most of these consequences will be indirect, and result from inter- action with particular kinds of environment'.[4] Both the evidence accumulating in the present study and the consensus of previous workers[5] would seem to confirm the claim made by Erik Erikson;[6] that boys and girls employ characteristically different modes of activity which are deeply rooted in their respective natures, and which ultimately can be traced back to the basic and genetically prodigious chromosomal difference which defines sex and compels the two separate biological functions upon which, in its various ways, the human race has proceeded to elaborate over the years. If boys all over the world are more active, thrusting, adventurous and aggressive, while girls are in contrast more compliant and nurturant, centring their interest in the cradle of their own body-frame, and, by extension, oriented towards person-relationships within a relatively closed environment, these are facts of life against which it should not be impossible for growth and rapprochement of role to take place. An acceptance of biological divergence is not incompatible with a condemnation of cultural persecutions which may have been its accompaniment.

*'She's **aware** that there are things in her that she likes to keep secret . . .'*
A phrase often used to describe the play of pre-school children (and frequently applied to our four-year-olds) is 'he seems to be in a world of his own'. This impression arises partly because the four-year-old's new-found fluency in language seems to spill over regardless of time and place, so that his thoughts tumble out in words addressed to no one in particular or everyone in general; although he needs to have other people around, he does not necessarily require their continued attention and co-operation. Thus, when he is secure in the knowledge of his mother's presence, he will often play happily for long periods, keeping up a running commentary of 'egocentric speech' which is as much for his own benefit as anyone else's; and this is one reason why mothers can tell us a good deal about their children's fantasy play at four. For the most part, the mother herself will derive considerable pleasure from listening-in on the four-year-old's monologues: a child in this mood is usually contented, making few direct demands on her, and she is proud of his increasing verbal skills, charmed and amused by his idiosyncrasies of speech, and in general reacts with tenderness towards the whole situation.

At seven years, things have changed somewhat. The mother is likely to regard the child's play with a more dispassionate eye;

what is sweet and clever in a four-year-old may even seem a little silly or odd in a seven-year-old. The child himself is aware of this; he knows that the lines of tolerance are now more closely drawn, and that his flights of fancy are quite likely to encounter indulgent laughter and even derision from parents and older siblings. What is more, where at four he would have been unconscious of the amusement he was causing, partly because of his own lack of social empathy and partly because his family would have taken greater pains to spare him embarrassment, now his pride is more at risk. Children of this age are becoming more sensitive to any suggestion of ridicule, and ridicule is the enemy of fantasy.

The child's imaginative play, whether with other children or solitary, thus begins to take on a certain quality of reserve from the adult world. Children engaged in role-playing games may carry on long and involved conversations with each other, using many different voices and portraying diverse emotions; but these at seven are private communications, not intended to be listened to by anyone other than the active participants, even though there may be adults around who cannot help overhearing. At four, mothers were commonly welcomed into the child's game, and often took an active part in imaginative play; but there were a few then who found that the child regarded their participation as an intrusion: 'sometimes she'll have a shop set up with all sorts of odds and ends, and she'll put some high-heeled shoes on and be chatting away; and I'll come and buy something and she'll *freeze* – and that's the end of the game'.[7] At seven, such cold welcomes have become the norm; in fact mothers seldom even offer to break into children's play in this way, and there is a deliberate attempt by children who are playing together to keep themselves to themselves, to exclude adults and less sympathetic older siblings, and to shut themselves off as far as possible from inquisitive eyes and ears. The fear of appearing ridiculous perhaps also explains the popularity at this age of dens, hide-outs, wendy-houses, tree-houses and so on, which offer a means of physical isolation and ensure some degree of privacy.

Children playing imaginatively together are partially protected from embarrassment by group solidarity. Solitary fantasy play is obviously much more susceptible to the possibility of ridicule. Nonetheless, it retains a major place in the child's life, particularly for girls. We asked: 'Does he ever have play-acting games *when he's on his own* – either being someone himself or making up a story with dolls or toy animals or puppets?' – and mothers were asked to describe these games.

As we pointed out when the children were four, the figures we present in this area must be considered conservative estimates, since there must be some children who keep their mothers entirely in ignorance of their fantasies; mothers themselves are aware that their knowledge is incomplete – 'I can't tell you, because it's all in his mind', said one – nevertheless, they are likely to know more than anyone else about these secret corners of the child's world.

Wholesaler's wife:
War! Yes, he has a cavalry fort, an old-time fort – but it's a pageant of history, all types of soldiers, Indians, cowboys, cavalry, the whole thing – everything goes together, and he plays the most intricate games with them. He has battles and he captures people; and we have several layers of conversation, you know, little voices going on – he has a complete master plan of what he's doing . . . . . This is the thing, these men, no matter what money he has, invariably he'll come home with some more of them. Not necessarily soldiers – he has a farm too, with animals, and men to look after the animals – it seems to be these *smaller* things that catch his eye, you see.

Lorry driver's wife:
She's got a vivid imagination; she'll, like . . . if she's upstairs, she'll be . . . you can hear her, talking and laughing and some- times crying; she'll play with herself, imagining there's someone there. Sometimes she'll cry, you know, she'll imagine something sad, you know, she'll pretend someone's crying and then make as though she's laughing, you know, making as though there's people with her. We often listen to her. She acts as . . . if you were listening outside the door, you'd think there was another child in with her; and you can hear them falling out, yet there's just the one voice, yet how she carried on you'd think they was falling out. She'd cry and she'll make herself better, you know, she really *thinks* there's someone there – I listen to her some- times.

Filing clerk's wife:
He doesn't play a story much with *other* children; but he talks a lot to *himself* – you can hear him making gun noises and all that. I often find him on the toilet talking to himself. We often listen and have a laugh – talking to someone who isn't there.

Works manager's wife:
Oh, he's a great storyteller to himself, particularly at night when
he's gone to bed. He really does, he goes at it, and he's everybody, and there's always the best one of course, and he's always
rescuing them; and I can hear this going off, and he's got his
head under the sheets you know, and he's going "Come on!
Matthew Ellis [child's name] is coming, hooray!" It really would
make you have a smile at it.

Cycle worker's wife:
He often tells me he can see magic pictures under the bedclothes.
He often says "I'm not getting upset, I'm watching a film", sort
of thing – I suppose it's his imagination underneath the bedclothes, and they're all in colour. 'Course, I sling along with it.

Student teacher's wife (herself a teacher):
It can be with any of the dolls, she's got small ones and big ones,
it can be with any. [Father:] *Five Dolls in a House*, she often
plays that at the moment, she's got a book called *Five Dolls in a
House*, and she's read that I should think twenty times, and she's
got five small dolls about this size, which she puts into a sewing
box, and this is their house, you see; and she sets them out, and
they've all got the right name, and she plays with those. I wouldn't
be the least bit surprised if that's what she's doing now [evening],
or reading *Five Dolls*. [And do they have any new adventures,
or are these the same as the book?] Well, I wouldn't know, because we only catch her occasionally doing this, she's not doing
this in front of us. [When you walk in, she stops?] Yes.

Metal polisher's wife:
He does [have play-acting games] with the cat! Well, he just
says to the cat "Now you're not allowed to come past this point!"
And he looks at the cat, "Now you're going to do as you're told,
now, aren't you?" – you know – then he'll start talking to his
tommy-gun, you know: "I've got you now!" and "What did you
do that for?" He just makes conversation with them. [And does
he talk *for* the tommy-gun too?] Oh yes – in a squeaky voice.
[Does he talk for the cat?] Yes, yes.

Grocer's wife:
They can be dolls, or . . . once when we were at my mother's she
was playing on the front, and my mother's got a lot of marguerites, out at the time, she had; well, they were her imaginary

children – going on, smacking them because they weren't paying attention! Then she'd run through playing a few chords on the piano – out again – and smack some more marguerites that weren't paying attention. She's adaptable! – if she hasn't got any toys there, well, she'll have a few imaginary . . .

Table 17 shows that nearly two-thirds of all children engage in solitary fantasy play of one sort or another; and the pattern of sex and social class differences is closely related to those found for imaginative play involving other children. In particular, the divergence between boys and girls is very marked at every class level; but the similarity of these findings to those on imaginative group play is especially clear when we compare the overall summary tables. Both tables show large and significant differences overall between the sexes, but they also indicate that this difference is greater overall for working-class children than for middle-class children.

In our study of four-year-olds, we discussed the question of class and family-size differences in fantasy production at some length. The figures for 'incidence of fantasies' given then are not, of course, comparable with those given here on 'solitary fantasy play', since the former refer specifically to *persisting fantasy creations* and not to fantasy play in general. The problem of interpretation of differences is the same, however: where class (or family size) differences are found, are we dealing with a true difference of incidence or with a difference in awareness of fantasy by the mother? Using other studies as checks,[8] we concluded at the four-year-old stage that a factor of better communication between mother and child was an important contributor both to the greater number of reported

Table 17 *Children who engage in solitary fantasy play*

| | social class | | | | | summary | | |
	I&II	IIIwc	III man	IV	V	I&II, IIIwc	IIIman, IV,V	overall popn.
	%	%	%	%	%	%	%	%
boys	61	59	47	43	46	60	46	50
girls	85	71	77	84	67	78	77	77
both	73	65	62	64	56	69	61	64

Significance: trend ↘ **   m.class/w.class p <0·07
              between sexes ****

fantasies in higher social classes and to the greater number reported among one- and two-children families and (especially) among singletons; but we also thought that class attitudes and life-styles had an effect on the actual incidence of fantasy. For the seven-year-old, the fact that an active interest in fantasy games is reported by such a high proportion of mothers of working-class girls hardly suggests that working-class mothers are incapable of recognising this behaviour in their children when it occurs. We must therefore conclude either that a disproportionate number of working-class boys manage to keep their fantasy play strictly private from their parents, or that their interest in fantasy is in fact steadily waning. While there is some evidence (see Table 18 below) that working-class boys who do engage in fantasy play are more embarrassed by observers than middle-class boys, working-class girls are equally so; and we must assume from this that Table 17 shows a real difference in the actual incidence of such play.

At four, we had found that 22% of all children had their own individual fantasy *companions*, either human or animal, defined on the basis that 'it must recur in the child's imagination from one day to another and must very considerably transcend any original factual basis'. At seven, only 3% were known to have an active imaginary friend.[9] Class differences would be difficult to show on such small numbers; but, as one might expect in this kind of idiosyncratic behaviour, there is no sign of them anyway. Girls outnumber boys by five to one (again not significant on such small numbers).

University teacher's wife:
    They've all vanished except Harry Tom. Harry Tom was her husband, and – er – he is still there in the background, but we don't see much of him now because he's supplanted by a real boy whom she loves very much – lives in Bristol, unfortunately – and clearly it's much nicer to have a boy you're engaged to than somebody imaginary who you're actually married to; and the doll who had Harry Tom as a father is grown-up, and no longer needs a father. If one asks about Harry Tom, then it goes on. She seems to have other people, but she doesn't talk about them so much now. One is aware that she *has* a world of her own and her dolls. It is all connected with dolls, the dolls she has.

Miner's wife:
    Janet – yes, *she* still knocks around – *she's* still here – plays with

her just as she used to. Never down here, always in the front room or the bedroom, she'd *never* have her down here; well, maybe once or twice she'd be *sitting* there, but not like it is upstairs or in the front room. Many a time I've thought my eldest daughter was in the front room. when I've heard her talking, and I've said "Where's Bess?" – "No, she's not here" – "Well, who is here?" – "Oh, it's all right, it's just Janet" – and I say "Oh, all right".

Cost accountant's wife:
. . . I don't know whether he was Long John Silver or who he was, you know, and he'll fetch all his cuddly friends, you know, down, and they'll be people on the ship – and then of course he'll have his two imaginary friends, Robins and Jelly. Now where they're from I do not know, but Robins, of course, he had Robins when I had an interview before; but Jelly, I think Jelly came when we came to this house. They're a hundred years old, and they're like Peter Pan, I'm told, and they know everything; I don't think we've anyone on this road who doesn't know about them, because he talks to them coming home from school if he happens to miss the other children, and he carries on this conversation with them, you know, in his own little world.

Chartered engineer's wife (working as secretary):
Sometimes he'll say "Lion told me this" – he's got a mate called Lion. [A purely imaginary thing?] Yes. He told me the other day – he had had to wait that evening – and he told me that Lion had said I wasn't dead – so you could tell which way *his* mind was made up! I was late coming in, and he thought I might have had an accident, but Lion told him that I hadn't, so it was a good job Lion was there!

Fantasy companions have a number of functions beyond that of companionship, for which they might well be valued and retained; 'Lion', for instance, has obvious comforting qualities to support a child on his own, 'Janet' acts as a scapegoat (see continuation of this quotation, page 168), and others whom we met when the children were younger were variously useful as vicarious power figures or as stand-ins for the child: 'She sometimes says "*I* don't love you, but Noddy does" '. In their main role as playmate, however, they have particular virtues of patience and amiability which can ease the child very gradually into the social relationships which eventually have to be worked out on a reality level with his less tolerant peers. A temperamental seven-year-old to whom social relationships came hard (page 41) was still using an imaginary boy as a retreat; his mother, a locomotive driver's wife, described him playing marbles by himself 'because he says he can play better with his imaginary friend – he invented a little friend to play with, you see; if he's playing with his brothers or other children he's in-clined to fall out'. Most children at seven, however, are much better able to enjoy group play than they were at four – perhaps because experience has taught them the benefits of social co-opera-tion. But playing in a group makes it not only unnecessary but also much more difficult to sustain the fantasy playmate, if only because each is idiosyncratic to its owner. If fantasy companions are in fact useful to the child as subsitute playmates (and the evidence of higher incidence among 'only and lonely' children seems to sup-port this), one would expect them to begin to disappear as soon as their function is usurped by the availability of 'real' friends; that is, about the time when the child starts school. This is in fact the case. We asked specifically at seven about every 'imaginary friend' of whom we had a record at four years – what had happened to the creature and, if it no longer existed, the manner of its dis-appearance. Three-quarters of imaginary playmates existing at four had gone, so far as the mother was aware, by the age of five-and-a-half – 'just faded out' was the usual impression – and of the re-mainder, half had gone before seven. Sometimes the development took place by a subtle transition from playing *with* to playing *at*: Jeremy's bedroom, for instance, no longer actually houses Teacher, but he still plays at school there:

Scientific research worker's wife:
[When he was four, he had an imaginary teacher whom he kept in his bedroom – does he still have her?] No, he doesn't. She's been replaced by a real teacher now. He still plays this game, but now it's Mrs Grant or Mrs Dillon, the teachers he really has. [He still talks about them being upstairs?] Oh yes, yes – he *plays* school. His old Teacher went after he started school, about six months or a year after.

Natalie, the first child below, has graduated from eight named imaginary friends at age four to real school playmates; Jimmy's mother, in alluding to his road sense, is making a rather similar point – that, being less geographically restricted, he can now fill his experience with real people and events. Social seclusion fosters

fantasy; out and about, there is less need to resort to invention in
order to make life interesting.

Merchandise supervisor's wife:
Never heard about them since she went to school – it was some
companionship she was needing. [Natalie:] I even *saw* them!
[Mother:] I think it must have been lack of something, don't
you?

Presser's wife:
He don't do it so much now; he'll say, well, "I've been to such
a place, you know, Mam, and I've seen so-and-so" – er, you
know, more or less like a dream; it's one of them things – but
he don't do it half as much as he used to do. But it were more
or less when were down there, I mean we were in that big yard,
you know, and he got time to think about it, where now he's not
afraid to cross the road or anything, he knows his kerb drill, well
he's more sense than our William had – you can trust our Jimmy
now as much as when our William were eleven.

The child's own feeling, that to present imaginary incidents or
people in precisely the same terms as real ones is somehow no
longer appropriate, comes over clearly in many of these accounts.

Manager's wife:
He used to, but he doesn't now; his favourite some years ago was
how he came from London, how he lived there and he had two
dogs. The curious thing is – er – the other day he was on about
this plane, it's too complicated for him to do on his own as you
see, and Daddy's helping him, and every time his Daddy comes
in David says "Daddy, can we do a bit more to the plane?" So
I said finally "It's a pity you don't go to London to that hotel
of yours for a few days, ha ha ha!" So he said "Well – I was
only young then, Mummy, I never *really* went to London". He's
rather sort of . . . he doesn't make them up now.

Student psychologist's wife:
I can't remember when, but at some stage he developed a sense
of humour, so that this sort of reporting of non-existent occurrences in fact then became jokes, which were told with a wry
grin with one eye on mother, half hoping she'll believe, half
hoping I'll see the funny side of it. When he was young he was
very serious, and we thought we'd produced a child without

humour and we should find this very difficult, but in fact his humour has developed since then, but it was very gradual.

The 'joke' as a gesture made by fantasy towards the claims of reality is a development to which we shall return shortly. The last five quotations have all referred to imaginative flights which at four were communicated by the child and accepted by the parent on a level of seriousness which recognised their *subjective reality* to the child; at seven, the child himself knows that this will not quite do. Partly he solves the problem by acquiescing to his fantasy's status as merely 'a game', while continuing to play it with great involvement, as we have seen from the accounts given on page 154. The difference is that the game is recognised as private play-acting, and there is a tacit agreement that it will not make demands on the imagination of the whole family; even the few imaginary companions who survive are more retiring than they were. Contrast these highly obtrusive personalities at the four-year-old stage: 'You have to go and answer the door and that, you know . . . often she [playmate] comes to tea . . .'; 'He asked me to smack Cat'; 'Sometimes we've had to go back to the gate and let him [playmate] in'; 'I have to carry it about in my arms'; 'If my lad sits too close, it's "You're squashing her – get off!" '; 'I think he can really see this dog. In fact, I said to my husband, I think *I* can see this dog!'

The fact that an individual seven-year-old continues to 'play-act' his private fantasies as a 'game' does not necessarily mean that he can comfortably tolerate adult observation of this. We were interested to know about children's reactions to adults' interest in their fantasies; therefore, if a child did have 'play-acting games' on his own, we went on to ask 'Does he mind you listening to these games, or does he stop when you come in?' Table 18 gives four categories of reaction to observation; 'sometimes each' refers to children who vary in their reaction. The second part of the table shows preference for privacy as a function of social class.

The majority of the 64% of all children who play in this way do not mind an audience, or even positively enjoy one (though very rarely to the extent of actively allowing it to participate, like the foreman's son below); but almost a third of them consistently seek privacy for these activities.[10] Working-class children and middle-class girls show no significant differences here; however, there is an interesting tendency for middle-class boys to be considerably less concerned than the rest to maintain privacy, as if they rather enjoyed showing off in this way. An explanation of this may be that working-class children generally are more likely to be discouraged from this kind of play, while middle-class girls, while not discouraged, are more socially aware than boys of the proprieties, and for this reason are shyer of attracting notice of this kind.

Table 18   *Reaction to audience by children engaged in solitary 'play-acting' (64% of total (randomised) sample)*

	likes audience %	doesn't mind %	sometimes each %	prefers privacy %
boys	27	42	4	27
girls	21	39	6	34
both	23	40	6	31

Children preferring privacy

	social class					summary		
	I&II	IIIwc	III man	IV	V	I&II, IIIwc	IIIman, IV,V	overall popn.
	%	%	%	%	%	%	%	%
boys	19	12	35	36	31	16	33	27
girls	35	43	32	29	42	38	32	34
both	28	28	33	31	29	28	32	31

No significant differences

Political worker's wife:
> She does make up stories, and I mean she thinks she's completely on her own; because, you know, she's got to the age when she's *aware* that there are things in her that she likes to keep secret – although I've never sort of laughed at her or anything because of this – I don't know – I suppose it's because she mostly lives in a grown-up world. A lot of our friends haven't any children, and they come here, and she's become quickly aware that there are things that you keep private, you know; and so, if she is telling a story to herself, she'll immediately shut up as you appear. No matter how you try and say that was a nice story, she won't.

Railwayman's wife:
> She knows we're laughing at her, sort of thing – you have to laugh at her, because I mean it seems peculiar for her to answer herself back, sort of thing – and she'll stop playing. She goes all red, you know, blushy.

Joiner's wife:
Oh no, he likes you to listen – he keeps shouting "Oh Mummy, look, look what I'm doing, look what we're doing" – he wants you to know.

Foreman's wife:
Oh no, he'll join you in! I mean, if he puts a man on there, and I'm sitting there, and he'll speak to that man: well sometimes – I don't look at him, like – I answer him, and tell him what to do to this man; and he'll *do* it, you know, he's quite happy for you to . . .

Lorry driver's wife:
He's lost himself. If he's playing with cars or anything – most games, if he's playing on his own he gets absolutely lost in it, and you can talk and talk and talk to him, and he's just not there. He doesn't always notice when we come in, but all of a sudden he'll look up, and he'll see me, and he'll sort of smile as much as to say "Don't I look silly?" – a sheepish grin. A couple of minutes later, he's lost again.

Scientific research worker's wife:
He's sometimes a little bit embarrassed for a few seconds, but then I think he thinks "Oh well, it's only Mum", and carries on.

Storekeeper's wife:
She usually stops when I come in. I think she gets a bit embarassed at times about it, but with a little bit of encouragement she carries on.

What we are witnessing here, then, is a development away from the unselfconscious expression of fantasy by the pre-school child towards a more sophisticated self-appraising stage which allows the child to see himself as others see him and guard in advance against possible derision. The younger child is unconcerned about being overheard, because he fails to appreciate the possibility that he might be creating a very odd or amusing impression in the eyes of the onlooker. By seven, this inability of the young child to put himself in the observers' place and look at his behaviour through their eyes has been partially overcome. His increasing awareness of self and his heightened social sensitivity combine to alert him to the possibility of being overheard and to the implications of this.[11] He will now understand in a practical way, as he might not have done at four, that a person in the next room may well be able to hear all you say, even though they are out of sight or not overtly reacting; indeed, he himself may be becoming adept at listening to interesting adult conversations without calling attention to the fact. The inevitable penalty of the growth of consciousness of self in relation to others is that the seven-year-old's fantasy play is correspondingly less vivid, lively and spontaneous.

Mothers who have positively enjoyed their children's fantasies and are sorry to lose them can be very aware of the child's developing reserve. 'I would listen, but I would pretend to be very busy; I wouldn't embarrass the child', said a newsagent's wife; and an executive's wife was equally careful of her little boy's pride.

> Well, he's lost – he doesn't – he isn't conscious of you. [Does he know when you come into the room?] Well, he knows, but he sort of – we never – we don't like to make him self-conscious; the other two ignore him when he's playing, because I've found with my eldest boy . . . I lived with my mother-in-law for three years with him, and everything he did, she sort of commented on it, and it made him terribly self-conscious. Well, I didn't want that to happen to Matthew, so I sort of – when they laughed at him, I've sort of shaken my head, and they've learned to ignore him. He's – well, he's lost sometimes, plays away there and doesn't know we're in the room.

Matthew's brother and sister are old enough to co-operate in saving his embarrassment; siblings are often more inclined to seize the opportunity to deride and deflate. Children who are only a year or two older than the seven-year-old are severe critics, because they have only recently outgrown this stage and need to assure *themselves* of their own more grown-up status. One sympathises with the small boy who in his imaginings 'doesn't start from scratch but *enlarges* a lot', and whose elder sister Sarah is something of a trial: 'Sarah always says "*That's* not right!" Sarah's always there at his elbow saying "*That's* not right!" '

For mothers who, like the railwayman's wife above, think that 'it feels peculiar for her to answer herself back', such a diminution of fantasy would seem not a penalty but a relief. We noted a group at four (including the same mother[12]) who were somewhat disturbed by the child's imaginary companion; and such worries seem more urgent at seven, even in relation to ordinary solitary fantasy play.

Trimmer's wife:

    I'm not a very strict mother, but I do like to control them to an extent, you know, if they're doing something really wrong, or getting . . . she starts talking to herself – like – I think, er . . . they start talking to themselves, you know, specially at this age . . . if she's in the house before she goes to bed she'll talk to herself and – er – I don't like it. I tell her to be quiet – watch TV or go to bed. [And does she stop when you tell her?] Yes. Oh yes, she stops, or she has to go to bed.

Foreman's wife:

    . . . the conversation finally got round to this woman saying she thought Patsy was a neurotic. Well, I mean she does dress up and live in this imaginative world, and she can be very dramatic when she chooses . . .

Clive's mother nicely expresses a commonly felt need for reassurance from the child that he does know the difference between truth and fantasy.

Maintenance worker's wife:

    Well, yes, I've often been worried about that. He – you know if he's on his own, he starts these imagining games; and he'll start talking to hisself, and then being the other guy you know, talking back, and I was worried a bit about it; till, you know, I sort of thought . . . listened to him one day, and he says "That was a good game of mine, wasn't it, Mam?" And I thought, well all right, he realises it *is* a game, and I might as well let him go on.

'She comes out with some fantastic things, but you take it with a pinch of salt . . .'

Clive's mother is, of course, not at all unusual in her basic underlying concern that the child should by this time have a reliable understanding of where reality ends and fantasy begins, in the sense of being able to recognise his own fabrications for what they are: otherwise how can he be taught to 'tell the truth'? And teaching the child to tell the truth is accepted universally as a major duty for those who bring up children. However, there is a difference of opinion, which is partly a class difference, between mothers who clearly distinguish between imaginative fantasy and telling lies, and who therefore willingly find a place for fantasy within a fairly

F

moralistic frame of reference, and those who suspect that fantasy is a form of falsehood which is not so very different from a deliberate lie and must at least be watched carefully if it is not to lead to habitual lying.

Any discussion of children's imaginative play must be interested in what the child's fantasy productions mean to him – that is, on what level of his subjective reality they exist. Psychoanalytic writers have assumed that they have meaning in terms of his real-life experiences, fears and desires; but this to some extent begs the question as to whether there is indeed any confusion for the child between subjective and objective experience: Winnicott has pointed out 'the possibility that in the total theory of the personality the psychoanalyst has been too busy *using* play *content* to look at the playing child, and to write about playing as a thing in itself' (italics ours).[13] McKellar[14] has suggested an intermediate stage when the child goes through a period of half-belief, in that he chooses to believe his fantasies because they are pleasurable to him; certainly this is verifiable in the attitudes of many children to traditional myths like Father Christmas, or family myths like (in the writers' family) the Easter cocky-olly birds.

Choosing to believe implies a fairly strong underlying doubt, however; and our own view is that children have far less difficulty in distinguishing between reality and imagination than is sometimes supposed. Thus we may say figuratively that a child is lost in the fantasy of his own imaginative world, but we do not mean by this that he himself is experiencing problems as to whether it is all true or not. Exceptionally vivid dreams or nightmares may, of course, appear uncomfortably 'real', both to children and to adults; but we must assume that, at the age of seven, true hallucinatory delusions occur only in altered states of consciousness (in delirium during fever, for instance, or in the partially conscious state that characterises night terrors): occurring in the normal waking state, they would be interpreted as psychotic episodes.

The confusion which undoubtedly does arise, and which disturbs parents if they feel unable to gain some control over it, is not so much within the child himself as *between* the child and those with whom he attempts to communicate. It is in fact a confusion which is likely to arise between any two individuals when there is a failure to make a clear distinction between information offered about reality and information offered about things imagined. In particular, trouble arises when the child makes a statement given and intended to be received on the 'imaginary' level, which is in fact received at its face value; or where the child bases his story on fact but moves on into fiction without making it clear that such a shift has taken place.

Lorry driver's wife:
You know at school, if she gets told off, she'll come home and she'll say "Mrs Martin smacked me today!" and I says "Smacked you! Whatever for?" – "Ooh, I was laughing and I was shouting", you know, or "I was talking when I should have been quiet". And there's no mark anywhere, you know – "She didn't half hurt me there when she hit me!" You know, you start thinking – I wonder if she did? – so I say to Sharon "I'll go down to that school and I'll be asking her about it". And she says "Ooh, you needn't bother, she didn't hit me really you know". She does tell some tales.

Locomotive driver's wife:
Well, he comes home from school and tells me the biggest stories about things that have happened at school – they're so impossible that I *know* they couldn't be true. When he starts, you see, I think it's something that *has* happened at school; but as soon as he gets sort of into it, I begin to realise it's a yarn.

Departmental manager's wife:
This comes out when Eric [elder brother] is saying something that's happened at school, something quite grown-up, and *he* can't be left out – he has to say his say – which you *know* isn't true, but you can tell that's the reason, that he *can't* be left out. And they go on and on and on, getting out of all proportion as time goes on. [Do you accept it?] Yes – yes – I just say yes; it's no good; sometimes I think, well that *can't* be true – but he only gets angry.

As communicators, children of this age have still a somewhat inadequate ability to stand back and listen to what they themselves are saying, despite their growing self-awareness. The child therefore fails to include in the conversation such vital orienting remarks as 'This is what actually happened' and 'This is what I then imagined'. Signals from the listener that his words are being taken too literally may not be received, or received too late to adapt the message. The ability to put oneself into the position of one's listener, which is almost indispensable to genuine human communication, is a sophisticated art which the child will require many years to perfect.[15] Even though it is already present to some degree (as we have seen) in producing an *inhibition* of behaviour patterns which he senses are considered inappropriate, the positive adjustment of speech content to social need is likely to take somewhat longer.

We are arguing, then, that in the first place children of seven confuse imagination and reality only in the sense that they lack the necessary insight and communication skills to make their meaning clear to other people by spelling out the necessary logical distinctions as they go along. However, there are all sorts of complications to this. The child does not simply come to realise once and for all that fact and fantasy must be handled differently. Parents themselves may distinguish between fantasies of private play, justifiable exaggeration in the cause of the raconteur's art, and a downright lie, and their own varied reactions in different situations may at first be somewhat difficult for the child to code and make sense of: although ultimately the parent who makes most distinctions is also looking for a subtlety of understanding in the child himself. In making these distinctions, they are largely concerned with the *motivation* of the child and with the *persistence* of the confusion between truth and falsehood. If the child is perceived to be 'just playing' – that is, in effect, if he has no ulterior motive for wishing to deceive – then his fabrications are tolerable, even though suspect as 'verging on a lie' to mothers at the lower end of the class scale. Similarly, if the fantasy collapses when challenged, all is seen to be well. Obviously, motivation and persistence are closely linked: a deliberate lie, either to procure private ends or in self-defence, must be persisted in to be effective. In a sense, in fact, a lie is partly defined by how far the child is prepared to go in sticking to it: a lie in the heat of panic, withdrawn as soon as challenged, is more like the expletive which 'slips out'. Two examples of motivated lies will suffice; the first is retracted as soon as offered, the second is a real lie because it is maintained.

University teacher's wife:

This happened last week – I found somebody had embellished one lavatory wall with geometrical designs, and – um – Daniel and Charles were in the same room, and I said "Have you been drawing in the lavatory?" They said "No", and Charles looked a bit guilty, and I said "Have you, Charles?" and he said "I might have done by accident", and then he said yes, he had, and when he had, and why he had. If he'd said no, and I was sure he had, I would sort of confront him with it – his honest soul sort of gives him away!

Nylon winder's wife:

He come home from school last week and says this boy had said he'd got a scruffy shirt on; and I says to him "You tell that boy you've had a clean shirt on this morning!" And he said 'He's ripped it, Mum!'" – and I'd only bought that shirt on the Saturday, and he'd ripped it all up the side. So I took him across to school in the afternoon; and it appears Stanley had done it himself, climbing on the apparatus! So you ought to have heard me when he come home. I said "You told me stories, didn't you! If you tell me stories like that again, you won't go out to play after tea!" So he sat in the chair and sulked.

Both these situations are different in character from the other fantasies described in this chapter, and are really included to point the contrast. It must be emphasised that we are here concerned with fantasies and embroideries; 'real' lies are very much seen by parents as problems of discipline, and attitudes then harden considerably.

One reason why parents begin to have doubts about fantasy at this age is that they have a genuine practical need to know how far to trust the child's communications now that he spends a large proportion of his life out of their direct observation. At four, most children were spending a negligible amount of time outside their mother's orbit; at seven there may be considerable implications for action in the child's report, with consequent risk of adult embarrassment if the report is make-believe. We have ourselves suffered this kind of discomfiture, having believed our daughter's story from school that 'Miss E. is leaving'. Miss E. being a much loved and exceptionally skilled teacher who had been in the school for thirty years, this was hot news which, via parent gossip and a teachers' centre, had spread irretrievably before we learned casually 'Oh, she's not after all – we just *thought* she was'. Many parents find themselves inquiring of adults and neighbours about non-existent events; some begin to wonder how their own home life is presented at school.

Lorry driver's wife:

She embroiders things. She was telling me about the boy next door that got knocked down on the road. She says "He was sat on the pavement and the car ran over his legs", she says, "he was sitting there, and the car went down, and it went right over his legs and hit him, and he'll have to go to hospital, and he'll have no legs no more, they're taking them off". So the following day when I saw his mother, I said "Er – is David all right?" "Oh", she says, "he was running across the road, and the car skidded and it sort of knocked him down with it". But Sharon was on the street when it happened, you see, and she tries to put a bit more to it, you see . . . . . She tells stories at school, you know; she brought her work-book home a few weeks ago, and in this book were some of the biggest tales you've ever heard in your life – "My father's a policeman" – er – "We've got a police dog at our house". [This is supposed to be true, is it?] Well, yes, it's supposed to be – on this page it was "What have you got in your house?", and they more or less started from children to furniture, and "Have you got a car? Have you got a dog?" Yes, you know, she put "We've got a police dog", and then it said "What does your Daddy do?", and she put "My father's a policeman". And I said to her, I said, "Fancy putting that!" – "Grandma's been today for dinner" – and she's been nowhere near the house, you know! – "My mother's been to the hospital", and, ooh, one thing and another, and I said to her "I don't know where you get these stories from". And she says "Well, you've got to put something down, haven't you?"

The next two children both present problems generally. Carolyn has never been an easy child (see pages 46–7), has always been intensely jealous of her younger brother and has always craved attention; she had a rich and complicated fantasy life at four,[16] and now both uses fantasy as her mother describes below and tells more obviously motivated lies. Mary's problem is more easily explicable in terms of circumstance; her mother has been separated from her father for more than three years, to which Mary reacted with great unhappiness;[17] she sees her father intermittently, and these meetings are extremely disturbing to her because of her father's disruptive and provocative behaviour: he wilfully upsets both child and mother, and appears to use all his relationships inter-destructively. Mary too had a satisfying fantasy world at four.[18]

Machine operator's wife:
Carolyn used to come home with "Ooh I *have* been sick at

school, ooh I *was* sick!'' Well, that went on for weeks, and finally I said to my husband "There must be something wrong at school, I've got to see what's frightening her into the state of being sick". So I said to Carolyn "We'll go up and see Miss Jones about this". So I took her up and spoke to Miss Jones – and do you know, she'd never been a *bit* sick! I felt such a fool – I mean, what got me was she'd let me waltz up the road with her to the school and never said a word! And I said to Miss Jones "I've got an appointment with the doctor about it and everything". So she said "Well, you keep that appointment and see what he says". Which I did; but he said all children do that to get off school, he says "My own children get a sore throat or earache if they don't want to go to school". But myself, I don't think it *was* that – because she never said she didn't want to *go*, she only said she'd *been* sick. And I think she thought I was going to tell her teacher off for it – who she didn't like – and she was all ready to watch me do it. [Yet she must have known you'd find out when you got there?] Yes – but you see that wouldn't bother her, because she's all out for attention, Carolyn is – anything to be the centre of attention, to be a sensation. It's this jealousy again – though I've tried and *tried* to explain to her, how your love is divided between people, but she won't have it. And I think she'd got it all worked out, you see, how I'd go up there and create a scene about it, and there would be Carolyn being a sensation. She's *got* to be in the limelight.

Lorry driver's wife (separated):
The teacher said "Mary romances a lot". "Oh", I said, "Yes, she does". Her latest craze is that she's told the teacher that we're going to have another baby! . . . . . and every time another mother sees the teacher, she says "Has Mrs Allingham had the baby yet?" Oh dear! – she does romance, you know. Mary really lives up to a thing if she gets something stuck in her mind. [Is it mostly things she would like to happen?] Yes – things that she'd like to happen, or – er – things that – um – if you'd promised her, like, you know, and you've p'raps not had time, you know. If her Daddy says to her "I'll take you out on Sunday". You know – and I think she tells all the school-children that Daddy's going to take her out. And if he doesn't come, she'll make it up herself, where they went, you know – her imagination's there where she'd *like* him to have taken her, you know, and she makes it up herself when she gets to school the next day. [Does

she talk about it to you?] No, she never tells me, only other people, because I know it's not true.

Notice that there is no question of Mary *actually* believing the fantasies that she would like to believe – she does not mention them to the person who could challenge them. Note too that both these mothers, despite the considerable embarrassment to themselves implied in their daughters' behaviour, recognise the children's special needs and do not regard these fantasies in the same moral light as straightforward lies.

Most mothers do feel it important that some recognition should exist between parent and child of the make-believe status of fantasies, exaggerations and embroideries. They therefore try not only to pick their way for their own information between the true and the not-so-true, but to make the child aware that they are doing so. A sharp or quizzical look may be enough; or the mother may be at pains verbally to sort out fact from fancy, and it is clear that this is not just an *ad hoc* investigation of 'where lies the truth on *this* occasion?' but a teaching exercise in microcosm on the whole concept of communication.

Car showroom foreman's wife:
If he's talking to me about something, and he gets so far, and it sounds a bit *too* . . . er . . . I think my expression, and his expression back usually makes me smile, and he'll say "Well . . . it . . ." – I don't actually believe in that kind of thing. [It's a sort of exaggeration he does?] Well, he does it very rarely because he's always stopped, you see.

Scientific research worker's wife:
First of all he tells them as if they were true, and then I can usually see in his face that they are not quite true, and I say to him "Well, is this a story, or did it really happen?" and he says to me "It *nearly* happened . . ." – and then he'll proceed to explain.

Insurance agent's wife:
Yes, romancing, yes. About school, er – a little boy at school did so-and-so, and you can tell it's not true, it's so exaggerated; I say, "Start again; what was his name, and where does he live?"

Miner's wife (*re* imaginary companion, Janet, page 153):
. . . "Oh, it's all right, it's just Janet" – and I say "Oh, all right" – but mind you [pause] – at first when she used to say that, I

thought it were very funny, I did, but not now she's getting older; 'cause she tends now, if anything happens in the front room, such as the stuffing come out of me cushions – 'cause she'd found a thread of it and she must've pulled it – "Janet done that!" When they're little, you know, you don't take much notice, really; I think once they start to get a bit older – now – I put it down to saying little fibs – sort of saying that now sort of to get out of what she's done; so now I say "No it wasn't, *I* saw you". Mind you, as I say, she doesn't come out with it as much as she used to.

Bricklayer's wife:
Yes, Roy's always done that. [He used to, I remember, he told you he'd fallen over a cliff once.] Yes. [What sort of thing does he tell you now?] Well, he'll tell me "I walked home from school today, and I went for a long walk, and I came back again". I said "Don't you tell me an untruth", and he said "I'm only joking" – you know, things like that. And, er, he'll say "In bed I was dreaming this and I was dreaming that, and while you was all sleeping I was doing this", you know – and it's naïve really, more or less a joke, it's not a lie. [But he tells it as if it were true? He doesn't start off saying "I'll tell you a story?"] No, he does it for me to believe; I've got used to him now, not to believe him. [What do you say?] I usually tell him to stop romancing – just romancing. Then he wants to know what romancing means, you know, he'll query it, what does this mean, what does that mean.

Roy illustrates the child's active participation in coming to an understanding of the degrees of truth and falsehood: the nice distinction between 'romancing' and telling lies. A further possibility which mothers offer their children is the joke. Here, what might have been classified as a lie quickly changes its moral character by having a humorous intention ascribed to it; the mother cannot seriously condemn it since it was not seriously meant. Once again, the criterion depends on questions of motivation (the child merely wanting to tease a little) and persistence (jokes are defined by the pay-off – if mother is not allowed to discover she has been tricked, amid astonishment and laughter, this was no joke). Sometimes, as in the first example below, the child's claim to be joking has the ring of a lame excuse for a lie found out. This is not really significant; what is significant is that he has learned that truth admits of a number of permissible deviations, *one* of which is the joke.[19]

Textile threader's wife:
> Well, he has done on one or two occasions, you know, and then I've found out different. I've believed him. "I got so many stars at school today for doing this", and "The teacher says that I'm the best reader in the class" – he goes rambling on, you know. And something's cropped up perhaps hours after, and – "I thought you said . . . . . !" – "Oh, I was only joking – I was playing!"

Unemployed labourer's wife:
> He still does it! He still does! He tells you ever so serious, it's ridiculous what he *does* say sometimes, and he stands there with his eyes wide, and I say "That's not true, don't tell me those fairy tales". "Honest, Mum!" – he says – "Honest, Mum!" I say "Now stop that romancing, I know it's not true", and he says "I tricked you, didn't I?"

University teacher's wife:
> She loves to have you on. Often she'll tell us something that's not farfetched enough to be *obviously* untrue, but dramatic enough to be a bit startling, and you look round at her with your mouth open, and she says "Not really!" and you know you've been caught again.

Cycle assembler's wife:
> Well, the other day he went to the shop just there for me, and he comes and he says "Flo [that's the shopkeeper], she'll owe me fivepence, she's got no change". Well, I was looking at him and I thought, No. Well – I carried on, I says "Well, I can soon make it right with my bread tomorrow" – "It isn't, Mum, it's in my pocket!" – you see. Well, it has happened before she's said she'll owe us a copper or two, you see. But I knew that he was romancing there, so . . . [Was he doing it as a joke, or did he want the fivepence?] A joke, just a joke – a bit of devilment.

In the process of pushing the child towards reality, the mother needs, of course, to have some idea herself of where the truth really lies, otherwise she cannot challenge him with conviction. Time and again in these accounts, it is clear that the child already has a good notion of true and false, in that he betrays himself by his own behaviour: 'She turns away and gives that little cough, or she laughs'; 'I can usually tell by her face'; 'He reddens'; 'You know when it's not true, 'cause she uses her hands a lot'. Because the mother is so much more experienced than the child in reading non-verbal signals, it must sometimes seem to him that she has an almost magical power in her knowledge of the truth. The last child's mother knew he was trying 'a bit of devilment' and let him play it out; talking of 'real' lies, however, she said: 'Well, I try and get it out of him, but I'm looking at him intently when he's telling me, and I sort of conquer, 'cause he has this look on his face – his Dad can't tell, but I can. I can tell when he's telling the truth or not. It's just an expression that he has on his face – and yet his Dad can't spot it'.

Chartered engineer's wife:

Well he did have a patch of that, and I've come to the conclusion that I've fooled him into thinking that I can tell by looking at his eyes whether it's true. He used to tell things from school – he told me once that his teacher was dead – things like that. He tells me as if it's true, he will say that it's true if you ask him, and then you say "Well, look into my eyes and I'll see if it's true".

Cold food packer's wife:

I don't have to find out with Nicky, I know! I do, it might sound silly, but I do. When he was in Mrs Keith's class before he went into this one, he used to come home from school, and I used to say "Why did the teacher shout at you?", and he used to say "How do you know?" . . . . . I said to him one day "Why did that lady tell you to come home?" so he said "How do you know that?", and I said "I know everything about you". So he says "Oh – do you?" – and he says – "Well, I was playing on the bank, and it's got nothing to do with her". Yes, it's a funny thing – I do – he's the only one, I know him through and through.

In the interests of getting at the truth, a number of mothers do in fact allow the child to believe that they have such powers: ironically, a few falsely claim to see external signs of falsehood. Obviously such stories can be effective at this age, not only in dissuading the child from lying by showing him that there is no future in it, but also, if he *has* lied, in eliciting real signs of guilt which *will* betray him.

Lorry driver's wife:
Oh well, I've got a thing for that. I always say to them, if they tell me any lies and they *know* they're telling lies, if I look at their tongue they've got big black spots on it. My friend did that with her child once, and it worked, so I've tried it and it has worked with them . . . . I say to them "Do you want me to look at your tongue?" – and if he goes [mouth tight] I *know* he's telling me a lie 'cause he won't let me look at his tongue!

Fitter's wife:
He's got a pet story about a little girl who told lies and – I made it up, actually – and, um, I often say "Now you know what happened to that little girl in the story who told lies" – her nose grew, you see, and he – er – I think it goes home; although he doesn't . . . I don't think he *really* believes his nose will grow, but I think he's not very sure, I don't think he'd like to try it out!

Here, however, we are moving beyond 'romancing', to the question of real lying. Both the above-quoted mothers are in fact very tolerant of 'play' fantasy; both enjoy listening to these children 'play-acting on their own', and the second one says: 'It's very difficult, because you've got to be careful, I always think, about *actual* lying and imagination; but – er – sometimes he does come home with some stories which I realise myself can't be true'. These fantasies, however, are not put to the lengthening-nose test.

Drawing together the threads of the argument, we can look at the seven-year-old's development of notions of truth and reality in terms of a time sequence. At the pre-school stage, the child is allowed and even encouraged to let fantasy spill over into everyday conversation. With young children this is charming and entertaining, and rarely causes problems: the mother spends so much time with the child that she can usually 'sort things out' with reference to her own knowledge. The four-year-old has little reason to tell 'real' lies, nor does he have the skill and sophistication to persist in them; real lies are condemned, however, where they do occur.[20]

Shortly there arises a period of crisis in the child's fantasy life, starting on entry to school, when fantasy *playmates* begin to be dropped, but confirmed around seven by the growth of self-awareness. Now the problem comes to a head, in that the child is very much in a transitional stage which confuses the issue. Sixty-four per cent engage in solitary fantasy play *involving speech*, which is seen by some mothers as a symptom that the child is not sufficiently in touch with reality; 65% are said to prefer role-playing games when playing with other children, which also involves considerations of the distinction between 'playing' and 'being'. At the same time, the child now inhabits a real world separate from that of his parents for about half his waking time, and has to bear some responsibility for indirect communications between home and school. Leading a more independent existence, he meets friends, neighbours and shop-keepers on his own, and his conversational reports of such en-counters therefore assume a new importance from the parents' point of view: if his imagination runs away with him on these occasions, the social implications are not necessarily trivial. For all these reasons, sympathetic parents will attempt to help their children com-municate effectively and accurately, and will try to explain the con-sequences of mixing fact and fantasy indiscriminately. Thus the problem is not simply to teach children the distinction between the rather slippery concepts of truth and falsehood; rather, it is a matter of bringing the child to an awareness of where he should draw the line and how he should present his communications to other people so that everyone knows just where they stand. Para-doxically, fantasy survives intact in those families where communica-tion problems can be solved without making too much of an issue over 'romancing'. Where mother and child can show tolerance and understanding of each other's difficulties in communication, trust can be re-established.

Teacher's wife (herself a research assistant):
He did say to me about last October or November, "Is there really a Father Christmas?" And so I said no, there wasn't, it was Bill and I and his relatives. And he then said "Well, tell me about the fairies that bring the sixpence when I have my teeth out", and I said "No, that's also pretend – that's me that puts that six-pence there". And I said "Now, those were the only things we've ever told you that weren't absolutely true". I said "There's nothing else we've ever told you that wasn't true, but we thought those were rather nice little games to pretend". I said "Do you *mind* that we've done them, or would you have thought it was better if we'd been quite as open about it as everything else?" – and he said "Oh no" – he thought they were quite good little games; and I said "Well, there's nothing else, only those two things; and now we've got everything straight".

As in the learning of other skills and concepts, playing with notions of truth and reality helps to confirm them in the child's understanding. The mother who is able to juggle with the child the different concepts of 'playing at', 'doing', 'telling lies', 'telling the truth', 'telling a story', 'little games', 'joking', 'tricking' and 'romancing' is giving him the subtlety to appreciate not only the spectrum of greys between the black and white of 'false' and 'true', but also those between 'right' and 'wrong'. In that sense, this stage may well be considered a watershed for the development of conscious moral ideas.

We are once again suggesting that seven years old is an age of swift-moving transition into social and moral and conceptual awareness on many fronts, backed by a deliberate parental impetus. At this stage, parents are consciously and explicitly trying to teach these understandings; earlier on, allowances could be made. Looking ahead in the child's development, there will come a point when the difference between fantasy and reality is so well established that there is no longer any need to draw attention to it. At ten, our daughter had a large family of ratlike or hedgehoglike animals made in felt or wool. 'Hush', she said one night, as one of us opened a cupboard in her room, 'be very quiet, they're hibernating'. And so they were – tucked away in dark corners, two inside the back of the piano. We were very quiet, shut the cupboard door and went out on tiptoe. We knew she knew she was playing. We could afford to play too.

NOTES

1 Not presented under these names to the mother unless considerable discussion proved necessary to elicit a preference order.

2 A count at a local toy wholesalers showed 114 different kinds of gun available there, not counting model kits, 'Action Man' accessories and small-scale battle sets.

3 Many a good drama has been constructed around the company's props. Louisa Alcott's Little Women based a regular theatrical programme on a slashed doublet, an old foil and a pair of russet leather boots; and, on a higher professional plane, Nicholas Nickleby's first commission as house playwright to the Vincent Crummles Company was to work out a tragedy around 'a real pump and two washing-tubs'. Louisa Alcott, *Little Women*, 1867; Charles Dickens, *Nicholas Nickleby*, 1839.

4 Derek Wright, 'A sociological portrait: sex differences', in *New Society*, vol. 18, no. 474, 1971.

5 E. Maccoby, 1967.

6 Erik Erikson, 'Sex differences in play construction of twelve-year-old children', in J. M. Tanner and B. Inhelder, *Discussions on Child Development*, vol. III, Tavistock, London, 1955.

7 J. and E. Newson, 1968, p. 170 (Pelican edn. p. 178).

8 E. B. Hurlock and W. Burstein, 'The imaginary playmate', *J. Genet. Psychol.*, *41*, 1932, pp. 380–92; M. Svendsen, 'Children's imaginary companions', *Arch. Neurol. and Psychiat.*, *32*, 1934. See J. and E. Newson, 1968, pp. 174–5 and 184–6 (Pelican edn. pp. 184 and 194–5).

9 Figures for these comparisons are based on a sub-sample consisting of all children seen at all three age-stages: one, four and seven years.

10 Taken together with those not known to play in this way at all, this means, of course, that rather more than half the *total* sample do in fact avoid this kind of adult observation.

11 Piaget discusses this in terms of the child's development out of ego-centricity; but Vygotsky suggests that the child now becomes capable of a *differentiation* between social communicative speech directed at other people and 'speech' directed inward for the sole benefit of the speaker. This inner-directed speech now becomes unvoiced and elliptical (just as reading for meaning progresses from the voiced and exact to the silent and discontinuous). L. S. Vygotsky, *Thought and Language*, Wiley, New York, 1962; J. Piaget, *The Language and Thought of the Child*, Routledge & Kegan Paul, London, 1948.

12 J. and E. Newson, 1968, p. 189 (Pelican edn., p. 199).

13 D. W. Winnicott, *Playing and Reality*, Tavistock, London, 1971, p. 40.

14 Peter McKellar, 'Thinking, remembering and imagining', in J. G. Howells (ed.), *Modern Perspectives in Child Psychiatry*, Oliver & Boyd, London, 1965.

15 G. H. Mead, in discussing the process by which the child develops his concepts of self and other, and eventually evolves the notion of the 'generalised other', makes an interesting suggestion: that the child's solitary imaginative play is directly contributive to this process. 'He plays that he is, for instance, offering himself something, and he buys it; he gives a letter to himself and takes it away; he addresses himself as a parent, as a teacher; he arrests himself as a policeman. He has a set of stimuli which call out in himself the sort of responses they call out in others. He takes this group of responses and organises them into a certain whole. Such is the simplest form of being another to one's self. It involves a temporal situation. The child says something in one character and responds in another character, and then his responding in another character is a stimulus to himself in the first character, and so the conversation goes on. A certain organised structure arises in him and in his other which replies to it, and these carry on the conversation of gestures between themselves.' G. H. Mead, *Mind, Self and Society*, University of Chicago Press, 1934.

16 J. and E. Newson, 1968, pp. 179 and 190 (Pelican edn. pp. 188 and 199).

17 *Ibid.* pp. 100–1 (Pelican edn. pp. 103–4).

18 *Ibid.* pp. 174 and 182 (Pelican edn. pp. 183 and 191).

19 It would be interesting to follow the aetiology of joking through the child's earliest years. We ourselves looked briefly at teasing at four (1968, pp. 451–2; Pelican edn. pp. 480–1), but we were concerned there with severe teasing, not very kindly meant, and provoking tantrums which would not facilitate subtle learning. Most children, however, go through experiences of very mild teasing ("I've lost your sweetie—oh,

there it is in your pocket!") which may be extremely functional in preparing them for the notion of verbal jokes. Much has been made of the peek-a-boo type of game and its use in helping the child towards the concept of object permanence; these games, and their development into 'tricking' games (such as hiding behind the settee when Daddy comes in – "Where's Jane?" – "I don't know *where* she is" – "Boo!" – "Oh, you tricked me!") may have equal importance in giving the child a flexible understanding of degrees of reality.

20   J. and E. Newson, 1968, pp. 446–7 (Pelican edn. pp. 474–5).

Chapter 6

Friendships and Quarrels

Let me play I beg you.
Go away we don't want you.
Oh please let me play
it's lonely with no friends
And I don't feel wanted.
They play nice games but I
can't play oh please.
No don't keep asking we shan't let you play
I can't play by myself.
Yes, you can you're only making things up so go and play.

When I go home I hear them saying
What shall we do tonight?
We can play cowboy and we can have my tent
Oh what can we have to sit on
we can have my mummy's old rug
So when I go home I read a book.
Susan Desborough, aged 7[1]

In Chapter 2, where we tried to draw up a brief overall appraisal of the seven-year-old condition, we made the point that 'while the child has for most of his life been capable of friendliness, he is now becoming much more conscious of the *process* of friendship'. Partly this is because his emergence from the egocentric stage allows him to stop taking his social world for granted as a small circle of relationships all appended to himself as centre, and to begin to be aware of himself from a different point of view, as an appendage to the social circles of others – with the possibilities this implies of rejection or acceptance. In addition, as we have seen, his greater geographical orbit immediately offers a wider range of potential friendships; and the other side of that coin is also a more recurrent risk of being rebuffed both by individuals and by the group.

Movement between home and school makes the peer group bigger, and thus choosing or being chosen becomes more of an issue; but, beyond this, the children's growing ability to use language to describe relationships both increases the complexity of relationship patterns and helps to formalise them in the individual child's awareness. At four, the child made do with the nearest available playmate, and often 'his friend' would be the *only* child of similar age within 'running round' distance; it would be largely a matter of luck if their temperaments turned out to have the compatibility which could produce a lasting friendship once more choice was offered. Thus mothers of four-year-olds tended to talk about 'his friend' rather than 'his best friend'. At seven, however, the 'best' or 'special' friend has real significance in terms of a mutual choice between children *who have other choices available*; and, because both parents and children find it appropriate to use such a verbal label in ordinary conversation, the status of 'best friend' (or the stigma of being no one's best friend) can now become a central feature of the child's image of himself.[2]

The use of the term 'best friend' by a given child at any given time does not, of course, necessarily imply more than the present intention of lifelong friendship. There still seems to be a moderate component of the accidental in friendships at this age; for instance, children living at one end of a school's catchment area are unlikely to be allowed to go on their own to visit children living at the other end, so that friendships formed at school may well not be kept up out of school hours. The child whose best friend attends the same school but lives too far away for casual visiting tends to be at a loose end on Saturdays and Sundays and during the holidays; for example, Leonard's mother takes him out with her a good deal because 'he's going through a lonely stage, and he's got nobody to play with, only girls'. Conversely, those whose best friends live in the neighbourhood but go to a different school will have fewer common interests to cement the relationship, since school plays such a dominant part in everyday life at this age. Thus some of those friendships will be the products of use, habit and expedience, rather than the marriage of true minds: Stephanie, wandering into the room at this point in the interview, commented 'She's my special friend, and I hate her usually!'

The mother's evaluation of another child as being 'special friend' to her own is likely at least to take into account some evidence of duration and stability up to the time of speaking; and 76% of them can name their child's special friend. Children who are said to have a best friend do not differ from others by sex or class. Rather more than half of these children see their best friend both at home and at school; it is perhaps surprising that as many as 40% of 'best friends' are so named despite the difficulties of their being available in only one of these settings. This is in fact an indication of how much best friends are an expected part of life at this age. That it is possible for the relationship to be very close indeed is indicated in a few cases where it has been broken by one of the families moving from the neighbourhood: 'I don't think Veronica will ever replace Jill until she's a bit older and has forgotten her', said Veronica's mother. This also underlines how dependent a seven-year-old's friendship is upon circumstantial support. It would be prohibitively difficult for most of these children to keep up a long-distance friendship by letter-writing, and adequate visiting needs more adult cooperation than is usually available. Moving house is one of those decisions which adults tend to take without much reference to children's wishes, and here children's helplessness is likely to continue, however 'democratically' disposed parents and society may become towards them.

Telephone engineer's wife:
Well, one little boy left – he was very good friends with him and his little sister, and then they left and went to Mapperley, and that seemed to upset him, and he closed in and didn't go out much at all – until *we* moved, he didn't seem to want to go out to play, and I told my husband, I think he was missing that little boy. He's not a child that makes a lot of new friends easily, but once they are, you know, he keeps them a long time.

Sales representative's wife:
Tania is that type of girl that she'd make a friend and it would be a lifelong friend if possible – she's not the sort for having a pal for a month and then dropping her off and having another pal next month. No, 'cause when we left Nottingham she did miss a little girl – ooh, every hour of the day they'd played with one another, you know, that was free for playing in – and she *did* miss her at first. And I think *that*, p'raps, was why she was a little slow at making friends at school, I mean, I did go by at playtime, just

to see whether she was playing, and she seemed to be standing on the side a little bit, watching. But I didn't push her. I didn't want to worry her into thinking, you know, that she'd *got* to make a friend. I know what she is – if she takes to someone, she can be friendly with them and she'll be a *real* friend to them, you know what I mean; she'll be a close friend and stick by them, no matter what they do to her; she'll stick to them. But she's not one that'll have a dozen friends and keep swapping and changing them. One definite friend, I think, or two at the most, would be close friends for Tania.

The 24% of children who do not have a known best friend are not by any means friendless; almost all of them simply have a number of friends of whom no single one stands out as especially close. Although 18% of children experience minor or major difficulties in making friendships with others, a point which we shall take up shortly, only 2% *never* play with other children in the neighbourhood.[3] Some of the 24% without a best friend have many good play contacts, and a few are exceptionally friendly children: 'He seems to make friends *very* easily', says Stanley's mother – 'mostly when he sees a child walking up the street he says "Hey-up! Hey-up, kid!"'

Engineer's wife:
Well, he plays very well with strange children, but particular friends he doesn't seem to make – anyone special. He'll play with any child quite happily, but no one in particular.

Insurance inspector's wife:
He has about three boys he's very pally with, but they vary from day to day as to which is the special one; and he also has a special girl who he's particularly friendly with, but he goes off her as well from day to day. I should think he's got about half-a-dozen close-knit friends, and he calls them the gang.

Student teacher's wife (herself a teacher):
Well, as an adult to an adult I would say it was an acquaintance-ship rather than a friend, if you know what I mean. Um – I don't think she's got – I don't know whether she'll ever have – this strong friendship with other children; time alone will tell. She needs their company, but I won't say that she actually needs their friendship. [Father:] Yes, but she will play rather quickly with anyone. [Mother:] Yes, she will. If we were at the seaside, she

would play with the children on the next bit of beach quite happily. [Father:] She wandered right down the beach at Shering-ham, playing with people.

Accountant's wife:

He's still got these two imaginary friends, and sometimes I do believe he'd rather play with those imaginary friends, you know; I have to say to him "Would you like to have Timothy in tonight?" It's very rare that he asks to have children in – it's usually me that says to *him*, you know – and yet I think he *must* get on quite well with children at school, because I've never known a child go to so many parties in my life: it costs me a fortune![4]

It is already clear from the quotations we have given that the child's own individual personality, in addition to the geographical and other social circumstances in which he finds himself, will contribute rather heavily towards the pattern of his friendships: further, it seemed to us that the mother herself was still capable of exerting some degree of control over the friendships maintained by the child at this age. Accordingly, the questions we asked around this topic were intended to shed light on all these aspects. Although the main questions on friendships and associations were asked as a block (Questions 32–45), the interview had already discussed play and spare-time activities, so that casual mention of other children had often been made quite frequently by this point; following these questions, there were also a number of other opportunities for renewed discussion of peer group relationships (questions on group play, fantasy play, independence and school activities, for example). The main block of questions is given below for convenience; their context can be seen in the full questionnaire, Appendix I.

32. You've mentioned other children a few times
    You haven't mentioned other children very much } : which
    does N like best – playing with other children, or playing by himself?
33. Who does he play with mostly?
34. Has he any special friends? – at school?
                     – at home?
35. Does he see his friends in the weekend? (*If NO*): Any particular reason?
36. Do they come and play at your house?
37. Does he go to theirs?

38. Are you happy about ⌠ his friendships?
    　　　　　　　　　⌡ this friendship?
    (*prompt for each mentioned*)
39. Have you ever tried to discourage any friendship between N and another child?
    (*If YES*): Any special reason?
    (*If NO*): Do you think you would ever do this for any reason?
40. In general, how would you say N gets on with other children? Does he make friends easily?
41. Does he stand up for himself, or does he let other children boss him around?
42. How do you feel about quarrelling at this age? Do you think quarrelling *has* to happen between children? (*prompt if necessary: between sibs; others*)
43. Does he do a lot of fighting – do his quarrels often come to blows? (*prompt: sibs; others*)
44. Do you (would you) ever interfere in N's quarrels and arguments with other children outside the family?
45. Do you ever tell him what he should do in his quarrels, or help him to manage them in any way?

Table 19　*Children who prefer to play with others rather than on their own*

| | social class | | | | | summary | | |
	I&II	IIIwc	III man	IV	V	I&II, IIIwc	IIIman, IV,V	overall popn.
	%	%	%	%	%	%	%	%
boys	71	78	84	80	84	74	83	80
girls	78	67	74	70	79	73	74	74
both	75	72	79	75	82	74	78	77

No significant class/sex differences

Table 19 shows the children's preferences for playing alone or with others. The percentages given represent children who definitely prefer playing with other children to playing on their own: 77% overall. Class and sex differences are not significant. The children who do not prefer playing with others are made up of 13% who are equally happy either way and 10% who have a definite preference for solitary play. It occurred to us that this last group might

Table 20   *Children said to make friends easily*

| | social class | | | | | summary | | |
	I&II	IIIwc	III man	IV	V	I&II, IIIwc	IIIman, IV,V	overall popn.
	%	%	%	%	%	%	%	%
boys	86	83	80	84	95	84	82	83
girls	80	73	83	73	87	77	81	80
both	83	78	81	79	91	81	82	82

(————81%————)   91%
Difference between Class V and the rest   *

consist of children from small families, or perhaps with no siblings in the age-range 2–11 years: there is no evidence for such an association, however.

The great majority of children at this age (82% overall) seem to make friends easily: that is, on a casual level they make easy social contacts with their peers, leaving aside the question of whether these are maintained and built up into close friendships. Table 20 shows this distribution: the marginal advantage of boys over girls is not significant, and the only indication of a class difference is that more Class v children (boys especially) are said to make friends easily. It seemed possible that this result might be due to Class v children coming from larger families, but on checking this theory no evidence could be found to support it. The most likely explanation in this case is that the figures reflect the high valuation which Class v mothers set upon their children being able to go out and find their own level in the neighbourhood group on the street.

The children who make friends less easily divide into 11% who find it 'not very easy' and 7% who seem to have real difficulty. Beyond the basic fact that their peer relationships are not smooth-running, these children do not seem to have a great deal in common as individuals; possibly one could usefully divide them (across the two groups) into those who have difficulty in the process of communication (knowing how to act and behave) which impedes their social advances; those who are too shy; and those who are too bossy and self-willed to be tolerated. The first group are highly idiosyncratic:

Signalman's wife:
Not very easily – he prefers to be on his own . . . he's got a lazy

eye, and he's inclined to be a bit deaf, and this makes a difference –
he shouts at people all the time, so . . .

Window cleaner's wife:
> She tries to fight them to get to know them. I know it's funny,
> but she shows off to get to know them, and then of course she's
> in bad books straight away, and that ends the friendship, you
> know.

Shy children are not without friends, but tend to have just one or
two well-tried friendships; not for them the easy 'Hey-up, kid!' of
the out-going Stanley.

Driving instructor's wife:
> No, he doesn't [make friends easily], no. He's all right – I think
> really Pat [sister] has had a lot to do with that; I don't think
> he'd have made as many friends if it wasn't for the fact of Pat
> pushing him forward, because you see he was *very* shy, he didn't
> want to mix, you see. But, um, he's all right now, as I say – just
> with his own particular friends, like – I mean he's not so good
> at making *new* friends.

Hosiery worker's wife:
> She does when she's got to know them, sort of thing, but she's
> rather jealous of her friend's friend playing in the backyard –
> she'll play with *her*, but if she's got another friend there she won't
> go out. She'll say "When are they going home, because I want
> to go out and play". It's shyness or jealousy or a bit of both, I
> think.

The over-bossy children who have difficulty in making friends do
not fail to make the first approaches, but seem unable to contain
their bossiness within the necessary limits of tact and discretion to
make it acceptable: they cannot be termed leaders, since they can
find no one prepared to be led (unlike the children described on
page 191).

Traffic warden's wife:
> [. . . Does she make friends easily?] Well, yes. I should say she
> does, like. [You don't sound very sure?] Not *very* easily, because
> I think she likes her own way too much.

Foreman's wife:
> That is a bit of a problem, as regards children, you see. Well, she

doesn't get on well with children. I don't know if it's 'cause she's the only one, but she *doesn't* get on with other children. I don't know if she's slightly bossy or what, but she's not a good mixer. She's soon in trouble with children. She's got one special one and they play together, but she goes out to join a group and she's either not talking their way or she doesn't mix with them or there's trouble. We don't know how to cure her . . . If you have any children in the yard, she'll tell them what we're going to play at and who's going to do what, all the time. Well, they don't want to do it that way, but you can hear Paulette's voice above the rest *telling* them how to do it that way.

Building worker's wife:
No, not very easy. We've had some new children moved in across the road, you know, and they came and called for June a couple of times, but they've stopped coming; I think she was too . . . inclined to be a bit bossy, and they sort of packed her in, you know.

*'If Carolyn's got threepence in her pocket, she'll give him half, always; yet if she sees the chance of giving him a nip, she'll **give** him a nip. Funny, isn't it?'*
Children who cannot find anyone to play with outside the family circle can usually fall back on a brother or sister. Eighty-nine per cent of the children in our sample have a sibling aged between two and eleven years, the age-range which we took (from parents' own accounts) to have reasonable playmate potential for the seven-year-old. In Class v there is a significant rise to 98% of children having a sibling within this range. With this exception, class differences in playing with brothers and sisters were non-existent. Discounting the children who have no sibs in the range given, only 4% of the total sample were reported as *never* playing with their siblings. Fifty per cent play with their sibs often, and 35% sometimes.

We were not deliberately trying to map a detailed pattern of sib relationships at seven, so that the impressions we received were by the way and collected mainly in the course of looking at the child's play and spare-time activities. The problem, as always in considering sibship patterns, is that from child to child the family position changes so markedly if all factors of age, sex and birth order are taken into account. In other words, it is perfectly possible to show from statistical analysis of forensic or educational data that such crude categories as first-born, intermediate or last-born are meaningful in terms of associated behaviour or achievement[5] but a study which aims at drawing nearer to the actual family experience of the child is inevitably frustrated by the knowledge of how different are the experiences of being eldest girl with two younger brothers, boy with three mixed siblings on each side, youngest of four girls, elder brother of one sister, and only girl preceded by three miscarriages. Thus we have not at this stage attempted to make more than the simplest of references to sibship patterns.

If 50% of our children are playing with their sibs 'often', and a further 35% doing so 'sometimes', it is already clear that the provision of an available playmate is a major function of sibship. In particular, however, sibs other than twins offer the different angle on friendship and play afforded by a different age-stage. On the whole, children tend to choose neighbourhood friends of similar age to themselves; and, unless their school is vertically streamed, they are likely to play at school almost exclusively with children from their own year. A very positive aspect of sibling play (with, obviously, its negative side as well) is the opportunity to play protectively or dominatingly on the one hand, or as satellite or follower on the other. Either can be a relief, or at least a change of scene.

University teacher's wife:
He plays with Alice [aged two]. He *sometimes* does things with Daniel [aged ten], but the relationship between Alice and himself is of a different type . . . um . . . he's very good and nice with her, but he's a little bit bossy and teasing, whereas if he plays with Daniel *he's* the one who's bossed. He and Daniel play on Sunday morning and Saturday morning, but they . . . Daniel is very critical of Charles's efforts, and so he tends not to have too much of it.

Car sprayer's wife:
He hasn't got a lot of patience, but it's better now since we had the baby 'cause he's patient with *him* – whereas when he was the youngest one he used to get all his own way.

Lorry driver's wife:
She's always with Margaret [aged ten], they're inseparable. There always seems to be a crowd of them, but mostly Margaret's age-group, not her age-group. She doesn't seem to stay very long with her own. She's inclined to cling a bit to Margaret – gets Margaret to fight her battles. With Margaret being the bigger, and always being together, she's always hid behind Margaret. If I shout at

her occasionally, she'll go to Margaret to be loved better; and Margaret says "Well, you shouldn't be naughty", and she'll love her better.

Foreman's wife:

Yvonne [aged five] is allowed to join in her games, but only as a five-year-old, you know; I mean, if nobody else can come, then she wants to play with Yvonne, but Yvonne can't play in the same range. She can only do what Patsy wants her to – so in actual fact she's not so much being *played with* as being *used*.

Of course, if a child is consistently snubbed or bullied by his only sib, this is unlikely to be without effect. A rejecting 'friend' may be avoided; a rejecting or dominating brother or sister cannot be dispensed with so easily.

Electrician's wife:

Jimmy [aged ten] will only play with him if he's got nobody else – that's the top and bottom of it. He likes Jimmy and he likes to play with him, but it's the other way round that's the trouble, I'm afraid.

Fitter's wife:

I don't think she's terribly good at standing up for herself really. [When she's with Charmian (sister aged nine), does Charmian always organise all the games?] Yes, because Charmian is always the dominant one. She's the dominant nature of the two, I'm afraid. [Does Judith mind?] She is minding at the moment. I think she's getting now that she wants *her* way. At one time with their play, Charmian was teacher or Charmian was always mother, or . . . At the moment they are arguing more than they've ever argued, you know, I've never known them argue so much. I think maybe Judith is retaliating a bit.

Departmental manager's wife:

He's got his brother who's four years older. They do play a lot together; but four years is too much, really, to expect . . . it's very frustrating for the younger one, I find. They want to keep up all the time. The older one doesn't want him all the time. [I think you said that when Peter was four.] Oh dear, did I, I must have been saying this since he was *born*! – but he's so anxious to do things that the older one does. He's not content to sit back and say "Oh well, I can't". He always has to *try* – which of course is a good thing, but of course he can't *do* it.

A more intractable problem arises when the competition or domination comes from a younger sib. To an extent, children expect their elders to be cleverer, stronger and more socially sophisticated, so that, even if the difference is very great, it can be tolerated so long as it is in the expected direction; the tradition of elder sib superiority is so taken for granted, however, that competition from below will be proportionally the more threatening. Once again, both mother and child are conscious that this is a permanent problem which will have to be lived with rather than evaded.

Student's wife:

He's not afraid of anything physical – his fears are attached to not being able to understand. He's said once or twice something that rather horrified me: "I don't understand, there must be something the matter with me". This is the business of his relationship with Katherine [aged five-and-a-half]. It's just simply that James is not so intelligent as Katherine, and he's cottoning on to this fact very quickly, and I don't know what to do about it. [Has he been conscious of it for some time?] I think so – since Katherine started going to school and came home with reports of what she'd done, what book they were reading. His initial response was "You couldn't have done"; and she said "We did", and proceeded to show him. He was absolutely devastated.

For this boy, a sympathetic mother who is prepared to give her unlimited and subtle attention to his problem – literally to talk him through it at moments of despair – is a necessity: for the source of this child's anxiety is his apprehension of a real discrepancy between his younger sister and himself.[6] Where the bone of contention is the mother herself, the situation is rather different. The dilution of the mother's attention which is necessarily a part of being brought up in a large family is likely to alleviate a little the bitterness which this kind of competition arouses in a two-child family; but one should not make too much of this, for from the child's point of view the large family organises itself into sub-groups and patterns in which some sibs will seem very close and have higher potentiality for friendship or enmity, while others will be more distant, aunt- or uncle-like figures. Thus for any one child there is likely to be one sib who is his most constant playmate, and one (often the same one) upon whom his rivalry and aggression are focussed. The presence of other sibs may make this particular relationship less claustrophobic than it might otherwise have been; but large family groups are not always the answer to social claustrophobia, as the commune advocates sometimes suggest, and certainly some children find the pressure of many brothers and sisters difficult to tolerate.

Building worker's wife:
   I'm afraid I haven't got an awful lot of time to treat them individually – you know? It's one of the disadvantages of having a big family [seven], you *can't* treat them as individuals, you've got to – sort of – everything you do is done *together* . . . . . I honestly do believe sincerely that June would be a lot better if there was perhaps just her and another one or two. I think the large family does overwhelm her, definitely. Well, that's been proved, because when she's with my sister – they've just got one little girl – or when she's at my mother's on her own, or out with us on her own, she's a different personality altogether . . . . . You do get this problem with a big family, you *can't* give them each individual attention, that is impossible; but as I say, the others, they *accept* this. It hasn't arisen with Tom or Heather or Derek – it's just June – yet she's a lovely kiddie; as I say, if we've got her on her own she's marvellous . . . . . To me she's the odd one out, she's different from the others entirely. [She's *got* to live in a big family . . .] Yes, she's *got* to accept us, so what can you do?

The question of jealousy generally is one that must arise in discussing relationships between sibs; however, we have, to our own embarrassment, no useful data on this for the present age-stage. When the children were four, we attempted to explore this topic with their mothers, and found a defensiveness about it – an unwillingness to admit jealousy in the child – which we did not then fully understand. Partly there seemed to be an idea that children who were being adequately mothered ought not to be feeling jealous, so that often the query on whether the child in fact showed jealousy was met by the mother's assurances of her own fairness, implying that the child had no justification for jealousy. Clearly our questions at four were inadequate in their function of stimulating the mother to speak freely on this particular topic; and (given the assumption that jealousy is indeed common between siblings) we should obviously have taken pains to improve our questions at seven. Instead, we rather disconsolately abandoned the attempt.[7]
   We cannot therefore make quantified statements on the extent or circumstances of jealousy. From the incidental evidence of the general discussion of sib relationships, however, we would see

jealousy as an almost functional part of the ordinary growing-up process of learning to cope with a social world. Anna Freud suggests this in her statement that 'the child's first approach to the idea of justice is made during these developments of the brother-sister relationship, when the claim to be favoured oneself is changed to the demand that no-one should be favoured, i.e. that there should be equal rights for everybody'.[8] The child's jealousy is an expression of his suspicion that someone other than himself *may* be being favoured; and since each child in the family views the web of family relationships from its own egocentric vantage point, each child will have a highly subjective notion of who the favoured person may be. Perhaps, indeed, the best a 'fair' mother can hope for is not a total absence of jealousy, but a distribution of it, so that every child is considered by one of its siblings to be favoured. One thing is clear, however: that care taken by the mother to avoid jealousy does not necessarily have its effect, for there are some children who are endlessly defensive of their rights. Both the following mothers have spent a disproportionate amount of time over the years accommodating to these particular (eldest) children, both of whom are 'negativistic' in terms of the description given on pages 40–2).

Lorry driver's wife:
    . . . She'll kick her shoes off in the middle of the floor, and you could fall over them and break your neck but she wouldn't pick them up. You see – whether she thinks that I carry these about, with them being little [twin babies and a toddler], and she wants me to do it for *her* as well – but I mean she's getting seven now, she ought to be getting a *bit* off hand. It *is* difficult. I mean, I say "Well, these are babies, Sharon"; and she'll just say "You're *always* nursing them, you never nurse me, just because I'm seven", she says, "nobody cares about me". You see she just can't see.

Machine operator's wife:
    She's *always* been jealous – right from the start – it's always been there. Now when I was in bed with the baby – my friends used to come, and they said "Now when you're up", they said, "you must get her to help you with the baby, ask her to pass you things, then she won't feel left out". So, first time I bathed him, I said to her "Just pass me that nappy, Carolyn, will you please?" She said "Right", and she picked it up and *threw* it at me and swiped him right across the face! Well, it's been like that right the way along. And yet she's very *fond* of him; they play together all the

time. And if Carolyn's got threepence in her pocket, she'll give him half, *always*; yet if she sees the chance of giving him a nip, she'll *give* him a nip. Funny, isn't it?

'I don't think she wants to lead, but she doesn't like being trampled on . . .'

In any children's social group, whether composed of siblings and thus subject to age-status factors, or made up entirely of age-mates, a power pattern will eventually be discernible based on the willingness or unwillingness with which one child will accede to another child's wishes. Very seldom will a so-called 'peer' group function in perfect equality; by seven the children already display traits of assertiveness or docility which establish their roles (although the pattern may shuffle and re-form over time), even in an outwardly democratic group. That is to say, the greater exercise of power by one or two members of the group does not necessarily produce disharmony, since children, like adults, themselves vary in the extent to which they *wish* to lead.

Mothers were asked 'Does he stand up for himself or does he let other children boss him around?' and their answers were divided into four categories which can be briefly designated as 'he's boss'; 'wants to lead but fails'; 'give and take'; and 'prefers to follow'. These categories can best be explained by illustration.

1. 'HE'S BOSS' – *this child succeeds in leading other children in the group; his ideas are followed, and in general he has things his own way.*   29%

Teacher's wife:
  No, he's the boss! I sometimes wish – I mean, one or two of them *will* stand up for themselves, but not very much; what Mark says, goes – even to the extent of him saying "say thank you", "say please"!

Printer's wife:
  No, she definitely stands up for herself, Maralynda does. She'd get a lot of children in the garden, she'd have to be the school-teacher, and I've stood there and I've really laughed at her, the way she's made these girls . . . and they've done exactly as Maralynda's told them to do, sort of thing, you know, and they really enjoy it – till some of them get a bit fed up!

See also Guy on page 38.

2. 'WANTS TO LEAD BUT FAILS' – *the child is unable to express his dominating wishes in such a way as to be acceptable to other children. Sometimes, in order to get his own way, he will deliberately choose to play mainly with younger children.*   8%

Machine operator's wife:
She's not really got any friends around here, not to say *friends*. She doesn't seem interested – she did have a few friends, but she gets fed up if they won't do as she says, and they *won't* do as she says, so she just doesn't bother with them. She's a really bossy child, you know, but they've got her beat around here!

Businessman's wife:
He doesn't really make as many friends as he should, really, but as I say, he *is* self-contained. I suppose he does let other children boss him around. [Does he seem happy about that, or do you think he'd rather be bossing them?] Oh yes – he would like to lead, but he can't.

Cook's wife:
She's inclined to be bossy. [She stands up for herself?] Yes, oh yes! [If she's in a group of children, would you say she's usually the leader?] She tries to be, yes; if they'll let her, all the time. I find that she does . . . well, in the summer . . . tend to fetch all the little children in, the tiny ones; ooh, she used to have four or five of them in the back, teaching them, playing with them. You see, she wants someone she can boss around, and tell what to do, and the little ones she knows will let her.

(See also pages 184–5).

3. 'GIVE AND TAKE' – *the child reaches a compromise with other children, in that nobody noticeably dominates the group; or perhaps there is an alternation of domination.*   46%

Widow in her own business:
Oh, he stands up fairly well for himself. If the boy's *bigger*, I think he finds some way of backing down. [What about when he's in a group of his own age?] Yes, I think so; but if the group turns nasty he'd rather get out than argue too hard. He's fairly – oh, what's the word? not placid, but he'd sooner calm a crowd than fight it, sort of thing. But if it's a friendly crowd, he loves to be leader, then he's bossy and overbearing; but if they're rather

an unfriendly group of children it does hurt his feelings, I should say he's a bit mardy[9] when it comes to that.

Class IV wife:
I think he's easy-go-lucky – if he finds hisself in charge, he'll take the responsibility; if he doesn't, he'll not worry.

Presser's wife:
She stands up for herself; it's fifty-fifty. She gets a good hiding one day, but gives it back the next.

4. 'PREFERS TO FOLLOW' – *the child seems to have no wish to make the decisions, and prefers a more passive role. Sometimes he will play mainly with older children in order to be able to adopt this role.* 17%

Engineer's wife:
Well, I think he lets them boss him around; because he's one of them that likes things easy, you know, he'll just join in whatever they want to do. He'll do it, he don't like trouble if he can avoid it. He likes to follow.

Fireman's wife:
She plays an awful lot with a girl across the way, and she's twelve or thirteen. Whether she likes – er – older company, you know; whether she finds that a child of her own age is not sufficiently intelligent enough to tell her what to do; whether she's the type of child that *likes* being told what to do – she likes being told what to do, and she's quite willing to do it.

Gypsum worker's wife:
She makes friends easily, but I think she gets on better with the older child than she does a child more her age; Bernice gets on better if she can look up to somebody.

The percentages given are overall figures for the whole group, and in fact there are no significant differences either between sexes or between social classes. It must of course be remembered that we are asking questions here about the individual child's usual inter-personal behaviour within his own peer group: which is to say that this is likely to be behaviour in a group both of his own sex and of his own or similar class. For this reason alone, we should not expect to find any considerable sex or class differences. The only indication of any difference at all is that girls of this age are consistently, but

G

not quite significantly, more often said to be bossy than boys, and this sex difference does in fact reach statistical significance in the skilled manual group. So small a difference could be fully accounted for by the fact that where observers perceive a characteristic (such as dominance, aggressiveness or 'bossiness') as being rather masculine, they are more likely to report its manifestation where girls are concerned simply because it appears more striking to them in the feminine context.[10] Although the danger of this kind of distortion is fairly small where the child is being rated against its mainly like-sexed peers, enough of it might remain to produce the results obtained here, and we therefore would not regard them as meriting any attention.

To sustain an enduring relationship with other children obviously calls for a certain amount of give and take, or at least an understanding of how to dominate in a diplomatic manner; and children of this age do not necessarily possess enough social perception to keep their friendships running smoothly all the time. It is difficult for a seven-year-old to make allowances for other children's needs and foibles, for his own egocentricity is a too highly motivating force to be easily disguised under a social veneer. We have already seen how, for 8% of children, an assertiveness untempered by tact or discretion produces a pattern of very unsatisfactory relationships with their peers; this is a small minority of children, but for the great majority intermittent quarrelling will form a part of the ordinary composition of friendship. At this age, feelings still tend to be expressed rather than inhibited; so that, when the mood veers from co-operation and affection to spite and resentment, the object of these feelings learns about them rather quickly. Boys in particular boil up to a physical fight; girls in particular resort to the dramatic announcement of formal hostility: 'I won't be friends with you no more'; 'I'm not asking you to my party'; or 'We'll just play together on our own, then, won't we, Sandra?' It is a moot point whether the well-documented verbal superiority of girls over boys is the reason for or the result of a richer female experience of peer group invective.

Be that as it may, for both sexes the concept of loyalty is as yet comparatively poorly developed, and allegiances tend to be fickle and subject to the emotion of the moment – which equally means that the blazing anger of lunch-time can subside into loving kindness in the afternoon. Tom will see nothing incongruous in ganging up with an older child, Dick, against his own best friend, Harry, all the way home from school, and then wanting to come round and play in Harry's garden again after tea. Characteristically, it is then Harry's parents, rather than Harry himself, who will take a dim view of the situation.

Quarrelling turned out in fact to be one of those topics which almost every mother recognised as relevant to her own child: 'they've got to fall out sometimes, I mean they wouldn't be children if they didn't'. Obviously some mothers have objectively more quarrelling to cope with than others, especially where sibs are at loggerheads: Mrs Lievesley, when asked whether Vicky played with her brother much, exploded: 'Play? You're joking, are you? They're fighting all the time. They are, honestly – that's what gets me down'; whereas Mrs Lockett's older children were too old to quarrel with Mark, and Mark himself inclined to withdraw from outside quarrels. Given that the majority of mothers experience quarrelling, however, do they feel that there is any possibility of avoiding quarrels? We asked them: 'How do you feel about quarrelling at this age? Do you think quarrelling *has* to happen between children?'

Ninety per cent thought that quarrelling was quite inevitable, and 6% that it was difficult, but possible, to avoid. Only a tiny handful (4%) thought that quarrelling was quite unnecessary. There were no significant differences either by class or by the child's sex. Nor was there any difference when mothers were asked to distinguish between quarrelling with sibs and quarrelling with other children outside the family. In general, quarrels were seen as an unpleasant but 'natural' fact of life that therefore simply had to be lived with.

Crane driver's wife:
  Well, I think *every* child fights – mine do all the time, and I imagine each child out on the street fights as well, so there's nothing you can do about it. I don't go out to stand up for him; if he tells me he's got hit or anything, I say 'Well, go back then, and fight your own battles'; I don't go out and fight them for him.

Car repairer's wife:
  Yes it does [have to happen] – it's an outlet. Yes, it is, it's an outlet. Because I mean they're at school, and they can't really let off steam there at school like they want to – well, something's got to go pop.

Lorry driver's wife:
  Oh, I don't know – I worry about it, naturally, because I haven't got anything else to do, and I don't *like* disagreeable children; but I think it *is* normal, you know, they have to find their own

friends for theirselves. They come in and moan and groan, and next time you see them they're together again. It's not always other people's fault, you know. I mean, she's not my blue-eyes-Mary, she isn't, you know!

Electrician's wife:

Well, I think . . . well, that again is the same as when you're married; if people say "We don't argue, we don't fall out" – I don't think you can be complete unless you have your ups and downs, you've got to have your arguments; and I think the children have got to have, although mine argue a bit too much sometimes, but I do think they've got to have their ups and downs, they *must* have them.

This last more positive view was elaborated by a number of parents. 'Well, that's children all over, isn't it?' said a miner's wife – 'I like children like that myself, I don't like children what's been brought up too spick and span, you know what I mean?' A baker said that he thought quarrelling was 'an essential part of growing up, other people's views'; and a foreman's wife pointed out: 'If there's no arguments, there's no opinions, is there?'

Miner's wife:

Oh yes – I think it makes a firmer friendship, actually, because all children quarrel and fall out, right from the age of . . . small age . . . they do, and I think that it's a good thing – er – it's a *healthy* thing – if they *don't* quarrel, they get morose and they – er – suffer *inwardly*, they seem as if they do, they get quiet and can't be bothered with anything, and I think that's when the trouble really starts; if they don't fight and get it all out of their system when they're young, I think they'll do it when they're older when they can do some damage. [Do you think this is true for brothers and sisters as well as friends?] Oh yes – my two sons, there's only eighteen months between them, and no one fights more than they do; but let them go outside and anyone say anything to them! . . . and they never go anywhere without each other, although they fight in the house.

Student of psychology:

It *does* happen. I find it makes me cross, tired and frustrated and I'd love to bang their heads together, but this sort of reaction doesn't help. Um . . . it certainly does happen a lot in our house, but . . . I just hope that when they're bigger they'll see things more objectively and think round things more, but they won't always do this. [Can you see any way of preventing it?] As a potential psychologist, I suppose I should produce some sort of answer! I think probably it's all part of growing up, that you have to fight with people before you can really learn a satis-factory way of getting on with them. I think this is the case. If one never fought with anybody, one really wouldn't have learned the technique of getting on with people.

On the whole, positive evaluation of quarrelling was specific to verbal 'fighting' rather than including the physical variety. We thought it useful to know how much actual physical fighting went on at this age. Although we had no figures for incidence of fighting at four with which to compare, the situations at four and at seven are not closely comparable in any case: four-year-olds, as one might expect from their more limited verbal ability, do do a lot of hitting, pushing, hair-pulling and even biting (the last strongly discouraged), but they are also weaker, more closely chaperoned, and more likely than seven-year-olds to be facing larger children than themselves once they leave their mother's side, which will make them wary. Seven-year-olds, on the other hand, can find plenty of children of their own size or smaller; and their strength, as we noted in Chapter 2, is immediately reflected in the seriousness of bodily damage reported by mothers (see pages 51–3). Thus 'real' fighting at this age cannot be passed off quite so easily as the four-year-old's more puny efforts.

We asked 'Does he do a lot of fighting – do his quarrels often come to blows?' – and here differences appear both between girls and boys and according to whether sibs or other children are involved. There are no significant social class differences, however. The percentages appear in Table 21.

Table 21 *Children who fight physically with sibs and with other children*

	BOYS		GIRLS	
	with sibs	with others	with sibs	with others
	%	%	%	%
often	33	7	25	2
sometimes	35	25	34	14
never	32	68	41	84

Significance: between classes n.s. between sexes ****

It is clear that, when it comes to actual blows, siblings are a good deal more likely than 'outside' children to be involved. Twenty-nine per cent of all children fight *often* with sibs, compared with only 7% who fight *often* with other children; if we include all the fighting in one category (*sometimes* plus *often*), sibs are still involved in twice as many cases (64% against 32%). Twice as many boys as girls are involved in fighting outside the family (again taking *sometimes* and *often* together, 32% against 16%, significance level ****). However, girls show their aggression much more freely within the family, and here the figures for boys and girls are a good deal more comparable, differences deriving entirely from the *often* category: that is, girls are as likely as boys to come to blows with their sibs *sometimes*.

These figures would seem to imply that while there is undoubtedly an underlying constitutional difference between boys and girls with respect to aggression and its physical expression,[11] there are also fairly strong cultural pressures mediating its control. That is to say, if sex differences in aggression were wholly constitutional, the differences between family and 'outside' behaviour would be parallel for boys and for girls, reflecting simply the normal tendency of people's behaviour to show less social inhibition where their intimates are concerned. The steeper rise in aggression for girls illustrates both the cultural factor and the subtle way in which such factors operate: it seems to us characteristic of families, and of parents as the conscious directors of family life, that although they are the most potent media through whom cultural expectations are transmitted to the child, they also deliberately provide a sanctuary, as it were, from cultural pressures. In the case of children fighting, there is a cultural understanding that it is neither seemly nor safe to allow little girls to brawl in public places (yet another indication of chaperonage in the lives of female children); but this sanction is lifted in the privacy of the home to the extent that feminine aggression, if not exactly accepted, is not totally forbidden.

It is, of course, a corollary of the private nature of such behaviour that, *because* it is hidden within the family, other families are not aware of how common it is and therefore feel themselves to be alone in not exerting firmer controls. Very many mothers express their feelings of inadequacy in the face of their children's quarrels in terms of the fact that their own children seem worse than anyone else's (the problem is greater still at eleven). A more accurate statement would be that the behaviour which they witness in their own homes is worse than anything *which they witness* in other people's homes. Such feelings of parental inadequacy are rather typical of areas of child behaviour which are seen mainly in family privacy, so that the total perspective of children in general is not fully available to the mother: the use of dummies in the first year,[12] the comfort bottle in the second year,[13] taking the child into the parents' bed,[14] and children's bed wetting[15] are all examples of such hidden areas.

*'I told all of them, "If anybody hits you, clout 'em back!"' *
The fact that a mother thinks children's quarrelling is unavoidable does not necessarily mean that she will not try to avoid it, or to do something about it once it has happened. We asked all mothers whether they ever interfered in their children's 'quarrels and arguments with other children outside the family', and whether they ever told the child what he should do in his quarrels or helped him to manage them in any way. An analysis of their strategies is given in Table 22. Sex differences are insignificant throughout, and figures for boys and girls are therefore combined. The table is explained by examples of the categories used.

'Interferes personally':

Twist hand's wife:
> If they start fighting, I bring them all in here and I give them a good talking-to, and I give them each a glass of orange, you know, I get round them that way, and then I make them shake hands, you know.

Driver's mate:
> [Father:] We have done. Well, the wife has done. If something's gone wrong, like, it's always Wendy – well, I mean, it's not *forced* to be Wendy. Well, it's always "I done this" and "I done that", and . . . [Mother:] I think it'd be a poor mother that didn't stick up for her own child.

Setter operator's wife:
> If they hit him, I stick up for him and that, 'cause I know he won't stick up for hisself.

Representative's wife:
> I tell her what I think's right. I mean, if a child's playing hop-scotch, she'll walk by ever so nice and then she'll poke her tongue out first, and then she'll kick the stone away; so I shout her back and I make her put the stone back in the ring, which

Table 22 *Mothers' strategies in dealing with children's peer group quarrels*

strategy predominating	I&II	IIIwc	III man	IV	V	overall popn.	remarks
	%	%	%	%	%	%	
interferes personally	24	24	23	24	41	25	Class v vs. the rest significant at 0·01 level (***)
	—24%—				41%		
counsels justice	15	19	7	11	4	10	Significant class trend ***. Middle class vs. working class ****
	—17%—		—7%—				
counsels diplomacy	8	4	6	6	6	6	No significant differences
urges withdrawal	11	7	8	8	5	8	Class differences n.s. Girls slightly more often urged to withdraw (significant at 0·05 only *)
	(boys 6% vs. girls 10%)						
urges retaliation	18	22	27	25	27	25	Overall class trend significant *** Middle class vs. working class at 0·07 only
	—20%—		—26%—				
refuses involvement	19	17	26	22	17	23	Class trend in expected direction, but not significant
	—18%—		—24%—				
other strategies	6	6	2	3	0	3	
'retaliation' and 'refuses'	37	39	53	47	44		Middle class vs. working class significant ***
	—38%—		—51%—				

she don't like – she don't like you to tell her – put the stone back and then say she's sorry and ask them if she can play. It embarrasses Angela to say she's sorry.

'Counsels justice':

Fitter's wife:

 I try to sort of talk to her about it, and let her see that she's, well, not always right herself, but then the other person is not always right, and you've got to come to a sort of compromise;

but then it doesn't always work, but I think it helps her sometimes.

Cabinet maker's wife:
I like to point out to Greg . . . er . . . well, I say "Now look here,
Greg, you can't expect the boys to play if you will insist on
having . . ." – he seems to think that things should be done just
exactly as *he* wants them doing. He's like that in everything he
does. I cannot for the life of me make the child understand that
other people are just as important in their ideas as he is in his,
you see. It's the same with Susan [younger sister], he'll say she's
this and that, and I say "But *she* has to have her own ideas, as
well as you have yours, and she's *entitled*". But it doesn't sink
in; it might do, I don't know.

Insurance inspector's wife:
Yes, I do, actually [help him to manage quarrels]. Probably
later, you know, I advise him as to what I think he should have
done or should not have done. [What is the general advice you
give him?] Um . . . um . . . I don't particularly want him to
argue with other people, so mainly I tell him that he ought not
to be arguing, but mainly his squabbles are over his bike or somebody else's bike which he wants to ride, and mainly to advise
give and take and share.

'Counsels diplomacy':

Hospital porter's wife:
Well, I always say to him if he *knows* he's in the wrong, then
he should admit it and say that he's sorry, you see, and then
everything's OK again and they're friends. But children don't do
that, not very often, do they?

Actor's wife:
If I sense that she wants to get out of a situation but she wants
to be polite as well, I try to suggest a way out that she could use.

Foreman's wife:
Well, we try to show her, you know, how to *make* friends rather
than fall out with them all the time. [What sort of thing do you
say?] Well, ask them if you can play with them, rather than
forcing yourself, and, er, do what they do. Don't try to be the
boss all the time, you know, do what *they* want to do – fall in,
you know.

'Urges withdrawal':

Car sprayer's wife (child too weak):
> I advise him, like; but I advise him if there's any trouble to keep away 'cause you don't get hurt then, but if you tend to join in you'll perhaps get the worst, and you've nothing to do with it. I don't like them to fight or quarrel really, but you can't help it sometimes.

University teacher's wife (child too strong):
> I've told him that if he feels himself getting really cross he should walk out of the situation before he comes to blows, because I've *told* him he has this strong temper and is a strong child, and that he certainly mustn't hit or frighten children smaller or not so strong as himself *because* of this. He understands this . . . er . . . and it's sort of one of the things he's learning to live with, as it were.

Lace worker's wife:
> I tell her to be kind, and say if they aren't kind back to her, to leave them, just not bother to play with them.

'Urges retaliation':

Stoker's wife:
> I always tell him to fight his battles, and if they hit him always hit them back. Never be frightened of anybody – of them hitting him.

Fitter's wife:
> Yes, well it all depends what they've done, you see. If, say, they've kicked him and he comes in crying, I say, Well go and hit them back then; if you can't hit them, kick them back; the same as they've done to you. I mean, it'll stop most of them doing it. If you don't stick up for yourself, they'll only keep hitting more.

'Refuses involvement':

Builder's wife:
> There's quite a few children on the street, and they all play together, and they fall out, they *do* fall out, but I mean it's no good taking any notice. I mean, if one's done some harm to her

one day, she'll do it to them the next day, you know how children are.

Hosiery presser's wife:
Oh no, no, no. I say that's up to her. If she causes arguments, she can patch them up again!

Labourer's wife:
He makes friends easily, but when they play together, I mean it's natural with all children, they fall out over one thing and another, and he comes in, "Mum, they've done this" and "they've done the other", and I don't take no notice; I mean I told him, I says to him "You're playing with them, you go and sort it out yourselves".

Very often a refusal to become involved also incorporates a suggestion, not just that the child should 'sort it out' for himself, but that this sorting out should be in the form of hitting back; and injunctions to hit back are frequently accompanied by an explicit statement that the mother does not wish to be involved. In coding mixed responses, we tried to judge which feeling was more emphasised; but the common association of retaliation and refusal of involvement is the reason for combining them in the last line of the table, and in this larger group the class difference is more clear.

It should be noted that different degrees of retaliation are subsumed under that heading. At one end there are the parents who feel so strongly that their child must learn to give blow for blow that they will punish him aggressively for withholding aggression. 'If they fall out and he comes in crying', said a disabled soldier's wife, 'I just give him a good hiding and send him out and tell him to hit 'em back'. Fathers and brothers often threaten boys in this way; but little girls are not excluded from such sanctions.

Railwayman's wife:
Well – let me tell you – she'll fight Kevin [brother, aged eleven] like *hell*; she really hurts him; but any other child, she'll come in crying. I can't understand that; I mean what *is* the reason, do you know? She'll fight Kevin, and she'll get the best of it; but then she lets the other kiddies rule her, sort of thing. I say to her "Now look, you know, if you don't hit them back I'll give *you* a good smack".

Labourer's wife:
She won't hit any other children – *very* little outside the family.

If they hit Ida, she runs in and starts crying. You shout at her – "You must go and hit 'em back – if you don't, I'll hit *you* for not hitting them back" – but she takes no notice.

The implication of threatening punishment for *not* retaliating is that it elevates physical retaliation to the status of the morally right rather than merely accepting it as an expedient necessary in an imperfect world ('hit them back, and they won't be so quick to hit you next time'). Thus the child is not only pushed back into the fray to cope with it himself, but is under heightened moral pressure to fight someone he has already run away from – where only expedience is at issue, the child is more free to decide what is expedient for *him*. This is rather different from parents at the other end of the retaliation group, who start from a position of disapproval of physical aggression and are then reluctantly brought to feel that the environment demands it. In particular, this attitude is expressed by middle-class or upwardly mobile mothers still living in an area which is rather below their own class status; otherwise, it usually arises with reference to the school peer group, where the situation is still less under the mother's control.

Greengrocer's wife:
He did let them boss him around a lot; he realised it, and my husband had to start and get down to him a little bit, you know, and say a thing I didn't want him to do. The thing I didn't want him to do was to start fighting, but – er – this Brian in particular used to attack him. So we said, well, what's going to happen if we don't do anything about it – he's going to be always afraid of him, and if they're in the same class while they're at this school, wherever Gerald is, that child is going to be quite the boss of him. So we had to change our ideas over that till my husband did show him how to look after himself a bit more, and now he does take a bit more care of himself. We try to instil into him, "Don't sort of *look* for trouble, don't be aggressive, play nicely, but if they hit you . . ." We've had to come to the idea that you've *got* to hit them back, which we didn't like the idea of at all.

Business executive's wife:
When he first came home from school and I thought he was letting people kick him, I told him he must say "Now don't do it, it's not very nice to do!" So he said "Well they *insist* upon

doing it". So I said "Give them a push or something, make them
see that you're not easily . . . you know, that you're just not
going to put up with it". And I've seen him do that since.
Nothing more than that, I haven't told him. I am really in an
awkward position, because he's been taught *not* to fight.

It may seem surprising that Class v mothers are significantly
more likely to interfere personally in children's quarrels, in view of
the fact that at four years they were markedly unwilling to intervene.
At four, taking only the 55% of responses which were definite and
unambiguous on this point, we compared the interventionist category 'Mother accepts role as arbitrator' with the non-interventionist
'Mother lets children settle own differences', and found a clear class
trend ranging from 37% in Class i and ii to 20% in Class v *for*
intervention, and from 19% in Class i and ii to 43% in Class v
against intervention.[16]

The change at seven, which at first sight seems anomalous, partly
reflects a true change in the situation of the child and partly is due
to our more detailed analysis of strategies appropriate to this
changed situation. At four, arbitration and verbal counselling tended
to involve personal intervention *at the time of the quarrel*;[17] in
order to be appropriate to a four-year-old's verbal and conceptual
level, advice given would necessarily be specific to the situation
under arbitration, even if its more general application were also
pointed out. It is also true that arbitration at four would often be
backed up by the mother standing by to make sure her decisions
were in fact carried out, and that sometimes she would underline
her suggestions by leading or putting the child where it was supposed to be, or physically holding combatants apart while her words
sank in. At seven the presence of the mother is much less necessary
in order to ensure that the principles she has taught are carried
out, and she may herself feel that it is more appropriate to the
child's growing social awareness at this age for her to pursue her
counselling role in the background: 'If he's outside my door', said
a showroom foreman's wife, 'and I hear a quarrel, and I know
Larry's definitely in the wrong, I wouldn't go out and tell him and
make him look small; but I would have it in my mind, to bear in
mind to mention it to him after'. Thus at seven it becomes possible
to analyse mothers' strategies, as we have here, partly in terms of
advice given verbally at a distance; and it then appears that those
who are relying on the rather complicated verbal advice involved
in 'counsels justice' are significantly more likely to be middle class,

and this group has moved away from direct intervention. If, however, a mother both finds it difficult to rely on verbal counselling and still wants to retain some control over quarrels (perhaps because her child needs defending against the larger children he is now likely to meet), personal intervention becomes more necessary at seven than it was at four; and possibly it is for this reason that Class v mothers, who are not much inclined to use verbal persuasion, now choose more often than before to interfere.

It should be added that the reason so often given at four, mainly by working-class mothers, for not interfering – that to interfere causes trouble with the other child's parents and that you 'can't afford to fall out over your kids' – was repeated many times at seven; we also collected a number of examples of what parents have in mind when they invoke this adage. It is interesting that mothers who describe experiences of falling-out over kids do so in a warning spirit – it is not at all the case that these are mothers who do not mind falling out.

Representative's wife (living on council estate):
I did [interfere] last week, but you don't like to because you don't like to fall out over children, but it's no use letting people always get away with it. My husband went to see this child's mother about it; and then, um, when was it? Wednesday, my husband had taken the children all out apart from Caroline [sister, aged four], and she was playing in the back, and I just looked out of the window, and this little boy came down the road. And he knew there'd been trouble, you see, friction between them, and he just spat at Caroline in the face, you see. Ooh, that made *me* angry, so I marched up the back, you see, and I told his mother: I said, you know, "I'm fed up", I said, "I'm going to keep my eyes on him, and every little move he moves wrong", I said, "I shall be up". Well, I mean, you don't want it, do you? I mean, there's enough tension trying to bring up five children decent, isn't there?

Baker's wife:
I find that you can't possibly fall out with children's parents, because while you're falling out with the parents the children are back together again . . . . . as a matter of fact, we had a court case, you see, over these children – I had to take the man to court – he struck Melanie – she's only seven – she didn't want belting, not by another man anyway. I took him to court, any-

way – he were fined two pound. It was his children that caused it, so I says to mine "Keep away from them", and that were it, and she has done.

'. . . I didn't sort of say **outright** *you can't bring her in again, but . . .'*

Melanie's mother solved the problem of trouble-making friendships by telling her children to keep away from this particular family; and because seven-year-olds are still somewhat restricted in their movements around the neighbourhood, and perhaps also still relatively amenable to this sort of edict, the mother does have some option of controlling the child's pattern of friendships by encouraging those she approves of and discouraging, or even forbidding, those she considers undesirable. There are a number of very understandable reasons why a mother might object to a particular child being friendly with her own. In Melanie's case, real trouble had already occurred, and the mother saw the other children as the root cause. In the case of Amanda, a miner's child, the whole interview was answered in terms of pre-Jimmy and post-Jimmy – Jimmy being a seven-year-old wanderer who had persuaded Amanda to wander with him all over the city, and whose final banishment from her friendship three months before the interview had apparently saved her parents' sanity. Barney, a labourer's son, was in danger of being terrorised into a life of crime by his delinquent 'friend' :

Well, this boy, he's been taking Barney to the shops, and saying to Barney "I'm going to smash your face in if you don't go in that shop and pinch money out the till"; and he come home one day, Saturday it was, and he come in, and he was crying, he was, and I said "What's matter wi' you?" And he says "Bill Barton's going to smash me face in". I says "What for? What's he going to do that for?" He says " 'Cause I won't go in Fine Fare and pinch money out the till". And anyway, I went down and told his mother, and she just laughed and sort of well-I-couldn't-care-less attitude. I says "He's not been used to it, and I'm not having it". I says "If he wants money, he can come and ask for it". I says "I've left my purse on the table", I says, "I've left it all over, and he's never attempted to take money out my purse"; and I says "You're to keep him away from him", I says, "because if you don't keep away from him", I says, "he's going straight to the police station, because I'm not having it". But *since* then, his mother's left, she's separated from her husband, she left like *that*; they've got no mother at the back on 'em, and his father's out at work all day, and when they come home they've got to be on their own till he comes home at seven o'clock . . . and the lady next door but two, she'd left the money out on the window-ledge for the Corona man, and when she went back he'd taken it off the window-ledge and kept it. That's how he's got, and I said I wouldn't let him go with him again. If he comes to the door now and knocks on the door for him, I says "He's not coming, you're to keep away from him!"

In general, however, if mothers have reservations about their children's friends, they are for much less dramatic reasons at this age: the other child is dirty or uses unacceptable language, he is rowdy or quarrelsome, or he is bad-mannered and cheeky.

Pipe fitter's wife:
There was a little child up at school who was a bit dirty. I try to teach them not to be snobbish, sort of thing, but on the other hand I'm always scared that they might get something in their hair – 'cause they've got terribly long hair, practically down to their waists, and I should hate to have it cut off, sort of thing – so I told her to be careful.

Lorry driver's wife:
There's some that live down the road. Well, they never seem to be at school, some mornings when I go to work they're outside on the pavement playing then. And I mean some nights at ten o'clock they're out. They're out on this field playing, and they're really rough. There's like all old people in these flats, and sometimes they'll start throwing stones at the windows downstairs, you see. I mean I wouldn't let her play with anyone like that, you know.

Engineer's wife:
I only have once [discouraged a friendship], and that was with a little girl, and in my ways she's . . . well, say, had it been Avril doing the things that she'd been doing, I wouldn't have liked it. She were one of them, she'd play with other folks' things and break them – you know, not sort of take care of them – and we had her in here once to play and she started fiddling with the television and noseying about. Well I don't like that in kiddies; and she used to sort of tell Avril to come in and ask me for lemonade or slices of bread. Well, I've always taught mine never to do that.

The standards of conduct which children of seven display are not yet very firmly based upon a consistent pattern of internalised principles. Because of this, in order to meet their parents' notions of courteous behaviour, they need constant reminders: 'Did you remember to thank Auntie May, to wash your hands, to wipe your feet?' etc.; or 'When you're at someone else's house, don't ask for things to eat – don't open their drawers and cupboards – wait till things are offered'. Parents expect a habit of acceptable social behaviour (including moral behaviour) to be acquired only gradually, by dint of their own reiteration of minor demands which will eventually create a consistent and binding framework for an understanding of what is and what is not permissible.

During this process of socialisation, parents are very much aware that the child remains vulnerable to outside influences, and that he may all too easily be swayed by children who do not share the same standards, particularly when the behaviour of the other child has the spice of novelty and adventure just because it is less controlled and less constrained by adult pressures. Sometimes the issue can be recognised by the parents as a clash of cultural values – no less potentially threatening for being understood in such terms.

Student's wife:
It's difficult to put into words, but on this rather rough estate where the school is there is a sort of feeling that seems to grow up – it isn't noticeable in the children until they're seven or eight – but from this time onwards there is a great and definite antipathy to *things as they are done*. I suppose when they grow up this crystallises into an anti-authority attitude – it isn't that at this stage, but it's a sort of general feeling of aggression and hostility, and not wanting to do things for no better reason than the fact that they are done generally by most people . . . um . . . and I have a feeling that if he goes on being very friendly with Michael, as they get bigger he will in fact pick up this attitude. If our relationship with James is sufficiently strong and satisfying, this probably won't be very important, and will be a passing if rather irritating phase. I think it *could* become a serious problem if one didn't keep an eye on it.

Sometimes, too, parents can accept that an issue is a trivial one stemming from individual differences in what a given mother or father will tolerate. 'The *Farndons* are allowed to lick their plates after their puddings', complains Becky to her mother, who replies 'Yes, well, bad luck, you're not – and I dare say you're allowed to do some things that *they're* not'.

Here it is appreciated that the two families differ only in detail as to what is acceptable, and the mother implicitly states both points – that her present demand is at once comparatively trivial and to be respected as something that she personally minds about. Where the disapproved child comes from a family of generally lower standards, however, the issue is a good deal more complicated, and the mother is both more concerned and more uncertain as to what line she should take. In particular, although 'dirtiness' is often mentioned, mothers are seldom unambiguously intolerant of dirty children, since they almost invariably seem conscious that such children are likely to be the victims rather than the villains of the situation. Thus where dirt (including nits) is the *only* complaint, they will usually worry but accept the child. 'Dirty habits', so called, are a different matter.

Bleacher's wife:

> There's only one – which *isn't* their fault, and I have to be very careful when I say these things, because children can repeat these things – next door the house is . . . well, it is *really* dirty – but you can't blame the children; and they're not dressed very nicely; but they have dirty heads, you see; and I do say to them – you know, I have done – I wouldn't like you to say this *to* them – I have *stressed* that it's not the *children's* fault, it's the fault of the mother more than anything, like, and we've always called the mother Fanny Fernackapan, and the children will say "It's Fanny Fernackapan's fault" . . . . . You know how you teach children to say "Auntie Dot", "Auntie Edith"? – well, I've always said "Mrs Williams", because I would be ashamed if on the front they said "Hello, Auntie Jean" . . . . . Well anyway, her children do come, and she'll say "We're going to do hairdressing" or "We're going to dress up"; and I always just shout to them, and say quietly "Now remember what I told you, don't put your head near to Diane's and don't swap things on your head, Edwina" – "I know, I know" – "That's all right then". But I don't want to stress it too much, but on the other hand it *is* important to me, I don't want . . . I mean, if she does say "Me head's itchy", I'm having a look *straight* away [laughed]. But as I say, I don't want to discourage the thing, because after all it's not *fair* to the other children.

Miner's wife:
> Yes, well, this little girl, she has rather dirty habits, I'm afraid.
> [What sort of dirty habits?] Well . . . looking at herself, you know
> what I mean – nasty little habits – I think "Poor little devil"; and
> especially if Karen was on the toilet, or any other little girl for
> that matter, she used to stand watching, well I don't like that sort
> of thing, I don't. And she was always scratching her head, you
> know, she was never kept very clean – mind you, I didn't hold
> *that* against her, not being clean – it was the dirty little *habits*.

Machine operator:
> She's one of eight children, and the parents are a bit lax about
> the sort of language they use – I don't necessarily mean *bad*
> language, but, um, the sort of English they use, you know. Ever
> since we've been up here [moved to council estate from central
> area], we've tried to bring ours on a bit, and, er, we know that
> Edgar slipped back a lot through this association. [Mother:] But
> she's very dirty, which of course the child can't help, we don't
> hold that against her, but they say such awful things, and coming
> from a child they sound horrible. [Father:] But we wouldn't want
> to break the association, because obviously they're such good
> friends. [Mother:] And she's one of those children whose beauty
> shines right through the dirt, you know.

Dirt plus bad language quite often give grounds for discouraging another child's friendship; but mothers can accept these if they
can be seen as superficial to a basically socialised child. It is when
these are the surface indications of a more deep-seated disregard
for all the standards which mothers are still trying to inculcate in
their own children that such a child poses a threat that cannot be
tolerated: 'it wasn't so much her language, it was just her *way of
life*, I think', as a forecourt manager's wife said. The mother is
faced with alien norms and assumptions in a child who expects to be
out and about at all hours, to wander freely long distances from
home and to play over-boisterously and destructively. Thus,
although a mother may dislike in itself the fact that her child's
friend is cheeky, her real reason for discouraging or forbidding
him is that he is unamenable to the ordinary social controls which
she has hitherto found effective, and that his defiance offers a
seductive invitation to her own child which, whether deliberately or
not, undermines her own hard-won authority. This is the root of
the matter, and one cannot dismiss her qualms as mere snobbery,

although she herself may well be defensively alert for such a reaction.

Salesman's wife:
One little lad I did [discourage]. I put me foot down about it. I told Scott to come in on one occasion, and this lad said "Tell her to shut her mouth!" – and I mean he was only a matter of six years of age, and I said "We'll have no more, go and play in your own street and your own house". He sort of looked at Scott, and he said "Take no notice of her, come on" – and Scott was between the devil and the deep, he didn't know whether to come in or whether to show he was clever and go with him. So afterwards I said "That's finished, he comes here no more". I've managed to ease him off.

Wholesaler's wife (living in council house):
Actively, no, I don't think I've ever said "I won't let you play with so-and-so again, you're *not* to play with him"; but there is one that I have tried to play down. This is an older one, there are three in the family, and they play with both Martin and Neill . . . . . Well, to be honest, I think the child is dishonest – I *know* he is, put it that way! And also the language that I've heard from him, quite honestly – well – bargee language – and he used it to his *mother*. And also, in this particular instance, one day I *saw* him take a bottle of lemonade from a lorry standing there, and his father was walking down behind him and laughed about it. Well – of course, that – it's a small thing in itself, but I felt that was entirely wrong. And the whole family attitude – although I speak to them, I mean we get on quite super-ficially – but the whole thing: you see I've heard the child say to Martin and Neill when I've called them, "Let's go somewhere, take no notice of her, *she* doesn't matter", sort of thing – which of course is infectious. And while I think – I *hope* – I can deal with this sort of thing at home at the moment, I don't generally want to *have* to. But it's so difficult. I just feel that I'm out-numbered by those three boys! These things are difficult to explain, but I do feel very strongly about it.

Most of the reasons given for discouraging or forbidding children can be subsumed under this general heading of threatening the mother's chosen values; but there is also a small group of children's friends who are rejected for individual personality traits which are seen as directly harmful to the child, either because they are undesirable in themselves or because they are unwelcome in conjunction with this child's own personality. Cruelty, hysteria, morbid interests, over-demonstrativeness, pugnacity, precocity and giggly behaviour are all occasional reasons for a child being discouraged; a more frequent worry is that the friend is generally dominating, and that, because the mother's own child is naturally submissive, the association is to be avoided.

Chemical worker's wife:
I'm not particularly happy about it, because at bottom Hazel's frightened of her. It might sound strange, but it's perfectly true . . . . . This girl Annette is older, you see, she's nine. And of course Hazel does as Annette tells her, all the time, you see – she's frightened to do otherwise in case Annette doesn't play with her. [Father:] She's a pretty forceful sort of girl, Annette. [Mother:] She's *over*-confident. But they can hit it off. But Annette can sit *down* and play, and I think if Hazel had her own way, she's a bit more wild – she'd sooner climb a tree or jump off a bank, or skate up and down the hill or get thoroughly dirty, you know . . . . . [Other children, not Annette, specified] I don't think she'd stand up for herself – do you? [to father]. [Father:] It depends – not in little things; things she might feel very strongly about, she might do then. [Is she *content* to let other children boss her a bit, would you say?] No she's not, it always upsets her. But I think if it was a choice of giving in to them *in order* to play with them, half the time she would rather give in, and play, rather than stand up for her own rights and be on her own. She must have people to play with, children to play with, no matter what it cost her. She would give in, sooner than . . . If they say "Come and do this, or we won't play", well then Hazel will do it.

Widow carrying on husband's business:
Just recently we've bought him a fishing rod and taken him fishing. We met a rather nice boy who we became very friendly with. He was about eleven, and they got on famously. Now this friendship I *would* try to break, simply because we realised afterwards that this boy, he's really charming, but he's got a quite cruel streak. He found a frog, he played with it till he killed it, and he broke its skin – tore it to pieces almost – and yet as I say he was a charming boy, and Simon really enjoyed his friend-

ship. Well – in that case the boy lived at Kegworth, we live here, we just don't find it convenient to go fishing there – we go else-where. [Suppose he lived round here, what would you do?] Well, if he lived round here, I would only allow him to go fishing with him if I was there; because you know it was quite a long time before we found out about this . . . . . If we met the boy, you know, *while* we were fishing, we'd be friendly, but we wouldn't really encourage it. [Did you discuss it with Simon?] A little – 'cause Simon said "Oh Mum, wasn't it awful, he made that frog's giblets come out!" I said "Well, it *was*, Simon, because that poor frog, it had feelings, it didn't deserve to die, did it?" and he said "It didn't, Mum, It just wasn't fair". And I said to him "Well, I don't think I would like to go fishing very often with Chris now, Simon". And we left it at that, and he hasn't really bothered since – it didn't prey on his mind and it didn't become a fixation with him, but I think he realised it wasn't nice himself. Perhaps it was a good lesson taught to him.

With some understanding of the feelings that might prompt mothers to curtail their children's friendships, we may now look at the actual numbers involved in this. Our introductory question asked whether the mother was happy about her child's current friendships: 85% were quite content, 11% had some reservations, and only 4% were definitely worried. No sex or class differences could be detected here. Obviously the fact that the mother is happy about the child's friendships *now* does not imply that she has always been tolerant of his friends: in fact, a mother's satisfaction with the present situation could well mean that she has successfully eliminated those she does not approve of. We therefore went on to ask whether she had ever tried to discourage a friendship between her child and another; if so, for what reason; and if not, whether she might do this and in what circumstances. The results of these questions are set out in Table 23.

The first half of this table shows the mother's action to restrict the child's friends in terms of what has in fact already happened; the second half, which adds in those who *would* take such action, but have not yet had occasion to, shows attitudes rather than behaviour: and the difference between 'have' and 'would' is in itself interesting. Overall, 35% of mothers have already intervened in this way, and actual intervention is more likely for boys than for girls. There is a suggestion of a class difference showing more discouragement of specific friendships in the middle class than the working class, but this comes mainly from a striking increase in intervention where white-collar parents' boys are concerned. An apparently anomalous figure also appears in Class IV, where the incidence of restriction for both boys and girls is higher than one might expect from the total pattern.

Table 23 *Mothers' active discouragement of specific friendships*

	social class					summary		
	I&II	IIIwc	III man	IV	V	I&II, IIIwc	IIIman, IV,V	overall popn.
	%	%	%	%	%	%	%	%
Has already discouraged								
boys	34	56	38	42	32	45	38	40
girls	39	37	25	36	31	38	28	31
both	36	46	32	39	31	41	33	35

Significance: trend not consistent   m.class/w.class *
                           between sexes **

Has already or would discourage								
boys	69	79	75	73	74	74	74	74
girls	80	80	66	64	54	80	65	69
both	74	79	71	68	64	77	70	72

Significance: trend $\searrow$ **   m.class/w.class n.s.
                  between sexes n.s. interaction *

Both these results are explicable in terms of the living conditions of families in these two classes. The problem of living in a neighbourhood where the way of life of most families is 'rougher' than this family finds acceptable is one which is especially pertinent to Class III (white collar) and to part of Class IV. We have frequently noted before that anomalous results in Class IV often arise as a result of the Registrar General's uneasy combination in this class of semi-skilled heavy manual workers (stokers, quarrymen, bricklayers' mates) with highly 'respectable', steady, almost clerical occupations such as postman, hall porter, storekeeper, telephone operator and bus conductor. Occupations such as these, together with those included in Class III white collar, have in common the fact that

middle-class values of law-abiding respectability and order combine
with low incomes which make it difficult for such families to live
in middle-class areas. Thus it is extremely likely that they will be
surrounded by families whose notions of child rearing are different
from theirs, and whose children behave in ways which might be
considered a threat to the standards of behaviour which they expect
of their own children. Often, in talking to these mothers, one has
almost the sense of a family beleaguered by alien forces: some make
the move with relief into a more sympathetic neighbourhood; others
cannot, and continue to struggle against their children's assimilation.

Sales representative's wife:
    I haven't [discouraged a friendship] in the last two years; um –
    when we lived on Blank Street, he used to bring some children
    home then, some roughs and scruffs – you know, it seemed as if
    he really collected them. And, er, I used to say don't bring them
    home and don't play with them – they weren't nice children. It's
    such a change here – we haven't had to. [They were just generally
    rough?] Oh yes, they had dirty hands, very noisy, we couldn't
    keep them in the house at all, and couldn't send them home.
    [If a child round here turned out like that, would you discourage
    it?] I'd try to, yes. [Family had moved from an isolated row
    of council houses in a very poor area to a pleasant suburb.]

Clerk's wife (she managed a grocer's shop before her handicapped
baby's birth):
    I'm not happy [about his friendships] up here, no; I do try and
    keep him away from them. It's a bad area; and the talk's *terrible*.
    [Is there any particular child you stop him playing with?] A
    little girl across the road, Denise; and one up the top there.
    Horrible children – bad language – cheeky – not just a roguish
    cheekiness, you know, *really* cheeky – they'd soon turn round
    and give you a mouthful. [In this case, mother giving up her job
    caused a temporary move to very inferior accommodation.]

Miner/fitter's wife (herself nursery-nurse trained):
    No, I'm not happy. I've been trying to get out for years. I'd
    like to get in a nice district where they have got some friends,
    but it's very difficult to get an exchange or anything else. We've
    been trying to think of a way to buy a place, but – you know –
    at the moment – it's very difficult when you've got three little ones
    to bring up. [Living on an older council estate with a high
    delinquency rate.]

The hypothesis that a mother is more likely actively to have discouraged a friendship if she lives in a community of families somewhat below her own in class status can easily be checked, by comparing middle-class children living in predominantly middle-class
districts (i.e. in the suburban belt) with those middle-class children
who live in predominantly working-class districts (i.e. the central
and council-estate areas). Such a comparison shows the hypothesis
to be justified: of 171 middle-class children living in middle-class
districts, 34% had already been restricted in their friendships, whereas of 70 middle-class children living in working-class areas, 54%
had had this experience (significant at the 0·01 level). A similar test,
looking only at the much smaller group of Class III (white collar)
boys, also produced a significant difference.

Being prepared to ban one's children's friendships is a majority
attitude in relation to both boys and girls; the difference lies mainly
in whether the occasion to do so has already arisen. In the middle-
class, mothers are rather more ready to restrict their daughters'
friendships, but in fact find it happening more with their sons. This
predominance of the actual restriction of boys' friendships in all
classes except the top and bottom of the scale is probably partly
because the girls are already more closely chaperoned and therefore less subject to undesirable influences, and partly because, of
'undesirable' children generally, boys are undesirable in more obvious
ways than girls. In working-class families, parents are both actively
and theoretically more wary of their sons' friends, for reasons
which begin to reflect the sex ratio for later delinquency.[18]

It is clear from the quotations we have already given in this
section, as well as from the statistical material, that the fear of
children being adversely affected by unsuitable companions operates
at every class level. Reading the interview transcripts, however,
there does appear to be a difference in the extent to which parents
feel they are able to control the situation. A kind of fatalism was
often expressed by mothers at the lower end of the social scale, even
by those who had already tried to select their children's friends:
'Whatever you do, if you stop them playing with one kiddy, they'll go
out and find one that's even worse', said a Class v wife; and a
mother in Class IV thought that 'children find their own friends,
no matter what you say – they'll go in the street behind your back,
won't they, so you just may as well accept it'. Middle-class mothers,
on the other hand, even where they were not very happy at the idea
of rejecting individual children, gave an impression of greater confidence in having the situation in hand.

Teacher's wife:
> There's one little boy I'm not so keen on as the others, but I shan't say anything directly; but I would do if it was someone I disliked – if the child were a rough, wandering type of child – wild and so on. I should hate Mark to become wild! So I should just – I think I'd stop him; I *might* say "I don't want you to play with him"; I'm not quite sure as to whether I'd do that, or whether I'd be crafty, and always have him busy when this child called. I'm not sure: I might do that.

A greengrocer's wife is worth quoting at length because she illustrates vividly the middle-class mother's security that, in the long run, her child's whole way of life will back up her own control over him.

> We try and impress upon Gerald how to choose his friends a bit more, we don't want to choose *for* him, but the point is to get him a little bit more discriminating about his choice. We don't want him to sort of get too rough, and – um – it's rather difficult, you've got to let them choose for themselves, but at the same time, if you give them *too* much freedom of choice of friend, you can be running into trouble later on. We haven't made an issue of it. There were two at his party in particular. One of them, we were not awfully happy when we knew he wanted to ask him, but we said "Ooh . . . well, yes": I mean, it was his party, he could ask who he liked and that was it. But he saw for himself, strangely enough, that they didn't fit into what he was used to. They were trying to do things that he knew *he* couldn't do . . . sort of wandering off upstairs . . . . . I saw him having a quiet chat with his auntie; well, she told me afterwards that he was explaining why he'd asked them – two of them, when Brian's gang attacked his, they'd come and rescued him, so he owed them something; and this other one, Brian, who was the one we were so much against, the reason he'd asked *him* was because Brian had given Gerald quite a few of his cards, you see, these little picture cards, and he felt he must ask him because he'd got to repay him . . . . . Most of them were all right, but as I say, there were two main offenders. But we didn't make an issue with him, we didn't, er, *say* that they were a noisy lot and that sort of thing, but he did realise *himself* that they were noisier here than he was used to.

Middle-class parents have two lines of defence: first, they tend to live in suburban areas, which makes it a good deal less likely that their children will ever meet the most 'rough', unruly and potentially delinquent children; and secondly, they tend to keep their children under closer control and supervision by making it possible for them to invite their friends in and by providing child-centred facilities which will keep the children content at home. So long as they are living in a community which accepts middle-class values as normal, they can afford to exercise control with both subtlety and confidence, since an unacceptable association rarely arises save where the other child's influence is effectively diluted both by 'nice' children and by the middle-class environment. As one descends the social scale, however, a more fatalistic attitude is justified by reality: overcrowding forces children out of the home, and the street peer group offers an attraction which parents feel progressively less able to oppose as the child's range increases. It is not true that the majority of working-class children are potentially delinquent: but it is true that those who incline in that direction can exert a disproportionate social influence upon other children in a neighbourhood where the street is the main focus for children's activities. In such an environment, the ability to make friends, which every mother wants for her child, can seem a risky talent.

NOTES

1 From *Children as Poets*, ed. Denys Thompson, Heinemann, London, 1972. Permission to use this poem is gratefully acknowledged.
2 It is a revealing exercise to talk to a seven-year-old about friendship patterns in the classroom. We have found that a very detailed sociogram can be built up by asking the child (for every classmate) 'Who would so-and-so choose to sit next to? Who would like to sit next to so-and-so?' The significance of this lies not in the actual patterns that emerge so much as in the fact that the child knows (or believes he knows) all the answers with some degree of certainty. Thus, whether his answers are objectively accurate or not, each child takes his place in a web of friendly or not-so-friendly attitudes of which he himself has a particularised awareness.
3 Seventy-seven per cent play with others 'often' (at least one session a week in term-time, but usually much more) and 21% 'sometimes'.
4 Children's parties in suburban Nottingham are almost as worthy of anthropological attention as the potlatches of the Kwakiutl. Mothers are willy-nilly drawn into the ritual of presents for the party-giver (with a birthday card, of course), a present (or even two) for every guest, a lavish tea *and* cake to take home in a napkin, prizes for the party-games, balloons, and all the heart-searching preamble of 'she asked me to hers, so I shall *have* to ask her to mine, so that makes seventeen!'
5 For example, J. P. Lees and John Newson, 'Family or sibship position and some aspects of juvenile delinquency', *Br. J. Delinquency*, 5, 1954.

6 In follow-up at eleven we found that James had coped with the situation most effectively (helped by intensive support from his mother) by becoming outstandingly successful in his chosen sport.

7 In returning to the children at eleven years, we have taken up the challenge again; and fieldwork in progress as this book is written shows that it *is* possible to get mothers talking about jealousy. Perhaps this is a function of the child's increased age, however.

8 Anna Freud, with Sophie Dann, 'An experiment in group upbringing', in *Psychoanalytic Study of the Child*, VI, Imago, London, 1951.

9 'Mardy', used of a child of this age, means peevish, soft, a bit of a cry-baby.

10 This kind of observer rating phenomenon is reported by J. W. Meyer and B. I. Sobieszek, 'Effect of a child's sex on adult interpretations of its behaviour', *Devel. Psychol.*, 6, 1972, pp. 42–8.

11 The greater aggressiveness of boys has been too consistently shown over too many studies of young children to be explicable without reference to constitutional differences. See the summary of such studies in E. Maccoby, 1967, pp. 323–6.

12 John and Elizabeth Newson, *Infant Care in an Urban Community*, Allen & Unwin, London, 1963, pp. 172–5 (Pelican edn. pp. 180–3).

13 *Ibid.* pp. 170–2 (Pelican edn. pp. 178–80).

14 *Ibid.* pp. 83–4 (Pelican edn. pp. 78–9); J. and E. Newson, 1968, pp. 277–80 (Pelican edn. pp. 293–7).

15 *Ibid.* pp. 326–39 (Pelican edn. pp. 347–61).

16 J. and E. Newson, 1968, Table XI, p. 114 (Pelican edn. p. 118).

17 A mother's choice of arbitration as a strategy immediately offers the child (i) extra interaction with her personally; (ii) increased language experience, both active (in the course of putting his case) and passive (in listening both to the other child's case and to her arbitration; (iii) rewards for competent use of language (presenting plausible verbal excuses). *Ibid.* pp. 436–8 (Pelican edn. pp. 463–4).

18 By the time the children reach eleven, working-class parents' preoccupation with peer group delinquency has considerably increased.

Chapter 7

Saturday's Child

Friday's child is loving and giving,
Saturday's child works hard for a living . . . .
                                        (nursery rhyme)

When we were considering the pressures for independence which
parents bring to bear upon four-year-olds,[1] we suggested that the
child's actual behaviour is probably limited more by his parents'
expectations than by his physical capabilities; and it seemed appropriate to compare four-year-olds in Nottingham contemporary
society with those of 130 years or so earlier, quite large numbers of
whom were expected by their parents to be actively involved in the
cottage industries of the lace and hosiery trades. Dr William Watts,
resident medical officer of the Nottingham Union, who gave evidence
to the Commission on Children's Employment of 1843, had
'observed in many instances, *especially in the houses of their
parents*, children at work, of four, five, and six years of age'.[2] The
subcommissioner who gathered evidence in the Nottingham area,
Mr R. D. Grainger, interviewed a family in Walker Street, in the
Sneinton area of Nottingham:

Mary Houghton, four years old: "Has drawn lace two years; her
mother gives her a penny a-week." Anne Houghton, six years
old: "Has been a drawer three years." – Mrs Houghton, the mother
of these children: "Is a lace-drawer and has four children;
Harriet eight years, Anne six, Mary four, and Eliza two years
old; of these the three elder are employed as lace-drawers.
Harriet was not quite three when she began to work, Anne was
about the same, and Mary was not quite two years. Eliza 'has
tried and drawn a few threads out.' " (Sub-Commissioner – All
this was interrupted with "Mind your work," "Take care," "Make

haste," "Now, Anne, get on," "Mind your work.") "Begins generally at 6 A.M. in the summer and 7 in the winter; in the former goes on till dark, in the latter till 10 P.M. The two biggest Children work with witness these hours; Mary begins at the same time in the morning, but she leaves off about 6 P.M. The Children have no time to go out to play; 'they go out very seldom.' . . . . . The Children are obliged to sit at their work; they sit all day. ('Mind your work.') The work tries the eyes; the black is the worst; 'it is dree work.' ('Now mind your work.') . . . . . The Children are very fine and pretty girls, and appear healthy; the two younger sit perched upon chairs, their legs being too short to reach the ground."[3]

By the time we come to consider the life-style of the seven-year-old, a perspective over the last century is still more significant: for whereas at four the working nineteenth-century child was in a minority, albeit of considerable proportions, at seven to work was usual for all but the privileged.

149. The Sub-Commissioner reports that "almost all the Children of the labouring classes in the Nottingham, Leicester and Derby districts are engaged in one or other of the several branches of the lace-manufacture and hosiery trade".[4]

And the Commission concluded:

From the whole of the evidence . . . . we find –

1. That instances occur in which Children begin to work as early as three and four years of age; not unfrequently at five, and between five and six; while, *in general, regular employment commences between seven and eight*; the great majority of the Children having begun to work before they are nine years old, although in some few occupations no Children are employed until they are ten and even twelve years old and upwards.

2. That in all cases the persons that employ mere Infants and the very youngest Children are the parents themselves, who put their Children to work at some processes of manufacture under their own eye, in their own houses; but Children begin to work together in numbers, in larger or smaller manufactories, at all ages, from five years old and upwards.[5]

Nor was this work in any sense equivalent to what we might think of as a hard school day in terms of hours expended; to quote again from the Commissioners' conclusions:

19. That in some few instances the regular hours of work do not exceed ten, exclusive of the time allowed for meals; sometimes they are eleven, but more commonly twelve; and in great numbers of instances the employment is continued for fifteen, sixteen, and even eighteen hours consecutively.

20. That in almost every instance the Children work as long as the adults; being sometimes kept at work sixteen, and even eighteen hours without any intermission.[6]

In addition, although most seven-year-olds (particularly girls) would have been working in their parents' own homes or in a nearby household under a 'mistress', a considerable group were already beginning to service the machines in the numerous small workshops; the average age for graduating to 'threading', for instance, was eight, and it is plain from the evidence that seven-year-old threaders were not at all unusual. The process is clearly described by Mr Grainger, whose skill as an observer of the Nottingham scene we salute fraternally across the years; the reader may usefully try to imagine some modern seven-year-old acquaintance at this task.

In this process the threaders sit before a table containing the bobbins which are to be threaded. In the most common kind of bobbin the aperture is sufficiently large to allow the thread to be drawn through it by means of a small hook, which is mounted on a stand and is placed immediately before the threader. But in the *spring-top bobbin* the opening or eye is so small that it must be threaded like a needle. Some idea of the nature of the occupation may be formed from the following facts: the average number of bobbins to be threaded for one machine is probably about 1800; the number of threaders to perform this work is usually two or three; the average time occupied in threading for a machine is two hours or two hours and a half.[7]

And this account must be set in the context of the way in which threading was organised. Mr Grainger took evidence from two Nottingham lace machine operatives in their twenties, who had been threaders as young boys; their description of the life perhaps throws our findings on chaperonage (Chapter 3 – *Out and About*) into a new perspective.

William Hinde: . . . Among the small masters, who have each one or two machines, it is the custom for one set of children to work for two or three masters. The masters often live a long way from each other; children have often to go one or two miles; from

Snenton [*sic*] to Radford is one mile and a half; from Snenton to Hyson Green two miles or better. They are always wanted when the machine comes off, whatever may be the hour of the day or night; they are required just as much by night as by day, unless the men will accommodate the children, which is very rarely done, especially when trade is good . . . . . There is no more regular time for sleeping than for eating; the children often lie down "in the middle of the shop floor when it is warm." Thinks hundreds have been sent to the grave by this work. It is enough to kill the children, going half fed and clothed to work in the night, at this time of the year. (The thermometer last night was 10°.) . . . . . Has seen children, when they have been stupid, from want of rest and food, knocked off the stool by the men. Has seen them knocked off the stool for dropping a bobbin; has himself many a time been served so.

William Pymm: . . . Was formerly a threader; began at eight years old . . . . . The number of threaders employed by the small masters is very great. Threaders begin to work when they are very young; many go as early as seven years old, others at eight and nine . . . . . When he was a threader, was obliged to go whenever the machine came off . . . . . If he got up at 3 or 4 o'clock in the morning, never thought of getting to bed again before night, "many a time not till 12 at night." This often happened; didn't think much about 4, but used to think it was rather hard to get up at 3 . . . . . After having been at Radford, has often had to come back to Snenton, then to go to other parts of the town . . . . . All the threaders and winders who work for small masters have to run about in this way. Used to get very much tired and sleepy; has many a time gone to sleep whilst at work. While waiting for the machine coming off, threaders often lie down to sleep on the floor and tables; "there is a good deal of that kind of thing." Used to get very cold in the winter at night.[8]

In our own time, the fact that there are legal restrictions upon the paid employment of seven-year-olds, based upon the assumption that the sole proper business of the young school-child is education alternating with recreation, does not mean that he is totally incapable of contributing to the family in either work or income. Although parents know that he cannot yet legally have a newspaper round or become a regular errand boy, they also know that, with a certain ingenuity, it would be possible for him to find small errands or other services to do for neighbours for which a few pence a time would be forthcoming; or, within the home, he might take a genuinely useful role in the day-to-day household labour, perhaps even helping to release the older members of the family for additional paid work outside. Some of our seven-year-olds do in fact find ways of earning money from people outside the family which involve them in a fair degree of effort and enterprise: but it is characteristic of our culture's current attitude to children's employment, first, that these children are very much the exception rather than the rule; and secondly that, where this does happen, the child is not expected to hand over any of his earnings to help out the family budget – though from his own choice he may indirectly ease the financial situation, either by providing small treats for the family, or at least by relieving his parents of the need to find him 'spending money'.

Nylon operator's wife:
I know what else he does like doing: he earns this hisself. Well, across the road they throw these big boxes out from the factory, and he loves to carry them home – put them on the yard and break them up with a hammer. These boxes, of wood, chopped up – at the shop, lady up there, you know, they give him sixpence[9] when he's brought all the wood up – does quite well out of it. Boxes thrown out – for nothing – then he struggles with them; swimming with sweat! He's got a big sledge hammer – chops them to pieces for his mother, but he loves to earn something for hisself! [Does he earn quite a reasonable amount?] Quite three shillings – something like that. [Does he do this most weeks?] Most weeks, yes, and then he buys flowers, quarter of tea, wasn't it? He's ever so good-hearted, like. [Could he earn extra from you or his Daddy if he wanted to?] Yes. I always give him little jobs to do, but let him know he's got to *earn* his money, you know what I mean? Let him do a little job – if I didn't *want* it doing, I'd give him a sixpence to do it rather than just giving it out of my purse, you see. Got to work for his money all through his life. [And when he's got money (earned understood), does he again usually spend it at once?] Well, he'll go and buy sweets; or like he did this week, buy flowers, and he was having a party, and he had two shillings, and he went straight down to the beer-off and bought two shilling cakes towards the party.

Machine Operator's wife:
The little girl up the road, Hazel, washes down gates for three-

pence, and Carolyn helps her; and I have to pay my threepence too, she won't do it for nothing! And one or two other things – Hazel's mother gave her a big bag of apples to sell; and my neighbour came past them, and she said to Carolyn "Ooh Carolyn, those apples do look lovely, will you give me one? I could just eat an apple now!" So Carolyn picks her out a nice one – "There you are: sixpence!" "I'm not paying sixpence for an apple!" "All right", says Carolyn, and takes it back; and she dipped in the bag again, and takes out a little one and gives it to her. So my neighbour says "Well, thank you, Carolyn". "That'll be threepence." "Threepence? A little apple like this for threepence? I'm not paying threepence!" "All right", says Carolyn, and takes it back and puts it in the bag again. But that's how she gets; but I think it's really Hazel that's got her into that way of going on, because *she* does a lot of getting spending-money that way.

Caretaker's wife:
They have about one or two shillings each, according to what people give them: they earn it. They take the tomatoes round, say, from the garden [i.e. allotment]; I have my own regular customers, you see, and they might get threepence for taking them round, and it works out between a shilling and two shillings each. Course, in winter he has to depend on what his Dad can give him.

The most common source of outside earnings is running errands, including shopping; but it is not always easy to draw a clear distinction between genuine earnings and more-or-less unsolicited gifts. For instance, when children are sent on errands they may be paid both by the person who commissions them to go and by the recipient of the message. If a child is willing and well-mannered, and has given up his own time to do something obviously useful, the grown-up often feels some obligation to reward him with a little gift either in money or in kind: as in the tipping of adult service workers, the money is given not simply in return for services rendered, but partly as a traditional act of semi-spontaneous generosity. The old, the infirm and the housebound, particularly in working-class areas where telephones and home helps are less abundant and where private cars are much less available to the women of the family, may in fact seriously depend upon the services of young children and be prepared to pay accordingly;[10] but other adults often seem willing to give a child money merely to acknowledge that he has *tried* to be helpful and considerate – or simply because they have enjoyed the pleasure of his company.

The family itself offers the child his chief opportunity of earning, yet here the distinction between earned and unearned income is still more blurred. It seems to be almost universally accepted that children need at least a token personal spending power, however small: only 4% of children receive no pocket money at all. However, the spirit in which this money is given varies, in that some (a small minority) of parents represent it as payment for the child's rather unspecified duties, and in this sense it is conditional upon his earning it, if only by attaining some vague standard of 'being good'. Or pocket money may be increased in consideration of the extra effort a child is now expected to make because of changed family circumstances (a new baby, or mother starting work, for instance), and here again the element of earning comes in.

Insurance inspector's wife:
He's supposed to have a shilling a week if he's good, but I'm afraid he hasn't had it for some weeks! You know it's quite silly, we only started giving it to him recently to give him an idea of the value of money, but he's had it very rarely. [It's definitely provisional on being good?] Yes – good – not being cheeky I suppose is the main thing; but he's not had it very often at all, and he doesn't come and ask for it. If I give it to him he accepts it, and if I don't, he doesn't bother at all. He seems to just know – it's ever so queer!

Loco fireman's wife:
Sometimes he'll go and help his Dad with the garden, but not a set rule; although I do sort of say that their pocket money – they are given it in return for running errands and washing pots and helping with the little ones. I mean, Saturday they have it, and they do two or three errands before they get their money – they get *them* done *very* quickly!

Wholesaler's wife:
We have a system. We both give them a shilling each, actually [per week]; and if they do little odd jobs in the daytime, then they can have an extra shilling. [How often does he earn his shilling?] Oh, he does it most weeks, just little things, lay the table, help clear up. [And this is a shilling for the whole lot?] Yes – in the first place, how it happened, it was with my going to the office,

and I said if they did these small jobs – and in those days it included washing themselves and that sort of thing, but now of course it's automatic – then they'd get this extra shilling; and if they refused, then I wouldn't insist but they'd just lose this money. But I find it's just done now, it's fairly automatic.

The first of the three statements above would appear to refer more to a notional pocket money which is then confiscated out of existence rather than to positive wages (indeed, it is not unknown for pocket money to be instituted for the express purpose of allowing the possibility of fining); the second describes a *way of regarding* pocket money rather than specific payment for individual jobs (similarly it was said of a doctor's child that her pocket money – sixpence – was 'really *meant to be wages*'). The third statement may be judged to refer to a regular shilling for pocket money plus a shilling usually earned: but the situation is in a transitional stage, in that the natural development from here will be two shillings regular unconditional pocket money within a habit of life in which the child expects to take certain unpaid household responsibilities (just as he no longer expects to be explicitly paid for washing himself). Only the third child in this group would be counted as earning for our purposes.

The means by which children earn money from their parents tend to reflect fathers' and mothers' traditional roles. The jobs which mothers offer are almost without exception rather prosaic and down-to-earth, closely linked with the day-to-day running of the household: bringing in the coal, dusting, washing-up or shopping errands.

Paint sprayer's wife:
Yes he does – he's started it. Penny a bed – he makes his bed for a penny. Sometimes he forgets it and then he'll have another go at doing this: penny a bed for so long, then he forgets to do it – then he thinks about it, and "Go on, I've made my bed, a penny!" Penny a bed, you see, a penny a job!

Postman's wife:
For doing jobs we give him perhaps sixpence in a week. He'll wash the pots and vacuum-clean – he'll vacuum-clean his own bedroom – he'll get coke in for you. [You pay him for that?] Not every day – probably by the end of the week you'll have given him sixpence. He'll rock the baby – that's one of his jobs.

Fathers will also sometimes hand out wages for housework, and include help in the garden and car-cleaning among the jobs they will pay for; but, over and above these, they are generous employers where personal service to themselves is concerned. Perhaps the bread-winner, especially when his wages are in his pocket, likes to present an image of indulgence and extravagance; it is certainly true that working-class fathers in particular offer rather high rates for small services made to themselves as opposed to the household generally.

Refuse collector's wife:
> If her Daddy asks her to do anything for him, he always gives her perhaps threepence or sixpence. [What kind of thing would she get that for?] Oh – perhaps fetch his shoes in, or fetch his shirt from downstairs, or his wristwatch.

Coalman's wife:
> Well, perhaps if his Dad says "Fetch me me pullover down", or summat like that – "and I'll give you threepence, or sixpence" – that sort of thing.

Miner's wife:
> He does for cleaning shoes, off his Daddy – threepence a shoe!

Fathers are also inclined to reward children for meeting their whims, in a way which would be rather uncharacteristic of mothers: not that mothers are ungenerous, but they would pay for a job or *give* money for a special purpose, rather than take the role of indulgent patron, like these two fathers:

Labourer's wife:
> Can she earn it? Well, *he's* sometimes, you know, going on that way. [What sort of things?] Oh – the other day he was on to Freda to do him a bit of a dance; and he says "Oh! That's all right!" and give her threepence for that. You know, little daft things like that.

Departmental manager's wife:
> Well, I suppose they *could* do if they wanted to; they do do errands, but they've sort of never done any work *for* money. He could but he hasn't – unless you can call tickling his Dad's feet for threepence earning! He does do that at times. I suppose you could call that earning, couldn't you – look a bit odd if you put

it down there, though! Oh yes, it's a thing his Daddy enjoys. *I* don't – but he does! All the children's done that. [This is a family thing, is it?] Yes, I suppose you could call it that – he loves his feet tickling, though, says it makes him feel lovely and relaxed. [How long do you have to tickle his feet for threepence?] Oh, you have to tickle both feet till he's had enough – not too long. Oh, they'll often come and say to him "Can I tickle your feet, Dad?" [And that's with threepence in mind, is it?] Oh yes, they won't do it without he pays them. That's been passed down. Jennifer [eldest, seventeen] *used* to do it for nothing, until she realised she could get money for doing it. Well, you'd do anything for a bit of spending money, wouldn't you?

The figures presented in Table 24 refer to earning from parents only, since we were interested in parents' attitudes on this question. Opportunities for earning money from outsiders vary according to the neighbourhood; but theoretically children start off equal in the possibility of earning the occasional penny or two from their own parents. Whether they do so or not will thus depend upon the conjunction of the child's inclination and the parents' approval. We asked (Question 91): 'Could he earn extra money from you or his Daddy if he wanted to? Does he ever?' Answers were coded into

Table 24   *Children's earnings from their parents*

	social class					summary		
	I&II	IIIwc	III man	IV	V	I&II, IIIwc	IIIman, IV,V	overall popn.
	%	%	%	%	%	%	%	%
Does earn								
boys	55	50	62	62	54	53	61	59
girls	52	35	50	56	51	44	52	50
both	54	42	56	59	53	48	56	54
Parents won't allow								
boys	29	34	30	32	35	32	31	31
girls	33	49	35	32	37	41	35	37
both	31	42	32	32	37	36	33	34

No significant sex or class differences

three categories: Yes, he does; He could, but doesn't; Parents would not allow this.

Overall, more than half our seven-year-olds do earn money from their parents beyond ordinary pocket money income; but neither social class nor sex differences reach significance level. The only noteworthy difference is the finding that shop and clerical workers' daughters are less likely than other children to earn, mainly because their parents won't allow it: 65% of them don't earn, and 49% would not be allowed to if they wanted to. We have no ready explanation for this observation.

What clearly emerges from the second half of this table, however, is that right across the class range there is a substantial body of parents who 'don't believe in' ever paying their children for jobs done. Their reasons boil down to the two questions of what is *right* and what is *expedient*: only in a very few cases is it a question of resources – 'We'd like her to, but we haven't got it' (disabled plasterer's wife). The idea that it is wrong to pay for children's services is expressed in answers such as 'I won't. I think that's bribery' (from a labourer's wife), or put more explicitly in terms such as this, from Ivan's mother:

School caretaker's wife:
> Well, we've never done it. To tell you the honest truth, I don't altogether agree, because I've seen so much of this "well I'll clean the windows for you, Mummy, for a shilling", but I don't agree with it. I do think that if there's any jobs to do they should be done freely and because they live in a community – which I've taught them that much. I mean everybody should help everybody else, and not do it for money. The same as if they go errands for other people, I do *not* like other people to give them money; it gives the impression that you can only do it for a reward, and I don't agree, I'm very much against it actually. [So if he asked you, you would say no?] No, I wouldn't have a job for money – I would encourage him to *do* the job, and if he was *told* to do a job I'm afraid he would do it . . . . . I always say this, well, if anybody's going to do anything, I want them to do it 'cause they want to, not because they've got to get paid for it. Well, it's right really, you know.

Ivan's mother applies her principle to *all* earning; but another version of this basic attitude is that children owe their parents a certain duty which should not be paid for, but that this does not apply to earning from other people. 'I don't believe in her running errands for money', says a market stallholder's wife, ' – not to their parents, but if she does it for someone else and gets money by it, that's all right'.

The question of expedience is in fact closely linked to the principle and is often mentioned at the same time, as Ivan's mother does in her second sentence: that paying for help might create a precedent which the child is likely to abuse.

Window cleaner's wife:
> To tell you the truth, I haven't done that *because* they'd fully expect it for ever, wouldn't they? Once you start something like that – I think that's wrong – once you start it, I mean they'd p'raps turn round and say I'm not doing that unless you give me so-and-so.

Lorry driver's wife:
> Not while he's so small – when he gets older, I mean. I don't believe in it when they're so small really – I think if they do a thing with a good heart . . . I mean, going an errand for you, I don't believe in saying "I'll give you a penny if you go so-and-so" – 'cause, you know, they'll probably come out with "Oh, if you want me to go an errand I want a penny!"

The idea that 'once you've started it, they expect to be paid for everything they do – you're best not to start it' was borne out by a number of mothers whose children had in fact reached this stage. 'He might just go an errand for me and I might just give him a copper or two or something like that', said a labourer's wife – 'in fact they wouldn't *do* an errand without the coppers'.

Bus driver's wife:
> She's got another habit – if her Dad'll say to her "Go and fetch some sweets for the children", crafty, she'll say "Eh? Eh? I can't hear you", you know; and he'll say "Right, you can have three-pence" – so that clears her deafness! She's dead crafty about that.

Railwayman's wife:
> Well, same as she says "I'll clear the table for you, but I want threepence". She's all there, you know, Vicky is! [Do you pay her the threepence?] Well, it all depends how bad I want the table clearing! She's spoilt, thoroughly spoilt, I think myself.

The idea that children do have some obligation, even if more honoured in the breach than the observance, to contribute without reward to the running of the household comes up again shortly when we look closely at children's regular unpaid chores; in terms of family obligations, however, a few mothers made a different objection to earning: essentially that, if the money was there to be earned, it ought to be freely available to the child as a full member of the family, and not conditional on his work.

Lorry driver's wife:
Well, I've never thought about that. I used to tell Lena [elder sister] "I'll give you two shillings if you'll wash the pots", but she never did, so it's a waste of time, isn't it? [Would you let Elaine if she asked?] I wouldn't mind, but I don't think it's right to exploit children. If she wanted it for anything special, I'd give it her, she wouldn't have to ask anyway. I mean, the others have grown up right and she's the same. They know how much you've got and that's it.

Technical sales representative's wife:
If she *wanted* to, yes. But we don't say that "if you do this for us you'll have threepence", or anything like that. If *she* said "If I do this, can I have threepence?" – well, she can do it. [But you wouldn't suggest it?] No. Because I wouldn't like her to think that she'd got to do jobs to get money – I don't believe in that. She's never asked to do it, but if she asked she could – to try and encourage her a bit to earn something.

The objection to 'exploitation' does not, it is clear, prevent the child earning if he wishes to (presumably under favourable terms of employment!); for these mothers, as for the rest of the two-thirds of the sample whose children could or already do earn money at home, earning gives the child an opportunity for independence and initiative, and is therefore to be encouraged. Children are rarely pushed into earning, however; the motive force normally comes from the child himself, and is taken up by the parent. Often the child will in fact lose interest when he finds that real effort is required of him, and parents then tend to leave it at that; but where the child really wishes to earn, parents who do not disapprove in principle will take positive steps to make it possible for him.

Sales representative's wife:
Oh yes, we make it easy for them, you see; they do earn, yes,

if we think there's something they want is worth having. [How do you make it easy for them?] Finding them jobs – he cleans the kettle for me, I give him threepence, you see, if he polishes that; and he helps Daddy clean the car sometimes, and he'll sweep the garden and path, and go shopping.

Student teacher's wife (herself a teacher):
Well, we've suggested this, but it doesn't really work, does it? [Father:] What did she do last summer? She said "I'll mow the lawn for you if you'll – " what was it? If you'll give me a shilling. [Mother:] And she mowed a quarter of it, and told him he owed her threepence! [Father:] And then she went on and did another quarter and made it sixpence! [Mother:] When the strength was back again! [Father:] But that's the nearest she's been to deciding whether she could earn anything, probably.

University teacher's wife:
I'll find her some little job. She doesn't very often. Very occasionally. She might do the dusting, or I have asked her to tidy her room in a way that's more complete than I would expect – I've once or twice said "Do the whole room really perfectly so that nothing has to be done, and you can have sixpence each". [You think this is a good principle?] I don't think it's a good principle that she should expect to be paid for doing jobs about the house, but if it's more than she's *normally* expected to do, then it's for the extra. I think it's a good principle that she should be able to earn money if she wants to earn money – I mean I would *manufacture* some job for her.

'Oh, she saves, don't worry, and she counts and counts and counts!'
'It's all gone by the time she arrives back here'
Finding out how much pocket money a child has at his disposal is not a simple matter of asking 'how much?' and being given a figure. Even when the distinction between pocket money and earnings has been sorted out, all sorts of complications remain. What is the basic sum per week? If given by one parent, does the other parent also contribute? What about grandparents, older siblings and other regular visitors – do they give a regular amount that should be taken into account? Is this child's pocket money supposed to cover regular legitimate expenses such as bus fares, Sunday School collections or school biscuits, which other mothers might budget for separately? If he saves part of the money, does he do so voluntarily? If he is obliged to put part of it away in

bank or even money box, can he draw out that money at any time and for whatever expenditure? Do all his sweets have to be bought out of his pocket money, or does his mother provide a basic sweet ration in addition? And so on.

We were looking for an estimate of the child's basic spending power, and we calculated this on the basis of any unearned money, from whatever source, which he could *count on* receiving and controlling each week. Irregular 'tips' were discounted, as were involuntary savings over which the child had no control; however, a regular savings stamp which the child could at his own whim withdraw was counted as pocket money. Regular expenses connected with school, classes, church or library were also deducted. The sweets problem was solved rather arbitrarily by adding five (new) pence to the basic figure if the parents provided sweets separately, without prejudice to whether the child chose to spend his pocket money on sweets. Teasing out a final estimate was still not easy, as can be seen from the following dialogue.

Bricklayer's wife:
Yes, at the weekends Dad gives him some money; I give him some money, well he'll spend it straight away, and the money their Dad gives them, well they save that. I get them a two-and-six saving stamp to put in their books. [So that's two-and-six for saving . . .] Yes, for saving. And at night, you know, the ice-cream man, they get icecream. If they see . . . well, if they've enough saved, and they see a toy in the shop window, well, if they want it really desperate, I really get there and let them have it, you know; but I make him lift his own money, I make him lift his own savings. [He *has* to save some?] Some. [And if he wanted to spend that half-crown his Daddy gave him at once, would you say "No, you've got to save it?"] No, well, I don't let them spend it *all*, you know what I mean. I say "Well, put *something* back"; because they need a shilling for Cub night, and I always make him save. It's not that I'm miserable, but I want them to understand, you know what I mean. I say "Well put some away for your Cub money, because Mummy won't give it to you otherwise, you know" – which they will do. [That shilling could come out of the two-and-six?] Yes. [How much do *you* give them?] Well, I give them money all the while, you know. At the weekend I usually give them two shillings. [Two shillings each?] Yes, they can spend that. [Is there anyone else who gives Roy money?] Well, when my friend comes, they usually give them

money, and I say don't spend that. Well, they spend so much and they put some away for Cub money. [How much?] Well, probably about a shilling each, you know, they need really two shillings for Cubs night. They put a shilling away each. [And this money from your friends they get regularly, they can count on that?] Oh yes, yes. Well, he comes up Friday night, he gives them some money; and they'll go to the shop and buy crisps and sweets Saturday afternoon. Or if they wash his car, well he will give them two-and-six for that. They do give that to me for the stamps, that's extra for the savings stamps for when they go to Ireland [in the summer], you know. [And the other money they get from your friend – the odd sixpence?] Yes. [Ever a shilling, one-and-sixpence . . . ?] Yes – I don't like them to have a *lot* of money. [You like them to understand the value of it?] The value of it, yes, 'cause otherwise they want a lot of money. [So he has to save, and he has some to spend, and if he wants to spend what he has saved, he can do so? What about the money he's saving up for Ireland?] Well, as I tell you, if he goes out at the weekend and he'll see a toy that he wants, well, I say "Well, all right, you can lift your savings money, and I'll give you the rest" – if he needs some money towards it, you know, I'll give it to him. [You'll give it as you can afford . . . ?] Yes. [And do you buy him sweets apart from these they buy themselves?] Well, I give them their biscuit money each morning. They have three-pence each morning, and that's not counted in their bus fare, and then they have a sweet or cake or whatever they want, coming from school – you know, they can't wait till they get home.[11]

In practice, the amounts given ranged from nothing at all (4%) to over 50p (2%) per week. In addition, there was a group who received no fixed pocket money but who were given small sums of money as and when they demanded it and their parents could find it. These we refer to as the *ad hoc* group: they are *not* children who are given a fixed sum in instalments through the week, but those whose parents cannot estimate the total weekly sum because it is in fact disbursed *ad hoc* and varies from one week to the next. '*Ad hoc*' children are excluded from the estimates of pocket money rates in Table 25 for this reason.

To round off our information, we also asked 'If he wants extra money for something, do you give it to him?' Obviously the *ad hoc* group was excluded from this question, since they had no basic sum to which additional money might be considered 'extra'. We

Table 25 *Children's unearned income and savings as a function of social class*

	social class					summary		
	I&II	IIIwc	III Man	IV	V	I&II, IIIwc	IIIman, IV,V	overall popn.
	%	%	%	%	%	%	%	%
No pocket money at all	3	1	5	5	4	2	5	4
Significance: trend	n.s.					m.class/w.class		n.s.
Ad hoc pocket money only	10	17	15	19	21	13	16	16
Significance: trend	↗ **					m.class/w.class		n.s.
Average weekly pocket money	13p	15p	17p	18p	18p	14p	18p	17p
Significance: trend	↗ ****					m.class/w.class		****
	%	%	%	%	%	%	%	%
Pocket money 20p or more weekly	21	30	43	45	46	25	44	39
Significance: trend	↗ ****					m.class/w.class		****
'Extra' given freely when possible	12	11	26	20	25	12	25	21
Significance: trend	↗ ***					m.class/w.class		****
Extra restricted, not forbidden	71	76	63	67	60	73	63	66
Significance: trend	↘ *					m.class/w.class		**
Compulsory saving	18	28	17	15	13	22	16	18
Significance: trend	n.s.					m.class/w.class		n.s.
Money always spent within the week	10	22	29	39	52	16	34	29
Significance: trend	↗ ****					m.class/w.class		****

ad hoc payments excluded

tried to discover whether extras would be given freely (within what the mother could afford) or whether limits of amount or purpose were imposed.

The most striking finding is that as we move down the social scale, although the family income tends to decrease, average pocket money tends to increase. Thus, while children in the professional/ managerial group were receiving an average of 13p per week at the time of the interview,[12] children of unskilled manual workers averaged 18p per week: the class trends are very clear and consistent, whether one uses average pocket money as the basis or takes the proportion of children receiving 'high' pocket money rates (i.e. 20p or more). The giving of 'extras' follows the same trend: far from low pocket money being made up for with extras, it is the children with plenty who are likeliest to be given more on demand.

The findings on savings compound the class differences which characterise working-class children as the big spenders on the seven-year-old scene. Although the minority group who are compelled to save show no significant class differences (other than an interesting and predictable rise in Class III white collar), the *habit* of saving is strongly class-influenced. Our criterion for voluntary saving was simply that the child should sometimes keep some of his money for at least a week before spending it, i.e. that he would sometimes allow an accumulation of one week's money with the next. On this not very taxing criterion, most children (71%) do save either voluntarily or compulsorily: but the class trend runs consistently from 90% in Class I and II to 48% in Class V. Put the other way round, and perhaps more succinctly, 52% of Class V children *always* spend their money within the week, whereas only 10% of Class I and II children do so.

We may briefly illustrate some of the attitudes behind these findings in the mother's own words.

The *ad hoc* group and those who give extra money freely on top of the basic sum both reflect a wish to indulge children while the money is available – not just available today in contrast to next week, but nowadays as opposed to 'in the bad old days'. 'Kiddies today *need* that bit more', said a lamp room attendant's wife; 'they're not satisfied with threepence a week!'

Unemployed labourer's wife:
He has about a shilling most weeks, sometimes two; but he doesn't spend it, he spends yourn! No, he hides it in this poly-

thene box he's got; and when the icecream man comes, he'll say "Mam, gimme fourpence for an icecream!" I'll say "Where's that shilling I gi' you, then, take some of that". "No", he says, "I can't spend that, I'm saving that, *you* give me some" – and you have to give him some more! But they all have about three-pence in the morning and threepence after dinner, for their sweets and that. [If he wants extra money for something, do you give it to him?] Ooh yes – for a little car or owt like that, oh I would. What I could afford, like – I mean I might not *have* it, but if I had it I'd gi' it him, I like to be generous. I think . . . I was brought up hard myself, my parents were separated, and I realise now what a struggle my mother had to feed us and that; but I didn't have anything, and I think when you remember that in your own childhood, it makes you want to give your own a bit more than what *you* had – to make up for it, like.

Driver's wife:
My mum and dad were very mean, and I never had much really, I hadn't, and I always said I'd try to give my kids more than what I got . . . . . Now I've got a few more coppers in my purse, now I'm working. I go to town every Saturday – you know, normally I couldn't afford to get her books, but now she gets something every week, and it's only through me working, like.

For these parents, meanness versus generosity is the issue: money is for spending while it's there, and you'd have to be pretty 'skinny' (as the children say) to deny it to your own child if you've got it in your pocket: 'Ooh aye', said a baker's wife, 'I don't begrudge him anything'. The child learns that there are good times and bad times to ask for money: 'If I'm a bit flush at any time, same as when the gas-man's been,[13] I might give her sixpence extra for ice-cream', said a railwayman's wife.

Crane driver's wife:
Well, he gets two-and-six on a Friday and then the odd three-pences and sixpences off and on in the week: about three-and-six altogether, or even up to five shillings if his daddy has a drink! They'll keep getting the money out of him then – saying "Come on, Daddy, give us some more money!" They're terrors!

At the same time, not every child understands that money given freely when it is there is simply not to be had on other occasions;

these parents often explicitly praise a child's acceptance of this situation. Sandy (page 44) is deeply appreciated because he doesn't, like his siblings, 'pester and pester – keep asking and asking', but just says 'Can't you afford it?' – 'I'll say "I'll give you something on Friday", and then he'll say "All right, Mum." ' Such a child is, in effect, keeping his side of the *ad hoc* bargain, and therefore deserves its benefits.

Miner's wife:
> I don't like to refuse her, I don't. Her Daddy doesn't, he doesn't refuse her either. Well, she doesn't say anything if we *can't* afford it.

As we move up the class scale, the amount of pocket money, while decreasing, is much more predictable in the sense that the child knows what he can count on and can theoretically work out his income for weeks in advance. Sometimes the amount will be subject to variation, but typically the variation itself will be controlled by fixed and sometimes highly complicated rules.

Professional engineer's wife:
> We don't give them much. We give them a penny per year of their age plus a penny, so she has eightpence a week. If at the end of the week she's spent it wisely, if she hasn't spent it on sweets, she gets a bonus of half the amount she hasn't spent: you know, if she hasn't spent *any* of her pocket money she gets fourpence bonus, so she'll have a shilling. We try to encourage them not to spend it on sweets. [What do you mean by 'wisely' – what would count for a bonus?] They wouldn't get a bonus if they spent their pocket money on icecream, but if they bought a writing book or crayons or something like that they get a bonus for it.

Clergyman's wife:
> The last six weeks before Christmas they are allowed to pay their money back in the Family Bank, and I keep a close account of how much every child has got, so that at the end of every week it's doubled; and it comes accumulative so that, at the end of three weeks, if they have a shilling in the Bank, then I put another shilling in and make it two shillings. By Christmas they've usually managed to accumulate about a pound to buy their Christmas presents.

The provision of 'extras' further up the class scale is also likelier to be hedged around with rules and provisos as to how much, what for and in what circumstances.

[If he wants extra money for something, do you give it to him?]

Electrician's wife:
Well, it depends what he wants it for. I mean, when he came out of school last night, he said "Can I have sixpence?" – I said no. I mean, I just don't part with it like that, you know. I don't believe in it. I don't think they want too much. But I mean sixpence, mind you, not a penny, sixpence! I said "Oh no, not today". So it all depends – if it was something special I would, but not just off like that!

Scientist's wife:
Well, it depends – supposing he wants something at about two shillings, and he's saved three weeks' spending money [6d per week], well, I put the other sixpence to it. We don't begrudge them money on books and things like that.

Widow in own business:
Well, it would depend what it was for. If it was for something I felt would be useful to him, I would give it him straight away – I would buy it *for* him. If it's anything like a car, that he doesn't really need and it's a whim, then I'd make him save half and give him the other half – and I make him save purposely to make him wait, in the hopes that the thing he wants he'll go off before he's got his money. I think I'm as crafty as he is!

Wholesaler's wife:
Well, it would depend what it was for – I mean if he wanted an extra soldier, well, he'd have to pay for it himself; but say swimming or some school activity, then I would pay for it. I mean, we introduced [pocket money] with the idea that they should have so much money to spend on their own things, but not just "I've seen so-and-so and I want it". If it was extra, it would have to be something sort of educational.

University teacher's wife:
It depends what it was for; well, shall we say he wanted the next set of Meccano, and there was something he wanted to build, and he'd got three-quarters or two-thirds of the money,

then I would *advance* it. [To be paid back?] I think so, because everything has to be fair in this family.

The principle of making loans against future expectations obviously stands up only in a context of predictable expectations plus a habit of saving: loans do not arise among the *ad hoc* group, since money for them is either there to be given or not there at all. That the child has made the effort to save is quite usually the precondition of a loan.

Research scientist's wife:
Sometimes I compromise, if it's something he wants *very* much and it would take him weeks and weeks to save: I might tell him to save up for four weeks, even if it is more expensive, because four weeks is a terribly long time to save [child has 6d per week]; and then I insist that he gives me the two shillings that he has saved during the four weeks, and perhaps what he has bought costs four shillings. But he doesn't realise the difference yet, and I think *he* feels that he has given me back what I have spent; and I think that is quite all right, as long as he realises that he can't just borrow from me indefinitely.

It is clear that the explicit purpose of a fixed rate of pocket money is not simply to give the child spending power – *ad hoc* hand-outs serve that purpose well enough – but to allow him to budget and plan his resources, and, in short, to make him understand that 'money doesn't grow on trees'. Loans convey the same deliberate message: 'He *must* pay it back, it may be hard, it's not for my sake, but I think it's to sort of, you know, teach him the value of money', says a tobacco worker's wife. A warehouse manager's child has 25p per week, but out of this must pay the expenses of his pet rabbit and also contribute some token amount to the bank account which was opened in his name when he was born: 'We've sort of explained to him that this is money in the bank and one day he'll want it . . . . . The idea of his money, I mean we don't give him pocket money to live on, we give him pocket money to make him realise that, you know, it's not a bottomless pit – he has to learn to get some sense of value for money'.

While the table shows a greater inclination to save among middle-class children, it does not indicate what the child is saving for. There is, however, some evidence from the transcripts that middle-class children tend to save up for some possession – an addition to a collection (Lego or Meccano parts, dolls' outfits, etc.) – or for a better toy than they could buy with one week's money, whereas the working-class child's tradition is to save 'for his holidays' – i.e. in order to have plenty of spending money for icecream, fizzy drinks and amusements on summer seaside trips. To have 'money to burn' in one glorious extravagant fling is a goal worth striving for: but it is also interesting that saving for the holidays is rarely mentioned by middle-class mothers, which suggests that incidental holiday expenses are one hidden benefit which middle class children receive independent of stated pocket money rates.

In fact, in interpreting all these findings we must bear in mind that children of this age tend to receive many benefits in kind rather than in hard cash, and that this will be particularly true of children further up the social scale. Play-space and equipment, reference books and outings are all more easily come by for the middle-class child; his home is much more likely to carry a supply of drawing and writing paper, pencils and crayons, and the other consumables of children's creative and educational activity, where a working-class child will usually have to buy such things for himself in expensive small quantities. Most middle-class mothers expect to keep a stock of fresh fruit – apples, oranges and bananas – as part of the day-to-day household stores, and will not object to the child helping himself within reason; many working-class children, however, buy fruit with their own money or do without. In general, the further up the class ladder, the larger the family stocks of any commodities in daily use: food storage facilities are better, money can be spent in larger quantities at a time, goods can be transported with ease; so that, while the poorer child needs money fairly frequently to buy snacks and titbits from the corner shop, children from more affluent families can simply go to the pantry or raid the fridge or the deep freeze.

It is important to understand, however, that class differences in attitudes to pocket money occur not merely in this context of differing standards of living but also as an expression of differing ways of life. Salaried workers normally receive their money on a monthly basis; it will be paid directly into a bank account, and decisions will then be made as to how much will be withdrawn each week to meet cash expenditure, how bills will be paid and so on. A large proportion of the money going in and out of a salaried worker's possession will never be handled as such, and transactions will be conducted in comparatively abstract terms. In such a context, it may well be more convenient to buy commodities in large quantities and to pay by cheque. The total pattern is conducive to taking thought for the morrow; and implicit in the pattern are a distrust for impulse spending, a habit of saving and an interest in obtaining value for money that almost amounts to a moral duty. What Brian Jackson calls 'the middle-class ethic of postponed pleasure'[14] can be seen sharply focussed in middle-class attitudes to getting and spending: but these form only one aspect of an ethic which holds good throughout the middle-class mode of life and is faithfully reflected in middle-class child-rearing patterns generally.

By contrast, the wage-earner will tend to have a rather less stable amount coming in but in much more tangible form. The notes and coins in his weekly wage packet are there for the spending, and most of them will in fact be paid out within the week for immediate needs. If he wishes to meet commitments extending beyond next pay-day, a deliberate effort will have to be made to put aside real cash. With little margin, sudden unforeseen expenses can be catastrophic; if there happens to be no urgent necessity of the moment, however, minor windfalls may be joyfully squandered on family treats. Having cash in hand is equated with enjoying the good life: the relationship between money and enjoyment is specific and direct.[15] In Richard Hoggart's words, 'the immediate and present nature of working-class life puts a premium on the taking of pleasure now, discourages planning for some future goal, or in the light of some ideal'.[16] The working-class child already begins to fall into this traditional pattern of life in his use of pocket money.

'He did start bringing the coal in because he fancied it, but this quickly faded out, he found it manly but boring . . .'

The question of the seven-year-old's work role has already been approached in relation to the child's possibility of earning; but to complete our picture of the child's place in the family economic system we wanted to know how far he was in fact expected to contribute any unpaid effort to the general work of the household. Just as we saw with children who put a lot of energy into earning money, those who take a really large share of the housework are the exception at seven, and they seem to do so entirely as a matter of their own choice: such a child is domesticated by inclination and busy by temperament.

Cook's wife:
As far as I'm concerned, she's a marvellous child in what she can

do; you can't name anything that she can't do. She can do almost anything – cleaning, washing pots; she makes the fire up, she tries to cook, which frightens me to death if I'm not there. I don't mind if I'm there to watch, but sometimes she'll try and mash a cup of tea when I'm not there, and it harasses me a bit, although I think it's wonderful that she can do this type of thing . . . . . Actually I don't think – I've never *told* Felicity to do anything. I mean, I've always been so independent myself, I like to get on you know, and I've sort of never encouraged them, but this one's turned out with no effort at all; she does everything. The other one, if he can get out of not doing any – I mean, now and again we have to make *him* do something, because *she* seems to be on all the time doing something. She's marvellous as regards that, I mean she's only got to look at the fire and see it's going down, and it's made up. Oh, she's very handy. I don't think I appreciated it before I went to work; but in the mornings it's marvellous, she'll wash the breakfast things up, and dry them, and put them away – well it's really a big help first thing in the morning when you're going out.

Prison officer's wife:
She can't sit still for a minute, always got to be doing something, I mean if it's only doing a bit of washing in the sink. Oh, you know she'll get the Vim and say "I'll wash the sink out for you" – that's one of her favourite pastimes.

Ex-army private's wife (husband now unemployed):
He washes pots, makes beds, polishes the brass, tidies the front room, sweeps the floor – he seems pleased to do it.

Essentially, the difference between working for money and doing one's regular chores is that the child can elect *not* to do paid work without incurring reproach, whereas regular allotted household chores *have* to be done (though it is not unknown for children of initiative to sub-contract their own jobs to younger siblings at sweated labour rates). Nobody worries if the child does not wish to earn; but a considerable proportion of mothers think that it should be part of the child's social development to begin to accept some responsibility in the home, at least for tidying up the mess that he himself has made. Fifty-five per cent overall expect the child to take some share in the ordinary household jobs; and 82% expect at least some help from the child in tidying up his own things, though only 65% actually get any. Table 26 shows the child's participation in regular household tasks, while Table 27 explores mothers' attitudes on whether the child should keep his

Table 26   *Children's household chores*

	social class						summary	
	I&II	IIIwc	III man	IV	V	I&II, IIIwc	IIIman, IV,V	overall popn.
	%	%	%	%	%	%	%	%
Job regularly done								
boys	25	32	28	22	25	28	26	27
girls	37	37	33	28	13	37	30	32
both	31	34	30	25	18	32	28	29

Sex and class differences not significant

	%	%	%	%	%	%	%	%
No help expected								
boys	43	35	48	51	56	39	49	47
girls	26	41	45	53	59	33	49	44
both	35	38	47	52	58	36	49	45

Significance: trend $\nearrow$ ****   m.class/w.class ***
                    between sexes   n.s.

own things in order. Household tasks were investigated by asking (Question 92):

> We'd like to know about the sort of jobs children do around the house at this age. Is there any little job you expect N to do now (without being paid)?
> Is that something he does as a regular thing, or just when he feels like it?
> Suppose he's too busy doing something of his own one day – what happens?

Additional questions were asked (see Appendix I) to discover whether the child took occasional responsibility for the care of younger siblings or full responsibility for looking after a pet. Answers were classified under three headings: jobs regularly done; no regular job, but child expected to help; no help expected.

Such sex differences as can be seen in this table are confined to the top and bottom classes: girls are more likely to have regular jobs in the professional/managerial class, boys in the unskilled group. The general inconsistency of the first half of this table made us wonder whether regular household chores were more closely associated with family size, family position of the child, mothers at work, or the area (central, estate or suburban) in which the child lived. All of these possible factors were tested for, but none gave significant results.

It must of course be remembered that the doing of a regular job has two components: the mother's expectations and the child's own inclination to do the job. Thus whether the job is in fact done is not an adequate guide to the pressures put on children, which are shown better in the second part of Table 26. Bearing in mind the residual third category, where the child has no special job but is expected to help generally with housework, the two halves of the table can usefully be compared. For instance, a difference between girls in the two middle-class groups now appears: at first sight, their position is similar, in that precisely the same proportions do regular jobs; but in fact among Class I and II girls the majority of those who do not have regular jobs are at least expected to help, whereas among Class IIIwc girls the majority of those without regular jobs are *not* expected to help. Girls in the top class are more likely than any other class/sex group to be pressed to help in the house, whereas girls in the unskilled group are least likely to experience this.

The social class gradient in favour of diminishing expectations as one descends the social scale is clear, and is of interest in that, on a simple economic hypothesis, one would expect more need of help at the lower end of the scale. Richard Hoggart has drawn attention to the inconsistency in economic terms of what he thinks of as working-class traditions of indulgence: 'the remarkable feature, in view of how much the mother has to do and how short is spare money, is that they [the children] are asked to do so little and that spare-time money-making is so often regarded as for their own pockets. How often do the children wash up? How often are they bought disproportionately expensive presents? . . . . . Parents expect and encourage the children, even in adolescence, to do little to support the house in labour or money . . . . . "ye'r only young once" '.[17] In the words of a maintenance worker's wife, 'Children are only children once, and if you're going to force them to do these things you're going to bring them up all wrong'.

One of the more obviously helpful things that a seven-year-old might be asked to do is to keep an eye on the baby or amuse a toddler for a little while; and the stereotype of the working-class girl child often seems to include an image of the little mother bearing responsibility beyond her years. If we look at the children

Table 27 *Pressure on children to tidy up their own toys*

	social class					summary		
	I&II	IIIwc	III man	IV	V	I&II, IIIwc	IIIman, IV,V	overall popn.
	%	%	%	%	%	%	%	%
Child does it himself								
boys	36	40	38	42	33	38	39	38
girls	34	29	41	41	44	32	41	39
both	35	34	40	41	38	35	40	39

No significant differences

Child/mother do it together								
boys	30	31	22	27	26	31	24	26
girls	34	24	26	35	10	30	26	27
both	32	28	24	31	18	30	25	26

No significant differences

Mother reckons to do it herself								
boys	9	10	23	17	33	9	23	19
girls	14	16	17	14	28	15	18	17
both	11	13	20	15	31	12	20	18

Significance: ↗ ****   m.class/w.class *
between sexes n.s.

who do in fact have siblings aged five or less (two-thirds of our sample), almost all of them take an occasional share in 'minding' them, but significantly more middle-class children (94%) than working-class children (82%) do so. Girls are rather more involved in this way than boys (90% against 80%). When it comes to leaving the seven-year-old in sole charge of the younger child, the figures drop to 45% and the small overall class differences disappear altogether; sex differences in the working-class group harden, however, to 53% of working-class girls occasionally given sole charge, against only 36% of working-class boys. Once again, working-class boys seem more able to escape responsibility if they wish to.

The main questions on which we based our data in Table 27 were:

27. Some children are careful with their toys when they are using them, but they leave them about carelessly so that they get broken that way. Does N do that?
28. Do you take any trouble to get him to look after his toys?
29. Do you expect him to keep them tidy himself, or do you reckon to tidy up after him?

Behaviour and attitudes were coded on a four-way classification: child does it himself; child and mother do it together; child expected to tidy but doesn't; mother reckons to do it herself.

Sex differences in this table do not reach significance. In all, 64% of children do clear up their own things (39% alone and 26% with their mothers' help), but in a further 17% of cases the child is supposed to help but does not do so in practice. 'I *try*, but I'm afraid it all falls on deaf ears', said a building worker's wife; 'It's all right for a day or two and then, bingo, we're back to normal!' Class differences are not significant where positive pressure to tidy is concerned, but the class trend reaches a high level of significance with regard to mothers who do not expect their children to do any tidying at all. Only 11% of Class I and II mothers have such low expectations, compared at the other end of the scale with 31% of Class v mothers. Among the mothers whose expectations are thwarted, the fact that they do have such expectations can also be class-linked: 23% of middle-class mothers fall into this group, decreasing to only 8% in Class v (difference between middle and working classes ****). There is a small but significant interaction effect between class and sex, in that more boys than girls in the working class are free from pressure to tidy up their toys, whereas in the middle class boys are more likely than girls to be pressed to do so ($p < 0.04$).

With these figures in mind, we can consider the real nature of the problem. For most mothers, getting the seven-year-old to tidy up is more trouble than it can be worth in here-and-now terms: more time and energy are expended in persuading him to do it (and in completing the job later to her own satisfaction) than in doing the whole thing herself without fuss.

Foreman's wife:

I try – I've tried. [Laughs] – I've tried shouting me head off, I've tried *all* sorts, but no; as I say, he's a charming child, and he just looks at you, and he says "Oh Mum, will you help me please?" and I automatically do. I think a lot of it's yourself, isn't it? – if you think to yourself, oh, it's quicker to do it myself than argue.

The phrases which mothers use in talking about this make it clear that they regard getting a child to tidy up as hard work on their part. Those who think they themselves are lazy are referring to their failure to insist on the child helping, not to their own refusal to tidy for him: 'I used to make him, but since I've had the last kiddy I've less patience'; 'I know it's wrong, but it's quicker'; 'I do have a concentrated effort [to make him help], but I'm afraid it falls away again and I forget'; 'I feel too old to be bothered with this – when you're older you haven't got the patience you see'; 'I think I tend to be a bit slack about it'; 'I haven't that much time to spare'. Children who are encouraged or pressured to tidy up are thus taking part in a deliberate training exercise which, except in a very few cases, is not expected to pay off for some time yet in terms of saving the mother trouble.

Transport manager's wife:

I try – I endeavour to – I think there comes a time, I hope by the time he's eight, when he *should* do a certain amount. I don't know whether it's going to work, quite frankly, but no, I do think that you should aim at this.

Greengrocer's wife:

Well, he has to have a good try . . . we know that he's not going to make a perfect job of straightening at this age, but if we don't start, then he won't make a perfect job of it if you start him at eleven, will he?

Coal merchant's wife:

It's no use *expecting* her to do anything, but I just keep persevering. I think it's better that she has somebody that perseveres.

Labourer's wife:

I think it's good training for them. If they learn to be tidy now, it'll stop with them.

Class differences can thus be accounted for as part of the pattern by which parents further down the class scale are less inclined to invest time and effort in projects which do not show immediate results. In the upper reaches of the scale, however, not only are long-term aims and long-delayed rewards part of the ethic and the way of life: so too is the idea of reciprocal duties and obligations, which, as we have seen,[18] forms a central tenet of the democratic principle of child upbringing favoured by the upper sections of the class continuum. Thus as one moves up the scale one finds greater concern that the child should begin to understand that life is a pattern of rights and responsibilities, binding upon both parents and children: on an issue such as tidying, he must learn that it is expected that people do not leave their own mess for others to clear up. Because this is a matter of *principle*, mothers further up the scale go to some trouble to convey these expectations, even if they do not suceed in obtaining the actual behaviour they want; they do not feel it right simply to opt out by indulging the child, though they know this would be easier in the short run.

It must be added, however, that material aspects of differing life-styles also contribute. If a child is 'off out' most of the time, for instance, he will not cause so much untidiness in the house; if he has very few possessions, again it is difficult for him to make things very untidy. A mother in very deprived circumstances said 'We've never bothered [to get him to keep his toys tidy], 'cause he han't had enough to bother *with*, do you know what I mean?' Similarly, a very poor household is less conducive to housepride than one in which tidiness and cleanliness are the context for a satisfying display of material possessions: 'Well, we're never straight here', says a mother who has settled for cheerful passivity. Children living in less cramped conditions, with more room to themselves and more facilities for their play, are in fact likely to make more work than the child whose play is with just a few toys on the living-room floor. In particular, the kinds of creative play sessions which emerge from a life-style of more space, more resources, more parental supervision and more parental interest in play as an educative activity[19] – dressing-up, puppet-making, painting and drawing, craft work generally – produce the kind of chaos which the mother cannot easily take in her stride. Children who engage in interesting and varied creative activities leave behind a great deal of interesting and varied rubbish!

NOTES

1   J. and E. Newson, 1968, Chapter 4.
2   Children's Employment Commission, *Second report of the Commissioners on Trades and Manufactures*, 1843, Irish University Press series of British Parliamentary Papers, facsimile reproduction, IUP, Shannon, 1968. Italics ours. Dr Watts is at pains to point out that the parents are 'generally very adverse to send their children to work so young, and nothing but necessity would induce them to do so'; nonetheless the *possibility* of such a course was not in doubt.
3   *Ibid.* Appendix.
4   *Ibid.* p. 21.
5   *Ibid.* p. 195 (italics ours).
6   *Ibid.* p. 197.
7   *Ibid.* p. 47.
8   *Ibid.* Appendix, p. *f*32.
9   All the interviews were completed before the introduction of decimal currency. Specific sums quoted in the transcripts are therefore given in shillings and old pence, but sums given in the text are in decimal currency.
10 Not only do the old and infirm have better access to communications in the middle-class areas, but middle-class children are less likely to be encouraged to take money for helping them. People on low incomes further down the social scale have a much more matter-of-fact attitude to paying money for services rendered: elderly mothers may, for instance, expect to pay their adult sons for doing household repairs and renovations, and, although charges will be kept low, labour as well as materials may be taken into consideration. We have noted this class difference before in relation to neighbours helping during the lying-in period (J. and E. Newson, 1963).
11 In coding this, all the child's stated income from parents is counted except 1s 'legitimate expense' for Cub night, since he clearly has full power over the rest of his 'savings'. An average income of a shilling from the family friend is also included, but possible earnings from the friend are not. The daily threepence for 'biscuit money' is not counted, but the fact that they also have money for sweets or cake on the way home means that the arbitrary shilling is added. The child's spending power is thus reckoned at 5s 6d or 27½ pence; since his mother is ready to give him extra as and when she can afford it and he particularly wants it, this is in fact likely to be an underestimate in this case.
12 The use of decimal notation is somewhat misleading here, possibly, since it helps to conceal inflationary changes. Pocket money rates, like other kinds of wages and salaries, undoubtedly are subject to cost-of-living adjustments; it is the variation across classes, rather than absolute figures in pence, that is of chief interest.
    For comparison, however, local authority pocket money rates to children 'in care' at the time of our interviewing may be cited. A survey of Children's Departments showed a range of 1s to 3s (5–15p) allowed to seven-year-olds, with a modal figure of 2s 6d (12½p) and a mean of 2s (10p). Nottingham at this time was giving 1s 6d (7½p) and was about to increase their rates as a result of this information (personal

communication to authors; R. B. Woodings, then Children's Officer, City of Nottingham, and subsequently Director of Social Services).

13 Although the gas-man's visit is to collect money, gas paid for by slot meter is over-priced, and a small rebate therefore accumulates. The gas-man is a welcome visitor for this reason.

14 Brian Jackson, Review of Ronald Goldman, *Breakthrough*, in the *Guardian*, 20 December, 1968.

15 A quotation from Sillitoe's 'long-distance runner' is perhaps apposite. Describing his Nottingham family's reaction to receiving a lump sum of £500 benefit after his father's death, the boy says: 'Now I believe, and my mam must have thought the same, that a wad of crisp blue-back fivers ain't a sight of good to a living soul unless they're flying out of your hand into some shopkeeper's till . . . . . Night after night we sat in front of the telly with a ham sandwich in one hand, a bar of chocolate in the other, and a bottle of lemonade between our boots . . . . . and I'd never known a family as happy as ours was in that couple of months when we'd got all the money we needed.' Alan Sillitoe, *The Loneliness of the Long-Distance Runner*, W. H. Allen, London, 1959.

16 Richard Hoggart, *The Uses of Literacy*, Chatto & Windus, London, 1957.

17 Richard Hoggart, 1957.

18 J. and E. Newson, 1968, p. 441f. (Pelican edn. p. 469f.).

19 J. and E. Newson, 1968, pp. 166–73 (Pelican edn. pp. 174–82).

Chapter 8

With Love and Kisses

When one is planning the form and content of a research interview, most of the questions will be deliberately desgined to flow logically and naturally one to another, to be easy to understand and comparatively straightforward to answer. On occasion, however, it can be valuable to ask a question which, while simple enough in its wording, is in a sense a conversation-stopper: it has so much resonance, as it were, that the mother is forced to take a deep breath and look at her child all over again. For very many mothers, the question 'Now that N is seven, what is it about him that gives you most pleasure?' had just this quality. To sum up the credit side of the balance-sheet of their relationship and draw out the major item was almost beyond some, but their attempt to do so often brought a new depth to the discussion.

Businessman's wife:
I really don't know . . . um [long pause and sigh] . . . I couldn't say . . . I suppose . . . I don't know . . . he's still an *awkward* personality; he's not someone who is amenable or generous – as I say, he's very much an individual. [At the moment would you say that the awkwardness is outweighing the pleasure as far as you're concerned?] Oh no; no, I suppose I've got to the state where – er – time goes on – you know what I mean – each day goes by, and I sort of don't think about this. I probably don't enjoy them as much as I should. [And if you suddenly – I mean, most of us occasionally, looking at the children, will see something that makes us feel *oh, you are nice* – you know – or if you suddenly feel a little sort of rush of love for him – what's he doing, or what's he looking like, or what is it that makes you feel suddenly fond of him?] I suppose you might think this odd

. . . but I suppose his ability. He has more ability than the others – it's just quite obvious that he has, you know; probably they have it in different ways, but – er – I suppose that is what I would feel *proud* of him for. He's – er – in a *way* he's quite independent . . . you know, he *would* go away from me, whereas the others wouldn't – they're far more clinging. [So in effect you don't feel quite so needed as far as he's concerned?] Hm . . . well – perhaps *more* so, because I don't feel *he* would find anyone to replace me. If I – it may sound odd – if I were to die, and the other two were to have a new mother, they would settle down: Oliver wouldn't.

Sometimes a mother would come to the realisation that the relationship was in fact bringing more pain than pleasure, and this in turn opened the door to a discussion of why this should be.

Unemployed plasterer's wife:
Well, a lot of things really. I mean, she seems that naughty, and yet . . . I shout at her such a lot that . . . I mean . . . I sit looking at her and I think it's a shame – you know – I could cry . . . I don't know. All my kids give me pleasure . . . but she's that mischievous, you know, and with me shouting at her such a lot, and saying "If you don't stop it . . ." [pause] I can't really say that they all give me such a lot of pleasure, you know, in my way of thinking.

Company director's wife:
God – impossible question! I don't know . . . I just don't know. [Do you feel he gives you a lot of pleasure, or is he . . .?] Not at the moment – no.

Works manager's wife:
Oh dear, that's a difficult question! I don't know really. You'd better put a blank for that! I can't think . . . I suppose they've got to grow up – I don't like to see them growing up. Well, I *was* anxious to see him grow up, but not the other one [four years old], because that's it now – they've both grown up, and I've had it now. [Do a lot of things about him give you pleasure?] I suppose so. Well, I don't really think about it, till I see some child that's deformed in any way, or mentally handicapped in any way – *then* I think I'm lucky, but other times I wish them anywhere!

It was not simply those who were in two minds about their own net gains from the relationship who found the question challenging; even when the answer was to be totally positive, the mother seemed to pause, take stock, and look at her child in a different light. 'I don't know what to say really'; 'This is the most difficult question'; 'It's hard to know'; 'What could I say at all really?'; 'Well – um – that's a damn good question, that is!' – all of these were the opening words to appraisals which were wholly in terms of the mother's pleasure in the child. And mothers who could answer without hesitation, in that they were already aware of the ways in which they enjoyed the child, still seemed to change gear, so to speak, when they tried to express the nub of the relationship as opposed to the circumstantials of everyday life: for them, responding to this question seemed in itself a strongly pleasurable experience.

Railwayman's wife:
For one thing – p'raps it's just my own opinion – but it's her dancing about; she's lovely – and she'll do it specially for me, and she'll put her whole heart in it, you know. P'raps I'm silly, taking any notice of her like that, but it's just . . . she's a lovely little dancer! She's ever so light on her feet! And when we're on us own, she says "Can I dance to you, Mummy?" – and I sit and look at her, and say "That's beautiful, my darling" and things like that, to give her encouragement. She wouldn't do it in front of *any*body.

Insurance inspector's wife:
I think you get an awful lot of fun out of them, because they're not babies and neither are they grown-ups, and they sort of live in a funny little world, and they're most comical really. And it's true that children do keep you young, because they keep on about things that you take for granted – you probably take him on the recreation ground and he'll mention to you about the leaves: "It's autumn now, Mummy, and the leaves are coming down" – things that *I* wouldn't normally notice, I've seen it every year and it's nothing new to me. All different things like that – they sort of make you more *aware* of things.

Civil engineer's wife:
He's full of life, and he says a lot of comical things – I can't get mad at him for long – he comes and says "Who loves you, who loves you?"

We did not this time attempt to analyse the terms in which the mother answered the question;[1] the chief reason for asking it was in any case to give as positive a background as possible for the questions on parent/child conflict that were to follow. A brief survey of the replies is thus impressionistic rather than quantitative, but still perhaps of value in expressing prevailing moods about seven-year-olds.

As with the four-year-old, much of the mother's pleasure lay in the child's capacity to be good company for her. The situation is rather different at seven, however, in that the child now spends so much of his time at school, whereas at four he was likely to be the oldest person sharing the mother's day at home; accordingly, the answers now tended to stress the 'grown-up' aspect of the child's companionship.

Research worker's wife:
Oh, I think everything about her – she's quite friendly, and she's quite endearing . . . full of fun, full of mischief; and she's quite a happy person, oh, she's quite a happy person. What would *you* say? [to husband]. It's difficult to put into words. What she sort of – you know – I think she's – she's nicer . . . I won't say she's nicer, but I think you can *get on* with her better now than when she was four: she's a person now, somebody, you know, you can talk to her and . . . [Father:] She's quite intelligent too, and you can really talk to her . . . [Mother:] She can hold quite a conversation. [Father:] And apart from the odd discipline, she's almost treated as an adult – she's quite grown-up for seven. I don't know whether it's a good thing or a bad thing, but she's quite a person on her own . . . got her own personality, hasn't she?

Political worker's wife:
Well, the fact that she's an individual – that she can . . . she can *argue*, she's got a mind of her own already – I think this is nice. The more independent children get from their parents, the nicer it is.

CID detective's wife:
Well, he's an easy-going little boy; he – er – I seem as if I can *talk* to him better; um – he didn't seem to bother at one time, as long as *he* wasn't troubled, you know, but I can talk to him now. I have a little conversation with him, that at one time was impossible when he was younger. All in this last month or two

– it's amazing when you think of how different he is. He really has altered a lot, you know, in every way.

Lorry driver's wife (separated since Mary was a toddler, no other children):

Well, I think it's having her as company, you know. I should be awfully lonely and lost if I hadn't got her, you know. My friends often say "Ooh dear, don't you wish you'd never had any children?" – and I've said "No". They've said "Well, you could at least go here, there and everywhere". And I says "Well, you look at it like this: I could p'raps go out and enjoy meself, go to a dance and have a good time; and", I says, "I'll have been at that dance for an hour, that's all, and then you come home and you're on your own". Mary, I mean I've got her all the while, she's real company, you know; and I don't have to sit and talk babyish to her, you know, I can sit and talk to her grown-up, and get a grown-up answer off of her as well, you see.

Machine engineer's wife:

There's really a lot, you know what I mean – there's quite a lot that she gives us pleasure out of. I mean just me and her in here alone – *lovely* company, you know, I wouldn't be without her for all the money in the world. She's really a comfort to me, and I don't mind now . . . I know at one time I used to really hate our boys to go out, and be alone when he's on nights – I hated it – but now, I could, I really could say cheerio, they can *go* out at night, I could say "Go off and see your friends", and I don't feel one bit lonely if she's in, because times when she's in I'm *not* one bit lonely.

Companionship was markedly emphasised by mothers of girls in particular, and this links logically with the fact that girls, as we have already shown, are more home-oriented and less likely to be 'off out' than boys. Often, however, the mother was quite explicit that it was the femininity of her daughter that she found satisfying, especially where she had already suffered a slight surfeit of sons.

Optician's wife:

Ooh well, just this – I've noticed it this last fortnight more: now our Jane has got very shapeless hair – I've taken her everywhere to have it cut, never makes anything of her – so a friend of mine gave her a roller perm, and she's had this slightly waved, and it's changed her altogether, and it's made her more self-conscious of herself, as I was saying to my older daughter – she's grown into a proper young girl now, she's got out of the little girl stage into the young girl. I do think that with having a daughter among three small boys it gives you a *lot* of pleasure . . .

Van salesman's wife:
I like to, um . . . I think a girl *is* more with her mother, you know; if ever I want to go into town, it's useless trying to take these two [boys], but with Moira she'll trudge around with me for hours and not complain. I think, um, you've got more of a companion with a girl – a mother has, anyway.

Publisher's assistant's wife:
[Laughed] Well, possibly . . . I mean she's getting that much older . . . I mean they get a bit more offhand and they get that little bit of extra age, and I suppose . . . it's nice having a girl and appreciating the fact that she *is* a girl . . . with having the boys, it's nice to have a . . . if you go out and that, a little girl seems to notice things that, you know, a little boy *won't* notice. I suppose it is nice having a little girl to dress and, you know, titivate up.

It is clear that, while little girls are nice to dress and 'titivate up', and can thus serve as dolls to their mothers, at seven this is much more a question of shared feminine interests and attitudes that have very deep roots. Yvonne, for instance, is something of a tomboy; but when her mother was asked 'what is it about her that gives you most pleasure?', she showed no hesitation at all.

Boiler fireman's wife:
To know that she's a *girl* [laughed]. The pleasure is not actually dressing her up, because you *can't* dress up Yvonne; but to know that she's a girl, that I can say to her *you and I are alike* . . . you know, we've got that little thing between us, that's what I like between me and Yvonne. I can't talk to the boys because they're boys – well, I can talk to them – but *we've got our own little ways* – that little closeness that the boys don't get.

Because the child is now so much more in contact with people outside the family, often unsupported by his mother's presence, greater independence and self-reliance are of conscious import-ance to the mother because they ensure that he will be able to cope in a variety of situations. These qualities of general trustworthiness, together with a strong element of pride in a child who could be relied on to do his family credit, were emphasised by a few parents.

Administrative assistant's wife:

Well, I like to see that he's got more self-confidence – he's getting independent now. I think he will – providing we can teach him the right things – I think he will be what we *want* him to be. He's . . . I mean no one ever complains about him, and when he goes anywhere they always say he's well-behaved and he's help-ful. He'll always help anyone, and I think that gives a good impression.

Car showroom foreman's wife:

I like to see him when he's smart, and I love to see him look in through the windows . . . watch him stroll down the street when he's holding his back up well – that sort of thing. He likes to have his hair combed a certain way, and we amuse ourselves at that – nothing in particular, more or less anything . . .

Foreman's wife:

Well, she's not a baby any more, you know, she sort of does things for herself, and . . . [Father:] Well, I don't know, I think now she's seven she's old enough for us to be proud of her when we take her anywhere. That's one of the biggest pleasures, you know; she's – in my opinion she's a nice girl, she speaks nicely, we dress her nicely, and we're proud to take her out as our daughter. That type of thing, that's what we get most pleasure out of.

On the whole, though, mothers' pleasure was more likely to be expressed in the intimate rather than the public aspects of the child's individuality, whether in the generally appreciative terms of 'she's such a personality for such a small age' or in a special savouring of idiosyncratic quirks which they found funny and charming, and which for them summed up the niceness of their child. A policeman's wife, for instance, said she didn't know what to say, but finally plumped for 'her enthusiasm – you feel you could hug her for it'; a foreman's wife softened at the thought of her son 'trying to shave like his Dad, cracking on he's a man already'; while a bricklayer's wife who liked dressing up her son particularly enjoyed his own appreciation of his smartness: 'He gets up on a chair and looks in a glass, he's a proud little monkey'. An un-

employed labourer's wife admitted finding attractive the fact that
her son was 'such a little demon – one that can defy you'; and a
lorry driver's wife was almost impossible to pin down – 'I don't
know, she's all right, I don't think about it, she just sort of fits in,
I reckon she's boss myself' – but eventually grinned with pleasure
as she said : 'She's straightforward, Elaine is; she's as straight as a
die, she don't care who she offends'.

Grocer's wife :
He's fun. He's such a little devil that I think you can laugh
about him and enjoy him completely all the time. [Even when
he's a devil?] Even when he's being a devil, 'cause he's got such
a way about him, you know.

Builder's wife :
I love him telling me anything, you know – what's happened at
school – it's not often that he does – and he explains it in every
detail, you know, and I really enjoy it. He explains *every* way
– with his hands, by frowning, and one thing and another – goes
through all the actions, you know.

Assistant supervisor's wife :
Offhand I think I like when she gets interested in doing something – she'll talk for hours about things, what we just listen to
and don't say nothing to her, and she rambles on; she doesn't
think about there's somebody there – in a little world of her
own!

Grocer's wife :
She's very loving, very affectionate nature – she's very humorous,
always telling jokes, she loves telling jokes. She's such a personality for such a small age! She's good company. Mind you,
I don't want her to grow up, she's the baby of the family.

The 'growing up' which in some ways is so much enjoyed is not
undiluted pleasure for the mother. No longer labelled an 'infant'
at school, the child's days as 'baby of the family' are numbered
even if he is the youngest. His very independence can intensify
the sweetness of the tender moments. We saw when the children
were four that the older mothers of youngest children were particularly likely to give them an 'indulgent bedtime', rocking them to
sleep or in other ways prolonging intimate physical contact; and
bedtime can still be a welcome opportunity for tenderness and

babying. A lorry driver's wife, describing Sheryl all clean and brushed and in her nighty, said 'I always get a kick out of that, even now'; and for a miner's wife the best part of the day was watching television in the evening with her nightgowned daughter: 'you know the way they sit with you and snuggle right up to you and stroke your arm – strokes me face, and arms round me neck, and it's nice!' Mrs Harwell, speaking of her youngest, put rather well the ambivalence of watching a child's growing independence.

Departmental manager's wife:
> You miss them being babies. I wouldn't say I want any more – I don't – but when you've had three or four, I think the youngest one doesn't seem a baby long enough. They grow up *very* fast. [You said that last time – already when he was four!] Did I say that then? Well they do, the youngest grows up *very* fast. You miss it – they sort of grow away from you quickly. I think you miss them sitting on your knee. [And he doesn't do that now?] Odd times – odd *times* he will do. [And this is what you miss – what about him *now* gives you most pleasure?] I think I'm pleased in a sense that he's so independent; but then you miss them having to rely on you for these things – though of course it's better for *them*. It's mixed. But with him growing up, he's considerate towards you. Now often in his little way he'll bring me a cup of tea to bed: if he's up first and we're still in bed, he'll bring me a cup of tea. It might be cold, it might be mashed with cold water or too much milk in – but he'll bring it you. I think that's what I like about him most at the moment, he's thoughtful.

Finally, for a few mothers growing up was a wholly positive affair, in that their children had presented major problems to which time appeared to be providing the solution. Normal development in itself thus seemed 'like a cloud going away from me', as one put it. For the mother of a child who had suffered from severe eczema, 'just to see him growing up and getting over his troubles' was her chief pleasure, and not just for his sake – 'I couldn't tell you how much I've been bound hand and foot'. And in the case of a girl who had been depressed after her elder brother's death, the fact that her mother could 'see her developing, showing much more interest in everything – shaping the right road to growing up' seemed then to mark a turning-point in the whole family's readjustment.

'She tells us she loves us both as much, but I think really it's me . . .'

How far is it possible to investigate the *feel* of the parent–child relationship: to discover the nuances of motherhood or fatherhood as perceived by those who experience it? Clearly, in the first place one should be asking fathers as well as mothers; and fathers were seldom available to us. Nonetheless, the mother has an intimate view of the father's relationship with the child, and a better opportunity than anyone (except, perhaps, the child itself) for comparing it with her own.

We asked a short series of questions designed to shed light upon, and perhaps contrast, the two parent–child relationships. They were asked in the context of a much larger group of about forty questions[2] which explored various activities of the child (conversation, drawing, reading, outings, church, holidays) which might be expected to involve the company and perhaps the active co-operation of his parents.[3]

147. Is there any special interest which you and N share – something which you both follow together?
148. Is there anything which he and his Daddy are both specially interested in?
149. Would you say he is closer now to you or to his Daddy?
150. Does your husband like doing things with him?
     Does he give N a lot of attention?

There is no doubt at all, of course, that either mother or father or both may develop a particularly close bond with their child of whichever sex. However, an overview of the transcripts suggests a qualitive difference in the relationships according to whether the parent–child pair is of the same or opposite sex. To simplify the picture – far too much – this can be described and illustrated thus:

Mother and son   The relationship is often characterised by a special warmth and protectiveness. The mother mentions that her son still likes cuddling or being taken on to her lap, often in private only. She is conscious of his having a special need of her if he is anxious or upset, even though he is outwardly independent. It seems in fact to be just this conjunction of tough exterior and vulnerable 'soft centre' that arouses the mother's tenderness towards him.

Instructor's wife:
    If something's happened at school, I can always tell when he

comes in . . . . . If I'm in the kitchen and his father's in here, he'll come in and close the door, and I know immediately then he wants to have a word with me. He always puts his arms round my neck and whispers in my ear, you know – I can't hear very often, you know! He always gets me round the back of my neck and whispers "Don't tell Daddy, will you? So-and-so happened at school today". Silly things bother him terribly about school, I think he thinks he's got to unburden himself about it – you know, like if he's been moved on to a different table . . . . . My husband is very much inclined – he's not hard-hearted, but he will like to get to the bottom of things and sort things out . . . I think Tim's afraid that Bill might, you know, try and sort things out a bit quicker than he *wants* them sorted out, sort of thing . . . . . Sometimes at night he'll say "I'm a bit worried", and I'll say "Oh yes, tell me what it's about", you know; and he goes all solemn, and I say "Well, have a cry and get it over with". And he'll sit there and cry – and I'm quite sure they're crocodile tears, you know, he's not really upset – he'll cry for a bit, you know, and then he'll say "Well, I'm all right now", you know, and I feel that it does help. Well, I know my husband wouldn't encourage him to sort of cry, 'cause he can't stand crying at any price – and I think that p'raps helps him a little, to have a little weep on my shoulder, just between the two of us, sort of thing.

Postman's wife:
When I kiss him "night-night", I've got to keep my face in a certain position so he can come up and kiss me – "Oh, I love you ever so much" – well, he wouldn't say that to his Daddy. That's the sort of thing that's kept in the dark, he won't show it in the light – he wouldn't kiss me "bye-bye" in the morning if Jim is there.

Mother and daughter The mother stresses companionship and shared interests, mainly those which are based in the home. Pursuits often emphasised are knitting and sewing, housework, drawing and story-writing, shopping and interest in clothes – mostly rather 'feminine' activities, in which the mother can expect to help and instruct the child. Conversations about people and relationships are often mentioned, and television programmes such as domestic serials, in which the making and breaking of relationships form the major plot interest, may be watched together. There is a strong

element of identification in terms of sex affiliation; although sometimes this very identification seems to impede protectiveness, as
if the mother knew the child's weaknesses too well to be wholly
sympathetic. In working-class mothers in particular, the element of
identification occasionally begins to have the feeling of a feminine
conspiracy which deliberately excludes men and boys.

Bleacher's wife:
> You know when she says things, it jogs my memory back to
> when *I* was little, you know. Dressmaking – makeup – well, she's
> only seven, but say we're going anywhere to town – makeup, to
> me she's not old enough, but I do give her the odd very pale
> little lipstick, and when we're getting ready, she'll, I'll *know*
> what she's going to say – I can read her mind. Like – she's got
> this pretty dress on, what I've made, and I remember what *I*
> felt in a new dress, didn't matter how cheap, it was *new,* you
> know; and I've done her hair in four rollers on the top, so it
> sticks up – "Do you think I ought to put some makeup on?"
> And I say "Oh, I don't know, duck – well, just a bit of lipstick".
> And you can tell she's watched me, and she – all this business
> [pulling her mouth taut]; and if it's very pale, well I don't say
> anything, 'cause she'll have it licked off in five minutes anyway
> . . . but the fact that I know she's thinking "I want to look
> nice". . .

Actor's wife:
> She's adult enough to have a grown-up, almost, conversation
> with me, and she's a real friend, and I can see myself in her,
> and know almost exactly her thoughts – it's rather charming,
> and I'll say "You're thinking such-and-such", and she'll say
> "How *did* you know?" and I say "You're recalling to me how
> I was at your age" . . . a nice comfortable feeling we have
> together.

University teacher's wife:
> Her sense of *style* is something I specially enjoy about her. She's
> got to an age where she's not content to know something's good,
> she wants to know *why* it's good – I mean if she does a picture
> or a story, I might say "I really do like this bit", and she gets
> very serious about it, and says "Tell my *why* you like it – tell
> me what's good about it". It's a real challenge to my critical
> ability, trying to pull out the essential thing and explain it to
> her in a way that she'll understand, and it's also very enjoyable

that I *can* make her understand and that she appreciates these rather subtle qualities – something that brings us very close, very much a shared interest.

Machine operator's wife:
She gets on my nerves when she gets sulky and pouting: she gets in her sulks, and she goes like this [rolls eyes up]. My husband can't see it, but you see I *know*, I can *see* it *because* I was just the same when I was Carolyn's age: terrible for sulks! I mean you know your own faults, don't you, and you don't like to see them in your own child.

Bus driver's wife:
We have our little secrets, just me and Evie, you know. You see, if I . . . well, when he's on lates, like, I often have a little natter at the top of the terrace with . . . well, my old man thinks they're me fancy men. I tell her secrets like that, you know. She'll keep them under her hat – she's never told anyone anything – she's, she's very secretive, is Evie.

Father and son   As in the previous like-sexed relationship, common interests are stressed either in the home in terms of the conventionally masculine activities of property maintenance and model-building, or outside mainly in sport and expeditions. Sport is a major topic of conversation, and TV sports programmes are jointly watched and discussed, often to the exclusion of females. Like-sex identification may be expressed either by collusion against the female element or, less comfortably for the child, by the father objecting to the mother's protectiveness.

Textile threader's wife:
Well, he doesn't see much of his Dad, but they do seem close; I'm sort of left out when they're together. I don't understand a thing about football – I know when it goes into the net it's a goal! But he knows all the players, and who's buying who, you know.

Scaffolder (father speaking):
You should have seen him when he caught his first fish! It was only three weeks ago, it was. Threw his line in, and I said to myself, oh, he'll not get naught there, see – I just shut him up, see, and in one minute the float went straight under – and pulling it in, ever so exciting, you know – and the fish only appeared from the water to the side . . . he threw the rod away and just

flew in, he made me laugh, and he caught it with his hands and all. The fish just come to the bank, and he was that interested to get hold of the fish, he threw the rod away and just dived under the water, and that was it! And me mate caught a little frog, same day this was, and he was just going to put a hook in it to catch a fish with it, and Teddy wouldn't let him do it – he said "No, I'm taking it home – you shouldn't do that". And then we was catching little fish, you know, for bait, and would he let us do that? "No" – he says – "it's cruel" – he said – "don't do it" – and he wouldn't let us do it, so we'd got to go on fishing on maggots – wouldn't let us touch anything like that.

Student's wife:
 . . . he has on occasion had a weep on my shoulder about this frightful girl [sister, aged six]. I have every sympathy, because she *is* frightful sometimes. I think he talks to his father more about this, and his father is a great believer in a strategy of cunning where women are concerned . . .

Lorry driver's wife:
He's got six big boxes of train-sets in the front room, and viaducts and stations, and oh, he and my husband have a marvellous time! My husband says he's going to have one big room built, just to take that!

Cleaner's wife (husband in prison):
Their Daddy used to be with them every night and every weekend, you see; I can't make up for what he used to do. 'Cause he was always on the Forest [common land] with them at weekends, playing football, and he took them places – well, I can't keep up with that, and that's why he's missing him so much. And these fights at night that he used to have; and you see at night-time he'll say "Sit and do these sums with me" – well I've got them all to undress, hot water bottles to do, their suppers to do, and I say "Oh, I haven't got time – wait", and I cut him off, see. And his Daddy could sit, once he'd come home from work and had his wash, he used to sit with him, you see.

Father and daughter The opposite-sex relationship again emphasises warmth and quiet comfort-contact. There is a tendency to protectiveness, indulgence and lenience, often 'giving in' where the mother would be firmer.

Security officer's wife:

Well – it's a different relationship altogether. Her Daddy she can twist around her little finger – she can do anything with him, any mortal thing. And yet it's me she *turns* to; although I'm much more strict with her, she knows very well she can't get away with anything when she's with me. So it's really quite a different relationship.

Insurance manager's wife:

She likes to go and sit on his knee and be made a fuss of, you know, she's a proper female, she knows how to get round her Daddy!

Labourer's wife:

She may not tell me everything, but she will her Daddy, she never keeps anything from him; she's very fond of her Daddy, and I mean he is of *her*, so he can get any kind of information out of her. Because he usually tells me, he says she wouldn't dare tell Mummy because "Mummy might be cross with me if I told her", you know . . . she always seems closer to her Daddy, I think she always will in that line. Sometimes he smacks her if she's been too rough and that – she'll come to me then – I say "I thought you were Daddy's girl?" "Oh", she says, "we've fell out now" – then five minutes later they're friends again!

Railwayman's wife:

He wouldn't bother smacking her. I thought she *was* going to get one last night, but it was only a threat *after* all. It's never any good telling her Dad of her, he's hopeless!

Warehouseman's wife:

. . . she'll sit on that chair-arm, and he'll sit there, and she'll comb his hair and put curlers in – just for about ten minutes – puts a cloth round him and wets his hair. [Father:] Some nights it's quite soothing!

In general, then, there seems to be a tendency for children to turn to the opposite-sexed parent to express dependency or to solicit indulgence, and to the like-sexed to enjoy more grown-up companionship on an equal level, sometimes with a spice of almost conspiratorial adventure for both the pair. By and large, this schema seems to hold true independent of male or female traits regarded as characteristic of fatherly or motherly roles (see pages 278–80).

Obviously, however, this description irons out the idiosyncratic bumps of individual relationships; for in practice there are wide differences between families in the way personalities mesh and bonds develop. One parent may be strict and the other lenient, independent of sex. Some fathers are always on hand, whereas others are away from home for long periods of time (and a few are separated from their families or have died).[4] Some fathers are deeply involved in their families, while others prefer to leave almost the whole of the handling of the children to their wives. Some habitually indulge all their children, irrespective of sex; some are seen by their wives as generally intolerant and over-strict, making too few allowances for youth: 'the big gaffer – he'll not stand no messing about'. Mothers too may be temperamentally soft-hearted or tough-minded, and this propensity may for them override the effect of the child's sex.

Interplay of personality can become paramount in shaping practice. The individual mother may react to the individual father, either 'making up for' his perceived over-lenience or over-strictness, or coming to a compromise with him in order to present a united parental front. Or the parent–child relationship may change and develop over time, so that, for instance, the father becomes more personally involved than previously, or than he had envisaged; or a special relationship may develop with one particular child which does not apply to the other children in the family. It must be stressed once again that the child is an active agent in the making of a relationship with a particular parent, whether their own relationship or that of a sib: when Mrs. Dean says 'Marian and I are mostly in step, but Rachel and I are out of step, I don't know why', the *contrast* between these two relationships is likely to contribute to the feel of either one of them. The size of the family will also have its effect: for instance, a special tenderness for the youngest child is probably more tolerable for its siblings in a large family than in a two-child family, and certainly the distance between sibs will affect the manner in which bonds and alliances are both created and perceived. The permutations possible are almost endless. Generalisations about trends in the pattern, such as we have offered above, must thus be treated with caution; they are of interest chiefly as an expression of a cultural 'ideal norm' against which to match any given parent–child relationship, with the implicit reservation that each of these will in fact be the product of features unique to itself.

The question 'Would you say he is closer now to you or to his

Daddy?' was asked in the knowledge that we would be getting a one-sided, subjective, but still valid view of the situation; and we were also conscious that there are explicit taboos against parents expressing preferences among their children or children between their parents. Children know that they are supposed to love their parents equally; parents often go to great trouble to declare equal love for their children. The word 'closer' was deliberately intended to bypass the notion of 'love', and does in fact meaningfully designate a rather different dimension of feeling, as was clear from the transcripts: although the mother might bring in the word 'love', it would be in *expansion* of what she said about closeness rather than as a synonym for it.

Table 28　*Child's comparative closeness to one or other of his parents*

| | social class | | | | | | summary | |
	I&II	IIIwc	III man	IV	V	I&II, IIIwc	IIIman, IV,V	overall popn.
	%	%	%	%	%	%	%	%
Closer to mother								
boys	28	28	45	39	45	28	43	39
girls	46	38	43	39	36	42	42	42
both	37	32	44	39	41	35	43	41

Significance: trend n.s.　　　　　　　　　　　　　　m.class/w.class
　　　　　　between sexes　n.s.　　　　　　　　n.s. (p <0·08)
　　　　　　　　　　　　interaction sex x class*

	I&II	IIIwc	III man	IV	V	I&II, IIIwc	IIIman, IV,V	overall popn.
Closer to father								
boys	16	28	22	16	14	22	20	21
girls	15	15	19	13	33	15	20	18
both	16	21	21	15	22	18	20	19

Significance: trend n.s.　　　　　　　　　　　　　m.class/w.class　n.s.
　　　　　　　　　　between sexes　n.s.

Table 28 analyses the answers to this question. Overall, 41% of children are said to be closer to their mothers and 19% to their fathers, which leaves 40% described as 'about equally close' to both parents. Sex and class differences overall are negligible; however, when sex and class are looked at in conjunction, it is of interest that middle-class boys as a group are less likely to be reported as 'closer to mother': 28% are so reported, against 43% of working-class boys. Reversing the coin, however, we find that this is not because middle-class boys in general are closer to their fathers: although white-collar boys have the highest incidence of being 'closer to father', this does not reach significance, while Class I and II boys gravitate not to the 'father' but to the 'about equal' category. It is also of interest that while only 14% of Class v boys are said to be 'closer to father', 33% of Class v girls are so reported.

Such differences as emerge from this table seem to reflect a greater expectation at the top of the social scale for the roles of mother and father to converge so that both parents may be considered equally close to the child; while at the lower end of the scale parental roles, like work roles, are more likely to be sex-typed. The low incidence of middle-class boys said to have a closer relationship with their mothers is interesting, and may perhaps be explained in terms of preserving their masculine image; that is, if middle-class boys are in so many ways (as we have seen) treated not unlike girls, this may need to be compensated for by placing heavy emphasis on their relationship with their fathers; whereas there is less doubt about the masculinity of working-class boys, who can thus better afford a 'spoiling' relationship with their mothers.

The child's greater social maturity at seven, combined with his increased exposure to concepts and knowledge that come from outside the family circle, make possible a genuine two-way exchange of ideas between parent and child; and this in turn implies that the child can have his own field of interests which may be similar to or different from those of his parents, but which anyway are not merely 'child's play' and thus have the potential at least of being shared with a parent. We have already seen how both parents comment on the sense of real companionship and understanding which emerges from the discovery of shared interests and which subtly alters the whole nature of the relationship; bonds of dependence and protectiveness, whose existence was based upon the accident of birth and the child's need to be nurtured, become reinforced *by choice* in the recognition of mutual enthusiasms and sympathetic personalities.

The sense of the two questions on interests, which were further explained to this effect if necessary, was that the activity mentioned must be at least to some extent particular to the pair: general interests which included the other parent or the rest of the family were ruled out of consideration here.

As one might expect, mothers share special interests with their daughters more frequently than with their sons (Table 29); but it is perhaps noteworthy first that this difference is not very great, and secondly that even in the middle class only half the mothers can think of a shared interest. The class trend is very consistent, shared interests decreasing as one descends the social scale, particularly where boys are concerned. An interesting finding, taking sex and class in conjunction, concerns the largest class group: skilled manual workers' wives align themselves with the lower

Table 29   *Children who share an interest with a parent*

	social class						summary		
	I&II	IIIwc	III man	IV	V		I&II, IIIwc	IIIman, IV,V	overall popn.
	%	%	%	%	%		%	%	%
With mother									
boys	43	45	28	31	23		44	28	33
girls	55	53	51	43	28		54	46	49
both	49	49	39	37	26		49	37	41

Significance: trend ↘ ****   m.class/w.class ***
                    between sexes ****

With father									
boys	72	79	66	68	60		75	66	68
girls	49	40	42	32	26		45	38	40
both	61	60	54	50	43		60	52	54

Significance: trend ↘ ***   m.class/w.class n.s.
                    between sexes ****   (p <0·07)

working class group in their low incidence of shared interests with their sons, but are more like the middle class in sharing interests with their daughters. The small proportion of working-class boys generally who have any interests in common with their mothers is especially striking; and this may have an important bearing on their socialisation, in as much as the mother is likely to be the most available parent.

It is part of the stereotype of a good father-son relationship in Western culture that they should share 'masculine' interests: the very pronounced sex difference in relation to the father is not unexpected, therefore. There is a class trend for both boys and girls which, if not very marked, is consistent and clear; but it also suggests a steeper drop in shared interests towards the lower end of the scale. This in turn suggests that family size may be a factor. When large (4+ children) and smaller families are compared, social class held constant, there is in fact a difference (significant at the 0·05 level) showing shared interests between father and child occurring rather more often in small families than in large.

Overall, the table shows girls and boys faring rather similarly with opposite-sexed parents, but boys doing very much better than girls when it is a question of sharing an interest with the same-sexed parent. One factor which may be operating here is the actual *identifiability* of different interests: for instance, football is an easily identifiable interest which the child can be clearly seen to share with his father, whereas cooking, because it is part of the housework, might not be dignified with the title 'special interest' even though the mother and daughter were closely involved together in it. Feminine interests which, like football, are readily identifiable – pop-star or doll crazes, for instance – tend not to be shared by the mother. Although such a factor may complicate the results slightly, however, they do not invalidate them since we are here concerned with interests which do indeed identify one parent and one child as a pair for this purpose in the eyes of the rest of the family.

'He'll often say to my husband "Do me some sums, Daddy, dead hard ones!"'
In many ways it is much easier to gauge the degree to which a father participates in the upbringing of this child when the child is very young. For a one-year-old baby, there are certain things which have to be done by someone – feeding, nappy-changing, bathing, attending to him in the night – and one can ask in detail whether the father will do these things as a matter of course or only in an emergency, and whether there are any specific activities at which he 'draws the line'. Similarly, the four-year-old has a perceived need for help with bathing, dressing and undressing, and for supervision in the house and on shopping expeditions. At seven, however, the child's needs are much more nebulous, and also more variable from one child to another. Thus the question asked must be more open-ended: we can no longer tot up scores for father's participation on the basis of how often he carries out which services for his child.

Table 30   *An index of father participation*

			Score
Q148	Is there anything which he and his Daddy are both specially interested in?	YES	2
		NO	0
Q149	Would you say he is closer now to you or to his Daddy?	DADDY	2
		MOTHER	0
Q150(*a*)	Does your husband like doing things with him?	YES (unequivocal)	2
		Sometimes	1
		NO	0
Q150(b)	Does he give N a lot of attention?	A great deal	3
		Quite a lot	2
		Not much	1
		None	0

Score range possible: 0–9

Distribution of these scores was examined and participation defined thus:

		% *in random sample*
'highly participant'	(scores 7, 8 or 9)	45%
'moderately participant'	(scores 5 or 6)	27%
'low participation'	(scores 0, 1, 2, 3 or 4)	28%

Note. On this index, distribution of father participation scores is skewed towards the high-score end of the continuum (72% of fathers score 5–9), which suggests that overall father participation is high: however, these criteria are much less demanding in terms of practical services than those used at earlier age-stages.

We arrived at an index of father participation on the basis of four questions, two of which were those on 'closeness' and 'special interests' which we have already discussed. The method of scoring is shown in Table 30.

That these four basic questions can elicit a quite subtle and detailed picture of the father's participation (and how the mother feels about it) can be seen in the following verbatim extract, which includes normal probe additions as prompted by the mother's replies.[5]

[(Q147) Is there any special interest which you and Oliver share – something that the two of you follow together – would you say?] Mmmmm . . . I don't *think* so. [(Q148) Is there anything which he and his Daddy are both specially interested in?]

[pause] . . . *No.* [No special thing . . . (Q149) Would you say Oliver is closer to you, or to his Daddy? . . . or is it about equal?] About equal . . . might be a shade towards me . . . [(Q150) Does your husband like doing things with him?] (sigh) . . . mmm . . . not really – no. [(pause) . . . How do you mean?] Well – I suppose he *does* like doing things with him, but opportunity doesn't often present itself. [I see – yes . . . yes] He's . . . he's . . . well, he's home tonight, but some nights he's not home till seven or eight, so he just sees them go to bed, really, and get up in the morning. [. . . yes . . . and does he give Oliver a lot of attention when he *is* here – would you say, um, about average, or more or less than most fathers?] Well, I sometimes think he could give *more* . . . ummm . . . he could perhaps take them *off* more – the boys – and play with them more. (voice rises) If the boys play games, they play games with *me!* [yes] This is what I find, you know? [I see . . . yes . . . yes . . .] 'Cause he's always . . . *out*, or *busy*, [. . . yes . . .] or *doing* something. [. . . yes . . .] I suppose it's circumstances . . . not deliberate . . . [You're sort of more available] Yes . . . yes . . . If we go to the cricket match – *he's playing* cricket – *I* play with the boys! (general laughter) [And the boys sort of *feel* really that you're more available – that, er, you're the person they play with, I suppose?] Yes! Now Oliver asks *me* to take him swimming – he doesn't ask his Daddy!

Table 31 shows father participation in terms of high scorers and low scorers. There is a consistent if modest class trend indicating, as one might expect from findings at four years and one year, that fathers become less participant as we move down the social scale. However, this overall trend is in fact almost wholly derived from the figures on boys: no significant class trend can be found if girls' fathers are taken alone. Thus the most highly participant fathers at age seven are those of middle-class boys, and middle-class boys also have the fewest low-participant or non-participant fathers. The importance of this in practical terms is that, for these boys, the father's active involvement is likely to compensate them for the fact that their mother is less inclined to share in their increasingly male-centred interests and activities. The corollary of this is perhaps that a significant number of working-class boys (more than a quarter overall, and 35% in Class v), having low-participant fathers, can only find such compensation by turning to their like-sex peers outside the family.

From the transcripts one also has the impression that 'low participation' has a different feel to it in different social classes: that is, the father's work-style affects the *manner* in which he withdraws from his children. The manual worker's wife tends to stress father's inactivity and lassitude when at home: Vance's mother, a labourer's wife, said that Vance very rarely asked his father questions – 'I mean, by the time his Dad comes home at

Table 31 *Father participation index scores as a function of sex and social class*

| | social class | | | | | | summary | | |
	I&II	IIIwc	III man	IV	V		I&II, IIIwc	IIIman, IV,V	overall popn.
	%	%	%	%	%		%	%	%
High scorers (scores 7–9)									
boys	58	62	46	47	46		60	46	50
girls	37	24	34	25	23		31	31	31
both	47	43	40	36	34		45	39	40

Significance: trend ↓ **   m.class/w.class   n.s.
                    between sexes ****

	social class						summary		
Low scorers (scores 0–4)									
boys	12	17	28	20	35		14	27	23
girls	28	31	26	31	28		29	27	28
both	20	24	27	25	32		22	27	26

Significance: trend   n.s.   m.class/w.class   n.s.
                between sexes   n.s.
                            interaction class x sex $p = 0.05$

night, and he's had his dinner and sat down to watch telly, they don't really ask him anything – he doesn't sort of give them the chance'. A bus driver's wife thought her husband was 'a bit of a misery' over never wanting to do anything, and a bleacher's wife gave an example of just one in a series of incidents when her husband's inertia had disappointed the children.

I should say less than average. I think, where it is, is – where I would put myself out, and if they said something that they'd set their heart on I'd go out of my way to do it – um – I don't think he would. Like yesterday – just to stress the point – he'd promised

Stuart he'd take him to Highfields, swimming; and he went to work just for a few hours, and of course I *knew* that when he came home . . . but I thought, well, he can't make excuses about the weather; but I kept saying "You'll not go, Stuart – don't set your heart on it – wait and see". 'Course, as soon as he come in, like – they'd had their dinner and everything early, and Stuart said "Well, are we going swimming, then?" And he says "Well – I don't know . . ." – you know. And I just – I don't like to do – but I think "Here we go" – and I said "*Don't* set them on these things", I said, "If you want to take them anywhere special, say we're going somewhere special, but don't *set his heart* on it. I *tell* you, and you *do* these things . . ." But by the time he'd sat down, and one thing and another, it was too late.

While non-participation in the manual group seems to be compounded of role differentiation plus physical exhaustion, in the middle class it is characteristically made up of role differentiation plus a high level of work activity at home. Like the businessman on page 275, this small group of fathers are always '*out*, or *busy*, or *doing* something'. A political worker spends most of his evenings out, and when he is at home is often inaccessible to the children because he is working; a grocer in his own business works late in his shop, does his books at home, and 'seems to be occupied *without* the children the odd times when he is at home'. This does not mean that all middle-class fathers who bring their work home are non-participant: some make deliberate arrangements to participate *more* with their children, especially if the mother is also working at home. The couple who are both at university make exceptional efforts to meet their children's needs – not altogether successfully, in their son's view: 'Recently', says this mother, 'he has expressed a resentment that I don't do enough with him – I perhaps come in here, shut the door, and I study – and although my husband is always available then, in fact I don't do it *unless* he's available, I think James feels he has been shut out of part of my life'. Eventually, of course, in these highly active, striving families, the family pattern is likely to settle down into one of communal labour: the children will be heavily occupied with homework and other extra-curricular pursuits, and the pattern of working at home will be supportive. While the children are younger, however, there is at least more opportunity for children (and mother if they are her only occupation) to feel excluded.

Transcending both the sex-linked parent–child bond-types that we have described and the class-linked attitudes on father's participation, the overall consensus can be reduced to three generally perceived differences between mothers and fathers in relation to seven-year-old children.

1. The mother tends to be the more familiar everyday caretaker of the two, even if father is highly participant, and familiarity to some extent does breed contempt: that is, the children tend to be more amenable to father's authority – which is galling for the mothers, who put in most of the effort.

Welder's wife:

My husband never smacks her. Her Dad's only got to say one word, and she does as she's told. Sometimes I have to tell her two or three times, and it annoys me to think, you know, one word from Daddy and that's it.

Builder's wife:

My husband won't smack them at all. Well, if you know what I mean, he don't have to – they're not scared of their Dad, but they know what he says is law. For me, they just couldn't care less. I went out one night – well, my husband says, there's no trouble with those children tonight. They got washed, they undressed and went to bed, and that was it, he said. But they really do play me up. He said "There's no trouble with them, I don't know why you're always going on about it".

2. The mother in the end is the nurturant, cherishing parent (as differentiated from an indulgent one): specifically, in illness or hurt the child turns to the mother, even when in other circumstances he would want the father. 'If it's anything *hard* they'll come to me', says the unemployed father of three boys and a girl, all under eight, 'but anything gentle, they'll go to their Mum. If they cut themselves and that – if they want a wash or have a bath, they'd sooner go to their Mum than me'; and the labourer's wife whose daughter has always been 'Daddy's girl' (page 268) adds 'She's fond of me if she's ill – all for me then'.

Checker's wife:

I would say they *respect* him more than me, because he's more firm with them and they do as they're told; but such as crying over hurts, it's "Mummy, Mummy" – probably because I'm there always.

Merchandise supervisor's wife:

> She always tells us she loves us both as much, but I think really
> it's me. You know, she doesn't mind Daddy being away, but I
> think she would if it was me.

3. The father because of his masculinity is better fitted to cope
responsively with the rumbustious side of the male child, which is
not often considered the mother's job: she may enjoy it as an
onlooker, as evidence of her son's masculinity, but rarely as a
participant by this age. The last two statements of Oliver's mother
(page 275) betray the characteristic resentment of the mother who
feels she has been pushed into this role. Gerald and Laura, the
student parents of James, express both the comforting role of the
mother and the father's role in accepting boisterous physical play.

> [Mother:] I think James *relies* on Gerald more . . . Gerald sees
> his point of view much more easily, and is more sympathetic
> towards his kind of approach to things, his problems, than I am
> . . . um . . . but in a queer sort of way he almost seems more
> *emotionally dependent* on me. It's a difficult question to answer
> clearly. [It's really a different sort of closeness, but about
> equal?] [Father:] If he comes home and he's worried, he'll ask
> if Laura is here. This fluctuates, it depends on whether he's
> what I call outgoing or ingoing. If he's outgoing and therefore
> rather masculine, and wants to roll on the floor, shout, create
> merry hell, so to speak, he's getting sympathy from Dad and
> therefore the harmony is there. At other times, when he wants to
> be put on your knee, then he'll go to Mum, I think . . . [Seven
> questions later: What sort of things make you get on each
> other's nerves now, you and James?] [Mother:] I think what
> really upsets me is the extreme masculinity; and when it rears its
> head, especially indoors, I find it very shattering. It may be that
> I'm tired and a bit edgy, because I'm working at full stretch;
> but the feeling that the space around you is *vibrating*, I find this
> awfully difficult to live with – and yet it's all part of being a boy.
> One shouldn't resent this, after all it is only him growing into a
> male creature; it's all quite in order.

Beyond these points, we do not have much to add to what we
said about fathers' roles when the children were four; although
we shall return to fathers briefly when we come to the question
of discipline (pages 327–9). For the child of the 'sixties and

'seventies, probably the most important thing about having two parents lies not so much in a differentiation of roles as in a differentiation of *people*: the fact that his upbringing is in the hands of two rather than one, who behave also in relation to each other. Alternatives of role and authority become available, influence and counter-influence operate, complexity and flexibility of negotiation between parents and children are the norm.

'If he isn't **shown** *love, he can't show love when he gets older, can he, really?'*
The frank display of affection between parent and child becomes less available to observation as the child grows older. It is easy enough to see a mother cuddling her baby in public places such as doctors' surgeries, trains or buses or in the park, and one can watch nursery school children being greeted with a hug and a kiss; but once the child is at 'proper school', these loving interchanges at the school gate rapidly decrease, or become formalised to a decorous kiss on the cheek. Quite apart from whether the mother has views on whether it is any longer appropriate to demonstrate her love publicly, the child himself (especially the boy) will be learning from the peer group subtle inhibitions in relation to behaviour which until now had seemed the natural expression of natural feeling.

Business executive's wife:
    I've had to drop that a bit, because he says "I don't like it"; you know, he says you have to wait until he's moved from his friends, you see! Anything like that, he's a little bit, um, you know – choosy.

Insurance inspector's wife:
    When he's going back to school, if I want to kiss him bye-bye, I've got to do it before he goes out – he doesn't want his friends to see. But he sits on my knee at night.

Teacher's wife:
    I always used to take her and fetch her [from school], not because she needed it, but just to think she was getting that bit of attention, you see; and – er – I got into the habit of kissing her; and she said "I do wish you wouldn't kiss me outside school" – you know, as if she was too grown-up for that sort of thing.

In general, it is perhaps ironic that reprimands directed towards children of this age are more freely observable than overt gestures of love. It thus seemed important to know whether cuddling was simply reserved for the intimacy of the home or was often inhibited altogether; whether mothers themselves felt that children of seven had in some sense grown out of the need for cuddling; and how far it was the child who decided the issue of whether he was cuddled.

The questions used (following the one about the mother's pleasure in the child) were:

154. Is he a child who shows a lot of affection?
155. Do you ever give him a cuddle nowadays, or do you think he's too old for that now?
(If too old): Do you kiss him at all now?

Answers to Question 154 were coded between children who showed a lot of affection, those who showed some reserve, and those who were reserved with everyone. The 'cuddling' question was coded in terms of those who were given frequent hugs and cuddles, those who received only formal kisses (i.e. at greeting or parting), and those who were no longer kissed or cuddled.

Three-quarters of all children in this age group are said by their mothers to show 'a lot' of affection. The results shown in Table 32 are notable for the absence of class or sex differences: the only sex difference is in Class III white collar, in which boys are nearly three times as likely as girls to be 'very reserved'. In this social class, as in the others, the sexes are equally represented in the residual category of 'some reserve', so that the differences that exist are in terms of extremes.

It seems particularly interesting that this is the only perceptible sex difference, in view of a heavy preponderance of boys over girls reported (in the transcripts) as objecting to public kissing. What this amounts to, in fact, is evidence that the 'taboo on tenderness' for little boys is one which they recognise and feel constrained to observe in the presence of their peer group, but which, like certain other cultural constraints,[6] they can afford to ignore in the privacy of the home. Bartholomew, for instance, won't even wave to his mother if anyone is watching, but sits on her knee in the evening and insists on his bedtime kiss. It is understandable that the casual bystander (or those whose contact with children is solely consultative) may underestimate the emotional dependence of seven-year-olds on their parents. At four years, the spectacle of a six-shooting cowboy with a dummy in his mouth points an obvious contrast; it is less easy to appreciate

Table 32 *Child's display of affection*

	social class					summary		
	I&II	IIIwc	III man	IV	V	I&II, IIIwc	IIIman, IV,V	overall popn.
	%	%	%	%	%	%	%	%
Shows a lot								
boys	70	71	78	67	74	70	75	74
girls	69	82	77	72	77	75	76	75
both	69	76	77	69	75	73	75	75

Significance: nil

Very reserved								
boys	7	17	6	15	14	12	8	9
girls	9	6	7	12	10	8	8	8
both	8	12	6	13	12	10	8	9

Significance: nil

that the playground tough may still enjoy a lap-cuddle when his friends are not there to see him. There is little evidence of inhibition in these children:

Building worker's wife:
> A very lot of affection, she does. She always shouts when she goes to school, or when Daddy goes to work – "Don't forget I love you!" Even when he goes to work, you know, she stands on the front doorstep and has to shout "Don't forget I love you!"

Clerk's wife:
> She's so happy, so loving – I look forward to her coming home, you know, because I always make it a rule that they both have a time separately when we're together; and Fiona's is when she comes home because there's nobody else in the house, and that is our time, we always have a little time together, we always have a little love, because she really is sloppy – I wish she'd always stay like it!

Turf accountant's wife:
> He's very loving in a way. He'll come and all of a sudden say "I *do* love you!" and give you a kiss. He gives a lot of pleasure.

Miner's wife:
> You'll be sitting down reading a book and she can be sitting over there with her dolls, and then she'll say "Gi' us a kiss!" – then she'll go and sit back over there again. Mind you, I've got one fifteen like that.

Table 33   *Mother's display of affection*

	social class					summary		
	I&II	IIIwc	III man	IV	V	I&II, IIIwc	IIIman, IV,V	overall popn.
	%	%	%	%	%	%	%	%
Frequent hugs								
boys	90	81	90	83	81	86	87	87
girls	91	92	85	93	85	91	87	88
both	90	86	87	88	83	88	87	87

Significance: nil

	I&II	IIIwc	III man	IV	V	I&II, IIIwc	IIIman, IV,V	overall popn.
No cuddle or kiss								
boys	6	9	5	9	11	7	6	6
girls	3	2	4	3	5	3	4	4
both	4	5	4	6	8	5	5	5

Significance: nil

Table 33 presents several interesting findings. First, a very high proportion of mothers – 87% overall – report that they cuddle their seven-year-olds 'frequently', despite the fact that the question was carefully phrased to make an alternative response quite socially acceptable. Conversely, only a very small group of children – 5% – do not get cuddled or kissed at all. Taking the residual category 'formal kissing only' into account for comparative purposes, 13% of mothers are now discouraging spontaneous hugs and kisses, compared with 5% when the child was four. Considering that the child's increasing age is often the reason given for the mother's reserve, this does not seem a very striking change. Sex differences (except, again, in Class III white collar) are once more conspicuous by their absence; still more noteworthy is the absence of class differences, which gives the lie to the rather glib and simplistic idea that educational and emotional deprivation both increase equally towards the lower end of the social scale. Emotional warmth towards children is not the prerogative of any one social class.

Production manager's wife:
  This cuddling in the morning [in mother's bed] gives me pleasure
  – I encourage him to show his feelings, 'cause I never could as a
  child.

Bricklayer's wife:
  I don't think you're *ever* too old to be kissed and cuddled really
  – I don't. I think that is a very important thing in a child's life
  really. I mean, a lot of people'll say "Oh, he's too old" or "He's
  a boy"; but I still don't think a boy is *any* different – because
  if he isn't *shown* love, he can't show love when he gets older,
  can he, really?

Dyer's operative's wife:
  Oh no! She'll never be too old for that!

Most significant of all is the data which emerges from combining
these last two tables. Eighty-seven per cent of the mothers cuddle
their children 'frequently'; only 75% of the children return the
gesture in the sense of themselves showing 'a lot of affection', i.e.
being cuddly. The obvious implication is that there are not enough
cuddly children to go round. This does not necessarily mean that
every cuddly child will have a cuddling mother: the mismatch
may happen in the other direction.

Sales representative's wife:
  I don't think he's too old, I think it's me sometimes. I think
  I sometimes feel a bit embarrassed, you know, to cuddle him. I
  don't think he's too old actually. I think I ought to do it more
  often, but . . . life seems such a pressure – everybody rushing
  around – these things get left, you know. But he's an affectionate
  child, and I think he likes to be shown affection.

A clear association can be shown between the child's willingness
to display affection and the extent to which the mother gives
cuddles and kisses, viz.:

Of the demonstrative
children (75% in a random
sample):

95% receive frequent and
spontaneous hugs and kisses.

Of the children who show
some reserve (16% in a
random sample):

75% receive frequent and
spontaneous hugs and kisses.

Of the 'very reserved' children (9% in a random sample):	42% receive frequent and spontaneous hugs and kisses.

This association is both highly consistent and highly significant statistically (chi-squared $= 80 \cdot 05$, d. of f. $= 1$, p. $< 0 \cdot 001$). Obviously this begs the fundamental question of which is cause and which effect: does the cuddling mother create a cuddly child (as would tend to be assumed by the psychological determinism which has shaped the history of child psychology), or does the child himself limit his mother's response?

Cuddly children are highly appreciated by cuddling mothers, and it is quite evident from the figures alone that some of these mothers are not as successful as they could wish in producing children who wholly appreciate their advances. The evidence of the transcripts more than confirms the view that mothers who are reserved in their show of affectionate gestures tend to be so mainly in deference to their child's expressed wishes. Often they cite in contrast their response to another child who does welcome their cuddling. We ourselves are inclined to see this group of uncuddly children mismatched with cuddling mothers (or with unwillingly non-cuddling mothers) as a reflection of fairly basic, perhaps constitutional differences between individual children; the absence of consistent social class differences in both tables supports this view.

Building worker's wife:
  At the moment she goes her own sweet way, you know. I mean she doesn't sort of come and sit on your knee and whisper things in your ear and things like that – she never *has* been like that. She'll come for a kiss goodnight when she goes to bed, but that's as far as it goes, you know. She doesn't throw her arms round you and tell you she loves you and things like that, you know. Now Tom will, and Heather will (ages eleven and ten), they'll say "Oh I do love you, Mummy" and things like that – well June won't. I don't get that from her.

Park superintendent's wife:
  He still doesn't seem that close to me . . . I've lost him, sort of thing, and I don't know *where* I've lost him. He's not a child that you could sort of go up and cuddle him – he'll not let you cuddle him.

Teacher's wife:

  I do kiss her, but she doesn't like it [laughed]. I mean I wouldn't dream of tucking her up in bed without kissing her goodnight, but I mean quite often it's, you know . . . she gets a funny look on her face, and . . . er . . . not really nasty, she's never really nasty, but as if to say "mind you don't go too far"!

Stoker's wife:

  I kiss him if I can – he's one of those children that doesn't like it. He thinks he's too old. It started just after he was six. I'd say "C'mon and have five minutes!" And he'll say "Oh no, I want to play, Mam". He sort of shudders you off.

Cycle worker's wife:

  Oh no, no, he isn't one for affection. You've got to sort of – if you want a kiss, you've got to ask him for one. He won't give you one voluntary, like. [Does he mind if you kiss him?] He goes red – he blushes . . . . . [Do you ever give him a cuddle nowadays?] Oh yes, I often say "Come on, let me get hold of you", you know. I don't think he's too old for that. *He* thinks he is, yes.

Stentor operator's wife:

  No, no, it just doesn't appeal to her, never since she was a baby. She's never been a child you could sit and nurse and love.

'Even though they're little, they deserve a little bit of co-operation – I don't think it should be all one-sided'
Let us repeat: emotional warmth towards children is not the prerogative of any one social class; nor is the child's expression of warmth towards the parent. Yet a class difference can be discerned in the loving, sharing, caring side of the relationship between parents and children, both in terms of the sharing of interests and, to a lesser extent at seven, in the willingness of fathers to participate. This led us to speculate further about the precise nature of the qualitative difference in parent–child relationships that differentiates middle-class from working-class parents; and we eventually concluded that the salient difference was to be found in the parents' degree of 'child-centredness'. To the extent that such a dimension informs the whole range of parental behaviour towards the child, even small class differences here must be reckoned important. The emergence of substantial differences would identify a major social class differentiation in child-rearing practice.
  What do we mean by 'child-centred'? In general terms, the key-

note to this attitude is the parents' recognition of the child's status as an individual with rights and feelings that are worthy of respect. In other words, although clashes of interest will inevitably arise between children and adults, child-centred parents voluntarily relinquish the authoritarian stance, and instead deliberately concede to the child the right to exercise choice and autonomy, to participate in decision making, and generally to be taken seriously as a member of the family community. Child-centredness is *not* to be equated with permissiveness or indulgence: for instance, the mother may insist on certain conformities which she regards as important or inevitable, while showing her child-centredness in her sympathy for the child's wish not to conform and in the trouble she takes to make conformity in these respects easier for him.

When the children were four, we brought together six items from the interview schedule 'chosen for their face validity as positive indications of child-centredness in the mother': the index thus devised reflected the mother's responsiveness to the child's attention demands, her wholehearted (i.e. equal-status) participation in the child's play, willingness to 'chat' during the night if asked, acceptance of the child's excuse of 'I'm busy', valuation of the child 'for himself', and willingness not to make a moral issue of the child's smacking her. Overall, a significant class difference was found on this index: middle-class mothers were more likely than working-class mothers to score high on child-centredness, and *vice versa*. The differences were not very striking, and were probably obscured at four years by the more nurturant role expected towards the pre-school child. In particular, however, they were interesting in their support for what we had already identified as a middle-class principle of reciprocity of rights as between parent and child.[7]

The data which made up the child-centredness index at four was no longer appropriate at seven, but on a similar rationale a further index was devised for this age-level, data again being drawn from questions scattered throughout the interview. We saw indications of child-centredness in ten specific items, viz.:

1. That the mother concedes the need for the child to have some place, however small, to keep his own things; a corner, a cupboard or a grocery box all count.
2. That the child can and does bring his friends into the house.
*3. That the child's reluctance to go to school is met with sympathy. Mothers are not, of course, totally free agents in this,

since it is their legal responsibility to get the child to school: we were thus looking for a sympathetic response rather than actual permission to stay at home.

*4. That the child's *pretence* of illness in order to miss school should also be sympathetically dealt with, even though he may still be sent.

*5. That the child's complaints of school should be taken seriously (irrespective of action taken).

*6. That the child's artistic efforts are taken seriously: mother shows she values them by displaying or keeping them.

7. That the mother shares some interest with her child.

*8. That the child has some voice in deciding on holiday activities (anything from 'Denmark or Spain?' through 'Skegness or Mablethorpe?' to 'Shall we take our tea to the park?').

9. That the child's 'rudeness' or 'cheekiness' to his mother is ignored or reproved, but not punished.

10. That the mother may occasionally apologise to the child for being cross with him: not when she has accused him mistakenly (this does not count), but when she has been rather crosser than she feels the situation warranted.

The actual questions and scoring system for the index follow in Table 34. Some of the topics to which these questions refer are discussed elsewhere in this book, and page numbers are given; starred questions are considered relevant to the child's educational experience, and are discussed in the volume subsequent to this, *Perspectives on School at Seven Years Old*.

Taken in isolation, none of these individual items, perhaps, would provide very convincing evidence of child-centredness. Since each question contributes only a single point to the overall score, however, we would argue that the total score does give a meaningful indication of the mother's present underlying attitudes. Table 35 presents high-scoring and low-scoring mothers analysed by sex of the child and social class.

The differences emerging in this table are too clear-cut to be ignored. Both sex and social class differences are statistically significant, and the social class trend is particularly striking: the proportion of highly child-centred mothers varies from 60% at the top of the class scale to 16% at the lower end, while for middle-class mothers as a group about one-half are highly child-centred, compared with only a quarter of working-class mothers as a group.

Table 34 *An index of child-centredness*

Question		Answer scoring 1
23	Does N have a special place of his own where he can keep his own things? (pp. 129–30)	Yes, however small; grocery carton counts
36	Do [his friends] come and play at your house? (pp. 95–9)	Yes, most weeks
*105	What do you do [what do you think you would do] if he says he doesn't want to go to school today?	Sympathetic attitude; whether child goes is irrelevant to score
*107	What do you do [what would you do] if he pretends he's not well, so as to stay at home from school?	Sympathetic attitude; whether child goes is irrelevant to score
*109	How do you feel about children's complaints of school? Do you think you should take them seriously?	Yes, irrespective of action
*135	What happens to his drawings when he's finished them?	Keep or display at least some
147	Is there any special interest which you and N share – something which you both follow together? (pp. 271–3)	Yes
*152	When you're deciding what to do during the holidays, does N have any say in what you choose?	Yes
184	What do you do when he is rude to you? (pp. 363–6)	Rebuke or nothing
195	Do you ever say sorry to *him* for being cross with him?	Yes: apology because of mistaken accusation excluded

Possible score range: 0–10

Conversely, well over half of Class v mothers score low on child-centredness, compared with only one in ten of Class I and II; as a group, nearly three times as many working-class mothers as middle-class mothers score low.

The overall sex differences, which are considerably less marked, show that mothers of boys are more likely to be low scorers than mothers of girls; but closer inspection shows that this sex difference is an exclusively working-class phenomenon. In the middle-class, mothers of boys are as likely to be child-centred as mothers of girls, but in the working-class group it is the boys whose mothers are least likely to have child-centred attitudes. Presumably this finding is related to the greater social contact which working-class girls have with their mothers through being kept more closely to

K

hearth and home. Interestingly, this difference between boys and girls is confined to the skilled and semi-skilled: Class v mothers, while emphatically continuing the trend away from child-centredness, do not favour their girls in this way.

When these index scores are subjected to other statistical analyses, a further significant relationship appears in terms of family size. Children from large families are less likely to have child-centred parents (p <0·001); but this is again influenced by social class, so that the family size effect *only appears clearly in relation to working-class children*. Among middle-class children, family size does not appear to be significantly related to child-centredness.

Table 35   *Mothers showing high or low child-centredness*

	social class					summary		
	I&II	IIIwc	III man	IV	V	I&II, IIIwc	IIIman, IV,V	overall popn.
	%	%	%	%	%	%	%	%
Low scorers (0–4)								
boys	16	16	44	51	60	16	47	39
girls	5	24	30	35	54	14	34	28
both	10	20	37	43	57	15	40	34

Significance: trend ↗ ****
between sexes **
                             m.class/w.class ****
interaction sex x class   n.s.

High scorers (7–10)								
boys	61	47	18	22	21	54	19	29
girls	58	39	32	33	10	49	30	35
both	60	43	25	28	16	51	25	32

Significance: trend ↘ ****
(non-linear trend **)   between sexes n.s.
                    m.class/w.class ****
interaction sex x class *

In this chapter we have been concerned not with snippets of behaviour (such as whether the child picks his nose, or whether his mother shouts at him for picking his nose); nor even with strands of development (such as whether he is becoming more independently involved with his peer group, or whether his mother tries to supervise his involvement with the peer group). Rather, our preoccupation has been with the much less graspable entities of love, pleasure, warmth, concern and empathy: concepts which endlessly frustrate the researcher into family life, because he finds them so elusive yet *knows*, with a certainty that goes back to his own babyhood, that they are of supreme significance because they pervade and colour every behaviour, every attitude, every response of the child-rearing pattern.

So we have done our best to disentangle the threads, and inevitably one must be dissatisfied with an account which one knows to be less subtly shaded than the pattern it describes. Nevertheless, a harsh light may give definition.

We have noted before[8] that psychologists and sociologists who try to investigate social class differences soon discover their own social problems in that it is often felt (particularly by liberal-minded middle-class people) that it is not very nice to discuss social class at all; but especially not nice to discuss social disadvantage, and downright bad taste to talk about the social disadvantage to children that might lie in their parents' attitudes as opposed to mere material misfortune. Things have changed somewhat, to the extent that (in this country alone) the research of Pringle, Butler *et al.*, Bernstein, Douglas and others, as well as our own, has made social class as a factor for advantage or disadvantage impossible to ignore; yet we still detect an uneasiness in exploring these topics, which often manifests itself in an appeal to certain stereotyped notions of working-class virtue. Prime among these is a strong middle-class belief in working-class *warmth*: which is probably partly sustained by an equally strong working-class belief in middle-class frigidity. Of course, the middle-class speaker who expatiates on working-class warmth is never prepared to include his own circle of friends among the chilly middle class, or to suggest that he himself might be experiencing special difficulty in relating to his children because of his own middle-class affiliation. As we have seen in this chapter, it is not in fact possible to distinguish the social classes in terms of the warmth and affection which they give their seven-year-old children; and we ourselves would be inclined to appraise these beliefs as sentimental myths, comforting to the working class and expiatory to the middle class, akin to the myths of compensatory talents that grow up around the handicapped.

But warmth in terms of the giving and receiving of affection is only part of the story: it only makes up one aspect of the ambience of love in which the child gradually learns his own identity. Warmth can be felt for any treasured possession – an animal, a plant, a place. It is when the mother's warmth is asked to subsume consideration, respect, reciprocity, recognition: it is then that the crunch comes. How this is resolved must surely be basic to the child's image of himself, to his understanding of the human pattern of rights and obligations, to his ability to identify and empathise with others, and eventually to his capacity to accept responsibility as a mature member, not just of the family community, but of society as a whole.

If all these things are contingent upon child-centredness, and child-centredness itself is contingent upon social class, what then? Can we indeed see these findings in any more optimistic light than as a self-perpetuating mechanism for the preservation of the existing class structure with all its inequalities?

NOTES

1 At four we categorised replies by whether the mother expressly valued the child for himself (80%), for his affectionate behaviour (12%), for his good behaviour (7%) or for his physical appearance (1%); in relation to seven-year-olds, the data seemed less amenable in any meaningful way to an analysis of this kind.

2 See interview schedule, Appendix i, questions 112–52.

3 Taking these activities to be the home contribution to the educational process, they are discussed in the volume following this one: *Perspectives on School at Seven Years Old*, Allen & Unwin.

4 One per cent of our children's fathers had died by the child's seventh birthday; in 3% of families the parents were now separated, the child normally – though not invariably – remaining in the wife's care.

5 Elsewhere we have used an analysis of this extract to illustrate a number of points of interviewing technique. J. and E. Newson, in M. Shipman, (ed.), 1976.

6 See pages 198–9, 402–3.

7 J. and E. Newson, 1968, Chapters 13 and 14.

8 J. and E. Newson, in M. Shipman (ed.), 1976.

Chapter 9

Coming to Blows

We emphasised in the last chapter that by the time they are seven most children are seen by their parents as having personality characteristics of a very definite and distinctive kind. Right at the beginning of the interview we asked 'How would you describe him now to someone who didn't know him at all?' The following are one hundred adjectives taken at random from mothers' descriptions of their child's personality:

. . . sentimental, inflexible, affectionate, bossy, charming, rowdy, competitive, adult, crafty, aware, overbearing, responsible, touchy, demanding, worried, co-operative, open, spoilt, awkward, jealous, kind-hearted, lazy, obstruculous, unpredictable, nervous, independent, defeatist, over-concerned, placid, lively, sensitive, easily led, happy, insecure, strange, strong-willed, wearing, imaginative, happy-go-lucky, understanding, temperamental, adaptable, precocious, sensible, timorous, bad-tempered, jolly, absent-minded, scruffy, aggressive, cheeky, shy, comic, honest, deep, definite, enthusiastic, highly strung, amiable, pig-headed, marvellous, sophisticated, reserved, changeable, gentle, appreciative, self-contained, moody, high-spirited, irritating, studious, accident-prone, difficult, quick, withdrawn, irritable, mature, rather sweet, a bit dumb, anti-social, lovely, lonely, argumentative, courageous, helpful, perfectionist, quiet, mardy, restless, self-confident, slap-dash, idle, logical, serious, cute, bold, easy, variable, agreeable – and "funny – can't really explain him – there *is* a word, I suppose, but I can't think of it at the moment".

In short, the children are now asserting themselves as persons in their own right, individuals who have their own strengths and vulnerabilities, qualities and faults: who can pay a compliment that means something, offer a genuine act of kindness and consideration towards others, express opinions based on experience gained outside the bounds of the family circle, and in general make a real contribution to the family's social life. On the whole, parents react positively to their children's individualistic traits as a sign of the maturing of personality. What these developments also mean, however, is that the child is fully able to express feelings and ideas of his own which can bring him into direct conflict with other people. Since it is fairly characteristic for both children and adults to behave with least inhibition in the bosom of their own family, situations of conflict between parent and child are hardly likely to diminish at this stage, even though they are probably of a more verbal nature than at four. Thus the positive advance from four years old that we noted in Chapter 2, that 'you can reason with them more at this age', does not signify a reduction of conflict itself: merely that the mother resorts less to physical propulsion ('Pick her up and put her where she has to be')[1] and more to verbal persuasion. If parents feel that this is an improvement on the situation at four, this simply means that, with Churchill, they regard 'jaw jaw' as preferable to 'war war', not that in fact the child is more docile and biddable.

Newsagent's wife:
> He's no more tricky than any other child, I suppose; I have to be very dogmatic with him, you know ,"You've *got* to do so-and-so", and eventually we win; but he's got . . . he's got very much a mind of his own – but it's no good expecting an adult with a mind of his own if you have a wishy-washy child, you just can't. If he's going to grow up with his "yes" being "yes" and his "no" being "no", he's going to have a mind of his own when he's young, isn't he?

At seven, simple parental techniques of distraction and suggestion have largely lost their effectiveness. While the child's displays of somewhat undifferentiated rage or 'temper' have declined in frequency (and also in uninhibited violence), he is now better able to present and sustain an oppositional stance. He can argue the toss, dig his heels in on a matter of principle, or resort to sophisticated stratagems such as procrastination or the manufacture of quasi-reasonable excuses. Children of this age are not only becoming adept at resistance: they are also beginning to discover how to bring pressure to bear on others in order to manipulate events their way. And this applies not only to the 'negativistic' children whom we discussed as a group in Chapter 2 (pp. 40–2); it is true at least sometimes of the majority of children. Sometimes the very characteristic which makes a child docile at school will resolve him to obstinacy in the more intimate setting of home: the timorous child, for example, may show extreme determination in *not* going to children's parties or on outings, or to school itself, but, once there, may seem exceptionally amenable. But even those who are thought of by their parents as particularly co-operative, easy children (see pp. 43–4) can have their moments of (characteristically passive) resistance. Mark's mother, for example, is annoyed by his 'very *slight* disobedience': 'at the moment it's always "Yes, I'm coming" – "Yes, in a minute" . . . I've always got to wait'.

The extent of seven-year-old resistance can be gauged by the answers to one of our early 'general personality' questions, 'Is he the sort of child who usually agrees with what you want him to do, or does he tend to object to things quite a lot?' Only 37% overall were said to be generally agreeable to parental requests; 37% were variable, and 26% of all children objected to things 'quite a lot'. Sex and class differences are insignificant but Class I and II boys tend to be less 'agreeable'. These findings are discussed later (pp. 373ff) in terms of general personality dimensions; but we can illustrate them here simply to make the point that conflict is by no means a dead issue at seven.

Publican's wife:
She objects. Objects very strongly. She's got a will, you know. She thinks that she won't listen to you, she has to do it *her* way. You have to clamp down on her to make her do it.

Milkman's wife:
Oh, he does object to things, and you've got to really put your foot down. Mainly it's about going out: *he* likes to play, that's his idea of heaven, he doesn't *want* to go out anywhere, out to tea or anything; and we sort of say "We're going", and we can't go without him 'cause we can't leave him on his own, and we *have* had tantrums.

Warehouse manager's wife:
Agree? Oh *no*! [laughter] I say he'll be a lawyer when he grows up – he can argue his way out of anything!

Miner's wife:

No, she has her own mind and she likes *you* to agree with *her* if she thinks she's right. [If you want her to do something, will she do it?] Well – she will if she thinks it's right. If she thinks she's put on, she'll change her mind. She's very helpful in the house, she does all the Sunday tea, that's her job, and she doesn't want anyone else to wash the lettuce or do the tomatoes, and she cuts the cucumber thick, but I have to leave her to it, you know.

Wholesaler's wife:

Well, so-so; it seems to me that when you're expecting that he's going to object you don't get it; whereas another time you think, oh this is going to be plain sailing, and he suddenly sort of digs his toes in, and you know you're going to have a bit of a struggle; and then quite suddenly he capitulates and decides that it's quite all right anyway!

Bleacher's wife:

No, she's like me, like I was – if she's in the right mood she'll do anything, if she isn't she'll see you in hell before she does it!

Estimating supervisor's wife:

It depends how you put it to her. I mean, as an example, if I get clothes for her or I choose something, *invariably*, what I like, she says "Oh! I don't like that!" But the other day I bought her a dress – instead of giving it to her or saying anything, I just put it on the bed, and when she went up and saw it she decided she liked it. But this is what I have to do – I mean I have to know how to *approach* her, sort of thing.

Coal driver's wife:

He'll agree, but his face'll disagree and he'll sulk about it – but he won't come out openly and say.

Before discussing the issues involved in open conflict, we must also remember that there is an area of sub-conflict, as it were, that bears on this: the mutual friction generated by parent and child. We asked, as at four, 'What about disagreements? What sort of things make you get on each other's nerves now, you and N?' Oppositional or 'disobedient' behaviour was in fact often cited in this context; but there was also a miscellany of annoyances which did not relate to amenability, but had more to do with the rough edges of irritation that can appear in the relationship of any two people living at close quarters. To the extent that general friction, whatever the source, can fuel open conflict, this seems relevant to the issue. The wording of the question also allowed the mother to volunteer examples of the ways in which she thought she got on the child's nerves; and the overall impression, once again, is of a two-sided impact. Obviously parents were sometimes using their authority to 'go on' at their children in an effort to curb behaviour that they found annoying rather than actually judged as 'naughty'; almost equally, however, children seemed to be going on at their parents. Nagging, in short, appears to be normal on both sides.

Business executive's wife:
When he's thinking about something, with pencils in his mouth, one foot's lifting this slipper on and off, like this, and we go on *so much* about these wretched slippers – "For goodness sake put those shoes on your *feet*!" Pulling at his socks – his shoes and socks, on and off, fidgeting – always pulling at his socks, and makes holes in them you know, constantly, and this is the main source of, er . . . I mean, I just go on and on about it, but it doesn't seem to have any great effect on him . . . . . I think that must be his outlet, thinking about it, because he does it so very much. I've never quite thought about it that way before. I shall have to put it to my husband, because *he's* absolutely mad with these slippers. I've *never* met a child like him for this.

Auto-electrician's wife:
A lot of little things. She doesn't like me to sing, because she says I've got an awful voice – and I say "I don't blame you"! – and she doesn't like me to shout at her in the street, I have to keep my voice well lowered when we're walking along in the street, because if I talk very loudly she says "Shush!"

Builder's labourer's wife:
She's really awkward at times, and she'll say "Can I have so-and-so dress on?" – well, it's probably dirty, ready for washing, and I'll say "No, you can't" – "Well, can I have me shorts on?" And I tell her, you know, that it's not suitable weather for them, and then she'll start showing off a little bit. Of course, she'll get a slap, then I feel easier then; and many a time she'll say to me "I'm leaving, I am!" And I'll say "Go on, then, the bag's upstairs". She'll say "I am, I'm leaving!" and I'll say "Well, all

right ten". But nothing ever comes of it, I think she just does it to aggravate me.

Builder's wife:
Well, if he says "Mam!" and I say "Just wait a minute" – "You're not listening, are you!" He likes me to answer *straight away*; and you're just there making the dinner, he'll say "Mam, I've got something to tell you!" I say "Can you just wait a minute?" – "Oh, just you listen to me *now*". That gets on his nerves a bit. He likes me to be just listening, drop everything and sit down and listen to him, you know. He'll say "Mam, look at this". I'll say "Yes, it's lovely" – "No, you didn't even look at it, you couldn't even know what it's like!"

Cook's wife:
Well, she must have her *say*; and you tell her to "shut up and don't answer me back". But she must say what . . . "I'm *not* being cheeky, Mummy", and I can't seem to get through that it *is* cheekiness. I just can't make her see – she thinks that she's got something to say, and so she's going to say it! [So she's really putting her point of view, as far as she can see?] That's right, yes, and in her little mind I don't think she realises how cheeky she's been – whether I'm wrong or not there, I don't know, but whatever the consequence is going to be for her afterwards, she must have her say and explain herself. [And it comes out to you as cheekiness?] Well, especially when you say "Now shut up, I don't want to hear another word" – "But . . . I'm only . . .", and she'll carry on, you know, you just can't get it through. "Now I don't want to hear anything else about it, and that's it!" But *no*, she will *not*, and you *will* hear it, it doesn't matter what you're going to do to her, you'll hear it; and it annoys me at times.

Soap processor's wife:
Drives me mad . . . the moment she starts reading – she's not reading to herself, she reads out aloud to *you*, you know – the *voice*! It goes on and on. I know it's a good thing, but it gets on your nerves when you hear it all the time.

'He knows what he has to do, but it's always prolonged, and agonising to me . . .'
A typical way for a child to frustrate his mother's wishes at seven is by almost infinite procrastination. On a number of counts it is

an effective strategy on his part. It gives him an opportunity to make verbal objections if he wishes, yet does not quite commit him to the risky course of outright refusal. It leaves his options open so that if his mother becomes dangerously impatient he can hastily comply, while there is a good chance that she will abandon the struggle and do the job herself, help him to do it, or even produce a bribe. And if he does misjudge his mother's tolerance and she 'clips him one to buck his ideas up a bit', he will at least have the satisfaction of protesting righteously that he was 'just going to do it'.

Being slow, is, of course, the other side of the coin of independence, in the sense that if nothing is expected of the child in self-help skills or small domestic jobs then he cannot be judged slow in completing them. At the same time, there has also to be some element of supervision involved: thus the mother is the more irritated by the child's slowness over washing, dressing and so on if she feels that finally she has to check him out as having satisfactorily completed the process. Obviously the constraints that come from the demands of society that members of the family should be in certain places at certain times will often exacerbate this.

HP collector's wife:

I keep telling him over and over again – like when he won't get ready, you know. Oh, he really gets on me nerves. It takes him ages – and then he'll *stop*! When he gets undressed for bed, it'll take him ever such a long time – it takes him ages just to get his trousers off, you know. "Oh", I say, "aren't you ready *yet*? Oh! . . ." [What do you do when he gets very slow?] Oh, I either say "Come on, *I'll* get you ready" – if it's getting late, like if it's in the morning and he's got to get to school – 'cause he goes upstairs and washes himself, you see, and after I've looked to see – I mean it takes him a long time, but it doesn't mean he's really had a good wash! It's just that he messes about in the water, and he's got some deep-sea . . . you know, frogmen, like rubber, and he puts them in the sink and does things like that, you know. He plays about. [And so you would do it for him, would you?] Yes, if he's late. If he's got plenty of time, I just don't bother – you know, if it's, like, at the weekend.

If one looks at the 'being slow' syndrome in terms of incidence, the children divide fairly evenly into three groups: those who do tend to take a long time over carrying out their parents' requests, those who are usually quick, and those who are variable in this. Rather more than a third (35%) are 'often' slow; rather less than a third (29%) are usually quick. Class differences are negligible except that Class v children are significantly less often described as slow in this respect: as we have seen, less may be expected of these children by way of chores, and they are also less subject to close supervision and control by their parents. There is no significant difference between boys and girls.

Minor class differences do arise when it comes to the mother's reaction to her child's dawdling. A minority (11%) would resort to physical punishment for slowness itself, and in this group there are neither class nor sex differences.

Sales representative's wife:

I usually clip him one, you know, that bucks his ideas up a bit. [It's being slow, not actually refusing?] Oh, he's not refusing, no – that's why I feel a bit awful when I've done it, you know; I've done it on the spur of the moment, but it does – er – bring him to his senses . . . . . You couldn't help getting cross with him. You know, I've sort of talked to him, tried talking and telling him . . . I've smacked him in a temper more than anything, not hard, but just to make him jump to it, you know, and he seems as if he's improving anyway.

The majority strategy is verbal rebuke: 'just talk sharp to him'; 'say "Come on, I'm waiting" in a very annoyed sort of voice'; 'chivvy her on a bit'; 'give a gingering-up speech'. 'I start with a gentle nag', says one mother, 'and then I sort of yell a bit louder, and then I shriek *RUTH* at the top of my voice, and she realises she's gone too far and she jumps to it then'. Seventy-five per cent would verbally reprimand the child. However, this majority group is slightly overweighted with middle-class mothers; and when we look at the third group, a small minority who would ignore procrastination altogether (Table 36), there is a steady class trend (significant at 0·001) towards greater willingness to ignore at the lower end of the scale. Possibly this again fits with the fewer demands made in terms of duties, the lower degree of adult supervision, and perhaps a less urgent family timetable further down the class scale. 'I dress her', says a lorry driver's wife, 'it saves ever such a lot of trouble, you know. I do a lot of things people don't do, for the sake of peace and quiet'; and an unemployed labourer's wife is equally relaxed: 'What's the use of taking any notice on him? I mean, he does it in the finish'.

The conflict about whether it is easier for a mother to do things herself rather than teach the child the necessary skill is no longer a central issue as it appears at four. There is generally not so much doubt now that the child is *able* to do as he is asked. Even so, he will still find it very difficult to carry out a task in the mechanical fashion that adults adopt when they mindlessly run through a well-practised routine while thinking of something more interesting. It is an established fact that children of this age are not as capable

Table 36 *Mothers who 'ignore it' when their children are very slow in complying with requests.*

	social class					summary		
	I&II	IIIwc	III man	IV	V	I&II, IIIwc	IIIman, IV,V	overall popn.
	%	%	%	%	%	%	%	%
boys	5	9	10	16	16	6	12	11
girls	8	10	15	25	18	9	18	15
both	6	10	13	21	17	8	15	13

Significance: trend ↗ ****   m.class/w.class **
between sexes n.s.

as they will be later on of doing two things at the same time or of planning the second stage of an operation while carrying out the first. Perhaps this is the root cause of the problem: that children realise when they are asked to do something that this will probably mean a prolonged effort of concentrating their attention on some activity of little intrinsic interest to themselves. In other words, it may be because children at this age have very compelling ideas of their own to think about that so many of them resist doing chores which will monopolise their attention until completed.

'I don't think it's easy to bring up a high-spirited little child, you know ...'
Although procrastination can come very close to a tacit refusal, both child and mother are aware that the situation is still open-ended, and that a showdown is not yet necessary. An explicit refusal by the child is quite another matter, as is immediately reflected in the proportion of mothers who say they would smack him in

response to this: 56% overall, compared with the 11% who smack for being slow. We asked 'What happens when he simply refuses to do what you want him to do?' A number of mothers said that this kind of outright refusal was not something they would expect at all. 'Luckily, she wouldn't', said a supervisor's wife – 'she'd go quite a long way, but not *that* far!'

Engineering foreman's wife:
Oh, there's no such thing as refusing in this house. I think from the very start, you see, it isn't just now, it's all through the years, you see – you start it when they're young, you tell them to do a thing, and she's got to do it and that's it – it grows with them through the years – they *know* when you tell them to do a thing it's got to be done.

Greengrocer's wife:
Well, he doesn't definitely refuse. [Suppose he did one day?] Well, if he'd got to do it, he'd *have* to do it, there'd be no beating about the bush, but I mean if it's a thing that must be done, then he's got to get on with it. [How would you make him?] Well, we just tell him that it's no use playing about, he's got to do it and that's all there is to it, you might just as well get on; and of course he knows when we tell him that he *has* got to do it, because we have had that idea with them right from the beginning – they *do* know, and I think it's the same with all children, they *do* know how far they can go; and of course we've been very firm about that sort of thing right from the start when they were very small. If we said something has got to be done, then it's got to be done – nothing in the world will stop it being done if we say it's going to be.

Sales representative's wife:
I'd nag him. I don't really think – perhaps I'm wrong – that a child *should* refuse at this age. I mean, er . . . although with Gordon, you know, we kind of go along with him and we want him to have a happy life, I still thank that, um, children shouldn't rule the parents, kind of thing. I think that there's that much trouble today that I kind of rule him very strongly . . . or perhaps I'm just kidding myself.

Others emphasised the rarity of real refusal as opposed to resistance: 'He doesn't usually refuse point-blank', said a university teacher's wife; 'occasionally he throws a great and mighty tantrum

– this doesn't happen very often, but when he's cooled off he usually does it'.

Tax inspector (father speaking):
When there's absolute defiance, what usually happens then is a flood of tears, and either she is sent upstairs, or more often she will withdraw upstairs of her own accord, and there'll be sobbing and sighing and all that, and half-an-hour later a rueful Hilary will reappear and say she's sorry . . . but this happens very, very rarely, she doesn't often get to that stage.

For one mother, the exceptional nature of her child's refusal was itself a warning to be exceptionally tolerant: 'Well, I'd realise there was something up then, because Juliet is very easy to talk into doing things – if she absolutely refused to do something, I'd think there was something, some reason, and do it myself'. Most, however, saw it as the moment for clamping down, sometimes after a brief re-consideration.

Instructor's wife:
Well, if it was something important enough it would be a slap; I mean, I don't mind him having a mind of his own and saying he's not going to do some things that don't matter – or at least that *I* think don't matter, I mean parents have different sorts of views on these sorts of things, don't they? But if it's something that I consider important that has got to be done – er – if he refuses to do it, he either gets a slap or he does it, you know.

University student's wife:
It very often develops into this: "You will wash" – "I will not wash". Um – I think, generally speaking, I win. [How do you win?] I'm not sure – I don't smack him or anything else like that. [Father:] The crunch is, she's very fierce. [Mother:] It's difficult to say how it happens – I don't know, but I think I can generally get my own way. [Father:] If the situation has arisen where in fact he's been asked to do something very unreasonable, I think *you* realise this at the same time, and perhaps you can sort it out. But if it's just that he's digging his toes in because it's Monday morning, then Mummy's just fierce and he'll resent you for it. He cries but he moves.

Unemployed labourer's wife (who takes no notice of slowness, page 301): He'll get his backside smacked.

Only a small minority of 8%, without class or sex differences, would neither reprimand nor punish in the face of the child's refusal: 'I've had that many kiddies, I don't bother now, I do it myself', said an unemployed labourer's wife. Obviously also a rebuke can sometimes be implied in the *way* a mother may say 'Don't bother, I'll do it myself': the child may receive the message that he is at best unhelpful and at worst immature. We can reasonably assume, then, that almost always the child's refusal is met by disapproval, which in more than half of these cases is expressed in physical punishment.

It seems relevant to emphasise that, at the moment in the interview when 56% of the mothers volunteered that they would smack their child in the situation specified, neither punishment in general nor physical punishment in particular had yet been explicitly raised by the interviewer. The questions at this stage were deliberately framed rather neutrally: in fact, looking again at the four questions which bring us to this point, it is feasible to imagine them all being asked the other way round, in terms of how the child might react if faced by a refusal. The mother's *disciplinary* function, as opposed to her social relationship with the child, is not predicated by Questions 156–9; and it is not until Question 160, when she has already had the chance to commit herself spontaneously to smacking, that this topic is introduced by the interviewer.

156. What about disagreements? What sort of things make you get on each other's nerves now, you and N?
157. Do you find that N takes a long time over doing as you ask him?
158. What do you do if he's being very slow over this sort of thing?
159. What happens if he simply refuses to do something you want him to do?
160. How do you feel about smacking children of this age?

These questions and parents' reactions to them highlight the basic issues which emerge when we come to consider differences in disciplinary styles. Some conflict between parent and child is almost inevitable: it arises because parents require children to do things, or to refrain from doing things, and this interferes with the child's autonomy as a person, with wishes and feelings of his own. In disciplinary conflicts, by definition, we have a situation where certain individuals exercise their rights as people of superior status (in age, power and presumed wisdom) to determine what younger and less experienced people, of inferior status, may or may not do. If the child complies willingly, of course, (even if his willingness has been engineered by offering him the illusion of choice) his self-esteem can be kept intact; but whenever he is forced into an unwilling compliance by the threat of sanctions, whether these be pain inflicted or approval withdrawn, he will inevitably suffer in some degree feelings of powerlessness and humiliation.

Punishment is the word we use when sanctions are enforced by one person on another in an effort to secure compliance despite resistance: or sometimes in order to re-emphasise the power relationship when it appears to be threatened by sustained resistance or refusal. In the latter case, it is the hope of the punisher that *next time* his power to compel will be restored.

Punishment can take many different forms, ranging from beatings of greater or lesser severity, through the token slap, deprivation of normal rights or privileges and deprivation of property, to social ostracism. If this discussion is to mean anything, it seems important to define as 'punishment situations' only those which involve a deliberate act in which a socially more powerful person demonstrates that he can subject a less powerful person to his will. In the context of human relationships, it can obscure the issue to label all aversive stimulus as punishment. The burnt child fears the flame, but it is stretching a point to say that a flame can *punish* a child; equally, if a wife says to her husband 'Do you think I did right?' and he replies 'Not really', this may be aversive but cannot under normal circumstances be usefully discussed as punishment.

The definitive boundaries are of course blurred; but at least we can say that subjection is always implicit (and often explicit) in punishment. Thus its effect is mainly to hurt the child's pride, whether or not it is physically painful. Punishments are directed at the child's sense of self-esteem, and are intended to deflate his ego, and this is so whether they consist in the mother deliberately turning her back on him or beating him with a broom-handle.

The other side of this coin is that punishment in some sense absolves the child from responsibility for his action. For the present it bears the message 'I am making sure you pay for what you've done'; and for the future it adds 'if you do it again, you'll pay for it again', with the corollary ' – so you might think it's worth it'. Now or in the future, the punishing parent thus accepts responsibility for settling the account, and thus *the child's conscience is bypassed*. To this extent, punishment can even be a refuge and a comfort to the child. We shall return to the ways in which some parents recognise this in the next chapter (see pages 341–4).

'Not many go through life without a smack . . .'
When the children were four, we tried to come closer to what was happening when a mother smacked her child by describing it in the following terms, which still seem to hold good at seven:

> . . . smacking happens as one element in a *pattern of under-standing* between the mother and the child. The mother has a fairly consistent set of principles, roughly corresponding to her authoritarian or democratic attitude, which she hopes in time to communicate to the child by her words and actions, and through which she expects to socialise him into the sort of person she values; and, within this framework of principle, she not only smacks but tries to evaluate for the child the meaning of her smack. It is probably true to say that the precise form of an aggressive act is less important than the fact that it has occurred; and it is certainly true that the objective force of a smack, is less significant to the child than the spirit in which it is delivered.[2]

In other words, we have argued that issues as to how often and how hard children are smacked may be less important in the child's socialisation experience than the impact upon him of the mother's general outlook upon the whole disciplinary situation; thus, unless children are physically cowed by harsh and brutal treatment (which the great majority are clearly not), smacking is more usefully considered as a kind of punctuation within the context of a continuing dialogue rather than as a simple aversive stimulus. *As* punctuation, however, it clearly has significance in altering the feel of the situation: just as the disciplinary confrontation in itself crystallises issues of power and status, so the use of physical punishment underlines a relationship of 'I'm bigger than you' as opposed to 'I'm wiser than you'.

It is also true that the significance of frequency of smacking is rather greater at seven than at four because of the age characteristics involved. At four, although the possibilities of verbal control are very much greater than at one year, they are still imperfect enough for some mothers to discount them altogether. This is reflected in the fact that 75% of all mothers were smacking once a week or more when the child was four. By seven, the verbal alternatives to smacking are more obviously available, and this proportion drops – to 41%. However, because they are now a minority group, if a large one, these mothers can be assumed to be more committed to a 'smacking philosophy' than the majority group, taken as a whole, who smacked thus often at four.

Again, frequency is likely to be indicative of the mother's philosophy because it distinguishes between those who smack as a day-to-day measure – as part of their normal vocabulary, as it were – and those who use it as a last resort because everything else has failed, because the situation itself is exceptional, or simply because they've had a specially bad day. The mother who says 'I suppose at weekends he gets more because he's at home more then' clearly has a different *approach* from the one who, asked when she last smacked James, says 'I seem to remember an argy-bargy in the bathroom . . . it *might* have been this year . . .'

The frequency of smacking also has significance for the child in terms of how he evaluates any individual incident: to extend the punctuation metaphor, an exclamation mark will have more impact if used once in a chapter than if it is sprinkled ten to the page. The mother who wishes to use smacking for dramatic effect will obviously have to set this against a general policy of non-smacking, and the smack itself can be relatively light: while the woman who smacks as 'just part of the daily routine' not only finds that 'children forget about it so quickly', but is likely to resort to harder and harder smacking when occasionally she does want to make a more dramatic statement.

Before looking at the way parents feel about smacking, then, we should give the issue perspective by considering how often smacking actually occurs at seven.

The categories given in Table 37 are exclusive, in the sense that no child appears in more than one. Eight per cent overall are smacked once a day or more often; a third are smacked at least once a week but not as often as once a day; 28% are smacked at least once a month but less than once a week; and almost a third are smacked less than once in a month or not at all. Sex and class differences can be most clearly seen in the 'once a week' and 'less than once a month' categories: it is very obvious that boys in general tend to be smacked a good deal more often than girls, and that smacking decreases considerably for both sexes as one moves up the class scale.

However, before asking mothers how often the child in fact was smacked (at Question 166), we had already asked a series of questions exploring mothers' subjective feelings about smacking as

Table 37 *Actual smacking frequency reported by mothers*

	social class					summary		
	I&II	*IIIwc*	*III man*	*IV*	*V*	*I&II, IIIwc*	*IIIman, IV,V*	*overall popn.*
	%	%	%	%	%	%	%	%
Once a day or more								
boys	4	7	12	14	11	6	12	11
girls	2	8	6	5	5	5	6	6
both	3	7	9	9	8	5	9	8

Significance: trend $\nearrow$ p = 0·06   m.class/w.class n.s.
between sexes *

Once a week or more, excluding those above

boys	35	40	41	38	53	37	42	41
girls	17	18	27	22	44	18	28	25
both	26	29	34	30	48	28	35	33

Significance: trend $\nearrow$ ***   m.class/w.class p = 0·08
between sexes ****

Combining above two sections, to show children who are smacked
at least once a week
trend reaches **** significance

Once a month or more, excluding those above

boys	26	31	22	22	17	28	23	25
girls	29	31	33	35	23	29	32	29
both	27	31	28	29	20	29	27	28

Significance: trend inconsistent n.s.   m.class/w.class n.s.
between sexes n.s.

Less than once a month

boys	35	22	23	26	19	29	23	25
girls	52	43	34	38	28	48	34	38
both	44	33	29	32	24	38	29	31

Significance: trend $\searrow$ ***   m.class/w.class **
between sexes ****

a principle. The first four of these questions asked them to consider smacking in general: the last, to gauge their emotional feelings upon smacking their own child.

160. How do you feel about smacking children of this age?
161. Do you think parents should try to do without smacking altogether, or do you think smacking is a good way of training children?
162. In general, do you think smacking has good results with children of this age?
163. Any bad results?
165. What effect does [smacking] have on you? Do you feel relieved or upset in any way, (or is it just a part of the routine)? [*Last clause omitted only if mother clearly does not smack routinely*]

In addition, we later asked two further questions which are worth looking at briefly at this point, since they also ask the mother to examine her feelings about discipline.

196. Do you find that how strict you are depends a great deal on your own mood at the time?
197. When do you most approve of yourself – when you're being strict with N, or when you're being easy-going?

Bearing in mind the considerable class and sex differences where actual frequency of smacking is concerned, the results from the 'attitude' questions are somewhat surprising. Neither social class nor the child's sex is a significant factor. The individual personality of the mother seems to have more to do with her answer than any class-affiliated principle. In Table 38, percentage figures are given for a total random population, since in each case sex and class differences fail to reach statistical significance. The answers for Questions 160–3 are combined to give a three-point scale, viz: mother *generally approves of smacking*; she thinks it *unfortunate but necessary*; she *generally disapproves of it*.

These results can perhaps be illumined a little by the mothers' own words.

Generally approves of smacking:

Bank cashier's wife:
  I think they should be smacked. I don't think they should do away with it at all, because I think you . . . it's over and done

Table 38   *Mothers' attitudes to smacking and strictness*

(Percentages based on total randomised sample: no significant
differences with regard to sex or class)

Data based on:	Category	%
Q160–3	Generally approves of smacking	46
	Thinks it unfortunate but necessary	27
	Generally disapproves of smacking	27
Q165	Unemotional – 'just routine'	20
	Feels relieved	7
	Feels guilty or upset	73
Q196	States strictness not mood-dependent	16
	Admits strictness is mood-dependent	84
Q197	Self-approval greater when strict	15
	Self-approval greater when easy-going	69
	Miscellaneous unclassifiable	16

with immediately. I think no harm's done at all – it just shows them the right and wrong of things, and I think to hold a punishment till the end of the day is altogether wrong, and I think I'd far rather slap a child soundly and get it done with, and then they know that's not to be done. I'm in favour of it.

Machine operator's wife:
I don't think it does them any harm. I think it depends how hard and for what you slap them. But I wouldn't have any qualms about slapping them. I still think spare the rod and spoil the child. There's too much psychology applied to children.

Unfortunate but necessary:

Maintenance man's wife:
Well, I don't really like slapping them at any age really, but that's impossible really unless you're going to spoil them and let them have everything they want. It's the only way to get out of it. I believe it does no child any harm, just as long as you know how far to go with the slap.

Sales representative's wife:
I think it's necessary . . . I think, with a mother particularly, talking can be a waste of time – mothers talk so much that everything is lost, you know, so they don't listen, you know. They

seem to be . . . I think you've got to be aggressive, and – er – smack them to get them to respond; I don't know whether you've found that, but I just can't get through to them sometimes, I talk *too much*, you see . . . . . [Question 161] No, no, I think it would be a wonderful, wonderful world if we didn't have to do it, but I don't see any other way out, with boys particularly. I wouldn't – if I'd got a daughter – I wouldn't, I think *now*, I wouldn't want to smack a daughter; but I don't know whether I shall change my mind or not, I don't know. It depends on the child, I suppose, because you can't account for outbursts of temper really, can you? Because there must be times when you *would* want to.

Generally disapproves of smacking:

Warehouseman's wife:
I don't like it, and I don't approve of it, and I think it's the last extreme – you know, the last thing that you should do; try everything else before that, talking and coaxing and everything. I don't like violence of any kind, a slap even – if I have to do it, I regret it afterwards; and when it's all over, I sit and say to myself 'I'll *never* do it again', you know!

Teacher's wife:
Oh, never, never, never! I think it's awful – I should be so upset if I ever did it. I cringe at the thought of someone using power over someone little. No, I could *never* do that. Whether I'd feel that if I'd had children who'd been naughty, of course . . . I think I would; yes, I'm *sure* I would. I've been lucky – it's never *got* like that, you know . . . . . It's so degrading, for mother or father, to do it . . . I should feel I'd lost all face with Mark, and I should feel he'd never think of me the same again.

Mother feels unemotional, 'just routine':

Baker's wife:
Oh no, I don't feel anything particularly, I just find that he's needed it and that's it. I don't feel anything in myself.

Policeman's wife:
Oh, routine. Sometimes I think I've been a bit harsh, but if I don't take a firm hand with him, he'll be taking a firm hand over me!

Feels relieved:

Grocer's wife:
Well, I don't know, because each child is different, but I always think that smacking is a way of relieving your own temper, not to sort of help the child . . . . . Sometimes perhaps you feel like smacking, but there again, as I say, it *is* the parents' relief, and *therefore* I don't, I hold back.

Assistant manager's wife:
It's a jolly good way of relieving my feelings.

Feels guilty or upset:

Electrician's wife:
Well, sometimes if I've smacked them I feel a little bit afterwards I'm sorry, you know; because sometimes they're sort of just being mischievous, they don't know what to do, and then I think I ought to be a little more lenient, you know. Such as today – when they're in and they're bored, they don't know what to do with themselves; they get into mischief, and you can't blame them really. They get me so het up, you know – "Stop doing this", "Stop doing that" – and in the end I give them a good rollicking, you know, and that's when I feel a little bit guilty afterwards, I feel sorry.

Jointer's wife:
She's defiant. *I'm* the one that's upset. I feel *awful* afterwards. If she's gone off to bed looking sorrowful, I think to myself, Oh, you rotten devil! It makes me really tired – I can't do *anything* afterwards. But next day it all starts again. Because I mean you *can't* let it ride – she plays up to such a pitch. It wears you down, you know.

Strictness not mood-dependent:

Sales manager's wife:
We have a set of rules mostly, you know, and I don't enforce more some times than others. She knows what she can get away with and what she can't.

Insurance inspector's wife:
No, I think it depends on the child, what *she's* like, more than anything.

Strictness is mood-dependent:

Bleacher's wife:
I think so – I think, say you've had a busy day and you're tired, or say like when I went to work, or anything like that: they can do one thing, and say it was dinner-time and you weren't tired, you would just say "Now pack it in". But if it was night-time and you were tired – you know, "For goodness sake, let's have you upstairs!" you know. It's in yourself how you react.

Electrician's wife:
Yes, sometimes now with me it does; as I say, my nerves get on edge quite a lot. Some days they can be ranting and raving, and it not bother me: some days they've only got to step just a little bit out of line and I'm off.

Self-approval greater when strict:

Foreman's wife:
I think I've enjoyed the results most when I've lashed her with my tongue and finally got her to see that she was wrong.

CID detective's wife:
Well, I think I feel better when I'm being strict and every-thing's going smoothly. I *like* to be going with them, but if you're too easy-going they tend to take advantage of you, so being strict I think you feel you've got them all under control.

Self-approval greater when easy-going:

Executive officer's wife:
I should say when there's a nice calm atmosphere in the house. I'm very easy-going most of the time, and it's only in these emotional crises . . . if it's calm, everything's calm, it's fine; in fact, when we've been upset I think, Oh, what a bore, you know, to have to do it whether you want to or not. I prefer to paddle along.

Chemist's wife:
I think when I'm being easy-going. I hate nagging of course, and I hate myself if I realise we're going through a phase where I'm doing it more than I wish. I'm happiest when we're getting on and enjoying life.

Unclassifiable:

Student psychologist's wife:
When I have a good reason for doing what I do. In other words, when I'm not being entirely pragmatic, I suppose. In a sense, when I have time to stop and think something out, and feel that the reasons for doing something are adequate reasons.

Caretaker's wife:
Well, sometimes one, sometimes the other, it depends on the mood – sometimes you feel more self-righteous by bashing around, and another time you think, well, isn't it nice of me being very kind!

Grocer's wife:
My conscience says when I'm being strict, but I feel more at ease when I'm just me! I feel *not me* when I'm being all strict, I feel that I am what I *should* be, and I'd rather be as I *am* than how I should be.

It would appear, then, that there are numbers of middle-class women who, while more or less accepting the principle of smacking, do not in fact make use of it very much in practice; while there is also a group of working-class women who smack quite often while disapproving of it in principle. Considering how relatively commonplace smacking still is at seven, it is interesting to see that almost three-quarters of all mothers are emotionally upset by it – 'feeling churned-up inside' is a typical description; multiplied by the number of children she may have of smacking age, this adds up to considerable and repeated emotional expenditure for the individual woman. The proportion categorised as 'feeling relieved' is a little understated, in that some described an initial feeling of relief that was quickly superseded by disturbing emotions: 'I feel terribly upset – it may relieve a certain amount of pent-up tension in me, but it makes me feel dreadful'.

'I think it does something to them a bit psychological . . .'
The rather poor fit between principle and practice is borne out by more detailed referral to the transcripts. There is a strong feeling of constraints imposed upon parents' inclinations by the demands of the moment, the personality of the child, their own personal inadequacies where they would have preferred 'not to let it come to a smack', and their worries about the future. This last is of course (as we saw at four) very basic to the socialisation process; parents

would often prefer to 'let things ride for the sake of peace and quiet' if it were not that they are haunted by the thought 'What will he be like later if I let him get away with things now?' Although it is true that middle-class styles of discipline, because more verbally based, place more responsibility on the child for *long-term* good behaviour (see pp. 341–3), it is by no means the corollary of this that working-class mothers have no eye to the future: their discipline may be short-term effective, but it is certainly long-term intended. Mothers generally in fact have in common *the aim that the sanctions they impose should result in a socialised child*, and each tries to follow what *she* sees as the means to this end. So central is this aim that we make no apology for quoting at length in illustration of the theme.

Gardener's wife:
If I didn't stop them, they'd be the gaffers of me all the while; so I've got to put my foot down one way, and shouting I don't always do it. So you might as well give them a good hiding and done with it . . . . . Well, I think if they never have a good hiding they think they can get away with a lot, now they do, when they get older. We had good hidings, yet we never did them things what's going off today, did we?

Foreman's wife:
They need a little bit – whatever they say about smacking, you can't give them all their own way, I mean you've got to have them a *little* bit frightened of you, haven't you? *I* think you have, anyway.

Business executive's wife:
I can't see where [smacking] has any effect, quite honestly. [You don't think this is a good way of training them?] No, I don't. I think it's much better to try and reason with them, even if it takes much longer; because after all, when they've been smacked the smack is gone, and they are more likely to forget what it's even for; whereas things you say are likely to come back in their minds a little bit.

Builder's labourer's wife:
If they get away with it once, they try it again. My brother ended up in a home because he was never smacked.

Painter's wife:
A smack now is better than prison later.

Designer's wife:

I *am* fairly strict with him, yes – only because I like to see a well-disciplined child, and I do feel that unless you're strict with them from the beginning all the way through, you can't expect them to behave in a reasonable way later on. I suppose, er . . . I don't take a *pride* in being strict, but it's the results I'm after. I'm trying to think it's going to be better for him in the long run.

Machine operator's wife:

I don't try to smack 'em an awful lot. In a way it's a difficult age, seven – if you hit 'em too much you can turn them the wrong way, but if you *don't* hit 'em you can turn them the wrong way as well, you see – you've got to try in between. I have to try and use my intelligence, if I've got any, and try and work it out myself.

Stoker's wife:

He *believes* in smacking, my husband; but he don't really have to do it, because they take notice, like, you know, of him. [He's stricter than you?] Ooh – yes! In fact my husband never falls out with me only over that. He says "I'm trying to bring them up right and you're too soft-hearted" – that sort of business. But I can't be hard enough, I've tried but I can't. Some people's very firm, aren't they? And that's what we really fall out about – I ought to be firmer. He keeps them in their place, everyone round here says so; while I'm making them rogues like they are – in a way by being kind to them, you know.

Jointer's wife:

It would be nice not to! I think they do need it. And yet it doesn't seem to have any effect on them. I mean, Cheryl and Tess – they just look at each other and titter: they do, they turn round and laugh at you for it. And that's why I wonder sometimes, is it worth all the exertion, just for them to laugh at you? They titter, they defy you. If you *don't* smack them, they just do whatever they like with you, but then if you *are* strict with them it seems to me they just get rebellious; and I think sometimes, when they defy me like that, that I just get myself worked up for nothing. I despair sometimes, really I do.

These last two mothers are expressing their feelings of inadequacy in dealing with children who are already frank problems: others who are much more in command can still feel that such confrontations find them irresolute and very fallible.

Student teacher's wife (herself a teacher):

Well, I'd say that this again [smacking] depends on our mood – sometimes we've got the strength to reason with her and sometimes we haven't. If we're feeling fed up . . . me out at work . . . [What you *do* depends on your mood, but what you feel about it might not; sitting down calmly thinking about whether one should smack children of this age or not, or whether it's useful . . . ?] I think there are times when it can be well used. Depends again on the child, I suppose – our best way of dealing with her in any difficulty is to banish her to her bedroom and us downstairs, and we calm down and she calms down; but just occasionally she does have a good slap, she did round at her friend's the other day, "for arrogance" as my husband put it. It did a world of good. [Father:] It did . . . I don't think smacking at every little turn is a good thing. [It has its place?] Well, that's right, it has its place, even if it only relieves you. [Mother:] I don't know that you gain anything by it except, as you say, by relieving your own tension. [But when you did this the other day, it had results?] It had. [And these results were what?] Satisfactory to us. [Father:] They were quicker than trying to reason with her. In some instances you need a quick reaction. [Mother:] We were out at friends and she was being abominable. [Father:] So terrible, that we . . . it was just one smack with my fingers. [This was a sort of show-off thing, was it?] Yes, well partially show-off, but it was going on, it wasn't just one isolated incident, it was probably the culmination of . . . I don't know if she [his wife] agrees with me? [Mother:] I don't think she's had a smack since then . . . . . [What effect does it have on you . . . ?] [Father:] Well, that last time I thought to myself, Keep your hands to yourself, *don't* hit her. I think there's some other way. I get annoyed with myself that I've got to that state where I've had to smack her. [Mother:] I just get driven up the wall by it, and afterwards I sort of feel, well, I'm the adult, I should be able to cope with this situation. I think that's how I feel most of the time – ashamed . . . no it's not . . . it perhaps *isn't* when I've smacked her that I feel like this, it's when we've had an argument or a disagreement. No – I think when I've smacked her, I *know* I've smacked her and that's it – the smack has finished her, I *know* I've smacked her and that's it – the smack has finished it, and we've both . . . the whole thing's closed. But when it's just talk and reason through, and I've won *by virtue of size*, or at least I think I've won by virtue of size, that's when I feel ashamed. I feel guilty inside. But I have a great power to feel guilty inside about all sort of things! Did as a child, and I do as an adult. [Father:] This smack the last time; I've wondered whether I smacked her too hard, and thought "you big bully" – but it did have the desired effect on her. But whether probably a good telling-off would have done the same thing, I don't know – you see I have my doubts. I probably think, well, I ought to have *tried* a good telling-off, a really good one, and it might have saved my smacking, I don't know.

'The desired effect' is, basically, to get through to the child fast, and this is often cited as the main function of a smack, either in the case of a particular child or in particular kinds of situations (typically those of cumulative conflict).

Loco fireman's wife:
I think it depends on the child, because my eldest boy, I haven't *got* to smack him – I haven't done since he was a toddler because there's no necessity; he sort of has sense enough to give in – not to provoke to a great extent. But with Larry it's very often the last resort – you've sort of got him up in his room, and he'll be screaming and dancing and coming down the stairs and throwing things – he picks things up and he's going to hit you with them, and he gets so violent that a smack across the legs will do it. A smack seems to pull him round . . . sort of pulls him up, you know. He'll start crying then, and he'll sort of dissolve on to the settee crying, but gradually he'll come round. It calms him down.

The message of 'I'm bigger than you' which a smack necessarily conveys is the deliberate intention of many mothers who believe in the authoritarian principle; the question of: 'Who's gaffer in this house?' is the issue as they see it, and they wish both the question and its answer to be made explicit in the smack. 'I mean, you've got to show them who's boss a bit, 'cause as I say, she would be the boss if you'd let her', says an engineer's wife. Nobody, however, pretends that the child likes to be smacked, and even mothers who fully subscribe to the authoritarian premise may be unhappy about the actual physical hurt that this sanction entails: 'I've always been against smacking them, because I've had beltings myself when I was a kid', says a labourer's wife who smacks her son between once a month and once a week – 'but of course, you've got to show who's the boss'. Simply by asking about the effect of smacking on the child, we obviously stimulated some thought about what smacking meant to him, but it was clear that some mothers were already very aware of possible undercurrents of emotion which were not within their own intentions. 'They don't like being smacked at that age, they think they're getting too old for it', said a stoker's wife; '*I* don't think they are, but *they* think so'. The two mothers quoted next have in common their concern for the child's view of smacking *in terms of the total relationship*: very different personalities otherwise, the first is socially confident, highly verbal, highly educated; for the second her feelings of personal inadequacy have run like a thread through her whole experience of motherhood as she has conveyed it to us since Dawn's babyhood, though it is only at this stage that she has been able to verbalise them so clearly.

Student psychologist's wife (herself in similar training):
Oh, it's undignified. One loses one's temper and feels absolutely frightful afterwards, much worse than one does with a small child. Not just undignified for you, it's undignified for the child. Recently I smacked my daughter [aged six], and she said "How *dare* you" – you just didn't *do* this. It's not a punishment, it's an indignity. I felt terrible. This is the only answer I can give. They're not babies any more, they're not totally irrational beings and unknowing, and one mustn't treat them as though they are . . . . . They feel they've been imposed on and made to look foolish, and nobody likes that. [Do you think this has a bad effect on the relationship?] Yes, I would – I'm not saying it couldn't be put right if it didn't happen too often, but it would be foolish to make a practice of it . . . . . [When did you last smack James?] I can't remember. I seem to remember an argy-bargy in the bathroom – it *might* have been this year. [Did you feel then that he felt that it was an indignity?] I have felt this, as a matter of fact, for some time; but it was this more recent occasion with Katharine where she verbalised this, so indignantly and so precisely that I felt, This is *right*.

GPO worker's wife:
Life goes by so quickly, doesn't it? I think they grow up too fast. That's what I always think, you see, and that's why it

worries me when I smack them. You want them to behave properly, and yet you want them to be happy, and it seems to be all smacking. I don't want them to look back and think, Well, my childhood's gone by and it was all smacking. That's what worries me. [It's her *memories* that worry you?] Yes – it is – I haven't the confidence, you see, after my own childhood. I mean, I do look back, and I know I didn't get the attention I ought to have had: I don't want mine to remember me like that. I mean, she comes and puts her arms round my neck, but I always have that doubt – is she just doing it for what she can get out of it? [You haven't the confidence to know that she loves you for yourself?] That's it – and life goes by so quickly!

The majority of children (67%) are in fact thought by their mothers to be emotionally upset by being smacked, as opposed to merely disliking it; but there is a social class difference in the proportion of mothers reporting 'upset', ranging from 74% in the middle class, through 66% in the skilled working class, to 54% in the unskilled group, a trend which is significant at the 0·001 level. Detailed results are given in Table 39. Obviously it is a matter for

Table 39   *Child's reaction to being smacked*

	social class					summary		
	I&II	IIIwc	III man	IV	V	I&II, IIIwc	IIIman, IV,V	overall popn.
	%	%	%	%	%	%	%	%
Child 'upset'								
boys	65	76	67	51	48	70	62	64
girls	80	77	65	72	61	78	66	69
both	72	76	66	61	54	74	64	67

Significance: trend ↘ ****   m.class/w.class **
               between sexes   n.s.

(Middle (residual) category: child 'merely dislikes')

Child 'doesn't care'								
boys	10	9	11	24	24	10	15	13
girls	5	6	15	8	16	5	13	12
both	7	7	13	16	20	8	14	12

Significance: trend ↗ ***   m.class/w.class *
               between sexes   n.s.

question whether the class differences lie mainly in the behaviour of the child or in the perception of the mother. The link between frequency of smacking and the child's reaction is further followed in Chapter 11 (see pages 392–3 and 396).

'I don't think ill-treating anything weaker than yourself is clever, do you?'
'I mainly use the strap for really bad things like cheeking the neighbours . . .'

Beyond a simple frequency estimate, a further way of assessing the salience of smacking in the mother's disciplinary repertoire is to note in how many different conflict situations smacking comes to her mind as her expected response. Thus the question of what happened when the child was being very slow over doing as he was asked (page 299) was only the first of a number of proposed situations of potential conflict to which the mother might say that she tended to react by smacking the child. Refusal was the second (page 301), and later on mothers were asked 'What do you do when he is rude to you?' and 'Has he ever picked up any bad language? . . . . . What do you think you should do when that happens?' (In two other proposed conflicts – child smacking mother and child telling lies – we were more interested in the mother's perception of the total situation, and therefore did not code smacking separately from other forms of punishment.)

Table 40 shows the proportions of mothers who spontaneously mention smacking as their response to 'rudeness' and 'bad language'. It can be seen from this data that the class differences shown in the frequency table are substantiated by reference to the ways mothers expect to handle specific situations. On the other hand, the sex differences in frequency are not reflected here, which suggests that mothers do not expect to treat girls more leniently in these situations, but simply that girls do not present these problems so often.

To a certain degree, asking the mother 'What do you do in such-and-such a case?' formalises the behaviour she reports, in the sense that she thereby identifies it as her normal, more-or-less *chosen* response, even if she is not altogether happy with it. To this extent, behaviour reported in this way probably has more significance to her style of child rearing (as perceived by herself) than sampled behaviour would, which might be more subject to the pressure of circumstance.

In the same way, the aggressive act itself can be gauged in terms

L

Table 40   *Mothers who would smack in response to 'rudeness' and 'bad language'*

	social class					summary		
	I&II	IIIwc	III man	IV	V	I&II, IIIwc	IIIman, IV,V	overall popn.
	%	%	%	%	%	%	%	%
'Rudeness'								
boys	29	30	50	57	49	30	51	45
girls	34	24	42	45	42	29	42	39
both	32	27	46	51	46	29	47	42

Significance: trend ↗ ****   m.class/w.class ****
            non-linear trend *   between sexes n.s.

'Bad language'								
boys	12	12	16	16	25	12	17	15
girls	0	4	11	16	31	2	14	11
both	6	8	13	16	28	7	15	13

Significance: trend ↗ ****   m.class/w.class ***
                    between sexes n.s.

of formality. Almost any mother may hit out in a fury when tried beyond her tolerance; differences here may be basically a matter of individual tolerance level. *Slowing up* the act of smacking, however, immediately invests it with purposiveness and underlines for the child her disciplinary intent. In the pre-school years, to say 'Wait till I get you home!', and to smack the child once they got home, had a similar effect of formalisation; now, to take down a boy's trousers or turn up a girl's skirt in preparation for smacking, to fetch an implement, or even to own an implement as such, all signify the mother's *acceptance of smacking as punishment* as opposed to her use of it as an expression of anger. To the extent that some mothers would never dream of formalising it in these ways, however hard pressed, this divergence represents a real difference in attitude rather than just degree – though, obviously, smacking is likely to hurt more on poorly protected skin or where an implement is employed.

Overall, 17% of mothers sometimes take a boy's trousers down (or turn a girl's skirt up) in order to smack. This behaviour happens slightly more towards girls than towards boys (significant at the

0·05 level), which probably reflects only the fact that the mother can turn up a skirt herself, whereas taking down trousers needs some degree of co-operation from the victim. Class differences are not significant except in one respect: 28% of Class III white collar mothers of boys, as against 13% in all other classes, are prepared to take down their son's trousers for smacking (class difference significant at the 0·02 level). Mothers of girls in this social class do not behave differently from other classes.

168. Do you ever take his trousers down (turn her skirt up) to smack him?

Administrative assistant's wife:
Oh yes, I make a job of it. Because it's the drama more than anything else that seems to have the effect on him. He's screaming and shouting long before I've even got his pants down.

HP collector's wife:
Er, no, I haven't done. I think his Dad has, you know, because, er – it hurts him more, you know. But, um . . . I don't think he likes you to do it, you know – take his trousers down and smack him – because even when he's getting dressed, he don't like anybody to look at him . . . you know . . . things like that . . . [mother a little embarrassed].

Of course, the baring or partial baring of the child's buttocks is intended to make the punishment degrading as well as physically uncomfortable; and it may be that, as in the last quotation, working-class parents in particular (whose sense of sexual modesty is more acute) may feel that this is going too far – they wish the child to be shamed, but not quite to that degree. Inhibitions of this kind do not apply to the use of implements as such, however. We asked this group of questions as follows:

166. How often does N in fact get smacked?
167. Is it just with your hand, or do you use a slipper or a cane or anything like that?
   (If hand only): Do you ever threaten to use something more?

We thought it important to ask about threats of this nature because once the threat had been made (or once the implement was known to have been used on older siblings, or to exist at all), it seemed to us that the issue of physical punishment had already moved into a new dimension: in a word, the dimension of beating, not smacking. We shall be discussing the question of unfulfilled punishment threats generally in the next chapter; but it is useful here to present data on the actual use of punishment implements in conjunction with data on their threatened use (Table 41).

Table 41 *Smacking: mothers who use, or threaten to use, an implement*[3]

	social class					summary		
	I&II	IIIwc	III man	IV	V	I&II, IIIwc	IIIman IV,V	overall popn.
	%	%	%	%	%	%	%	%
Implement already used								
boys	29	26	27	20	25	27	25	26
girls	22	18	19	17	10	20	18	18
both	25	22	23	18	17	24	21	22

Significance: trend   n.s.   m.class/w.class   n.s.
                              between sexes   *

Implement threatened only								
boys	51	71	68	60	67	60	66	65
girls	29	37	38	56	59	33	44	41
both	40	54	53	58	63	47	55	53

Significance: trend ↗ ****   m.class/w.class p<0·06
                              between sexes   ****

Implement threat or use								
boys	80	97	95	80	92	87	91	91
girls	51	55	57	73	69	53	62	59
both	65	76	76	76	80	71	76	75

Significance: trend ↗ ***   m.class/w.class   n.s.
                              between sexes   ****

Twenty-two per cent of all seven-year-old children have received corporal punishment via some implement; a further 53% have been threatened with this, making the remarkably high total of three-quarters of this population for whom being struck in this way is at least within the bounds of conscious possibility. This overall percentage is consistently high in all social classes, except that Class I and II mothers are less likely to *threaten* with an implement; they are, however, just as likely as other groups actually to use one. There is a perceptible sex difference in actual punishment with implements, and a much bigger sex difference when it comes to threats of their use: combining both tables, 91% of boys are either threatened or actually hit, compared with 59% of girls. A breakdown of the type of implement used suggests that cane and stick are rather more favoured by middle-class parents, and strap or belt by working-class parents. Slippers and other more *ad hoc* implements such as yardsticks, wooden spoons and the dog's lead appear in too small numbers to analyse their social class distribution.

The last few of the quite typical quotations which follow suggest that the threat of cane or strap may not necessarily have prognostic significance as to actual use. Nevertheless we reiterate that, at the very least, the mother's appeal to its existence does in fact subtly alter the feel of potential conflict situations between her and her child: just as the cane in the corner of the junior school headmaster's office colours the collective perceptions of his schoolchildren even if it has not actually been used within the memory of any child.

Metal polisher's wife:
I don't use me hand. Me husband says you mustn't use your hand, just use a belt and give him a good hard slap. 'Cause *he* says you can do more damage with that hand than you can with one belt.

Unemployed labourer's wife:
He'll sit and sob [when he doesn't want to go to school]. I've often had to run him out wi' a stick, many a day – and he'd stand there and he *wouldn't* go.

Sales representative's wife:
Well, usually I think I use my hand; but if I have a stick I can wave it about and it has a great effect, but I don't like smacking with a stick. [Do you sometimes?] Yes, I have smacked them with it sometimes on the bottom.

Presser's wife:
Oh, I threaten many a time. I threaten my yardstick. I've got a yardstick in that corner, you know. I threaten that, many a

time [Have you ever used it?] No, never. [Do you ever intend to use it?] No, I don't, I might break it.

Lorry driver's wife:

I've got a stick there, but that's a warning – a be-gooder-or-else!

Labourer's wife:

Yes, I do, I often have the strap there, but I never use it – I just show them, and say "you know, this hurts". The master at the school they're in – he has a strap, and he used it on the boys. I says "You know, straps are sometimes used on girls, as well as boys!" – "I know, Mum, but *you* never do!"

Builder's wife:

Yes, I threaten 'em with a strap. I keep saying I'm going to buy a strap. I keep *saying* I'm going to get a strap, but I never have got one yet.

Lorry driver's wife:

I say I'll go and buy a cane, and he laughs and says he'll break it then.

'I just think it's cruel – cruel and unnecessary'
'You've got to be cruel, to make 'em understand what you're doing'
Although we have distinguished between the incidence of physical punishment and the formality with which it is administered, and have pointed out that threats of an implement do not necessarily lead to its use, we thought it meaningful to combine these various aspects into one comprehensive index which would measure the degree to which corporal punishment featured in the lives of individual children: whether this was because it was frequently resorted to, invoked in many different situations, formally ritualised or merely threatened. Internal comparison of scores on these various points did in fact produce a significant degree of consistency (****): the measures of incidence (items 1–5 in Table 42) were found to correlate at approximately 0·3 with the measures of formality (items 6–7). Table 42 shows how the index of corporal punishment is made up; and Table 43 analyses this population in terms of high and low scorers on this index and their distribution by social class and the child's sex.

The most obvious conclusion from Table 43 is that physical punishment is invoked considerably more for boys than for girls at this age. Though slightly less marked, there is also a distinct and significant tendency for physical punishment to feature more

Table 42 *An index of mothers' reliance on corporal punishment*

Item		Based on question	Mother's response	Score
1	158.	What do you do if he's being very slow . . . . . ?	Physical punishment	1
			Verbal rebuke or ignores	0
2	159.	What happens if he simply refuses to do something . . . . . ?	Physical punishment	1
			Verbal rebuke or ignores	0
3	166.	How often does N in fact get smacked?	1+ per day	3
			1+ per week (<1 per day)	2
			1+ per month (<1 per week)	1
			Less	0
4	184.	What do you do when he is rude to you?	Smack	1
			Other punishment/reprove/ignore	0
5	185.	Has he ever picked up any bad language? . . . . . What do you think you should do . . . . . ?	Smack	1
			Other punishment/reprove/ignore	0
6	167.	(*If any smacking*): Is it just with your hand, or do you use a slipper or a cane or anything like that? (*If hand only*): Do you ever *threaten* to use something more?	Implement used	2
			Implement threatened only	1
			No threat or use of implement	0
7	168.	Do you ever take his trousers down/turn her skirt up to smack him/her?	Yes	1
			No	0
				(*Range 0–10*)

strongly as we descend the social class scale. In particular, physical methods of controlling behaviour are much more likely to be stressed among families in the unskilled manual group, and their girls enjoy a lesser degree of comparative favour than do girls in other social classes. A further analysis of the index scores, to ascertain whether the salience of Class v might be mainly a function of family size, shows no such relationship.

It is our impression that the main burden of the maintenance of discipline at this age rests firmly upon the mother. This is partly because she is more often around when such issues arise, but also because it is much less acceptable nowadays for mothers to appeal to fathers as the ultimate sanction. Fathers themselves, in line with

Table 43 *High and low scorers on corporal punishment index*

	social class					summary		
	I&II	IIIwc	III man	IV	V	I&II, IIIwc	IIIman, IV,V	overall popn.
	%	%	%	%	%	%	%	%
High scorers								
5+ *(top 31%)*								
boys	29	33	44	41	44	31	43	40
girls	12	20	24	21	36	16	25	23
both	21	27	34	31	40	24	34	31

Significance: trend ↗ ***   m.class/w.class ***
           between sexes ****

	I&II	IIIwc	III man	IV	V	I&II, IIIwc	IIIman, IV,V	overall popn.
Low scorers								
0, 1, 2 *(bottom 38%)*								
boys	41	29	29	27	21	35	27	30
girls	57	51	45	47	33	54	44	47
both	49	40	37	37	27	45	36	38

Significance: trend ↘ **   m.class/w.class *
           between sexes ****

their greater participation in nurturing functions, seem unwilling to be cast in the traditional role of avenging judge with mother as prosecuting counsel; and, on the whole, mothers too reject the 'wait till your father comes home' technique as unfair and inappropriate to the modern view of fatherhood. Table 44 shows the data obtained in answer to the question 'Who smacks most, your husband or yourself?' It is clear that the contemporary father's increased participation in child rearing falls short of the disciplinary role, and that this is true through all social classes at age seven, though there are rather more fathers at the lower end of the scale who still wield the heavier hand.

That mothers generally do accept this division of roles is shown by their answers to a further question. Where one parent did tend to smack more than the other, we asked 'Is that because you [husband and wife] disagree about smacking, or is it just that you are/he is more often there when it's needed?' Only 14% of these respondents disagreed with their husbands about the principle of smacking, and there were no class or sex differences. The circumstances of disagreement are indicative, however: the couple were four times as likely to be in disagreement when the husband was the major smacker as when the wife was.

Most of this chapter has been concerned with confrontations between mother and child in which the mother's superior strength as opposed to her greater moral wisdom has in the end been invoked – whether by an act of violence on her part or by drawing the child's attention to the possibility of such an act. Either way, her physical mastery has been made explicit.

Many mothers would say that this chapter has therefore been a story of defeat, and not on the child's side either: 'I have failed if she has to be smacked', says a clergyman's wife. Although, as we have seen, most mothers smack at least occasionally and most also imply some approval of the principle by at times threatening the use of an implement of punishment, it must be understood that the role of smacking remains a means to a more important end than the immediate conflict: it serves the need which parents feel to maintain their credibility as power figures who must undoubtedly win in any significant battle of wills. The inevitable occasional clash

Table 44 *Who smacks most, mother or father? (equal smacking by subtraction from 100%)*

	social class					summary		
	I&II	IIIwc	III man	IV	V	I&II, IIwc	IIIman, IV,V	overall popn.
	%	%	%	%	%	%	%	%
Mother								
boys	78	80	74	78	70	79	75	76
girls	73	81	88	79	71	77	84	82
both	76	81	81	79	71	78	79	79

Significance: trend n.s.   m.class/w.class n.s.
                                     between sexes n.s.

Father								
boys	3	12	12	13	17	8	13	12
girls	9	6	6	8	16	8	8	8
both	6	9	9	10	16	8	10	10

Significance: trend ↗ **   m.class/w.class n.s.
                                     between sexes n.s.

of interests between parents and children may become testing-times, when parents suspect that their long-term ability to influence their child's behaviour (a basic notion to the parental role) could be irretrievably diminished if they are seen to lose.

Controlling the child's behaviour thus often becomes a kind of game in which parents try to choose strategies appropriate to what they see to be at stake; and for most parents the stake is, to a greater or lesser extent, the myth of their own invincibility. In other words, few parents really want to maintain their authority wholly by brute force, because this would in fact tend to undermine their additional credibility as benign charismatic powers who do not need to punish their children in order to gain their co-operation and respect. Parents would like to be obeyed because of their superior wisdom and experience, because the child acknowledges that they have his long-term interests at heart, because they love him despite his faults, and because they choose *not* to exercise all the power they have to compel his submission.

It is when the child challenges them on these grounds that they need to demonstrate their invincibility, and this they may do in ways which are partly dictated by expediency. How they feel about resorting to a show of physical strength at this point will depend upon whether their child-rearing attitudes are deeply based in the democratic principle, when they may well fear that they are betraying their ideals ('I have failed if she has to be smacked'; 'I should feel I'd lost all face with Mark'); or upon whether they believe strongly in an authoritarian stance, in which case they have little reason to have moral worries about the showdown which 'makes him understand who's boss'.

Once again we have to reiterate that smacking happens, not in a vacuum, but as a part of a continuing dialogue of words and behaviour in which the mother's intent is conveyed in many and various ways. Hugs and kisses are one kind of message; smacks carry another; words are the vehicles for others again. It is to the verbal aspects of conflict that we now turn.

NOTES

1 J. and E. Newson, 1968, p. 418 (Pelican ed. p. 444).
2 J. and E. Newson, 1968, p. 410 (Pelican ed. p. 435).
3 Actual implements used are not here distinguished. In both use and threat, order of preference is: first, strap or belt; second, cane or stick; third, slipper; fourth, miscellaneous objects.

Chapter 10

Artillery of Words

Punish, *v. trans.* To cause (an offender) to suffer for an offence; to subject to judicial chastisement as retribution or requital, or as a caution against further transgression; to inflict a penalty on.

Shorter Oxford English Dictionary, 1965

The whole question of smacking is, as we have seen, bedevilled by the ambiguity of the situation in which it arises. For many parents, the smack is an impulsive response to conflict or to the child's defiance, given in the heat of the moment and generated by that heat; but it is also (often simultaneously) regarded as an acceptable act of discipline. Perhaps the clearest finding to come out of the last chapter is the mothers' ambivalence on this issue: if 41% smack once or more per week, 75% threaten or use an implement, 73% feel guilty or upset when they have smacked the child and 69% approve of themselves more when they are being easy-going, then the very least that can be said is that this is an emotional area of considerable dissonance.

At this point, then, it is useful to move a little away from the fraught arena of violence and to look more closely at mothers' attitudes on punishment generally. Once we have established an overview, as it were, of the punishment issue, we can go on to tease out the strands of controlling behaviour which are uncomplicated by violence (which is not to say that they are uncomplicated).

The means by which we quantified our data on attitudes to punishment was by devising an index to the mother's 'Acceptance of the Punishment Principle'. The items which make up the 'APP score' are presented in Table 45. Although, as we have pointed out, the emotional component of the smacking situation contaminates the notion of smacking as punishment, it would obviously be

Table 45 *An index of mothers' acceptance of the punishment principle*

Item		Based on questions	Mother's response	Score
1	160.	How do you feel about smacking children of this age?		
	161.	Do you think parents should try to do without smacking altogether, or do you think smacking is a good way of training children?	Smacking approved Unfortunate but necessary Generally disapproved	2 1 0
	162.	In general, do you think smacking has good results with children of this age?		
	163.	Any bad results?		
2	165.	What effect does [smacking] have on you? Do you feel relieved or upset in any way, or is it just part of the routine?	'Just part of the routine' Relieved Guilty or upset	2 1 0
3		(Positive answers to following questions are summed, maximum score 6. If *total* is 3 or more, item scores 2. If total is 2, item scores 1. If total is 1 or 0, item scores 0).		
	172.	Do you ever say that if he's naughty he can't have something he likes – ice-cream or television, something like that?	(Yes = 1)	
	174.	Do you ever keep back some of his pocket money?	(Yes = 1)	
	176.	Do you ever threaten him with someone else – his teacher, or the doctor or a policeman – someone like that?	(Yes = 1)	
	178.	Do you ever threaten to leave him or send him away from home?	(Leave = 1) (Send away = 1)	
	182.	Is there any other punishment which you use, or threaten to use, with N?	(Yes = 1)	
4	184.	What do you do when he is rude to you?	Any punishment Reprove, ignore	1 0
5	187.	What do you (would you) do if he tries to smack you?		

Item		Based on question	Mother's response	Score
		(*If M shows disapproval in any way*): Is that because you don't like him striking *any*one, or because you don't like him being disrespectful to his mother?	Dislikes disrespect Dislikes striking anyone/ignores	1 0
6	185.	Has he ever picked up any bad language? . . . . . What do you do?	Any punishment Reprove/ignore	1 0
7	194.	Do you expect him to say he's sorry to you when he's been naughty or rude? (*If YES*): Would you make him do that, even if he didn't want to?	Insists on apology Expects, doesn't force/ doesn't expect	1 0
8	196.	Do you find that how strict you are depends a great deal on your own mood at the time?	Strictness independent of mood Mood-dependent	1 0

Score range: 0–11

extremely artificial and misleading to omit it for this reason: we have therefore included items on smacking which deliberately attempt to exclude the element of emotion, and to explore the mother's principle or intention. The data on which item 6 is based was also used in the index of mothers' reliance on corporal punishment (Table 42): it is differently scored here, however, in that we are now looking for punishment of *any* kind, while in the previous index corporal punishment only was scored.

Basically, this index measures the mother's belief in adult-mediated authoritarian disciplinary control rather than the establishment of internal controls through democratic means. The authoritarian attitude is, of course, implicit in punishment of any sort; but it also asserts itself where punishment is not necessarily resorted to. In item 5, for instance, the mother might or might not punish the child, but we are interested in whether she reacts to the child's hand being raised against *mother as person* or *mother as authority*, and we score on this basis. Similarly, in item 7 'saying sorry' may be seen either as a democratic obligation between persons or as a duty from dependent child to *mother as authority*, and to be enforced as such. Mood-dependency is rather more controversial in this context: the argument for including it in this index is that acceptance of an external principle of punishment involves a certain rigidity in the enforcement of discipline which deliberately attempts to minimise personal mood factors on either side.

Half of the sample fall into the middle category of medium scorers; taking the high and low scorers separately (Table 46), a social class difference emerges of the kind one might expect, and this is more clearly defined among the low scorers. Middle-class mothers are less likely to believe in punishment as a necessary or effective principle, and are less likely to practise an authoritarian style of discipline than are working-class mothers.

The sex difference, showing that mothers tend to rely more heavily on the punishment principle where boys are concerned, is striking in the data for high scorers; it disappears for working-class low-scoring mothers, but is in fact still more obvious for middle-class low scorers. Taken together with our data on the chaperonage of middle-class girls (Table 9), it seems very consistent that their mothers are able to rely on the closeness of their

Table 46 *Acceptance of punishment principle as a function of social class and the child's sex*

| | social class | | | | | summary | | |
	I&II	IIIwc	III man	IV	V	I&II, IIIwc	IIIman, IV,V	overall popn.
	%	%	%	%	%	%	%	%
High scorers (7–13)								
boys	25	28	37	31	39	26	36	33
girls	20	18	25	19	38	19	25	24
both	22	23	31	25	39	23	31	28

Significance: trend ↗ **   m.class/w.class *
                        between sexes ***

Low scorers (0–3)								
boys	29	21	22	21	16	25	21	22
girls	38	35	16	29	26	37	20	24
both	34	35	19	25	21	31	20	23

Significance: trend ↘ **   m.class/w.class ***
                        between sexes n.s.

relationship (see also Tables 28 and 29), rather than needing to resort to punishment, which is the strategy of distance in relationship and poor identification. One might wonder on these grounds whether family size might be a significant factor: an analysis of variance, which confirms the same broad trends, does not however implicate family size as contributive.

'I can smack him till I'm blue in the face, but it doesn't do a thing to him. If I deprive him of something he really likes, it works wonders'
The 'Acceptance of the punishment principle' index is of additional interest because it brings together punishing measures which *might be considered to be alternatives*. One might suppose that parents accepting the principle would then go on to choose among the punishment options open to them: that those who smacked would not feel the need to use deprivation of sweets, TV, pocket money, etc., that those who did not smack would turn to deprivation instead, and so on. But this is not so. Seventy-five per cent of all mothers use deprivation, and class differences are minimal:[1] but this overall 'depriving' percentage varies in terms of 71% of mothers who smack less than once a month; 79% of those who smack at least once a month but less than once a week; 82% of those smacking at least once a week but less than once a day; and 88% of those smacking at least once a day. Thus the more often a mother smacks, the more likely she is to use deprivation punishment *as well*; this relationship is significant at the 0·01 level.

Once they have accepted the principle of punishment, mothers seem to search around among the non-smacking punishments in a rather pragmatic way: what they use tends to be what has proved expedient with this child. Obviously, withdrawal of television, sweets, spending money, playtime, etc. is intended to be effective: for this reason a mother may deliberately monitor her child's reaction to a particular deprivation and choose the more disliked one; or she may abandon something she has tried simply because the child seems unconcerned.

Paint sprayer's wife:
He was naughty last night and Daddy said he'd got to get in his pyjamas; and he said "Oh no, Daddy, I'd rather go without my sweets for the weekend", so Daddy says "Right, you can stop in" – of course, we picked the one Angus *didn't* want. Angus wanted to miss sweets for a whole week, so we thought, well,

therefore the greater punishment was to stay in, there and then, in his pyjamas. "You needn't go to bed, but you get undressed immediately, put your pyjamas on and dressing-gown" – but he still cried and said he'd rather go without sweets. But Daddy said "No, you can *not*, you're going to get undressed and not go out to play", like: always that one, the one that's going to punish him most.

Nylon winders' wife:
Well, now we've got Goose Fair coming on, I can get him to behave just like lightning! I say "I'm not going to take you up Goose Fair".

Gardener's wife:
Say as she wants some shoes – you know, she likes these point-toe shoes; well, if she's been naughty I say "Well, I'm not buying you none". Well, I let it run about a fortnight and *then* get them – when she's made up for it.

Company director's wife:
Well, I think his pocket money isn't regular enough, and he wouldn't miss it anyway, so that means nothing to him. I think that would be suitable for an older child, but I don't think it would be any good now.

It is rare that deprivation of privileges is rejected on principle ('I don't think I would, because that's *his* money, isn't it?'); apart from ineffectiveness with a particular child, the reason given for *not* using deprivation is almost always because in practice it would be difficult for the mother to carry through.

Sales representative's wife:
Well, say one of them's naughty and I say "Well, you can't watch television", well, often it is a bit difficult, especially when you've got others. You can't deprive *them* of watching the television, can you? So you've more or less got to send them off upstairs to bed, where they'll probably stand at the top of the stairs listening, or crying.

Foreman's wife:
Pocket money, well no, because she only has it the one day, it's not spread over the week; so I can't say "Well you'll not get it tomorrow", and usually it's only once or twice a week she's that bit naughty, and you can't . . . by the time the end of the

week's come, she's perhaps done two or three really good things
that's overridden the bad things – you can't stop pocket money
then.

Lorry driver's wife:
  If I *have* threatened, I usually carry it out; but all the others
  have to suffer as well, because I just can't bring myself to bring
  the other two something and not him. I can't do that, so they
  all have to go without.

We used the phrase 'deprivation of privileges' above because this
is the form of words normally used in the literature of child rearing;
but we are not altogether happy about it because it seems to assume
the despotic view that the child's *normal expectations* of incoming
assets (sweets, icecream, pocket money) and of pleasant occupations
(TV, playing out, staying up until his usual bedtime) are not his by
right but only by favour. From the child's point of view, these are
benefits which he has come to expect as part of everyday life: so
that to have them taken away is a very clear confiscation of property
or rights, rather than the mere withholding of bonuses, and must
underline the authoritarian relationship and his own lack of status.
It is *status* which Mrs Hutchins concedes to her child when she
says 'I don't think I would, because that's *his* money'.
  A more precise example of deprivation of actual privileges is the
mother's threat that a treat, which was to have happened, now will
not because the child has been naughty (and therefore has not
deserved special favours). The child who was threatened with not
going to Goose Fair comes near to this – except in so far as every
Nottingham child regards a visit to Goose Fair at Michaelmas as
his inalienable right, so that 'no Goose Fair' is a threat of the
same order as 'no Christmas presents'.

Company director's wife:
  I sort of say, "If we go down and see Louise [sister at boarding
  school] I might bring you a small present back"; and I say "Well,
  if you aren't good we won't be able to get anything". They seem
  to recognise things like that more than anything else, material
  things.

Sales representative's wife:
  Well, as I say, he likes to go to his Nana's; and I say "You
  know, if you aren't a good boy, when holiday time comes, well
  you won't go".

Miner's wife:

If we promise the circus and he's naughty, we threaten not to take him, but of course we do – it's only we *hope* to get a bit of quiet!

Occasionally a mother admits to having started giving a child regular pocket money in order to have the possibility of fining him; and in the same way, treats are sometimes thought up on the spur of the moment in order to have something to withdraw.

Surveyor's assistant's wife:

I suppose we have used "We're not going to Granny's", but that's if we've had no intention of going in the first place.

In this midway area between reward and punishment where treats are being offered and withdrawn, we come much closer to a commerce between parent and child in which the currency is the 'little bit extra' which parents delight in giving their children. In the pleasure of being in a position to hand out treats lies the parents' downfall, of course – to give up the treat of a circus is a punishment for parent as well as child, but equally uncomfortable for many is the role of implacable mother who won't give her child the simple pleasure of an icecream.

Sales representative's wife:

You see I'll probably say "That's very naughty – no icecream!" – then the icecream man comes round and tinkles his bell, and Veronica comes and says how sorry she is and may she have an icecream, and when she looks at me I melt.

'I'll carry out my threats half-and-half', says a clerk's wife – 'I camouflage it by saying "You've improved". Well, she'll go off and she'll cry, and she'll look at me with her big blue eyes, and I'll melt, and I'll say "Well . . . you *have* improved" – I would have to *camouflage* it, you know'. In camouflaging her own lack of adamance, what this mother is doing is to behave *as if* the child's part of the bargain struck between them has been fulfilled, and thus she avoids loss of face on either side. Jimmy, below, negotiates more explicitly; the balance of power teeters, and ends up (we think) just tipped in his favour.

Presser's wife:

It's just if we've promised to buy him summat, and then he shows off: we say to him "We shan't buy it you!" – and then he'll say "Well, you promised, and if you don't keep that promise I *will* show off until I gerrit", you see; and if we do keep to us promise, we find that he is all right.

The promise of a reward as such in return for good behaviour (rather than withdrawal of treats which were not originally given as rewards) may or may not be viewed as one end of the punishment continuum. Certainly it is class-loaded in the same direction as acceptance of the punishment principle, and more heavily so: that is, more mothers promise rewards for good behaviour as we descend the social scale. Nearly half of all mothers use the reward strategy, but this rises to 54% in Class v and is reduced to 25% at the top end of the class scale; both class trend and middle-class/working-class difference are significant at the 0·001 level. There is no sex difference discernible except in Class iii white collar, where boys are rather more likely to be promised rewards than girls.

On the whole, mothers seem to feel a little guilty about promising rewards. Many of them re-worded the question in terms of 'bribery', a more value-laden epithet, or talked of rewarding in terms of 'Yes, I'm guilty of that, I'm afraid' or 'Well, I must admit . . .' Some gave retrospective rewards but were careful *not* to promise them in advance, the criterion which we were using.

Foreman's wife:
I don't in a money sense, but perhaps a little outing that had already been planned. I know she likes going to the shops with me. If she's been particularly good, or if she's done something that wanted doing and doesn't have to be asked – that little outing is *then* told about – not as a reward – and she appreciates it. I don't believe in bribing children with money.

Supervisor's wife:
Well, I have, because she's been so thoughtful and helped me such a lot. We don't promise her that we'll get something *if* she's good, but we will plan to get her a gift *as* she's been good, you know. I think really it's a bad thing to hold a carrot in front of the donkey's nose, because I think it can lead to bad habits.

Reluctance to offer rewards for good behaviour and the deprecation of 'bribery' are strongly founded in the belief that children ought to be reasonably co-operative and compliant as a matter of course, irrespective of any material benefits they may receive. Sometimes the mother's emphasis is on her fear that the child may come to demand a reward for *every* co-operative act: 'You're going to be paying out all the time, aren't you?' The logical implication of reward is that co-operation is not the child's 'natural' response, and the mother does not wish him to feel this: 'I don't think I'd promise him a reward for being good – I *expect* him to be good', says an architect's assistant's wife. To the extent that the expectation of co-operative behaviour is part of the notion of reciprocal obligations which middle-class mothers are at pains to instil, the rejection of rewards on principle understandably has a middle-class bias; just as these mothers are more likely to expect household jobs to be done without reward, so they also take the line 'I behave reasonably to you, why shouldn't you behave reasonably towards me?'

This fairly widespread concern with the *meaning and implication for the child* of the appeal to rewards is extended by some middle-class mothers to the whole question of deprivation as a sanction. The next two mothers are both, as well as their husbands, professionally dependent upon their ability to employ words with subtlety and precision: in their dealings with their children, they are concerned to make them aware both implicitly and explicitly of the logical framework in which their sanctions operate.

Student psychologist's wife (taking same course):
No – although fairly frequently I point out the consequences of not being good, this is not a threat, it's a sort of *logical* consequence. For example, on Saturday I throw them in the tub, it's the only day I really have time for this, and they come down in their dressing-gowns to watch television, and my weapon on this occasion is that if the bathing isn't got through, the television will be over. [This is because "television will be over if you're a long time", not "you won't have television because you've been a naughty boy"?] That's it. Occasionally – if they're being particularly reckless with something that's breakable, in the kitchen with cups and saucers, I do threaten that if they do break one I may use their sweet money to buy some new ones. This has the effect of making them very much more careful! In this sense it *is* a threat, but it *is* a logical consequence.

University teacher's wife:
I don't really think in terms of punishment at all. I don't think

it's a relevant concept to me as far as children are concerned. If I hit out, it would be for the same reason as she might hit me – lost temper! I *have* used fines, but only for one purpose, and in fact they were damages, not fines at all. We came to a point where they were hitting each other I thought unnecessarily often, and to cope with that I evolved a system where for a more-or-less unprovoked hit the attacker had to pay a penny to the victim, and a smack on the face cost sixpence. It worked well, because the one who got smacked got compensation and the attacker sometimes thought it was worth the money, so it led to more good humour all round. Um . . . I wouldn't think it right to fine someone and keep the money myself – as I say, in *my* mind I draw a very clear distinction between punishment and compensation. The only thing is that I'm not certain how clear the distinction really is to the children, because we were talking about it one day, and one of them said "*You* may not think it's punishment, but to us it *feels* like punishment"!

'I make him realise, you know, we do mean what we're telling him . . .'
Once again – punishment of any kind, even when it is very frequently resorted to, is the punctuation of the dialogue of socialisation, not its be-all and end-all. Punishment very rarely takes place otherwise than within a verbal exchange. Smacking is likely to be only the end-point of a verbal build-up of directives or warnings (except where it is the swift response to 'cheek', 'bad language' or the child's own violence); and in all cases it is likely to be followed in turn by verbal justification and expansion: 'There, that's all I'm standing from *you*!' – 'And get out of here or you'll get another!' – 'You're very very naughty!' – 'Don't you dare speak to me like that!' Other punishment is also usually preceded by warnings, and necessarily has to be expressed in words in order to happen at all: 'No more sweets this week, then' – 'You'll sit still on that chair and you're not going out now till after tea.' The child's normal protest will in turn elicit further justification: 'I don't give *that* much what Julie says to her mother, you're not saying it to me' – 'I told you you were working up to a smack, and now you see you've got one' – 'No good moaning now, my lad, I said no sweets if you came in late and I meant it'. These statements do not have a solely here-and-now significance: they are deliberately intended to make the child understand the unacceptability of his behaviour both now and for future reference.

It would be very much an over-simplification, then, to suggest that middle-class parents mediate discipline verbally while working-class parents do not. It is perhaps true, though, that middle-class parents emphasise the *verbal elaboration* of the issues which they are trying to follow through with the child, so that it is much more difficult for the child to escape the moral implications of his action. 'I often, very often, make him repeat what I've said to make sure it's gone in', says a business executive's wife; 'I don't sort of soft-soap him, I make him realise, you know, we do mean what we're telling him. I do go on a bit, I go on about ten minutes at him, really making it sink in, but I think this is more effective, myself, than smacking'.

Scientific research worker's wife:

Often I feel that just punishing him for something and not saying any more about it perhaps doesn't quite do the trick, and I perhaps come back on the subject. Perhaps a day after I'll say "You know yesterday you did this or that, and I gave you a smack", and explain to him *why* it's not very nice; then he usually feels sorry, and says so; or perhaps doesn't say anything, but just thinks about it.

Perhaps words have such potency not just because they invest actions with explicit meaning but because, while few humanitarian parents can keep on smacking a child, the artillery of words can pound away until the mother is satisfied that an impression has been made. This is seen particularly clearly in the more minor conflict situations, where the mother is not so angry and therefore can concentrate on getting her message over to the child. The quotation that follows describes what might be thought a very trivial incident; it is of great interest because the mother is able to follow through and recount to us the subtly developing processes of thought that go to make up one deliberate sequence of socialising interaction. What is important here is the way in which this mother takes up her child's peccadillo and gives it significance by setting it in a moral framework for the child's consideration. In this example, the mother also uses non-verbal communication – 'I just kept sewing', 'I looked at her' – *in conjunction* with words, and the potency of the exchange is emphasised by its low key. Compared with this, punishment seems a blunt and ineffective instrument. The mother in question is a socially mobile skilled worker's wife, on the point of entering the middle class.[2]

This soft icecream van came round, and she was stood here – she'd just come home from school; and I said "Ooh, a soft ice-cream", I said, "Go and get two cornets quickly" – and off she went. She came back with a Zoom for herself and a choc-ice for me, and she said "Here you are, I've brought you a choc-ice". I said "No, I don't *want* that, Edwina, I would have sent you to the shop for that"; I said "I just wanted this *soft* icecream". I says "Well, you've bought it, well you can eat it now". I wasn't that upset, but I pretended, 'cause I thought she's not gone for what she was *sent* for, you see. And I said "I just *fancied* some of the soft icecream", I says, "well, *you* have it now, Mum doesn't want it – so go and stick it in the fridge till you've eaten your own Zoom thing, and have that as well". So she walked away, never said a word; and I thought "Aye, and you don't care, Edwina, you don't" – you know? So off she went; and she came back, ooh, a few minutes after, and she says "Well, it's icecream, isn't it?" I says "Yes, but that's not the *point*, Edwina, Mum wanted the *soft* icecream". I said "You could have gone across to the *shops* and got the other – and the point is, when I send you for a thing, you get what I say and not what you think you'll get". Well, off she disappeared again, and I thought, well, not an "I'm sorry, Mum" or anything; so I thought, *No*, I'm *not* going to say "It's only icecream, never mind, Edwina" – I'm just going to see. So after a bit she came back – and I just kept sewing, you know, didn't take any notice – and she said "Mummy I'm sorry I didn't bring you that . . ." – I said: "Sorry doesn't always do, Edwina, you must try and do as you are told to do, as far as you possibly can". She said, "Well, are you going to eat it?" So I looked at her, and I thought, Well, I really think she's learned a little lesson, you know, and maybe next time she *will* do as she's asked. So I said "All right, go and fetch it" – and when she came back she nearly burst into tears, and she said "I *am* sorry, Mum". And she said "Never mind, we've ended up laugh-ing, haven't we, Mum?" – and then she was all right. But I thought, Well, I've carried it through just to see how she *would* react to this thing.

Words are a part of every mother's armoury, and basically they are intended to make the child *think*: to evaluate his actions, or their consequences, in terms other than might be suggested to him by the simple smack which *on its own* carries only the message 'You displease me'. Words, because they have precision, also give

the mother the opportunity to choose between a number of different
levels on which to approach the child's behaviour. She may choose
to emphasise the *behaviour itself*, in terms of moral absolutes
('Using swear-words is just very very wrong'); or in terms of its
deviation from what is accepted in society ('Nice children don't use
words like that'); or in terms of its deviation from what is acceptable to her personally ('I don't care if Harry's mother doesn't mind,
I mind'). Or she may choose to emphasise *consequences* by appeal-
ing to society's attitude ('People won't like you if you behave like
that'); or to her personal attitude ('You're going to make Mummy
very unhappy if you don't improve, you've already given me a
headache'); or to punishment decided by herself ('Do that once
more and you'll be up to bed for the rest of the day'); or to
punishment mediated by society ('If you touch things that aren't
yours, you'll be in trouble with the police'). Because language is so
flexible a tool, it can be used not just to make statements but more
obliquely to call a child's attention to indirect implications. Moreover, since words themselves have the power to hurt and dismay,
they may be used almost in the role of punishment in their own
right: the mother may regularly threaten as a control technique,
without having any intention of carrying out the threat. Taking this
one stage further, words may be used to threaten or suggest sanctions which it is not actually possible to carry out, so that the
child is controlled by virtue of the fact that he does not realise
that his mother is bluffing. In the remainder of this chapter we will
explore these various uses and misuses of language.

The interview schedule includes a number of examples which
were offered to mothers as the *kinds* of things they might say to
the child in certain circumstances. In practice, these categories
seemed to cover the majority of verbal sanctions used, other than
the straightforward discussion of individual incidents with the
child. Obviously some mothers have their idiosyncratic forms of
appeal which they find effective, however, and these we asked
about: 'Is there anything else you say to him which stops him
being naughty, or which makes him sorry when he *has* been
naughty?' A few replies are given below in illustration, first of all,
of this rather miscellaneous group.

Architect's wife:
  Well, we have a little joke with her occasionally, I say to her
  "Primrose, I think you'd better go into the pantry and change
  your face". This is perhaps if she's scowling or unco-operative.

The humour of this is, she will go into the pantry and come out quite cheerful.

Executive officer's wife:

I've got a saying, "My mad is coming up" – and I don't know why, but this terrifies them, and I say "My mad is up, Roger", and I can feel it as soon as I say it that he knows he's gone too far. I don't know why, 'cause it's not half so bad as smacking, but he's gone in a flash. I don't know what secret it is, but I just said it once and found it worked.

Labourer's wife:

If he's naughty, I say "We'll have to buy a new baby now"; and he says "No, Mam, no, Mam, you've got me, love *me*". I say "All right, you'll be a good boy?" He says "Yes". [Sister: Sometimes she says "I'm going to the hospital to fetch that new baby now".]

Charge hand's wife:

I say "Do you think Jesus would have done that?"

Car repairer's wife:

I sometimes say "Would you like it if Jesus done that to you?" specially if he's done something to hurt me – and, er, little scriptures like that: "Well, Jesus wouldn't love you, and he's watching every little naughty move you make, and it doesn't make him love you any more". Sometimes I'll say to him "Oh you've got the devil in you today!" – "What's the devil, Mummy?" – "It's a naughty little man that makes you do naughty little things, and you mustn't". Or I'll perhaps look miserable – perhaps put me head down, lower me head and he'll think I'm crying. Then he'll think he's upset me; "I'm sorry, Mummy" – that's when there's nobody else in, but he wouldn't say he's sorry if there was anybody else in.

Milkman's wife:

Sometimes I say to her "You ought to be ashamed of yourself" – you know, probably if it's been a fit of bad manners – "you've been taught different, I expect different, and I think it's high time you pulled your socks up". Mostly that will pull her around, you know.

In all but the first two of these (which in their different ways have a ritual, magical quality), the child's self-esteem is particu-

larly appealed to, either positively ('I expect different') or nega-
tively ('it doesn't make him love you any more'), or both. The
child is intended to feel that his behaviour is not up to his mother's
expectations, and therefore to be ashamed of himself: or worse,
that she despairs of him, and might even take steps to replace
him.

Appeals to self-esteem – which are usual in any verbally mediated
discipline other than simple threats of punishment – essentially involve a comparison between the child as he is *now* (a 'naughty'
child), and the 'ideal' child that he either 'normally' is or might
become: the mother offers the child a hypothetical model to
emulate, or perhaps a negative one to avoid ('Nobody likes rude
little girls'). If there is a suitable real-life model available, however, she may well feel that to draw her child's attention to the
desired or condemned qualities in another child will engage his
sense of self-esteem still more effectively. We asked the question
both ways round, thus:

180. Do you ever hold up another child as an example?
     What do you say?
     (Prompt either way as necessary):
     What about the other way round? Do you ever say:
     'Look how nicely so-and-so behaves!'
     'You don't want to be like so-and-so, do you?'

Fifty-one per cent of all mothers would not hold up another
child as an example at all: like rewarding or 'bribing', they felt
that there were moral overtones to the question – that this was
something one *ought not* to do.

Tobacco worker's wife:
  Well, I mean each child is sort of an individual, you know, on
  its own; I mean, if Nigel was untidy and Paul wasn't, well, Paul
  might be a little devil when he's out and Nigel might be good;
  so you can't compare one child to another. I mean, *all* kiddies
  have got faults and that, and some of them are sort of different,
  so I think it's completely wrong to, you know, compare children.

Thirty-three per cent overall would cite another child as a positive 'good' example:

Food packer's wife:
  That happened only yesterday, Richard's stopped wetting the

bed and he's only three, and Nicky's seven – so I had to explain to him that if Richard can stop wetting the bed at three, I'm sure he can stop at seven, so I said "You must try, otherwise Richard's beating you" – you know, that sort of thing, talking their way.

Scientific research worker's wife:
If we go somewhere – on a bus, for example – and he is repeatedly naughty and won't sit still, and puts his feet on the seats or bothers other people; and there might be another child who is definitely much younger than he is, behaving perfectly well: then I might say "Look at that baby, how good *he* is!"

Machine operator's wife:
Yes, I'm awful for that! "Hazel does it for *her* Mummy", I say "Why can't you do it for me?" And mind you, I've no idea whether Hazel does it or not!

Twenty-nine per cent overall (some overlap with the 'positive' group) would hold up another child as a negative, 'bad' example:

Doctor's wife:
She has a cousin Felicity who's an awful winge-er [grizzler]; and if *she* winges, we all say "Ooh! – look at Felicity!" – and that stops her straight away, she doesn't want to be like her.

Lorry driver's wife:
Well we did, because we had a big girl living with us, my husban's niece, she got in trouble with the police and everything; 'cause she kept running away from home, started from Mablethorpe and came here five different times, we'd got policemen up here all day and it really upset me at the time: but as I tell you, when April was playing up and she started to be a bit cheeky, I said "You don't want to turn out like that, do you, nobody loves her, because even her mother and father have told her to clear off".

The use of models in so explicit a way is not related to the sex of the child. Differences between middle class and working class are not striking: they fail to reach significance in the case of 'bad' examples, and are significant only at the 0·02 level in the case of 'good' examples, which are used by 40% of middle-class mothers compared with 31% of working-class mothers. However, if we look at the group who *never* use either kind of example, we find a class trend which is significant at 0·01 increasing steadily from 39% in Class I and II to 54% in Class V; using models appears to be a temptation which mothers generally think should be resisted, but which those at the top end of the scale find more irresistible. A deterrent to using negative examples is that they usually apply to children outside the family, and might therefore teach one's own child to be intolerant, rude or snobbish: as one mother said of a neighbour's children whose dirtiness she had criticised, 'You're not sure what to say, because I don't want to discredit the kiddies, because after all it's not their fault.' There is also the difficulty that use of a neighbour's child as a bad example might percolate back to the neighbour! The problem with good examples, on the other hand, is that between siblings they can cause jealousy (as many mothers remembered from their own childhood experience); while other children may be known better to the child himself than to the mother – 'If you give her an instance of how good her friends have been, she'll tell you how bad they've been!'

'If she's only touched on the outskirts of being naughty, I probably give in...'
We have already seen that threats of deprivation of icecream or television can be difficult to carry through because of the demands of other children in the family; but the fulfilling of threats generally, like the fulfilling of promises, needs a certain commitment of time, energy and determination on the mother's part. Threats are usually made in the heat of the moment; once the moment has passed, even though the child has still not obeyed, the mother will begin to simmer down, inertia takes over, and to pursue the matter through to the end hardly seems worth the expense of effort and argument. Overall, 28% of mothers 'often' or 'usually' fail to carry out their threats to the full, and 20% 'sometimes' do; most of them deprecate their lack of stamina.

173. Do you carry out a threat if you've warned him, or do you usually let it go?

Window cleaner's wife:
Well, I keep it up for so long and then I forget it. I'm silly – such as this cup of tea lark, you know, they have a cup of tea every morning in bed; well yesterday they was fighting, her and Diane, and she tugged at the sheet and upset the cup of tea.

So I said, that's it – no more tea in bed! Well, I didn't take one this morning, but no doubt by the time next week comes round I shall be taking them up again. Once I've got over it, I'm as daft as grease again, like.

Actor's wife:
No, they usually talk me round, or else they're terribly good for the next half-hour and I feel that they've earned their position back again – I'm very bad at that.

Building worker's wife:
Well, I *say* it, but I don't always carry it out. There again, I know I'm in the wrong and that, but I get very soft, I sort of give in in the end, you know. I'll say "Now just for that you're not going to so-and-so", or "You'll go to bed at six o'clock" – but she doesn't, she'll stop up till her usual bedtime. That's it more often than not – as I say, it's very wrong, but I just – well – you know, that's *me*, that is!

Obviously there may be persuasive reasons (like 'they've earned their position back again') for not following through. Nonetheless, the fact that mothers generally feel it to be a weakness probably means that, among those who 'usually let it go', threatening has become a sanction in itself.

The fact that only 52% of mothers (see Table 47) can say that they usually carry out the threats they make will not surprise most practising parents; though it may be of interest to those who advocate the more widespread use of behaviour modification techniques in normal child rearing and teaching. Yet within the subtle interchange of mother/child communication, socialisation can take place effectively without precisely calculated schedules of reward and punishment. We would indeed regard absolute consistency in disciplinary matters as neither feasible in practical family life nor particularly desirable. Parents who hope to sustain honest and open relationships with their children through childhood into adulthood come to see a certain advantage in letting the child understand from an early age that emotion as well as reason enters into all real human relationships. Children need to realise that total consistency or predictability of behaviour is hardly possible in the hurly-burly of everyday life, and that much more important is the establishment of some kind of consistent moral philosophy or set of ideals for the evaluation of human conduct. The weakness of the behaviour modifiers' position is that it places all the emphasis

Table 47 *Carrying out threats*

	social class					summary		
	I&II	IIIwc	III man	IV	V	I&II, IIIwc	IIIman, IV,V	overall popn.
	%	%	%	%	%	%	%	%
M normally carries out threats								
boys	67	60	42	49	33	64	42	48
girls	68	57	61	44	33	63	54	56
both	67	59	51	47	33	63	48	52

Significance: trend ↘ ****   m.class/w.class ****
between sexes p = 0·08

M most often 'lets it go'								
boys	16	16	30	23	47	16	31	27
girls	8	20	33	33	49	14	35	29
both	12	18	32	28	48	15	33	28

Significance: trend ↗ ****   m.class/w.class ****
between sexes n.s.

upon behavioural conformity: and this sterile concept is rarely sufficient as an aim in normal child rearing.[3] Rather, parents are most concerned to pass on to their children the ideals, beliefs and values which they themselves cherish: in the last analysis, the consistency of what parents say in interpretation of their own actions is probably more important to the child than the consistency of their day-to-day behaviour – at least so long as the credibility gap does not widen to become an unbridgeable chasm.

The most striking feature of Table 47 is the steep social class trend. Twice as many mothers in Class I and II, compared with those in Class V, normally carry out threats; four times as many Class V mothers, compared with Class I and II mothers, normally 'let it go'. We would relate this to the strong value placed by middle-class mothers upon words *as the agents of truth* which we noted when the children were four;[4] that is, once an idea is formulated in words, this invests it with substance which must not then be negated. Thus it is an integral part of the middle-class philosophy that a threat should only be put into words if parents are also prepared to carry it through into action. 'Stick to your guns with a child, that's the main thing', says a teacher's wife: 'You must never promise a child or threaten a child anything if you feel that you can't fulfil it'.

Working-class mothers, and in particular lower-working-class mothers, are on the other hand rather more likely to be prepared to use words as expedients for short-term aims, with less per-nickety regard for their content in terms of truth. This we illus-trated in a number of ways at four; and to an only slightly less marked extent we can do so again now by referring to threats which *cannot* be carried out and which therefore leave us in no doubt as to the user's intent to bluff and bamboozle the recipient.

'Bamboozle (v.): to deceive by trickery, hoax, cozen; to mystify'
(Shorter Oxford English Dictionary)

The essence of a 'bamboozling' threat is that, while having little basis in reality, it must carry some degree of conviction to the child: otherwise there would be no point in using it. In as much as seven-year-olds are considerably more expert than four-year-olds in judging what is plausible or feasible and what is not, one may expect attempts at bamboozling to decrease as the child grows older and wiser.

Presser's wife:
If I said to him "I'm going to the Bobby about you", he'd say "Why, what's up wi' you? – the Bobby comes to school, he's supposed to be our friend, so *he* not do nowt!" You see, he's got an answer for you. I tell him I'm leaving him – it doesn't make no difference. He says "I know you'll not go". I say "All right, then, you see if I don't!" He says "I know; I know, 'cause me Dad wouldn't let you go" – you see!

Engineering worker's wife:
I threaten a policeman. I threaten to take him down, you know, to see him, and normally he says "Come on, then, let's go" – be-cause he's well in with the policeman that goes to the school with the projector and that, he's always talking about it. You see he's not *frightened* of him [said in the tone that he should be frightened of him but isn't].

Railway driver's wife:
I say "Oh Vicky, if you don't shut up you'll drive me into Mapperley [mental hospital]". She says "Ta-ra, then!" – she does, honestly! She couldn't care less. She gets beyond me at

times. She's wilful, you know what I mean? . . . . . [Do you ever
tell her you'll leave her . . . . . ?] Yes, I do: "I'm going to
leave you, find another Dad for you". You know the other
week – I said "I'm going to leave you"; she said "Well, when're
you going then?" I don't think they could care less, kids, nowadays! She knows I wouldn't, you see.

Car showroom foreman's wife:
Well, as a child as big as Micky [age two] I might have said
Mummy won't love you, but not now, because I think it's wrong
to say to a child of seven – I mean I think Scott realises that
he's my little boy, and . . . it's just one of those things, I don't
think I could say it to him now because I think he's old enough
to question it – and how could you answer when you don't
mean it? It wouldn't be true, would it?

Some mothers are still trying; others who were bamboozling at
four have now given up in the face of the child's increased sophistication. At the same time, because seven-year-olds are less physically
controllable, and because boys in particular – being less subject
to supervision than girls – pose more of a discipline problem to
their mothers, a reverse trend cuts across this, tempting mothers
to look beyond the household in their sanctions and to appeal to
authority figures outside the family in their dealings with boys
especially. Table 48 shows the proportions of mothers who threaten
their seven-year-olds with an external authority figure. The class
difference is very marked, as it was at four; but we now have a
strong sex difference which did not exist at four. The proportions
for four-year-old boys and girls combined are given for comparison; it is remarkable how similar the four-year-old working-
class figures are to the seven-year-old figures *for boys only*.
  Policemen, as at four, remain the most-used external authority,
though the transcripts show that the public relations exercise which
they carry out in primary schools can be effective in neutralising
their exploitation as bogeymen. As the possibility of delinquency
in law becomes more real for child and mother, obviously the
policeman is a less idle threat: 'I told him, never touch anything
belonging to anybody else, otherwise if a policeman has to come
he might get into trouble', says a rigger's mate's wife. Comparatively reality-based threats of policemen tend to spill over into
other areas, however: 'I say "If you don't behave yourself, I'll
fetch a policeman to you and he'll take you away" ', says this

Table 48 *Threats of external authority figures (teacher, doctor, policeman, etc.)*

| | social class | | | | | summary | | |
	I&II	IIIwc	III man	IV	V	I&II, IIIwc	IIIman, IV,V	overall popn.
	%	%	%	%	%	%	%	%
At four:[5]								
boys+ girls	6	17	23	26	39	11	25	22
Significance: trend ↗ ****						m.class/w.class		****
At seven:								
boys	12	24	24	27	40	18	26	24
girls	0	4	14	17	13	2	15	11
both	6	14	19	22	27	10	20	18
Significance: trend ↗ ****						m.class/w.class		***
between sexes ****								

same mother. This form of words is fairly frequently used; the alternative is the less severe threat of getting a policeman to 'give you a good talking-to'.[6]

Driller's wife:
> On Sunday I was going to take a walk and find a policeman that'd have to come and talk to her.

Hospital porter's wife:
> I say "I'll send you up to the policeman"; and he says "Oh, don't, Mam, I'll be a good boy".

Labourer's wife:
> Yes, I say "I'll fetch a policeman and tell him to lock you up in the police station and give your Mum a rest".

Policemen are also invoked, along with the 'school board man', specifically to counter the child's reluctance to go to school: the difference here is that the mother threatens *her own* removal. Although it is not the policy of the Educational Welfare Office to recommend prosecution except as a last resort, the general threat of trouble with the authorities clearly has some basis in reality: equally clearly, mothers who threaten in this way exploit for their own convenience their child's uncertainty of what might happen in such a case.

M

Nylon winder's wife:

He sometimes cracks on he's got a headache. I say "Come on, you'll have the school board man after me" – because we did, over the girl of fourteen – "and if *he* keeps coming, you know, you'll have me in prison". And he bucks up straight away as soon as he hears that.

Plant manager's wife:

I say "If you don't go to school, the policeman's going to come and fetch Mummy – it isn't you that he'll fetch, it's Mummy". That *would* worry him if I said that.

Welder's wife:

Well, I'd do to her what I'd do to the youngest boy, tell her that a policeman will come and take *me* away if I don't send her to school.

Teachers, seldom involved at four, are the second more frequently threatened external authority at seven. Here again, there may be some substance in such a threat. 'He doesn't like the idea of your ever going to the school – if you say you're going to school to see his headmistress, he doesn't like that at all', says Roger's father, and Roger's mother quotes herself: ' "Are you like this at school? We'd better go and see whether you're like this at school" – we don't *threaten* him with the teacher, we just say we'd better go and *see* about it'. Many parents will have experienced their children's dismay at the thought of being discussed, with the best of intentions, by parent and teacher together: in the above context the threat of consultation is as it were a middle-class version of the authority threat. The first example below goes one step further, and more obviously bamboozling examples follow.

Window cleaner's wife:

Sometimes he'll say Mrs Martin said he'd been particularly good, and then he comes home here and he starts – I say to him "I think I'll go back this afternoon and tell Mrs Martin what you're *really* like". I don't actually *threaten*, I don't say I'll tell the teacher this or that or the other.

Hosiery cutter's wife:

She's a devil for not wanting to get up in the morning, and then

I've usually said "Do you want me to fetch Miss Campbell, and let *her* shout you down?" She's said "No!" and come barging down.

Headmaster's wife:
  I think teacher's been threatened, headmaster's been threatened; I pretend to go and ring the headmaster up.

Other external authority figures were rare; doctors made an occasional appearance where the child was thought to be malingering, but this is not so much an idle threat as a deliberate check by the mother on whether the child feels that he has symptoms acceptable to an expert eye. We would not regard it as a threat unless the mother herself so regarded it: 'I'd tell her I'd take her to the doctor's – that'd soon rally her round, she don't like doctors'.
  It must be firmly borne in mind that mothers who threaten in this way are a small minority; as we found at four, those who had never used such threats felt this as a strong matter of principle. 'No, no, definitely *not*', said a railway fitter's wife – 'that's a terrible thing to do – a doctor or a policeman, a most stupid thing to threaten a child with, because they are both really important people for a child to get on with'. A departmental manager's wife said, 'Oh, *heavens*, no – do any parents do that?' Some had unhappy memories of their own childhood fears, and therefore avoided evoking fears themselves.

Accountant's wife:
  . . . as for sending for the policeman, I was scared stiff with that when I was a child, so I would *never* do it. My husband was the same, we were both threatened as a child with being sent away and that sort of thing, and he said we'd never do it. I wouldn't dare – I know the effect it had on me and my sisters.

On the whole, those who do threaten authority figures do so for expedience without expressing any particular guilt about it. Threats to leave the child or send him away were regarded as especially hurtful, however, and although a few used them precisely *because* they found the child vulnerable to them, most of the minority group who threatened this were unhappy about doing so. Children themselves were often reported as showing disturbance or distress in response to these threats and, as at four, there were mothers who for this reason no longer used them, though they had done so earlier.

Builder's wife:

Oh, I often threaten for me to leave – that upsets him terrible. "I'm going to leave you if you're going to be naughty boys." [What would you say that for?] Noisy – been fighting with one another; one of those days when they won't do anything at all. I'll say "That's it, now, then!" Oh, they do believe me, 'cause they get serious you know. But Roy's been complaining recently about the next world – "You know the next world, Mam, the end of this world, the *next* world, am I still going to have you for my Mam?" And Andy [eight] says "No, you're going to have a big ugly Mam and she's going to smack you!" Well, this upsets him. I don't know what's brought it on now, it's just recently he's been asking me this – "Am I still going to be with you, Mammy, 'cause I don't want any other Mammy". I say "No, darling, you're still going to have your Mammy", you know. It plainly bothers him, you know.

Lorry driver's wife:

I say "I'm leaving! – I'm not coming back no more", and she'll say "I'm coming with you". And I say "Oh no, you're not, Sharon, when I go I shall take nobody with me". And that *does* upset her; because I've always tried to say to Sharon, "Because you're the eldest, because you was my first child, my first baby, you're rather special really". [So when you say that, it makes her feel she's not special after all?] Yes, yes – I suppose so really. I've threatened all of them, I've said they'll all go. I've said they'd all go away – I should leave here and they'd all go in a home. When everything gets on top of you, you know, and you feel as if you can't stand it another day.

Jointer's wife:

Well, I've always threatened to put them in a boarding school, but they never take any notice of me. They know now, if I win the football pools, where they're going – it's accepted as a joke.

Hosiery worker's wife:

Well, we did, yes, quite truthfully, we threatened we'd put him in a home. A little while ago he was being very troublesome, and we said we'd have him in a home, and, er, I think it made his nerves bad; and, er, we both of us said we'd never do it again, because we didn't think it was good for him.

Milkman's wife:
> I say the Welfare lady will come and have him put in a home for bad little boys.

Postman's wife:
> Well, I have once – um – it was the day your letter came the other day. Over breakfast, I was really upset over her, and I said "Oh, I'll have you sent away!" I did – and she was quite upset about it; and then your letter came and she brought it in to me, and she says "What is it?" Well – I knew what she'd think, you see, so I thought I wouldn't tell her just then. But she went on asking, so at the finish I did say "Well, it's about you, the lady coming to see about you." Well, that did worry her quite a lot, thinking I *was* going to have her sent away. So I had to explain, and I said "She came when you were four, but you don't remember." So she said "Yes, I do remember, you sat in the front room" – so she did remember, and after that she didn't bother.

Although mothers threaten the child with separation from themselves without particular reference to reality, these warnings are not simply dropped into a vacuum, and there is often the chance that something may happen to reinforce the threat. In the last example this something was the interviewer's visit, and the mother did not wish to take the threat further, so tried to defuse it; we noted other examples, however, where chance letters, visits or news-items were deliberately used to underpin a threat, or where the interviewer was unwillingly cast in such a role. 'I often tell him I'll send him off to a home somewhere; he pays no heed to it, just looks at me', said a crane driver's wife: her husband, holding the eighteen-month-old little sister, warned her at this point – 'No, not on the table! That lady'll take you away!' A nylon winder's wife told her children, 'You know the other night there was a woman in the paper walked out and left all her kiddies – well, I'll do that with you lot soon!' (her seven-year-old commented, 'Ah, you say that, Mam, but you never do!'); and a driver's wife, whose nephew *was* in a children's home, used this fact to back up her threat – 'Perhaps you'd like to go and have a taste of what *he's* getting'. We have suggested before[7] that the use of chance events to back up idle threats is rather characteristic of the style of upbringing which relies on bluff as a disciplinary technique, and we have no reason to change this view.

A minority of 16% of mothers overall would use a threat to

leave the child; 14% threaten to send him away. Although this reduces to 11% and 7% in Class I and II, with such small numbers class differences do not reach significance level (p <0.02 is found for the class trend on threats to send the child away). The difference that emerges from the transcripts is a qualitative one: working-class mothers tend to threaten with children's homes whereas middle-class ones prefer boarding schools, and the middle-class score is increased by the greater number who specify that they will have to leave the child to go into hospital. We did in fact look separately at mothers who told the child he would make them ill if he was naughty, whether or not hospital was specified: a third of all mothers did this (the smallest group Class I and II at 25%, the largest Class IIIwc at 37%) and there were no significant class or sex differences.

The use of threats not to love the child is more subject to social class variation. It must be made clear that we were here concerned with quite explicit threats to withdraw love: the questions asked were 'Do you tell him you won't love him if he's naughty? . . . . . When do you say that?' Other workers have tended to use 'withdrawal of love' as a blanket term for a range of much less explicit behaviours; for instance, Sears, Maccoby and Levin included looking coldly at the child, turning her back, refusing to listen to him, telling him she didn't want to look at him till his face was smiling and pleasant, isolating in a separate room, threats of separation, statements that he was making her unhappy or hurting her feelings – all under the heading of withdrawal of love: 'all these actions, on the mother's part, we regard as manifestations of one underlying process: the mother is indicating to the child that her warmth and affection toward him are conditional on his good behaviour'.[8] In the present study, as we have made clear in this chapter, we have thought it important to distinguish statistically between these rather different behaviours; and, whereas Sears, Maccoby and Levin found it difficult to obtain admissions of using specific threats of love withdrawal, perhaps because their sample was more biassed towards the middle class, we did not find this a problem, though it was quite common for mothers to express guilt in doing so.

Plasterer's wife:

Yes, I do say that, but I never did ought to: I don't think that's right. I say "Oh, I don't love you" – but she just laughs at me, she don't take it seriously.

Railway driver's wife:
Yes – she'll start crying and saying "You don't love me" – and
she takes a hell of a lot of consoling, Vicky does. [What would
she have done?] Oh, anything that's naughty, you know, such
as putting her tongue out and that – I just can't stand that, you
know. I say "I won't love you if you do that". Sometimes she
says "I'm not bothered" – but she is all the time.

Dairy worker's wife:
Oh, that upsets him if you tell him you don't love him; he says
"Mummy, please, *please*, Mummy", he says, "you're not going
to leave me", and he gets hold of me – and it's unbelievable the
grip, for a child, that he has.

Class IIIwc widow:
I probably would, but I don't suppose I'd mean it, you know.
Not so much now – but as I say, when we went through this
period of me being so keyed up, then I said "I don't love you
any more". Not so much now, because I know it means so much
to her.

Table 49 shows mothers who do sometimes tell the child they
won't love him if he is naughty. Less than a quarter of all mothers
say they would do this, but class differences are striking: middle-
class women, especially in the professional and managerial group,
are a good deal more reluctant to put such a threat into words.

Mothers who use this threat quite often volunteer that they do
so when they are under stress – which may well mean that the
child is too, as in the last case quoted where the 'keyed-up' period

Table 49 *Mothers who threaten the withdrawal of love*

	social class					summary		
	I&II	IIIwc	III man	IV	V	I&II, IIIwc	IIIman, IV,V	overall popn.
	%	%	%	%	%	%	%	%
boys	6	24	24	35	30	15	27	23
girls	9	8	27	40	28	9	30	24
both	8	16	26	37	29	12	28	24

Significance: trend ↗ ****   m.class/w.class   ****
                    between sexes   n.s.

was associated with the father's protracted illness and death. The fact that boys in Class IIIwc are three times as likely as girls to be so threatened may be an indication of mothers being 'driven to it' by male obstreperousness. On the other hand, for those who do not believe in using such a threat, stress does not come into it because it lies beyond consideration: they answer in terms of 'I *couldn't* do that', 'That's something I'd *never* do'. Often they are aware of the child's possible interpretation of their displeasure, and will verbally explain that they love the doer though not the deed; or, more subtly (perhaps too subtly), they will try to distinguish between loving and liking:[9] 'I often say to him, "It's a good job I love you, because I don't like you at the moment" – I'd *never* say I didn't love him', says a civil servant's wife.

An important point of difference between our own analysis of this area and that of the Sears–Maccoby–Levin study is that they attempted to measure the *frequency* with which the mother used withdrawal of love (and found their measure, as they admit, unsatisfactory). Our own method was to ask only whether each individual threat was within the mother's normal repertoire, without reference to frequency; and we justify this on the basis that there is a very real gulf between using this kind of technique at all, however infrequently, and simply not contemplating it. It is the gulf which is important in this area, rather than a frequency count of once a day, once a month and so on; in fact, as some pointed out from experience, the more frequently such threats are used, the less weight they carry. Jimmy's mother, who 'threatens him with everything under the sun' and can give us an example for every one of our categories, told us: 'I say to him "You *are* a bad lad, why don't you do as you're told? I shan't love you" – he says "Well, if you don't, me Dad will, or our Nancy" '.

There are, of course, significant individual differences in how prone children are to the anxiety which might make them take threats of love withdrawal seriously. But there is also a general vulnerability in this age-group, in that seven-year-olds still find it difficult to bridge the discrepancy between emotions of the moment and long-term feelings. Many children when they have incurred serious parental disapproval will seek reassurance that their parents have not permanently turned against them, and many seem to welcome forgiveness, either verbal or shown by the mother's hug or smile, as a sign that love still underlies the relationship. Clearly, it is very much open to parents, if they wish, to capitalise on such insecurity feelings as a deliberate disciplinary strategy. It must be emphasised that the exploitation of children's anxieties is not approved of by the majority of mothers in any social class group: but mothers at the upper end of the scale are a good deal more likely to reject on principle a method of control which manipulates their natural fears and which does so by misrepresenting what is feasible.

Rather than attempt to measure how often or in what proportion the mother uses this group of strategies, then, we have chosen to measure the number of different aspects of the group which she accepts into her disciplinary repertoire. However, because we are concerned not just with discipline but with the total understanding between mother and child, we have also chosen to subsume these strategies, not under 'warmth conditional on good behaviour', but as indicators that the mother is to some extent prepared to put expedience and her own convenience before honesty and truth. It was on this basis that we devised an index which, for want of a grander name that expressed what we meant equally well, we called a measure of 'bamboozlement'. Table 50 shows the six items which contribute to this index: they consist of the strategies which we have discussed above, together with one which is more fully dealt with elsewhere[10] in terms of the child's educational experience – the issue of what the mother does if the child asks her a question which she cannot answer (i.e. she does not know the answer, rather than does not wish to answer). Here the mother might react in a number of honest, whether more or less constructive, ways: 'Say I don't know', 'Tell him to ask his Daddy, 'Tell him to try

Table 50   *An index of 'bamboozlement'*

Question	*Answer scoring 1*
115 Can you always answer his questions? What do you do if you can't?	M conceals her ignorance from child
173 Do you carry out a threat if you've warned him, or do you usually let it go?	Usually 'lets it go'
176 Do you ever threaten him with someone else – his teacher or the doctor or a policeman – someone like that?	Policeman (threats of others do not score as they *might* not be idle threats)
178 Do you ever threaten to leave him .....? or to send him away from home?	Yes Yes
179 Do you tell him you won't love him if he's naughty?	Yes

Possible score range: 0–6

his encyclopaedia', 'Take him down to the library' and so on; however, some mothers who wish to preserve their image of authority in the child's eyes will be primarily concerned to conceal their ignorance from him.

Lorry driver's wife:

I pass it off with something else. [This is when you really don't *know* the answer?] Yes, I'd pass it off: "You wait till you get a big girl, I'll tell you when you're bigger, you're not old enough to understand".

Although, as we have pointed out, the seven-year-old is less amenable to being bamboozled than he was at four, Table 51 shows that this is by no means a dead issue. By bringing together, under one index, those maternal strategies which involve bluffing or duping the child, a pattern emerges which meaningfully distinguishes class styles. A bamboozling score of nil, which is a majority score for the professional and managerial group, applies

Table 51   *'Bamboozlers' and 'non-bamboozlers' analysed by social class and the child's sex*

	social class						summary		
	I&II	IIIwc	III man	IV	V		I&II IIIwc	IIIman, IV,V	overall popn.
	%	%	%	%	%		%	%	%
Bamboozlement score									
Zero:									
boys	71	46	33	31	14		59	31	38
girls	65	51	35	29	28		58	33	40
both	68	48	34	30	21		58	32	39

Significance: trend ↓ ****   m.class/w.class ****
                                    between sexes n.s.

2 or more:									
boys	15	25	30	40	46		20	34	30
girls	8	14	34	39	33		11	35	28
both	11	20	32	39	39		15	34	29

Significance: trend ↗ ****   m.class/w.class ****
                                    between sexes n.s.

to only half of white-collar wives, one-third of the skilled and semi-skilled group and less than a quarter of the unskilled; consistent bamboozling, in the sense of using this kind of strategy in more than one way, while it is a minority behaviour in every social class at seven, rises steadily as we descend the class scale from only 11% to 39%. Sex differences are negligible: the only contrast of interest is in the middle class, where nearly twice as many boys as girls are bamboozled (this difference is significant at 0·05): perhaps this represents once again a more desperate search for any way that offers for dealing with this less amenable sex.

These figures support those we presented at four on mothers' willingness to 'evade or distort the truth'.[11] We speculated then that, because the mother is likely to set the pattern for a child's later attitudes towards authority, her willingness to use bluff and bamboozlement may sow the seeds of distrust of later authorities, such as teachers in the first instance and the agencies of law and administration later on. It is as true at seven as it was at four that 'the most widely used [disciplinary] deception in Class v is the idle threat of authorities outside the home . . . so that many children must initially meet these personages as allies of an angry mother, whose own falseness they must soon discover'. Since mothers are only intermittently angry, however, we particularly questioned the effects of the child coming to realise, as he inevitably must, that it is a supposedly *benevolent* authority who has deliberately used trickery in her dealings with him: this one might expect to have a more subtly powerful influence than would deception from a frankly malevolent source. The findings of this chapter do not yet give us any firm answers; but they do make us feel that continued conjecture in this vein is more than justified.

'We try to instil in him a sense of good manners . . .'
In a battle between parent and child, the artillery is not confined to one side, and we can hardly end this chapter without some consideration of the child's verbal contribution and his mother's attitude to it. It was already clear at four that the availability of words as a medium to exert control over the child is paralleled by the child's increased ability to influence or perturb the mother by his own use of words. Verbal 'rudeness' and 'cheek' were already a source of conflict at four; to the extent that a cheeky four-year-old can be considered sweet or cute, while at seven the sweetness has worn off a little, this becomes a sharper issue as children grow older.

In asking 'What do you do when he is rude to you?', we did not specify what we meant by rudeness: we were looking for the mother's response to what she perceived as such. As at four, rudeness is largely in the ear of the listener. Twenty per cent of these mothers felt that they had to cope with 'a lot' of rudeness from their child (there are no significant sex differences here), but we have no way of knowing how much and what this consisted of in objective behavioural terms; from the transcripts we can assume that what one mother finds objectionable, another may not. 'There's so much rudeness flying around the house with all the children, it doesn't mean very much', says a university teacher's wife; whereas a cook's wife complains that 'she must have her *say*; and (I) tell her to shut up and don't answer me back'.[12]

Teacher's wife:

I don't know – I suppose you'd have to distinguish between rudeness and just a lively mind. I mean, if he said *"I won't"*, I'd just turn that into a joke, I wouldn't take umbrage. I wouldn't *like* it, but there again, you see – answering back – that might be just a lively interest in a subject, mightn't it? And there's no reason why that should be rudeness. I mean, when I climb over him to get at the Teasmade in the morning, he says "Big Fat Mum!" – well, I mean some people wouldn't like that at all, but I just take it as an affectionate remark.

Policeman's wife:

I think you've got to let them have their say, but . . . um . . . if he told me to shut up and things like that – which he doesn't . . . you know, I sometimes wonder if I'm doing right, 'cause I *do* stop him saying things, you know, and yet I don't want him to be *frightened* of saying anything. I let them have their say as long as they're not cheeky.

The subjective perception of rudeness is, as these quotations illustrate, not just a matter of differences between greater or lesser tolerance in individual parents, but the dilemma which parents individually face as to where to draw the line between what is 'lively' and what is 'rude'. Most parents want their children to have lively minds; most also want them to be courteous and reasonable: to balance these is the problem. An awareness of the 'changing times' is another factor.

Political worker's wife:

Well, it's a strange sort of rudeness – *disrespectful* rudeness – and

I find it hard to cope with, because I would have never *dreamt* of talking to my mother like that, you know; not even *thinking* that way! It's so strange, and I've just come to the conclusion that children today are *like* this, you know – all the children down the street are like this, and she can't help it . . . This relationship with parents, it's completely different – and I'm not sure which is best. It's lovely for the children; but – um – you know, I can remember thinking that the way I thought about my mother was quite nice, you know! Yet I wouldn't have dreamt of cheeking her the way Nanda cheeks me, because I know it would have hurt her more than anything . . .

An important element for most parents in deciding whether apparent 'cheek' is tolerable is the child's intention: whether he meant to be rude, whether his manner was unpleasant, whether he was just trying out his independence: 'You expect it really, don't you, in the art of growing up', as a sales representative's wife put it.

Lorry driver's wife:
You see, a lot of children don't realise they're being rude, they think they're being straightforward. I mean, there are a lot of *adults* where they say they're being blunt and straightforward, the people they're being blunt and straightforward *to* tend to think they're being rude . . . It's only if he's been *too* rude over anything that he'll have a smack – when he *knows* he's been doing something wrong.

Policeman's wife:
It's the tone of voice in what they say – the attitude they take up – I think it *is* the tone of voice. If I felt she was treating me really disrespectfully, I wouldn't tolerate it. But I like her to think of me as another human being. I was young when I had her, and I haven't sort of achieved maturity. It's difficult really to sort of put on a stern mother act too much, yet – um – she knows when she's expected to obey, and I wouldn't ever tolerate open defiance, *ever*.

The question of what the mother does in response to what she perceives as rude becomes essentially a matter of whether she believes in an authoritarian style of upbringing. This belief will contribute to her response in two ways: it makes her more likely to appeal to the punishment principle, and it also will make her see rudeness as requiring action, since rudeness to herself directly undermines her authority. A more democratic style can (indeed perhaps must) accept a degree of rudeness, because implicit to the democratic principle is the verbal method of persuasion, which allows for various forms of arguing and answering back which then need to be met by verbal justification rather than repression. This class-affiliated authoritarian/democratic difference in attitude emerges quite strongly in Table 52, which shows mothers who respond punitively to rudeness; such sex differences as appear do not reach significance.

Table 52 – *Mothers who punish a child for being rude to them: rudeness subjectively defined*

	social class					summary		
	I&II	IIIwc	III man	IV	V	I&II, IIIwc	IIIman, IV,V	overall popn.
	%	%	%	%	%	%	%	%
boys	34	35	58	63	53	34	58	52
girls	37	27	49	51	47	32	49	44
both	35	31	53	57	50	33	54	48

Significance: trend ↗ ****   m.class/w.class ****

between sexes n.s.

Responses to rudeness and cheek were deliberately confined by the terms of our question to the situation of the child being rude to his mother, and it is certain that for her this comes somewhere between the greater offence of being rude to other adults and the lesser one of being rude to other children: rudeness necessarily involves someone on the receiving end. 'Bad language' seems much more of a criminal act in its own right: a child's muttered 'bugger!' can give him the satisfaction of a daring wickedness even if totally undirected, while his mother is likely to be somewhat discomposed even though no one but herself overhears. The utterance itself has magical properties separate from its intention: mothers whose children had in fact 'picked up any bad language' were asked 'Can you tell me what it was?' and many refused to pronounce the word aloud, whispered (although no one but the interviewer was there), or resorted to half-spellings ('He's said one or two words beginning with B, and occasionally he's come home with an F!').

The dilemma this time is different. While answering back could be interpreted as the sign of a lively mind, and valued accordingly, none of the mothers wanted her child to use swear-words: the best she could say in his defence was that he was 'using it innocently' – 'They don't know what it means, I suppose, but they always say it at the wrong time, don't they?' There is therefore agreement that swear-words have to be discouraged, and the main question is how? The knowledge that there is an element of bravado in the situation may incline the mother to think that the most effective method may be deliberately to play this down by ignoring swearing: 'If you tell him about it, then he'll do it more, so I just let it slide and he'll not do it, he'll forget all about it'. Others take a coolly rational but firm approach.

Student teacher and primary teacher:
[Father:] Didn't Antonia come home once and say "What does B – O – G . . ." [Mother:] . . . Yes she did, she spelt "bugger", but she spelt it incorrectly, didn't she? [Father:] She said "What does that mean?" and I said "It's a word when you get annoyed, you say that, and it means nothing, so you might as well not bother saying it, *we* don't use it, so. . ." [Mother:] "*We* don't use words like that, so there's no need for you to use it." And we've never heard anything since. Just that once, and she didn't know how to say it either, she spelt it, and she spelt it incorrectly.

Grocer's wife:
Yes, he has: "Oh, you're bloody this" and things like that. [What did you do?] Asked him what it means – I say to him "Well, what does it mean?" If he doesn't know, I say "How silly, what a silly word, you don't know what it means". Nine times out of ten it works. They feel such fools if they can't explain themselves at the time they use it. [Are you willing to explain to him all the words?] I would do if he . . . yes, I'd have to, I think. I'd have to, and tell him there was a better way of expressing it.

Lorry driver's wife:
I got him out of it – stuck it as long as I could – held my breath every time we went anywhere . . . He tripped once on the stairs at school one day and I was talking to the headmaster, and he tripped – "Oh, fucking hell!" he said straight out – "I *beg* your pardon?" I said. And he said it again, he thought I hadn't heard him! He used to come out with that a lot. [How did you get him out of it?] "Why do you say that, Julian?" – and he said "I

dunno". I said "Have you ever heard me use it?" and he said "No". I said "Well, don't you think if it was a nice word Daddy and Mummy would be using it?" And he said "Yes", and I said "Well, we don't, do we – so it can't be very nice, can it?" – and he's never used it since, thank goodness.

Parents know that they can be badly 'let down' by their child if he swears in public – the reader may remember that Roger's parents at one time couldn't go out to tea because 'he used to sing "bloody *bug*-ger, bloody *bug*-ger" to the tune of Z-cars while he was sitting on the toilet' – and many therefore react much more severely than to other misdeeds.

Jointer's wife:

> She got a real good hiding for that. I was fetching her from school and another kiddy came up to her to take something off her, and she said "You fuck off!" Well – I know I say *some* words, but I don't say anything like that, I mean that really is the worst, isn't it? And there was a lady just passing and she looked at Cheryl and she looked at me, as if *I'd* taught it to her. Well, that stopped pretty quick; but lately my big girl's been saying she's said it again, not out loud, just under her breath. And I caught her at it on Sunday. She was in the yard and falling out with another kid, and I saw her through the window, not *saying* it, just miming it with her mouth, "fu . .". Anyhow, my husband whipped her in in a minute, and said "Well, we've caught you at last, have we?" And she got a clip round the ear and a kick in the pants up to bed – and that was it, I hope.

BR driver's wife:

> I'd tell her how wrong it is, and if she does it again to my knowledge I'll give her a damn good smack, harder than I've ever given her.

Labourer's wife:

> Well, I just said "Don't let me hear that again or I shall cut your tongue out" . . . I wouldn't do that *really*, you know [*sic!*], just you say that to frighten them more or less.

Lorry driver's wife:

> She *would* get punished for that. She'd probably get sent to bed – I wouldn't smack her, I'd tell her, 'cause she knows when I'm talking very, very seriously, and I would say "Now, listen to what I'm going to tell you, because I'm just going to tell you

this once" – and then she *knows* that it's something really bad,
'cause with children you've got to have what I call your nice ways
and you've got to have your firm ones as well. That's one thing
I *don't* hold with, children swearing, and that was a really bad
thing up Broxtowe [former neighbourhood], and I'm very very
lucky that I didn't have the whole lot coming out with it, 'cause
it was a shocking place.

Table 53 shows the proportions of mothers who would ignore
bad language and those who would punish for it; the residual
figures are those who reprove the child, and these make up the
majority, 57% overall. The comparatively large number of Class v
mothers who punish (34% compared with the middle-class 12%
and the overall figure of 19%) may be partly due to their acceptance of the punishment principle, but also to a heavier exposure
of their children to bad language: the last respondent's indictment
of Broxtowe as a 'shocking place' is echoed by other mothers of
other places, and it is obvious that in some neighbourhoods children
quite simply cannot be protected from a repeated barrage of unacceptable language shouted up and down the street by older

Table 53 *Mothers' response to their children's use of 'bad
language'*

	social class					summary		
	I&II	IIIwc	III man	IV	V	I&II, IIIwc	IIIman, IV,V	overall popn.
	%	%	%	%	%	%	%	%
M punishes								
boys	17	20	23	24	33	19	24	23
girls	5	6	15	16	36	5	18	14
both	11	13	19	20	35	12	21	19

Significance: trend ↗ ****   m.class/w.class ***
between sexes ***

M ignores								
boys	25	21	26	20	21	23	24	24
girls	35	29	26	17	15	32	23	25
both	30	25	26	19	18	28	24	25

Significance: trend ↘ **   m.class/w.class n.s.
between sexes n.s.

children, teenagers and others. Here of course we are referring to the *amount* of bad language in a child's daily experience, of which the mother is conscious because much of it is in her experience too. Interestingly enough, there were no significant class differences in *whether or not* the child had picked up such words: 59% of boys had done so, compared with 37% of girls. Possibly this reflects girls' greater amenability (or sense of discretion) as well as the fact that they are less 'out and about' than boys.

The figures shown in the table combine actual responses to children who had used ' bad language' with anticipated responses to those who had not yet done so; and we wondered whether the actual situation changed anticipated behaviour. A comparison of the 'has already' and 'not yet' groups showed a close correspondence, with one exception: Class I and II mothers were nearly twice as likely to choose 'ignoring' if they had not yet had to deal with bad language from their child. It may be that these mothers' comparative insulation from overheard profanity makes them less realistic about their ability to ignore it when the child eventually faces them with the offending words.

These two chapters have focussed upon parents and children in conflict. Given a situation in which parents attempt to socialise their children to be acceptable to society, while children are encouraged by the contemporary climate in both child rearing and child education to think for themselves, it is likely that there will be conflict and that it will be open. The reader may have found the catalogue of violence and other sanctions depressing; but one might ask whether the more equal battle of today is not more healthy than the earlier spectacle of the righteous parent with God (and later Truby King) firmly on her side.[13]

What is not new is the basic attempt to bring the child to a discrimination of right and wrong (however these may be defined) through some form of manipulation of his own self-esteem. Whether this is done by a physical demonstration that mother is bigger and stronger than he is; or by a threat which he believes he cannot prevent being carried out; or by an appeal to pride ('You're not going to let Mrs Jones see you in that paddy, are you?'); or by praise for conformity or for achievement: the child's wish to be worthy of love, approbation and attention is the prime force in his own socialisation. And because words are more subtle and diverse and flexible than blows, they must ultimately have the prime effect in his shaping. 'Sticks and stones may break my bones, but words

can never hurt me!' cries the child with bravado. Hurt you?
They'll mark you for life.

NOTES

1 The only sex difference is a heightened incidence of use of deprivation
   in relation to working-class boys: 83%, compared with 72% for
   middle-class boys and 71% for girls generally.
2 It is an interesting sidelight on the class issue that we have many
   examples of upwardly mobile families where affiliation to the new class
   was apparent to us in the mother's child-rearing attitudes before the
   move had actually taken place in terms of the husband's occupation.
   We would see this as an additional indication that attitudes to child
   rearing form just one part of a total integrated life-style; in other
   words, it helps a family to *be* socially mobile if they already hold
   some of the values and beliefs which are appropriate for the class
   group to which they aspire.
3 We ourselves believe that the calculated scientific manipulation of
   the behaviour of one human being by another, while not totally un-
   justifiable in all cases, needs to be continuously and critically moni-
   tored as to its motivation and intent. Full clinical responsibility must
   be borne in such undertakings; further, operant conditioning methods
   should only be employed where the ordinary means of interpersonal
   communication have completely broken down, and where the hope
   that the use of manipulative techniques will help to create or restore
   them is a major motive.
4 J. and E. Newson, 1968, pp. 459–76 (Pelican edn. pp. 488–507).
5 At four we calculated threats of authority (which included the father)
   and *idle* threats of authority (i..e. external authority) separately.
   Figures quoted here are for external authority only. J. and E.
   Newson, 1968, Table 49.
6 According to Françoise Dolto, for French children this would not be
   an idle threat (at least, not at the time her article was written): 'Society
   takes part in this continuous intimidation . . . . . Policemen are glad
   to threaten, upon the parents' request, children on whom the *martinet*
   [whip] has lost its effectiveness or to whom the parents don't dare give
   hard spankings.' 'French and American children as seen by a French
   child analyst', in M. Mead and M. Wolfenstein, *Childhood in Contemporary Cultures*, University of Chicago Press, 1955.
7 J. and E. Newson, 1968, pp. 472–3 (Pelican edn. p. 503).
8 R. R. Sears, E. Maccoby and H. Levin, *Patterns of Child Rearing*,
   Row, Peterson & Co., New York, 1957, p. 342.
9 See J. and E. Newson, 1968, pp. 495–7 (Pelican ed. pp. 528–30).
10 J. and E. Newson and P. Barnes, *Perspectives on School at Seven
   Years Old*.
11 J. and E. Newson, 1968, pp. 468–76 (Pelican edn. pp. 498–507).
12 See page 298 for the whole of this quotation.
13 A discussion of the moralities that have informed child-rearing attitudes will be found in J. and E. Newson, in M. P. M. Richards (ed.),
   1974.

Chapter 11

Dimensions of Difference

It is an accepted truism that no two children are exactly alike, and that this holds even of small babies; yet child psychology continues to propagate the notion (though presented in many very different theoretical guises) that the individual child is largely a product of the way his parents have treated him. Little attention has been given to the equally relevant proposition that parents are unavoidably influenced by the sort of child they find themselves with and the way he treats them.[1] It cannot be stressed too strongly that socialisation is always a two-way process.

Although young adults at the outset of parenthood may think they know their own attitudes towards child rearing, and may indeed have made certain firm decisions about what they *won't* do, they are hardly likely to have well-formulated contingency plans mapped out in advance; nor can they in any meaningful way anticipate how they would react in specific situations before they have experience of the child in question and the real-life setting in which events take place. Parents' deep involvement with their own children – precisely the quality which makes parents different from other, more 'professional' caretakers – colours day-to-day events to a degree which they can hardly foresee. In such matters we all, even if professionally trained in some area of child health or child education, start out as novices.

Nor does anyone nowadays pretend that there exists a body of knowledge which can provide parents with simple and foolproof recipes for bringing up children. Advice on child rearing in books and magazines is less authoritarian and directive than it has ever been; at the same time, there is some evidence that while upper-working-class parents are moving towards the more democratic attitudes of the middle class, the middle class itself may be partly caught up in an anti-permissive backlash. Certainly fashions of advice to parents perceptibly shifted during the 'sixties and early 'seventies. In a period of such fluidity, it is particularly difficult to predict the eventual outcome of parent–child interaction – just as it is almost impossible to know in advance how a particular marriage will work out. In as much as child rearing is concerned with human relationships between unique individuals, we should not expect the result to be predictable in any obvious scientific sense, and perhaps it is fortunate that it is not.

The point we are making here is that parents are essentially pragmatic. Within the limits of their own personalities, they are constrained to react to their children's natures and to the demands which they make. Out of this most subtle interaction process, a certain pattern or style of relationship will gradually emerge. How to incorporate the facts of individual differences into some coherent account of the process of child rearing as it is actually experienced, without simplifying almost beyond recognition, seems to us an unsolved problem. A conventional strategy in this field is to describe the child's personality in terms of certain generalised traits or dimensions and then to relate such dimensions to various aspects of parent–child interaction. This is the procedure which we too shall follow in this chapter. We are only too painfully aware, however, that the resulting analysis can do scant justice to the richness and variety of personality, circumstance and their interplay. We must also add that it is one thing to point to a relationship between some aspect of the child's temperament and how he is treated by his parents, and quite another to know whether or how much one is the cause or effect of the other. Possibly, indeed, it is quite misleading to look at such questions with cause/effect assumptions in mind.

*'If there's a choice for her to make, she says "Which would **you** like me to have?"'*
'He's very objective – he objects all the time!'
A convenient starting point for this discussion is the notion of the 'easy' or 'difficult' child. Even at the four-year-old stage of the study (and indeed when the children were still babies), parents repeatedly drew attention to differences between their own children in terms of their compliance or lack of it. Several of our questions at seven were designed to have a bearing on this issue, while Question 198 raises it very directly; we can briefly look at these individually, and then combine the data into an index of 'amenability'. The relevant questions are as follows:

6. Would you say he was a placid child, or rather temperamental?

7. Do you find him easy to manage, now he's seven – or is he
a bit tricky, do you have to feel your way with him? [all asked
as one question]

8. Is he the sort of child who usually agrees with what you
want him to do, or does he tend to object to things quite a
lot?

157. Do you find that N takes a long time over doing as you ask
him?

198. I think everyone agrees that temperamentally some children
are much easier than others. Compared with other children,
would you say that N is very easy, or fairly easy, or fairly
difficult, or very difficult?

Just over a third of all children were described as placid by
their mothers:

Company director's wife:
She's not a child for asking a lot of questions, I think in that
respect she is some ways a bit lazy. She just tends to, you know,
plod along and take life as it comes.

A surprisingly high proportion are judged to be temperamental:
44%, the largest group on the three-point scale.

Locomotive driver's wife:
Oh yes, he's very up and down, cries very easily, gets very
tender-hearted; overwhelming generosity, you know. Very temperamental. [See also p. 41.]

This leaves only 19% in the in-between 'varies' category. There is a
very slight indication of a class trend to a greater number of
'temperamental' children at the lower end of the scale; but we suspect that this is contributed to by a slight misunderstanding of the
wording by some lower-working-class mothers, a few of whom
began by answering the question in terms of 'prone to tempers'.
In any case there is no significant difference between middle class
and working class. However, girls are more likely than boys to be
described as placid (significant at 0·05) and boys more likely than
girls to be called 'temperamental' (significant at 0·02).

'Easy to manage', because it was opposed to the idea of 'having to feel your way with him', evoked slightly different answers from the more global 'easy/difficult child' continuum. Mothers appeared to recognise the situation of 'having to wear kid gloves', or 'having to wrap things in tissue paper' with certain rather touchy children.[2] Thirty per cent of children were regarded as tricky in this sense, but this ranged from 24% of girls to 35% of boys, a difference which is significant at 0·01.

Advertising manager's wife:

> We have discovered that the easiest way to deal with Duncan is to humour him – I don't mean give in to him, but, er, to say rather, "Duncan, I'd love you to do such and such for me". The sweet approach works wonders with Duncan, you know.

Forty-nine per cent of children (44% of boys and 54% of girls) are said to be easy to manage, and the remainder (21%) are variable. Class trends and middle-class/working-class differences are not significant, although shop and clerical workers are an anomalous group in finding their children more tricky to handle than do other classes.

In the question on whether the child tended to object or usually agreed to requests, we were looking for some degree of the kind of negativistic outlook expressed by the child who 'objects in principle and then considers the matter', as contrasted with an attitude which *expects* to co-operate as a general rule, though circumstances may force exceptions. After all the data on conflict in the last two chapters, it may not seem surprising that a quarter of the children are rated as having a general tendency to object. Thirty-seven per cent were said to be generally agreeable to requests, though some of this agreeable front can hide the passive resistance that we noted earlier in the form of slowness. Overall sex and class differences do not reach significance, though Class I and II boys are rather less inclined to comply.

The final question contributing to this index appeared fourth from last in the interview schedule, and was intended as a general summing-up question which would allow the mother to make an overall assessment of her child's temperament in relation to all the different socialisation situations already covered by the interview. In a much more formal way than occurs anywhere else in the interview, we asked mothers to rate their children on a four-point scale of ease or difficulty. The formality of this task was obvious in the way the question was phrased, and in the fact that the mother was thus made aware of our coding scheme; nor was she permitted to offer a middle category. As this question was concerned not so much with specific aspects of behaviour (compared with most of the earlier questions) as with a total impression, it is perhaps not surprising that there was some reluctance to use the two 'difficult' categories, which carried the implication of an adverse final judgement on the child: mothers who had bewailed their child's unco-operative behaviour in many different situations would, when faced with this summing-up question, fall back on 'Well – I suppose he's about average really', and when constrained to a choice between 'fairly difficult' and 'fairly easy' would plump for the latter. The corollary is that the children named as difficult are likely to be quite markedly so. Oliver and Richard are two children who contrast with their more amenable siblings, presented major problems of handling earlier on, and are still negativistic;[3] both are described at this point as 'fairly easy'.

Businessman's wife:

At the moment, Oliver's fairly easy; but whether this is because I cater to his needs I wouldn't like to say. He's not a child who is easy by nature; he does have definite preferences, and if it doesn't suit him, he won't fit in with you. Probably we seem to be having a very quiet patch anyway. [You found him very hard work at four, didn't you?] Yes he was, but I find him much easier now. [Because you've learned to cope?] Well, I think half of each. I think he himself has learned more to deal with other people, and he's not so demanding – perhaps he finds more to occupy himself, perhaps at four he was bored . . . . . the other two make friends much more easily and fit in generally much more easily, you know, but he does seem to be . . . well, *different*.

Baker's wife:

Well, fairly easy I should say. It's . . . um . . . I mean, there must be . . . you see I'm going by Michael next door. I can only go by him. Well *he* won't stay school dinners at all, not at the moment he won't, and he's having to have lessons at private school because he can't read very well. I mean, when I've got a kiddy like Richard with just three or four difficult phases, I can't grumble, can I? So I should say fairly easy. I mean if you can't get over two or three things like that . . . if the child is dead perfect, I should begin to think there was something wrong with him.

The proportions of mothers answering in these different categories (overall population) were: *very easy*, 28%; *fairly easy*, 57%; *fairly difficult*, 13%; *very difficult*, 2%. In presenting the analysis in Table 54, these last two categories are combined, which in practice gives us a group of 100 difficult children, of whom 66 are boys.

Table 54 *Mothers' ratings of their children as 'very easy' or 'difficult'*

| | social class | | | | | summary | | |
	I&III	IIwc	III man	IV	V	I&II, IIIwc	IIIman, IV,V	overall popn.
	%	%	%	%	%	%	%	%
'Very easy'								
boys	19	21	26	22	23	20	25	23
girls	37	35	28	36	33	36	30	32
both	28	28	27	29	28	28	28	28

Significance: trend n.s.   m.class/w.class n.s.
between sexes ***

	I&III	IIwc	III man	IV	V	I&II, IIIwc	IIIman, IV,V	overall popn.
'Fairly' or 'very' difficult								
boys	28	19	21	15	5	23	18	19
girls	6	14	13	9	5	10	11	11
both	17	17	17	12	5	17	15	15

Significance: trend ↓ ***   m.class/w.class n.s.
between sexes ***

Departmental manager's wife:

Well, I'd say fairly difficult, because as I say, some days he's ... there's only got to be one slight little thing that goes wrong, and that's put him in a difficult mood for the rest of the day. I mean I couldn't say he was easy, or fairly easy – I would say he was fairly difficult but I should think there are some worse! I mean I *can* get through to him – there are some children that whatever you do, you don't, it just doesn't make an impression; I mean, so I've heard, I haven't really come across them. I mean I do think there's some hope!

Computer programmer's wife:

I'd say she was fairly difficult compared with some children, but then I don't altogether mind; sometimes I think it would be marvellous to have a placid child, and then I think I wouldn't really like a placid child because some of them are so placid they're uninteresting, you see. She's an interesting child: although she's difficult, she's interesting, and in a lot of ways I wouldn't like her any different really. I think it's because she's intelligent that she's difficult.

Electrical engineer's wife:
Fairly difficult; well, you could say *very* difficult, I suppose, but put fairly difficult!

Executive's officer's wife:
[On interviewer's arrival, Roger's mother, who rated Roger as *very difficult*, said:] Last time you asked me what gave me most pleasure about Roger, I couldn't think of a blind thing after recounting all the troubles I had with him; but this time I'm not going to be caught out, and I've thought out an answer in advance!

Both in terms of especial ease of upbringing and in terms of difficulty, sex differences are clear: more girls are said to be *very easy*, more boys to be *difficult*. Class differences are not conspicuous, though professional-class people apparently find their girls particularly easy and their boys particularly difficult to socialise. Very few Class v children are considered difficult, possibly because these children are less in contact, and hence less in conflict, with their mothers.

The questions we have discussed separately so far can now be brought together to form an index of amenability or compliance for each child. This is defined in Table 55, and the scores analysed in terms of sex and social class in Table 56. In the latter, cut-off points have been so chosen as to divide the total distribution into three roughly equal groups of low, medium and high scorers.

The difference between boys and girls continues to be the most clear-cut finding on the combined measure of amenability: boys are significantly more likely than girls to be rated as difficult to manage. However, in the 'very easy' group the slightly greater representation of girls does not reach significance. Class differences are variable and inconsistent. An analysis of variance based on the whole range of individual scores confirms the results shown in Table 56; there is a sex difference significant at 0·001 and no significant class difference. This analysis also shows a relationship

Table 55 *An index of amenability*

Based on		Mother's answer	Score
Q6	. . . a placid child, or rather temperamental?	Placid	2
		Varies	1
		Temperamental	0
Q7	. . . easy to manage, or tricky, have to feel your way?	Easy	2
		Varies	1
		Tricky	0
Q8	. . . usually agree with what you want, or tend to object?	Agrees	2
		Varies	1
		Objects	0
Q157	. . . takes a long time over doing as you ask?	Usually quick	2
		Sometimes quick	1
		Usually slow	0
Q198	Compared with other children, . . . very easy, fairly easy, fairly difficult, very difficult?	Very easy	2
		Fairly easy	1
		Very or fairly difficult	0

Score range: 0–10
Mean score approx. 5

Table 56 *Children scoring high or low on the index of amenability*

	social class					summary		
	I&II	IIIwc	III man	IV	V	I&II, IIIwc	IIIman, IV,V	overall popn.
	%	%	%	%	%	%	%	%
High Scorers								
(7, 8, 9 or 10)								
boys	38	29	35	32	32	34	34	34
girls	46	33	35	44	31	40	37	37
both	42	31	35	38	31	37	35	36

Significance: trend n.s.   m.class/w.class n.s.
between sexes n.s.

	social class					summary		
Low scorers								
(0, 1, 2, 3 or 4)								
boys	38	33	35	33	21	35	33	34
girls	18	27	23	20	23	22	23	22
both	28	30	29	27	22	29	28	28

Significance: trend n.s.   m.class/w.class n.s.
between sexes ***

between amenability and family size, in that children from large families (four or more children) are on the whole more amenable than those from smaller families (significant at 0·05): this finding holds independent of social class.

'She has a cough when she's upset – it's a real cough, but it comes on quick!'

A second dimension on which we can place individual children is one which brings together the child's dispositions towards shyness, anxiety and 'nervousness', along with his proneness to habitual 'tension habits' when he is feeling worried or overtired. Mothers certainly recognise that in this sense some children are more 'highly strung' than others, and we were satisfied that we were here talking about something which is meaningful in practical child-rearing terms. A dimension of this kind has of course been recognised by a number of previous workers, who have variously labelled it 'neurotic disorder', 'emotionality', 'manifest anxiety', etcetera. We will refer to a dimension of 'emotional stability', without however making any assumptions as to its clinically prognostic value: we would have used 'highly strung' if it had a noun form, and do prefer to use this term in opposition, rather than 'emotionally unstable'.

Again, we can look briefly at the contributing elements of this dimension, before combining them to form an index of emotional stability. The questions which mainly elicited this data follow; their context can be seen in Appendix I.

9. How does he manage in new situations? Does he enjoy them, or is he bothered by what he isn't used to?
10. What about new people? Is he shy?
11. In general, does he take things as they come, or is he a bit of a worrier?
40. In general, how would you say N gets on with other children? Does he make friends easily?
55, 60–65, 68 (see Appendix I for full wording): We're interested in the various odd habits that children seem to have at this age. Does N have any little habits you can think of? *(Various prompted; tension habits of interest here are nailbiting, compulsive swallowing or throat-clearing, pulling at ears, face, etc., picking other than functional, blinking or eye-screwing, stammering or stuttering, observed masturbation, headache following excitement or anxiety, vomiting for similar reasons.)*

The child's reaction to new situations and new people are of particular interest when looked at together. It might be thought that
there is not so very much difference between coping with situations
and with people, and that the operative factor would be the new-
ness. However, class differences are revealing here. Table 57 shows
first the proportions of children who are 'bothered' by new situations, secondly those who seem 'shy': these are the *unequivocally*
'bothered' or 'shy'. Those who 'vary' amount to 11% and 16%
respectively; overall, 67% positively enjoy new situations and 56%
are at ease with new people.

Clergyman's wife:
 She *is* bothered, but she's courageous and will cope with anything – but she takes it out on us afterwards.

Presser's wife:
 Going anywhere new, he gets all excited and he goes sick – he
 doesn't *mind* going, it's just he gets all worked up, as though

Table 57 *Children's responses to new situations and new people*

	social class					summary		
	I&II	IIIwc	III man	IV	V	I&II, IIIwc	IIIman, IV,V	overall popn.
	%	%	%	%	%	%	%	%
Bothered by new situations								
boys	29	19	24	26	12	24	23	23
girls	32	22	14	27	15	28	17	20
both	31	21	19	26	14	26	20	22

Significance: trend ↘ *   (non-linear trend *)[4]   m.class/w.class n.s.
between sexes n.s.

	I&II	IIIwc	III man	IV	V	I&II, IIIwc	IIIman, IV,V	overall popn.
Shy of new people								
boys	14	22	35	28	30	18	33	29
girls	25	20	28	36	31	23	30	28
both	20	21	32	32	30	20	32	29

Significance: trend ↗ ***   m.class/w.class ***
between sexes n.s.

he's never been anywhere before, but he's dying to go, you see what I mean? He seems as though he gets all worked up, all that week before we're going, and then you know two or three days he's got a sick headache and he's flat out for a couple of hours . . . . . We've got as we don't tell him until more or less the night before, only he keeps saying "How many more days before holidays?" I keep saying "Oh, we got to save some money first, before we go" – and that's how we've passed it off; because you see more or less every time he's got that worked up he's sick, and we've stopped telling him. And yet he's as cool and calm as anything *when* you're going; he's a good lad, he'll do as he's told.

Executive officer's wife:
That does bother him, he becomes withdrawn . . . . . He goes quite pale – in fact when I took him to the school medical, he'd been to the toilet to pass water, and before he'd got in he'd started to wet his pants, and that's how he is – anything like that – he is really a nervous child; everybody thinks he's full of confidence, and I have to keep explaining that to everybody. [. . . Is he shy?] No, he likes new people: if they'll give him an intellectual answer and he can show off with his knowledge, and if they show an interest in him.

A minority, but a sizable one at 30%, has problems either with new people or with new situations; a further 11% has difficulty with both. What is interesting about this data is that the class differences are in reverse directions: that is, more professional and managerial class children are said to be bothered by new situations, while more working-class children are shy of new people. Presumably this is partly to be explained by emphasis on verbalisation in the middle-class child's upbringing which might make him more able to cope with the social demands made by encounters with unfamiliar people. It may also be true that more verbalisation on the child's part makes the mother more keenly aware of his apprehensions about new situations, while shyness does not have to be verbalised to be apparent: the reverse, in fact. Sex differences do not reach significance.

Fears and worries were approached in two different ways at different stages of the interview: the early exploration of the child's general personality asked whether he seemed to be 'a bit of a worrier', i.e. whether he had a temperamental tendency to meet life in this way; while later on we asked for the *specific* fears and worries that were chronic for this child. Sex differences were almost nil, with the exception that a 12% difference in Class I and II, and a 19% difference in Class III manual, were found in relation to specific fears or worries reported: in both cases girls predominated over boys. The sexes are combined in Table 58.

Table 58   *Fears and worries of children*

	social class					summary		
	I&II	IIIwc	III man	IV	V	I&II, IIIwc	IIIman, IV,V	overall popn.
	%	%	%	%	%	%	%	%
Child generally 'takes things as they come'								
	46	53	52	53	64	49	54	52
Significance: trend ↗ **						m.class/w.class		n.s.
Child 'a bit of a worrier'								
	40	26	33	32	16	33	31	31
Significance: trend ↘ *** (non-linear *)						m.class/w.class		n.s.
Mother aware of specific chronic worries								
	63	58	53	49	45	60	52	54
Significance: trend ↘ ***						m.class/w.class		*

Just under one-third of the children are regarded as 'worriers' (17% come into the 'varies' category); just over half have worries which can be specified by the mother. The class trends on worrying as a temperamental trait and worries as specifiable entities are consistent: in both cases, children seem more likely to worry as we ascend the scale, especially in Class I and II, and less likely to do so further down the scale, especially in Class V. However, this statement may compound the children's actual emotions with the mothers' awareness of them: it may well be that the class trend derives in part from a differential in their alertness to children's problems. As in the case of children's fantasies, evidence suggests that it is the middle-class mothers in particular who would be the most likely to encourage their children to discuss their inner feelings, and the more educated mothers who would be most concerned with the psychological implications of children's fears and perhaps misconceptions, and the therapeutic value to the child of being able to talk them out.

Separated middle-class mother:
[Long pause] . . . I think – I think she has a fear of my going away. She has a [toy] dog called Pickering that she's had from about eighteen months, and if . . . if something is distressing her I notice – well, he'll always go to bed with her, but then she'll go to sleep cuddling him; but this week-end when I was going away, she was being terribly polite and saying "I *do* hope you have a nice time, Mummy, it'll be a lovely change for you". I said "You don't really want me to go, do you?" She burst into tears and said "No, I don't want you to go". I think she's rather frightened I won't come back; this may be that I'm her one parent, I can't think of any other reason.

The issue of whether a child makes friends easily or not might seem somewhat tangential to the dimension of emotional stability; we have taken only the group who experience real difficulty in making friends and allowed this to count one single point in the index. This group includes some children who have such problems because they are withdrawn and inward-looking, but also some who are too overbearing and bossy for other children to tolerate, or who are 'odd' in various ways. Eighteen per cent of all children are said to have these difficulties; class and sex differences are not significant. The topic has been discussed in more detail on pp. 183–5.

The inclusion of what we have characterised as 'tension habits' assumes that these are indicators of maladjustment and, in fact, emotional tension. We do not make this assumption altogether blithely. Imitation is one factor which gives us pause: children have been known to adopt other people's blinks and twitches in a purely experimental frame of mind. Habituation is another source of confusion: a 'behaviour symptom' which originally appeared in response to stress may persist as a self-sustaining mechanism which is no longer symptomatic of anything except lack of motivation to change. This is especially true also of what we would define separately as comfort habits: thumb sucking and dummy sucking tend to have their roots so deeply in the child's babyhood, and at seven are usually so closely linked with withdrawal into sleep, that we did not feel justified in including them under tension – although undoubtedly they sometimes appear at moments of stress.

Mothers were asked specifically about a number of tension indicators, and were also given the opportunity to add other more idiosyncratic habits. No social class differences were found with respect to any of them. Nailbiting was the most commonly reported habit, occurring in 24% of all children, significantly more often in girls.[5] The 'nervous cough' and 'nervous headache' came next, each reported for 17% of children, with no sex differences. 'Pulling and picking' occurred in 13%, blinking or screwing-up of eyes in 12% and observable genital play in 11%; a sex difference only appears in the last of these (16% of boys, 5% of girls), presumably because boys' genital play is both more obvious and more frowned upon. Disturbance of speech was reported for 8% of children, for boys significantly more often than for girls: 11% and 5% respectively. Seven per cent of children were subject to vomiting in response to stress.

This catalogue by no means exhausts the nervous habits described by mothers, and other examples were offered by 48% of them. Ellis sings in 'a sort of hum, not an actual song but just a noise he kind of makes if he's a little bit tense – a form of embarrassment'. Henry sniffs hard when his mother scolds him and 'ties his fingers into knots' when he's watching something exciting on television. Antonia hitches her tights – 'I think it may have *started* with the elastic being slack, but I'm quite convinced it hasn't finished up like that'. Patricia shakes her head when tired or watching television, and does it all the more if somebody comments on it. Felicity likes to feel somebody on a fleshy part – 'If she's playing with flesh, she's quite happy!' Stanley sucks his teeth and June twists her face and glowers. Clive rubs his knees together – 'he's got big bones in his knees and you can hear them clipping and clapping'. Vince has to smell everything he touches, Cyril 'licks his finger-ends and smells a lot of things where there's no smell at all', and Claudia keeps compulsively touching her arms. Betty bites her handkerchief, Larry bites his sleeve and Vera licks her handkerchief wet through every day. Simon used to shrug his shoulders, gave it up after six months, and went on to shaking an imaginary quiff out of his eyes.

A number of these habits are examples of some children's difficulty in staying quiet and still without fidgeting: they are labelled

N

as 'a nervous habit' by virtue of a particular movement becoming repetitive enough to engage the mother's attention. Subsequent repetition tends to become more irksome and irritating to both parents, but reprimands seem to have little lasting effect and are often said to increase this behaviour. Beyond the question of irritation within the family, parents often find such habits potentially socially embarrassing on two counts: the situation, they fear, reflects on their competence as parents, either because they have demonstrably made their children nervous and anxious, or because they have not managed to inculcate acceptable standards of self-control and good manners – or, of course, both. In addition, some mannerisms seem deeply disturbing in themselves to parents because they cast doubt on the child's mental health.

Precisely half of the overall population of children currently had two or more 'nervous habits' of the kind specified, and some children had as many as six. Social class differences are not marked, and merely show a slight difference between middle class and working class significant at 0·08, with rather more such habits reported by middle-class mothers. Overall, sex differences are of nil significance.

Before using incidence of 'behaviour symptoms' to contribute to the index of emotional stability, a check was made to determine whether children who had the worries and social difficulties probed in the earlier questions were also in fact more likely than by chance to exhibit behaviour symptoms. A positive correlation of 0·23 (significance**) was found which, while not very high, seemed sufficient basis for the combination of these two kinds of scores into one index. The scoring of this index is shown in Table 59.

If we now define 'emotionally stable' children as those with scores of 9 or more on this index, and 'highly strung' children as those with scores of 5 or less, we find ourselves with three more or less equal groups: 29% emotionally stable, 31% highly strung, and 40% somewhere in between. In terms of sex and social class affiliations, the data shows almost no patterning: there is a slight tendency for rather more highly strung children to be found in Class I and II and rather less in Class V, significant only at 0·05. More detailed analysis of variance confirms the absence of sex and class trends, but shows up a just significant difference (at 0·05) between children in large and small families: children in large families tend to have less of the 'highly strung' characteristics, and this in fact partly accounts for the lower proportion of highly strung children in Class V. We may conclude that the index gives results which

Table 59   *An index of emotional stability*

Based on		Mother's reply	Score
Q9	New situations . . . enjoy them or bothered?	Enjoys	2
		Varies	1
		Bothered	0
Q10	New people . . . Is he shy?	Not at all shy	2
		Varies	1
		Shy	0
Q11	Take things as they come . . . or a bit of a worrier?	Take as come	2
		Varies	1
		A worrier	0
Q40	How does he get on with other children? . . . make friends easily?	Easily or fairly	1
		Difficulty	0
Q51	Has he any fear or worries?	None	1
		Chronic worry specified	0
Qq55–68	Odd habits . . . things children do when a bit strung up . . .	No tension habits	6
		(1 subtracted from max. score 6 for each tension habit specified)[6]	

Maximum possible score: 14
Actual score range: 0–11
Mean score approx. 7

are independent of sex and social class once family size has been taken into account.

'. . . a relief to their feelings – but you want to find out what the feelings were that they were trying to relieve . . .'
The third dimension which it seems appropriate to construct is one which reflects the extent to which the child displays aggressive behaviour, and is outward-going and tough. Information contributing to an index of temperamental aggression was gathered at many different points in the interview; some of this data has already been discussed in other contexts. The following are the main eliciting questions for this index:

15. Would you call him an indoor child or an outdoor child?[7]
25. Is he careful with his toys, or do they seem to get broken rather quickly?
43. Does he do a lot of fighting – do his quarrels often come to blows?[8]
46. What sort of games does N mostly play with other children? [coded in preference order for rough and tumble play, con-

structional play, and imaginative role-playing with a plot][9]

164. What effect does smacking have on N?[10]

191. Does he ever seem to get a kick out of smashing something up?

193. Does N ever get into a real rage – shouting and stamping and banging doors? *(Prompt)*: About how often does it happen? What usually starts it off?

The questions on the child's destructiveness of material objects were asked in two different contexts (see Appendix 1), but were brought together for coding. We were interested in whether the child was generally destructive with his own possessions, whether he merely enjoyed smashing up expendables like old bottles but would be more careful of other objects, or whether he was a generally non-destructive child. There is of course a group of children who are inquisitive and exploratory as to how things work, and whose play involves taking things to bits in the expectation that they will be able to put them together again – an expectation which is often not fulfilled because of their lack of skill.

Miner's wife:
He likes to take them to pieces to have a look, but he likes to put them together again. [Does he always manage it?] Sometimes he'll manage it, sometimes he'll come and ask us, "Can you help me, I want to do this". A man gave him an old transistor . . . . . he's played with that and he still plays with it, but he's had it to bits and put it back and had it to bits again and put it back, and he can't understand why he can't get any sound out of it.

Scientific research worker's wife:
He is careful with his toys, but occasionally he decides that he wants to break this and see how it's made, and then he intentionally breaks it. He will do that with a brand new toy – last summer my mother-in-law gave him a rather expensive little crane with a lot of moveable parts, and he was quite intrigued by this. He played with it for half-an-hour, then he decided he wanted to know how it was made. He started by removing the tyres, and very gradually one piece after another. I felt quite embarrassed, my mother-in-law was watching him, and I didn't feel like stopping him because obviously he was very interested in it – I think probably he had the idea he could make one like it.

These children are not counted as destructive, since they are essentially constructive in their longer-term aims. Contrast the following descriptions:

Cotton winder's wife:
> Oh, he loves it, he loves smashing windows round us, he loves it, he loves to see how long something can last. "You see this, is it breakable, can it break?" So if you say it's unbreakable, well Tony wants to prove it, he'll get a hammer to it, and he'll smash it until he finds that it *can* break.

Railwayman's wife:
> Oh, she's *ever* so destructive – *very* destructive! . . . . . [Do you take any trouble to get her to look after her toys?] No, what's the use? I have tried, but she still goes breaking them up. It's a wonder she hasn't broke that typewriter up yet – she can't have thought about it! [six weeks old birthday present] I have to tidy up after all of them in this house. I'm a sludge-pump for them all!

Bricklayer's wife:
> Last night we bought two biros [ballpoint pens], and he squashed the other little feller's, not his own, he squashed it by putting it through the mangle: there was ink all over the new paint, you know. His Dad gave him his wages and he bought a biro and squashed it. [How do you feel about children doing that sort of thing?] What's the use of shouting?

Car repairer's wife:
> No, they get broken – I don't believe in them keeping them if they want to break them to vent their spite on their toys, and I think that gets rid of a lot of their burnt-up frustration in a child.

This last view, that destructiveness is the expression of frustration or in some other way a symptom of psychological stress, was very widely held but not usually expressed in this very tolerant manner. Much more representative were opinions emphasising the need for some kind of corrective action.[11]

Baker's wife:
> Well of course it's psychological, it's something inside them wants to be free, isn't it? I don't really know what to think. What can I think about this – the lads have never really done it – I suppose I should object if it was anything of importance. To do it pur-

posely, I think there's something wrong there, you know, I don't think they should do it deliberately. [Father:] They want talking to, to find out what's . . . what's the cause of it. [This is how you'd deal with it?] [Mother:] You would, you see, it would be deep.

Turf accountant's wife:
I wouldn't like it. I would think there's something wrong in the family, wouldn't you? I should think you'd need a doctor's advice – unless it's really temper, and then you've got to stamp that out.

Research chemist's wife:
I think I'd be a bit bothered . . . um . . . I'd rather they had things like sand and water and the usual things that help them to work this sort of thing out. I'd go out and buy seven pounds of clay; and if it was a book she'd torn up, I'd be *very* unhappy – I would think it was a red light if she did that.

Table 60 shows the proportions of children who are generally destructive, compared with those who merely enjoy smashing or breaking expendable objects; both are small minority groups, and 76% of children are not destructive in either way. In relation to sex and social class, the comparison is interesting. Despite the fact that so few children (11% overall) are generally destructive, sex and class trends are equally clear-cut: boys are more likely to be destructive than girls, and children are more likely to be destructive as we descend the social scale. Thus, to take extremes, Class v boys are twelve times as likely as middle-class girls to be rated destructive. In terms of destructiveness with expendables, the class difference disappears and the sex difference is reduced.

Because the seven-year-old spends a large part of his day at school, where temper tantrums are considered by others and by himself to be inappropriate, there is less time actually available than at four for the display of rage; on the other hand, if a tantrum is typically an explosion of pent-up emotion, one might possibly expect the constraints of school to ferment tantrums, to be released on the child's return home. Certainly it does work this way for a few children.

Departmental manager's wife:
The back door opens, from school, and you hear the *lot* in about three seconds flat. One thing on top of another – you've got to

sort it all out: everybody at school ought to be in prison – the headmaster is this and somebody else is that. If something has gone wrong at school, it's all in one go, it comes out in anger, always in anger – cap goes from one end of the kitchen to the other, something else on the floor, and then it COMES OUT – literally it *has* to. I suppose it's a good job it does.

Table 60 *Children's destructiveness*

	social class					summary		
	I&II	IIIwc	III man	IV	V	I&II, IIIwc	IIIman, IV,V	overall popn.
	%	%	%	%	%	%	%	%
Generally destructive (inc. own toys)								
boys	4	16	12	26	35	9	17	15
girls	3	2	5	12	15	3	8	6
both	4	9	8	19	25	6	12	11

Significance: trend ↗ ****   m.class/w.class *
between sexes ****

	I&II	IIIwc	III man	IV	V	I&II, IIIwc	IIIman, IV,V	overall popn.
Likes smashing expendables only								
boys	18	18	15	11	11	18	14	15
girls	8	10	13	3	13	9	11	10
both	13	14	14	7	12	13	12	13

Significance: trend n.s.   m.class/w.class n.s.
between sexes p = 0·09

However, the development of self-control is in fact gaining ground, and children who have frequent tantrums (one or more per week) are fewer: a reduction from 36% at four to 22% at seven. Also the descriptions suggest that many of the tantrums themselves are less overwhelming at this age: 'She stamps every step up the stairs and slam goes the bedroom door'; 'He'll bang off and slam off and go and stand somewhere in a corner'. Stamping and slamming fading into the distance, even with an abusive accompaniment, create less of a disturbance than screaming and kicking on the floor. Social class differences are low and are also inconsistent: Class I and II have the fewest children showing frequent tantrums

(17%) and Class iiiwc the most (28%). Sex differences are also non-significant overall, though in the middle class boys are more prone to frequent rages than girls (29% compared with 16%). At the other extreme of behaviour, children who have tantrums less than once a month or never are in fact the majority group at 57%, and again class and sex differences do not reach significance.

Table 61 shows the scoring system for the index of temperamental aggression, and Table 62 analyses these scores in relation to sex and social class. As before, the sample was divided as nearly as possible into three equal groups, defining these as high scorers (5 or more points) low scorers (2 or fewer points) and intermediates.

Unlike the first two indices we have looked at in this chapter – amenability and emotional stability – temperamental aggression is strongly associated with the child's social class and sex. The wide and consistent divergence between girls and boys, showing that boys

Table 61   *An index of temperamental aggression*

Based on		Mother's reply	Score
Q15	Indoor child or outdoor child?	Outdoor	1
		Indoor or both	0
Q25 coded with Q191	Careful with toys, or get broken quickly? Does he get a kick out of smashing something up?	Generally destructive	2
		Expendables only	1
		Neither	0
Q43	Lot of fighting – quarrels come to blows?	Often fights	2
		Sometimes	1
		Hardly ever or never	0
Q46	What sort of games does he play with other children?	'Rough and tumble' 1st choice	2
		'Rough and tumble' 2nd choice	1
		'Rough and tumble' 3rd choice	0
Q164	What effect does smacking have on N?	'Don't care' attitude	2
		Merely dislikes	1
		Emotionally upset	0
Q193	Does N ever get into a real rage? How often?	1 or more per week	2
		1 per month, less than 1 p.w.	1
		Less than 1 per month	0

Maximum possible score: 11
Actual score range: 0–10
Mean score approx. 4

Table 62 *High and low scorers on the index of temperamental aggression*

	social class					summary		
	I&II	IIIwc	III man	IV	V	I&II, IIIwc	IIIman, IV,V	overall popn.
	%	%	%	%	%	%	%	%
High scorers (5 or more)								
boys	22	38	33	52	53	30	39	37
girls	14	12	28	27	28	13	28	24
both	18	25	31	40	40	21	34	30

Significance: trend ↗ ****   m.class/w.class ***
between sexes ****

	I&II	IIIwc	III man	IV	V	I&II, IIIwc	IIIman, IV,V	overall popn.
Low scorers (2 or less)								
boys	35	26	17	12	14	30	16	20
girls	60	47	36	39	33	54	37	41
both	47	36	27	26	24	42	26	30

Significance: trend ↘ ****   m.class/w.class ****
between sexes ****

display more aggressive behaviour than girls, is perhaps not unexpected. A marked increase in aggressive behaviour as we move down the social class scale might also have been anticipated as a culturally determined personality trait, given a social milieu which, as we have seen at both four and seven, expects a child to play out at an earlier age and fend for himself against other children, and offers him less practice in the verbal settling of quarrels and a more extended model of physical aggression and authoritarian dominance. By contrast, as we move up the social scale, children are exposed to socialisation pressures tending to emphasise talking out rather than fighting out, following indoor educational and constructive pursuits rather than following the gang, and generally inhibiting overt aggression or at least cloaking it in a democratic guise.

Analysis of variance confirms these emphatic class and sex differences; no significant difference is found between large and small families when children are compared class by class, nor does residential district appear to be a factor independent of class.

'*We keep saying it's a sort of passing phase, but unfortunately the phase is not passing . . .*'

Looking now at these three indices together – amenability, emotional stability and temperamental aggression – there seem to be certain differences in the *kind* of dimension which they define. In the first place, there is the chicken-or-egg question: has the child always been like this, at least to some extent, or has his upbringing imposed the pattern upon him? The class/sex differences in the data on temperamental aggression suggest at least a strong environmental influence on this dimension; the lack of class differences in amenability and of both class and sex differences in emotional stability does not, of course, prove that such characteristics are wholly innately determined, but it does suggest strong predispositions here in the child which are not easily shaped or manipulated by external cultural forces. It would, of course, be somewhat difficult to trace aggressive elements back to babyhood, since this kind of behaviour is less available to the small baby: [12] the irritable, highly strung baby is easier to identify, however, as are amenable babies, and here it will be possible to trace children's personalities back over time, as well as forward into adolescence. Because we *are* moving forward with these children, we have chosen not to look at data longitudinally until we have a fifteen-year perspective; thus the indices of temperament which have been devised on the information gained at seven serve more as an indication of future possibilities for analysis than for a final analysis in themselves.

In the second place, there is a difference in the point of focus for these dimensions. Although all of them can be gauged and illustrated largely in terms of the child's social relationships, emotional stability or lack of it seems to be especially closely centred in the child himself, and even temperamental aggression can be expressed in terms of attitudes to things, to the world, and to life in general, rather than as a personal interchange. In contrast, amenability is all about how the child reacts to the chief socialising influence in his life, his parents, and in particular to the demands of his mother. From this point of view, it seems useful at this stage to bring together the three dimensions to see how they relate to each other.

Table 63 shows the proportions in which aggressiveness and emotional stability combined, and expresses these combinations in terms of how amenable the children were thought to be by their mothers. In each dimension, one extreme is used against the rest of the dimension: i.e. in the dimension of emotional stability we are looking at the 31% most 'highly strung' children against the children of average and above average emotional stability; in that of temperamental aggression, we are looking at the 30% most aggressive children compared with the average and non-aggressive children; and in each case we have stated what proportion of the group is judged 'non-amenable' (scoring 4 or less on the amenability index).

Table 63 *'Amenability' scores of 'highly strung' and 'aggressive' children*

	Highly-strung children	Not specially highly-strung children	Both groups together
Aggressive children	(N = 69) 48% are considered unamenable	(N = 148) 39% are considered unamenable	(N = 217) 42% are considered unamenable
Not specially aggressive children	(N = 144) 28% are considered unamenable	(N = 335) 18% are considered unamenable	(N = 479) 21% are considered unamenable
Both groups together	(N = 213) 34% are considered unamenable	(N = 483) 25% are considered unamenable	*All children* (N = 696) 28% are considered unamenable

Note. In this table, proportions given are based on the actual cases and not on a notional randomised sample.

On the basis of categories defined in the way described, there is no evidence to suggest that children who are highly strung are any more or less likely than other children to be aggressive. Forty-eight per cent of all children are neither aggressive nor highly strung, and of these only 18% are considered unamenable. Children who are aggressive but not highly strung and children who are highly strung but not aggressive appear in the population in almost precisely equal numbers (21% each); either characteristic appears to contribute to parental problems of socialisation, but more strongly so where aggression is concerned: 39% of 'aggressive only' children are considered unamenable, compared with 28% of those who are highly strung but not aggressive. However, if it is difficult to cope with a highly strung child and still more difficult to cope with an aggressive child, what about the child who is both highly strung *and* aggressive: who is anxious and tense as well as forceful and easily angered? One in ten of all our seven-year-olds is this kind of child, and 48% of them are considered definitely unamenable.

Analysis of variance confirms that the differences in amenability between highly strung and not so highly strung children and between aggressive and less aggressive children are highly significant (both ****). The analysis shows that these two effects are of comparable magnitude and operate independently in relation to amenability in the population as a whole (i.e. there is no significant interaction effect), but that the two effects are additive.

If we now bring into the analysis two indices of mothers' attitudes – 'acceptance of the punishment principle' (Table 45, p. 332) and 'reliance on corporal punishment' (Table 42, p. 327), we find that there is no relationship between either of these and the dimension of emotional stability. By contrast, however, the mothers whose children are temperamentally aggressive are both more likely to rely on corporal punishment and more inclined to use punishment generally; and this relationship holds independent of social class (temperamental aggression : reliance on corporal punishment $r = +0.38$ **; temperamental aggression : acceptance of punishment principle $r = +0.27$ **). This does not, of course, tell us whether the mothers are more punitive because their children are more difficult to control or whether the children become more aggressive because their mothers are more punitive. The association could even be explained in terms of an inherited trait of aggressiveness shared by mother and child!

Once again we would reiterate the caveat which we entered in our introductory chapter (pages 24–6) against the too facile reification of the concepts of temperament which we have been discussing here. Having constructed a statistical measure and given it a plausible label, psychologists tend to be too readily seduced into the belief that a more profound level of understanding has been achieved. When one goes further and begins to consider statistical relationships between hypothetical constructs, the opportunities for self-deception are greatly increased, together with the opportunities for impressing the less mathematically sophisticated with data that has been manipulated out of the domain of reality. We would put on record here and now that the further we go from what mothers actually said in the face-to-face situation, the less confident we are in our interpretations.

NOTES

1 Comparatively recently this begins to be recognised as a vital factor in relation to handicapped children, and specifically to autistic children: too recently, however, to save a generation of autistic children's parents from the ambivalence of an accusatory psychiatric stance.

2 'Touchy' is a better word than 'tricky' for what we were trying to get at. 'Tricky' to some suggests an element of cunning, and we substituted 'touchy' at the next stage of interviewing.

3 See earlier descriptions: Oliver, p. 254; Richard, p. 41. See also quotations at four, J. and E. Newson, 1968: Oliver, p. 219; Richard, p. 325 (Pelican edn. pp. 231 and 346).

4 The non-linear trend is not reflected in the reverse of this category ('enjoys new situations'), where there is a consistent upward class trend significant at 0·001.

5 A similar preponderance of girls was found by the Isle of Wight study (M. Rutter, J. Tizard, and K. Whitmore: *Education, Health and Behaviour*, Longman, London, 1970): interesting, in that mothers tend to deal with it in terms of appeals to vanity, the offer of manicure sets and varnishing of nails, which one might expect to be more successful with girls.

6 In practice very few children had six such habits, and none had more.

7 Table 1, p. 71.

8 Table 21, p. 197.

9 Table 16, p. 144.

10 Table 39, p. 320.

11 Thirty-three per cent of mothers overall express tolerance of some degree of destructive behaviour, and there is no difference in their attitude associated with whether or not they have experienced it in their own child. Class I and II mothers are significantly (****) more tolerant than the rest of the class scale.

12 —or possibly simply less easy to identify as such. Psychoanalytic writers have been very ready to talk in terms of anger in babies (and indeed in foetuses); but how far is this a kind of adultomorphism, ascribing to babies the emotive connotation that the same behaviour would have in adults? The description of infantile passionate love as sexual derives, we would suggest, from a rather similar conceptual confusion: but that is another story.

Chapter 12

Towards an Understanding of the Parental Role[1]

Every so often, we are asked by someone with a taste for the didactic why we do not end our books with a kind of recipe section on how to be a good parent. One could, no doubt, go on in an uplifting way for a long time describing the ideal parental role – what parents ought to be to their children, the benefits that should rightly flow from parent to child – and one would no doubt invoke the rather vague, yet still valid, concepts of love, security, respect for individuality, intellectual stimulus and so on. Alternatively, one might focus upon the problems that we all know to exist: the parents who by any standards must be considered inadequate, and who, perhaps defensively, adopt a fatalistic, don't-care attitude; those whose nurturing role seems to have gone sour on them; and articulate parents who find it an impossible and traumatic task to reconcile their respect for the child's rights with the need to impose reasonable social restraints.

In fact it is highly typical of the parental role in modern society that parents themselves, as well as professional workers in the field, should be so aware of a gap between the ideal and the reality. Indeed, the shortfall is partly created by the very process of delineating the complexities and subtleties of the child's needs, which thus heightens the demands that are made upon parents. It was comparatively simple for a parent to satisfy society's demands when the emphasis was upon hygiene and affectionate firmness, and when the parental ethic included the dictum that mother knew best; it is much more difficult when parents are asked to recognise the child's emotional and egotistical needs as valid while still giving him a moral framework of principles – and, moreover, to present the whole in a democratic context which acknowledges that mother might *not* know best.[2] To quote Johnson and Medinnus on the modern mother: 'Her feelings of inadequacy are matched only by her undying efforts'.[3] On top of this, parents are expected to derive a relaxed enjoyment from their dealings with their children: in Martha Wolfenstein's phrase, 'Fun has become not only permissible but *required*'.[4]

We are professionally and by inclination observers of the contemporary scene (although participant observers, by virtue of our own parenthood); we do not comfortably take up the advisory posture, nor are we political activists primarily bent upon change and improvement – though obviously one hopes that one's observations will point the need for change where it exists. Thus we make no apology if we neither describe our own picture of the ideal parent nor offer panaceas for the problems of parenthood. Rather, we will end this book with some not altogether random comments on the parental role in the upbringing of young children as it is shaped by the day-to-day conditions of contemporary family and community life.

In this society (and indeed it cannot be otherwise where the family exists as the basic child-rearing unit), it goes without saying that the first function of the parents' role is to bear responsibility for the children they produce. The biggest criticism that we can make of parents as parents is to say that they do not care about their children, and to assume that they are not interested in the child's upbringing. In fact this criticism is too often made hastily about so-called inadequate parents without justification, in that not being able to cope with one's responsibilities is not at all the same thing as not accepting them. In our experience, parents of every social stratum and every level of adequacy have in common the basic knowledge that, because they have produced this child from their own bodies, society requires them to see the job through, and judges them accordingly: almost without exception, parents accept this while the child is young, even if they also know that they themselves are poor practitioners of parenthood. (As the child grows older, the parents' sense of responsibility diminishes in direct proportion to the perceived influence of other people over the child: so that the child who is early subject to the influence of the street peer group, for instance, is likely to induce an earlier sense of fatalism in his parents as to how far they are any longer capable of affecting his development for good or ill. But that is another story, and one which we shall certainly come to when the children reach eleven.)

The responsibility which society enjoins on parents for their young children is quite different from that which it expects from teachers, nurses and other professionals. For one thing, it has no fixed hours. It is a truism to say that parents of pre-school children never go off duty; but it is also true, in terms of responsibility, for the parents of older children. If a child behaves badly in school, it is the parents who will naturally be blamed, not the teacher. Nor is this just a question of naughty or anti-social behaviour; if the child is unhappy, or shy, or over-assertive, or too passive, or lacks confidence, the first suspects are the parents who must have made him that way. And if by chance the child's behaviour is different at home, and unsatisfactory only at school, parents far too often are met with polite disbelief rather than an interest in why this should be.

Parents are in fact chronically on the defensive over their parental role because the responsibility laid on them is not only limitless but also supremely personal. Our children are a walking testimonial or advertisement for the sort of people we are – doubly so, since they advertise both their heredity and their environment – and this is fine so long as they are feeling in a social and civilised mood and ready to do us credit. Young children do not always choose the most discreet times for testing their parents' strength, however, and parents are particularly vulnerable to situations which bring the child-rearing process under public scrutiny, as it were. This can be seen in all sorts of ways. At the four-year-old stage, for instance, we were struck by the repeated use of the phrase 'She shows me up' or 'He lets me down' by mothers discussing many kinds of behaviour, from table-manners to tantrums, which might take place outside the home. Again, at the same age we found a stepping-up of the socialisation process aimed at fitting the child for a more public world, and this stemmed from a quite conscious anxiety: if he can't button his coat/blow his nose neatly/ speak up and answer politely/get on with other children, what will his teacher think of *me*? And at all ages in childhood, in an ongoing and more specific study of incidents of conflict between mother and child, we are finding a complication and exacerbation of the mother's feelings wherever an onlooker is involved.

This last example refers specifically to mothers, and it must be observed that (even in this age of vastly increased involvement of fathers), where young children are concerned mothers remain more vulnerable to social criticism. This is not just because women are more sensitive to social pressures anyway; in the end, criticism of the upbringing of a young child is still primarily aimed at the mother. If the children are aggressive, mother will be blamed by the neighbours for not controlling them better; if they are namby-pamby (or mardy, as they say in Nottingham, meaning spoilt and grizzly), it is her fault for being over-protective; if they are scruffy and unkempt, again mother will be found guilty, even if both parents have equally demanding jobs. Fathers are not expected to take public responsibility for either the behaviour or the appearance of very young children, and blame will be transferred to the mother even where father has voluntarily accepted the major involvement; more often, the mother's heavier day-to-day responsibility is all too real – as a labourer's wife said bitterly to her husband, 'You get your coat and you're off on your own, but if I get *my* coat, there's five of us going!'

Parents' awareness of personal responsibility is very closely linked to their emotional relationship with the child. This again is especially clear in the mother, particularly during the first year of life. We tend to think of the parental role as a flow of activity from parent to child, and to forget that the child himself is both a 'behaver' and an instigator of behaviour in others from his very earliest weeks. The baby with severe colic, for instance, who will not be comforted, may arouse in his mother feelings of anger and inadequacy for her failure in her basic mothering role of comforter – feelings that themselves shock and bewilder her: young mothers are often ill prepared for the violence of their own feelings, which stems from the threat to their own sense of worth from the very person who could make them feel most needed, and in a situation which is finally inescapable because of their unique responsibility for carrying it through. As the child grows older, parents continue to marvel at his ability to 'get under their skin' and arouse their emotions in incidents of minor conflict which they could face with equanimity were anyone else's child involved.

Again one can usefully compare the teacher's role. The relation-ship between parent and child often becomes violent and stormy *because* it is so deep; but it also contains tender intimacies and loving closeness which enable the child to use and build upon the conflicts in a constructive and lasting way. The child's relationship with his teacher, on the contrary, even at the infant school stage, is less intimate, more formal and much less permanent. A good parent–child relationship is in fact very unlike a good teacher–child relationship; yet because the roles have certain *ingredients* in common, though in different proportions (nurturance, discipline, information-giving, for example), they are sometimes confused by the participants themselves, to the misunderstanding of all concerned. The child's more emotive displays of egotistic wilfulness offer a case in point. Few children throw temper tantrums when in conflict with their teacher, because unbridled rage is essentially (as in adults) an emotion one inflicts only on one's nearest and dearest; but four-, five- and six-year-olds do sometimes have temper tantrums in conflict with their mother or father *in the presence of* a teacher, nurse or some other adult. If the mother anxiously tries to calm the child (because he is 'showing her up'), she may have little effect; whereupon the teacher may suggest that the mother leaves it to her – 'he'll be all right when you've gone'. Mother leaves, and the child recovers very quickly – not because the teacher has magic powers of calming him, but because it is no longer appropriate for him to have a tantrum in this less intimate company. But teacher feels that she is efficient where mother is inadequate, mother knows that teacher thinks she is inadequate, and the lines of communication about their different roles become more firmly blocked . . .

Because their relationship with the child is both intimate and permanent, parents can afford to show a degree of flexibility and indeed inconsistency which more formal educative relationships cannot. It is often suggested that parents ought to strive after consistency at all times: fortunately most are human enough to fail in this unnatural aim. For it must surely be within the circle of the family that the child must learn to adjust to and cope with living among other people in all their inconsistency and moodiness. In as much as we want our own children to learn sensitivity to the immediate needs of others, we think it important for them to respond understandingly to the snappiness of either of us on a bad day, or to their father's or mother's occasional abstractedness, and thus we do not feel constrained to show a consistent parental amiability at all times; and we try equally to be sympathetic to their moods, though sometimes we fail (hopefully, not both on the same day). Moodiness, understanding and failure to understand are all a part of the ordinary human condition, and the parents' role is to present and interpret these things to the child within a permanent loving relationship which offers plenty of time for mistakes to be made and to be forgiven on both sides.

The whole process of socialisation – the integration of the child into the social world – is the cornerstone of the parental role. Later on, the child will learn from other children, other parents, adults with more specialised roles towards him; but in the early years it is the parents' task to mediate cultural expectations and beliefs and to ease him out of the total egocentricity of babyhood into modes of behaviour which will be acceptable in a wider world. The parental role as socialiser is much subtler than this might imply, however. In teaching the child the inner controls which are expected of him, parents also modify their expectations to suit the individuality of the child, and in all sorts of ways make it clear to him that the standards which prevail in the world outside can be relaxed a little to meet his private needs within the family circle. In a sense, parents strike a bargain with their children that, in return for 'socialised' behaviour outside, a sanctuary will be preserved within the home in which the child can revert to his more uncontrolled and primitive self. Thus the parents at once uphold a dual role: as advocates of society's demands, and as defenders of the child against those same demands once he is in the privacy of his family.

Numerous examples of this can be found in early upbringing, over and above the displays of rage which have already been mentioned, and which are usually simply ignored if they take place privately. In many, many families, for instance, infantile behaviour such as comfort-sucking of bottles and dummies goes on in private long after the mother has made the child understand that this indulgence is not for the public eye. Similarly, we have seen that between four and seven children are allowed to 'play' with truth and falsehood in the form of fantasy within the home when it is considered both inappropriate and risky to stray from the exact truth outside the family. Even when the child is spending a high proportion of his day in an outside environment, the family remains the place where he knows it is permissible to behave in a less inhibited way than is expected elsewhere. One example at seven is that the cultural pressure for girls to do much less physical fighting than boys, upheld where fighting outside the family is concerned, is relaxed in the privacy of the home; so that feminine aggression, while not approved, is not entirely forbidden.[5] The seven-year-old's own view of the home as the place for more dependent and clinging behaviour has been illustrated by the children who reserve both their 'little weeps' and their kisses and cuddles for its privacy.[6]

In offering this small degree of escape from the pressures of socialisation, parents show themselves to be more aware of the child's individual needs than society as a whole can ever be. Another very significant way in which they do this is by acceding to the child's more idiosyncratic foibles and whims for no better reason than that he has these whims and the parents know of their existence and accept his evaluation of them as important. For instance, we saw at four that one child in three both demanded *and was accorded* a regular bedtime ritual which parents followed exactly every night without fail:

> Half an hour's love, then we have to jump her up every stair, then she sits on the toilet and Teddy sits on the shelf, and we have to wind him up and he sings to her, you see, while she's on the toilet; then we have to hop her into the bedroom on one foot, then she says her prayers, then she jumps into bed. Then we have to give her three kisses and one squeeze, then "God bless you", and she's off to sleep. That's what she does *every* night, it's always the same.

The bedtime ritual is only the most common example of idiosyncrasies which parents quite habitually take into account in their everyday dealings with their young children: some children like their shoelaces tied in a particular order, others have rituals about how an orange or an apple is prepared for their eating, others again set enormous store by sitting in a particular position at table or sharing in a special way in some regular activity of a parent (father's shaving, for instance).

That parents are in a unique position both to know about such idiosyncrasies and to indulge them must be of enormous importance in the development of a child's personality. By knowing about them, they establish the child as an individual; by recognising his need through their indulgence, they help to build up in him that sense of worth which is essential for a well-adjusted personality. Just because the child is so small in relation to those about him, and because he has to spend so much of his time learning to subordinate his own desires to cultural demands, his parents' willingness to concede him some small arena of individual power is of irreplaceable value.

In a not dissimilar way, the child is dependent on his parents' role as a memory bank to which he can continually refer for evidence of himself as an individual with a history. One of the means by which the ordinary child achieves a sense of personal identity is through his store of memories going back into his own past, in which he himself and his close family play central roles; but it must be remembered that the child does not maintain this store of memories on his own, but has them repaired, added to and embroidered upon in everyday conversation with his own family, the sharers of his memories. Most mothers know that, right up to adolescence, children love to hear stories of their own doings; 'tell me about things I once did', Little Bear's request to his mother,[7] is the classic request of every child. But in fact the invitation is not necessary, for the greater part of mothers' conversation with other mothers, with the children listening in, tends to be concerned with the past doings of children and family. In addition, the minutiae of family jokes and comment also tend to set the child in a long-term family context: 'Red hair and bad temper, just like my Aunt Ethel'; 'funny you don't like cheese now, you used to love it when you were little'; 'she was born at dinner-time, and she's been hungry ever since'; 'Billy never had a dummy, but Jane kept hers till she went to school'; 'that's the ornament Granny brought back from Scarborough the year before last' – and so on. Even the comment '*that* happened before you were born', which so many children find annoying, places the child firmly in a personal perspective. Remarks like these occur over and over again in the child's family experience, establishing him as a person with a past that others know about and make real by their sharing of it. In contrast, the child who is deprived of parents may in fact have *no single person* who shares his own most basic and important memories, no one to confirm whether these memories are in fact correct or figments of his imagination, no one to polish up a fading memory before it is too late. Parents' intimate knowledge of their child over the years plays a part in the shaping of his self-image which can hardly be adequately supplied by any other means.

What all this adds up to is a concept of parents as a uniquely caring force in the child's development. Parents have an involvement with their own child which nobody else can simulate. In this lies both their strength and their vulnerability. The crucial characteristic of the parental role is its *partiality* for the individual child. This is why all the other caring agencies that we can devise can never be quite as satisfactory as the 'good-enough' parent (to use Winnicott's term). The best that community care can offer is impartiality – to be fair to every child in its care. But a developing personality needs more than that: it needs to know that to someone it matters more than other children; that someone will go to *un*-reasonable lengths, not just reasonable ones, for its sake. This is the parental role which may well be of the greatest importance of all; and this is the role which society is unlikely to replace successfully, in whatever directions it may develop.

If we stopped there, this chapter could be re-titled *In Praise of Parents*, and we could end with three cheers; but, although we believe that parents are irreplaceable, we are not totally optimistic about every aspect of the parental role. It is a major part of that role to mediate and interpret cultural expectations to the child; but cultural expectations, as the reader will have noticed, do not come in one big convenient package. They vary within the culture, so that parents in one social group are likely to pass on the attitudes of that social group, while parents in another will transmit a sub-cultural package that differs in various ways. An obvious example that we have hardly yet touched on is that attitudes to literacy vary so much from one social group to another that a child's progress through school is significantly predetermined before he even sets foot in the place.

The implications of systematic variation in the principles of child discipline held by different social groups, and in the means by which they try to enforce it, are no less important for being less obvious. Parents at the upper end of the social scale are more inclined *on principle* to use democratically based, highly verbal means of control, and this kind of discipline is likely to produce personalities who can both identify successfully with the system and use it to their own ends later on. At the bottom end of the scale, in the unskilled group, parents choose *on principle* to use a highly authoritarian, mainly non-verbal means of control, in which words are used more to threaten and bamboozle the child into obedience than to make him understand the rationale behind social behaviour: and this seems likely to result in a personality who can neither identify with nor beat the system. In short, privileged parents, by using the methods that they prefer, produce children who expect as of right to be privileged and who are very well equipped to realise those expectations; while deprived parents, *also by using the methods that they prefer*, will probably produce children who expect nothing and are not equipped to do anything about it. Thus the child born into the lowest social bracket has everything stacked against him *including his parents' principles of child upbringing*. Because we do not see how we can easily change principles which are honestly and firmly held, for this group of children we are pessimistic about the nature of the parental role. All we can hope is that studies such as ours do contribute little by little to a more critical self-awareness in society, and that this in itself will act as a small prod against social inertia.

NOTES

1 This chapter, in slightly different form, was originally presented as a paper to the Annual Conference of the National Children's Bureau, 1972.

2 A fuller discussion of the moralities which have informed didactic influences on parents will be found in J. and E. Newson, in M. P. M. Richards, 1974.

3 R. C. Johnson and G. R. Medinnus, *Child Psychology: Behaviour and Development*, Wiley, New York, 1965.

4 Martha Wolfenstein, 'Fun morality', in M. Mead and M. Wolfenstein, 1955.

5 See pages 197–8.

6 See pages 263–4, 280–1.

7 Else Minarik and Maurice Sendak, *Little Bear*, World's Work, Kingswood, Surrey, 1958.

Appendix I

The Interview

(*Note:* F in margin denotes a follow-up question tailor-made for the individual child)

UNIVERSITY OF NOTTINGHAM
CHILD DEVELOPMENT RESEARCH UNIT

District.....................................
Interviewer at 1:0.....................................
Interviewer at 4:0.....................................
Interviewer at 7:0.....................................

Date.....................................

GUIDED INTERVIEW SCHEDULE
(For mothers of children aged 7:0)

A. BACKGROUND

Child's full name...
Address ....
....
Date of birth............................ Sex: Boy/Girl
Family size and position (for each child in family, indicate sex and age; include foster children, marked F, and deceased children, marked D)

sex ....
age ....

MOTHER   Age............... Not working/working part-time/full-time
Occupation if at work...

1. Did you train for a job before you had children? (*details, including untrained jobs*)
   FATHER   Age............... Precise occupation...............................

2. Does he have to be away from home at all, except just during the day? *Home every night/up to 2 nights away p.w./3 nights + p.w./normally away/separation or divorce/dead/other*...............................

Shift work? YES/NO   What shifts? ....

3. Does any other adult live here now, apart from your husband and yourself?

    YES .... */NO*

    If YES: How does N get on with him/her? Are they good friends?

4. Has N ever been separated from you for more than a day or two since he was four? – has he been in hospital, for instance, or have you been in hospital since then? (*Details: age at separation, how long, etc.*)

B. GENERAL PERSONALITY

5. Well, now – it's three years since you last told us about N, and a child can change a lot in that time. How would you describe him now to someone who didn't know him at all?

6. Would you say he was a placid child, or rather temperamental? *Placid/varies/temperamental*

7. Do you find him easy to manage, now he's seven – or is he a bit tricky, do you have to feel your way with him? *Easy/varies/temperamental*

8. Is he the sort of child who usually agrees with what you want him to do, or does he tend to object to things quite a lot? *Agrees/varies/objects*

9. How does he manage in new situations? Does he enjoy them, or is he bothered by what he isn't used to? *Enjoys/varies/bothered*

10. What about new people? Is he shy? *Shy/varies/not shy at all*

11. In general, does he take things as they come, or is he a bit of a worrier? *As they come/varies/worrier*

12. Does he try very hard to understand things that puzzle him, or does he just let things pass over his head if they're difficult? *Tries/varies/let pass*

13. Is he happy to sit still so long as he has something to do, or is he one of those children who can't keep still for a minute? *Will sit/varies/can't sit still*

14. When he's on his own, is he a busy sort of child, or does he easily get bored? *Busy/varies/gets bored*

15. Would you call him an indoor child or an outdoor child? *In/both/out*

C. ACTIVITIES

16. We should like to know something now about what sort of things N likes doing when he's not at school. What about in the

morning? Does he have any time to himself between waking up and leaving for school? *YES/NO*
(*If any*): What does he usually do in that time? How does he amuse himself?

17. What about when he comes out of school in the afternoon? Do you fetch him usually? *YES/NO*
   (*If NO*): Does he come straight home, or does he play out or go somewhere else before coming home?
   Straight home first/plays out, unspecified/elsewhere.....................
   (*Prompt if necessary*): Do you have any rules about coming straight home? *YES/NO*
   Are you usually here when he gets back from school? (*If not, state arrangements made, if any*)

18. When he gets home, what does he do with his free time until bedtime?

19. Some children seem to spend a great deal of time doing one or two special things, like reading or drawing or making models. Has N a special hobby of this sort? (*specify*)

20. Has he any (other) special toy or game that takes up a lot of his time?

21. Has he anything he collects, or anything that he gradually adds to?
   (*e.g. Lego, dinkies, train set, doll's clothes, etc.*)
   (*If bought*): Does he spend his own money on this?
   YES/NO/not bought

22. (*If any siblings*): Some parents like children to have their own special toys, and some think that all the toys should belong to the whole family. How do you feel about that?
   Separate/communal/some of each

23. Do the children (does N) have a special place of their (his) own where they (he) can keep their (his) own things? (*specify*)
   (*If a general room, ask*): Do they keep things in their bedroom?
   YES/NO

24. Does N play there a lot?
   (*prompt if necessary*): Which room does he mostly play in?
   Child's play-space: sep. playroom/bed-playroom/special corner/ no special play-place

25. Is he careful with his toys, or do they seem to get broken rather quickly? *Careful/break/other*...................

26. Some children seem to enjoy pulling their toys to bits more than actually playing with them – is N like that? *Destructive/not*

27. Some children are careful with their toys when they are using them, but they leave them about carelessly so that they get broken that way. Does N do that? *YES/NO*

28. Do you take any trouble to get him to look after his toys?
Much/some/No

29. Do you expect him to keep them tidy himself, or do you reckon to tidy up after him?
Himself/M reckons to tidy/M expects but he doesn't/both do it'

30. Now that N is at school, does he have enough time to do all the things he wants to do at home?   *YES/NO*

31. What about days when there's no school? What does he do with his time mostly? (*Include those occupations which child has on any average weekend, and prompt 'inside?' or 'outside?' as necessary*)
Inside:
Outside:

32. ⎰ You've mentioned other children a few times;
    ⎱ You haven't mentioned other children very much;
which does N like best – playing with other children, or playing by himself?   *Others/alone/equally*

33. Who does he play with mostly?   *Sibs: often/sometimes/never*
                              Other: often/sometimes/never

34. Has he any special friends? – at school?
                               at home?

35. Does he see his friends in the weekend?   *YES/NO*
(*If NO*): Any particular reason?

36. Do they come and play at your house?   *Most weeks/sometimes/No*

37. Does he go to theirs?   *Most weeks/sometimes/No*

38. Are you happy about ⎰ his friendships ⎱ ? (*prompt for each*
                        ⎱ this friendship ⎰   *mentioned*)

39. Have you ever tried to discourage any friendship between N and another child?   *YES/NO*
(*If YES*): Any special reason?
(*If NO*): Do you think you would ever do this for any reason? (*specify reason*)

40. In general, how would you say N gets on with other children? Does he make friends easily?
YES/not very/some difficulty making friends

41. Does he stand up for himself, or does he let other children boss him around? *He's boss/give and take/child prefers to follow/wants to lead but fails*

42. How do you feel about quarrelling at this age? Do you think quarrelling *has* to happen between children? (*prompt if necessary: between sibs; others*)

Sibs: inevitable at 7/difficult to avoid, but possible/quite unnecessary
Others: inevitable at 7/difficult to avoid,but possible/quite unnecessary

43. Does he do a lot of fighting – do his quarrels often come to blows? (*prompt*) *Sibs: often/sometimes/little fighting*
    Others: often/sometimes/little fighting

44. Do you (would you) ever interfere in N's quarrels and arguments with other children outside the family?   *YES/NO*

45. Do you ever tell him what he should do in his quarrels, or help him to manage them in any way?   (*specify*)

D.   *FANTASY AND TENSION*

46. What sort of games does N mostly play with other children?
    (*Place in order of his preference; prompt all if necessary*)
    ....*Rough and tumble, climbing, kicking ball around*
    ....*Construction – building, making*
    ....*Imaginative games: role-playing, 'house', 'school', etc.*
    (*criterion is* plot)

47. Does he ever have play-acting games *when he's on his own* – either being someone himself or making up a story with dolls or toy animals or puppets?   *YES/NO*
    (*details*)

48. Does he mind you listening to these games, or does he stop when you come in?
    Likes audience/doesn't mind/prefers privacy/sometimes each

49. Does he ever make up stories for you about things that haven't actually happened?   *YES/NO*
    (*If YES*): Does he tell them as if they were true, or does he explain that this is a story?   *As true/as story*

F 50. *Fantasy* (*follow up for individual child*):

51. Has N any special fears or worries? (*specify*) *YES/NO*
    (*If YES*): Has he had that for a long time?   *Since.....................*
    Did he come and tell you about it, or could you see that he was afraid?

F 52. He used to be afraid of...when he was four.
    Is he still afraid of that?

53. Does he ever seem frightened at night?

54. Do you feel that you *know* about most of his thoughts and fears, or do you think there's quite a lot that he keeps to himself?

55. We're interested in the various odd habits that children seem to have at this age. Does N have any little habits you can think of? Does he bite his nails, for instance?   *YES/NO*

F 56. When he was four, he used to suck his thumb. Does he do that now at all?* *YES/NO*
(*If NO*): When did he stop doing that altogether?........................

F 57. Does he ever suck his dummy now?* *YES/NO*
(*If NO*): When did he finally give that up?.............................
Did you have to do anything about it, or did he just drop it himself?

F 58. Does he ever use his bottle now?* *YES/NO*
(*If NO*): When did he give that up finally?.............................
Did you have to do anything about it or did he give it up himself?

F 59. *Transitional object* (*follow up if child had transitional object at four*)

56A, 57A, 58A, 59A *(*If YES to any of the follow-ups above*)*: Have you tried to stop that, or are you quite happy to let him go on as long as he seems to want it?

60. What about the things children do when they're a bit strung-up? Does he ever clear his throat or swallow as a nervous habit?

61. Does he pull at his ears or mouth, or pick at his face?

62. Does he blink or screw his eyes up?

63. Does he ever stammer or stutter when he speaks?

64. Does he play with his private parts, as far as you know?

65. Is there anything else he does as a habit – when he's overtired or worried, perhaps?

66. (*If ANY HABITS*): Have you noticed whether he.....................
(*prompt back separately for each*) at any special sort of time, or when he's in a particular mood?

67. Have you tried to stop him..............................(*prompt back separately for each*), or are you just expecting him to grow out of it? (*If STOP*): How?

68. Does he ever have a headache or a temperature because he's anxious or excited? (*Prompt*): Is he ever actually sick out of excitement or worry?
(*If YES to either*); Have you tried to do anything about this?

F 69. I think he was still wetting his bed sometimes/quite often when he was four. Does he ever do that now? (*If NO, check*): Never at all? *YES/NO*
(*If NO*): How long is it since he last wetted his bed?.....................
Did you do anything to get him dry at night?
(*If YES*): About how often does he have a wet bed? *Most nights/ 1–3 nights p.w./less than once p.w./less than 1 per month*
Are you doing anything about it, or just waiting for him to grow out of it?

F 70. You said he sometimes had wet pants in the daytime when he was four. Does he ever do that now? *YES/NO*
(*If NO*): When did he get quite dry in the day?............................

F 71. *Soiling (follow up if applicable at four)*

72. A lot of children of this age have their own superstitions – things they must do or mustn't do in order to feel safe, like doing things in a special order, or not walking on the lines of the pavement. Has N any superstitions like that? (*specify*)
(*If YES, prompt for each*): Do you know where he got that from?
How long has he had it?
Does it seem very important to him?

73. Does he ever talk to you about magical things happening? (*details*)

F 74. When he was four, you said that at bedtime you always had to
....
Do you still do/say that? *YES/NO*
(*If YES*): Would he mind if you didn't one night?
(*If NO*): Do you do anything else of that sort at bedtime now? (*specify*)

F 75. Does he still take his............................to bed with him?
YES/NO
(*If NO*): Does he take anything else instead? (*specify*)

F 76. Does he take anything to bed with him now (instead of his dummy/bottle)?

E. *INDEPENDENCE*

77. Could you tell me now what sort of things N does on his own?
Does he ever go on a bus on his own?
Not at all/to school only/otherwise (specify)............................

78. Does he play or roam around in the street at all? *YES/NO*

79. Does he go to the shops on his own? *YES/NO*

80. Do you trust him now to cross busy roads on his own? *YES/NO*

81. Can you always find him when you want him?
Always/not always/often can't

82. Do you have any problem over his wandering off so that you don't know where he is?

83. Do you have any rules about telling you where he's going before he goes out? *Yes, firm/would like, but he doesn't/no rules*

84. Have you any rules about how far he can go on his own?
Yes, exact/yes, vague/ad hoc, he'd ask/no rules, up to him

85. Does he ever go to a park or recreation ground by himself?............

swimming bath alone?.................. pictures alone?..................
anywhere else?...................

86. Does he belong to any clubs or organisations like Cubs/Brownies
or a church club – anything like that? (*specify*)

87. Does he ever stay the night at someone else's house without you?
YES/NO   (*specify*)

88. Does he have any pocket money of his own? (*Prompt: Who gives,
how much, regular fixed sum(s)? Exclude school expenses and school
savings*)
Is there anyone else who gives him money fairly regularly?............

89. Does he usually spend his money at once, or does he save any of it?
Does he *have* to save any of it?   *Voluntary saving/compulsory/none*
Is there anything he has to spend it on (like fares or Sunday School
collections, etc.)? (*Specify*)
Do you buy him sweets, apart from any he buys with his pocket
money? *YES/NO*

90. If he wants extra money for something, do you give it to him? For
what sort of thing? *Freely, if can afford/no/only less than 6d/
only for............................*

91. Could he earn extra money from you or his Daddy if he wanted to?
YES/NO
(*If YES*): Does he ever? (*details*)

92. We'd like to know about the sort of jobs children do around the
house at this age. Is there any little job you expect N to do now
(without being paid)?
(*Prompt for each*): Is that something he does as a regular thing, or
just when he feels like it?
Suppose he's too busy doing something of his own one day – what
happens?

93. (*If younger sibs*):
Does N ever help you by looking after { his brother/sister?
{ the younger children?
Do you ever leave him in charge of them for a while?
Does he ever take them out with him? *Only under supervision/
alone in house for short time/away from house/in sole charge for
periods over an hour* (*ref. sibs aged..................*)

94. Has he any animals of his own? *YES............................/NO*
(*If NO*): Has the family any pets? *YES............................/NO*
Does he look after it/them at all, in the way of feeding and cleaning?
Is that his job, or just a thing he does sometimes?
Responsible/sometimes/NO

F. *SCHOOL AND INTELLECTUAL*

95. We should like to know something now about how N gets on at school. Does he like school?
    Very much/well enough/not much/strongly dislikes

96. Which school does he go to?...
    (*If M demurs, ask what type*) *Private/L.E.A./other*.................

97. Does he stay for dinner? *YES*.................*per week/NO*
    (*If YES*): Does he like that?
    (*If NO*): Is that because he doesn't want to?

98. Do you know what he enjoys most at school?

99. Do you know what he *doesn't* like?

100. Does he naturally come and tell you about school, or do you always have to ask him? *Loves telling/average/have to ask*
    (*If ASK*): Does he seem to dislike talking about school? *YES/NO*

101. Does he seem to get on well with his teacher? *YES/NO/so-so*

102. Has he changed his class teacher in the last twelve months? *YES/NO*
    (*If YES*): Did that upset him at all?

103. Does he ever complain about anything special at school? (*specify*)
    (*If YES*): What do you say to him about that?

104. Does he ever say he doesn't want to go to school today? *Often/ sometimes/never*

105. What do you do? *or* What do you think you would do if he did?

106. Does he ever pretend he's not well, so as to stay at home from school? *Often/sometimes/has tried, not in last 12 months/never yet*

107. What do you do? *or* What would you do if he did that?

108. (*If any reluctance to go to school*):
    Has he ever *refused* to go to school?
    Often/occasionally/not in last 12 months/never yet
    (*If YES at all*): Do you know why?
    What happened?

109. How do you feel about children's complaints of school? Do you think you should take them seriously?

110. Does he often take things to school to show his teacher?
    Often/occasionally/NO
    (*If YES*): What sort of things?

111. (*If child does take things*): Do you encourage him in that – would you suggest that he should take something if he didn't think of it?
    Encourages/no special encouragement/discourages

112. Does he ever come home and start doing something he's been shown at school? *YES/NO*

o

113. Does he ever ask you questions about something he's heard of in class? *YES/NO*
(*If YES*): What sort of things?

114. Apart from school, what sort of questions does he ask you and his Daddy? What interests him?

115. Can you always answer his questions? *YES/NO*
What do you do if you can't? *or* What would you do if you couldn't?

F 116. One question $\left\{\begin{array}{l}\text{you } \textit{didn't} \text{ want to answer}\\ \text{he hadn't yet asked}\end{array}\right\}$ when he was four was where babies come from.
Does N know about that now?

F 117. (*If YES*): Did *you* tell him, or somebody else? *specify*.................
How old was he?..................
(*If NO*): What age do you expect to tell him?..................

118. How good is N's reading? Can he read well enough to enjoy a book for its story? *YES/NO*

119. When he's reading a book to himself, does he say the words aloud or read silently? *Aloud/mouths/silent, no mouthing*

120. Have you tried to help him with his reading at all? In what way?

121. Does he $\left\{\begin{array}{l}\text{read}\\ \text{look at books}\end{array}\right\}$ much at home?

122. (*If he can read*): Does he ever read a book which has more story than pictures? *YES/NO*

123. Does he belong to a library? *YES/NO*

124. $\left\{\begin{array}{l}\text{Has he any books of his own?}\\ \text{Have the children any books of their own?}\end{array}\right.$
About how many?........................
(*Real books, not comics. Count total of probable interest to N*)

125. Do you get him any comic or magazine regularly? (*specify*)

126. Do you often read to him? About how often? (*Daddy counts, but specify*)

127. What sort of things do you read to him? (*If long books*): Can you tell me some of the books you've read to him which he specially liked?

128. Do you or his Daddy ever help him with other things, like sums or writing, or any other school work?

129. In general, would you say you're pleased with the school N goes to – I don't mean is it a good school, but does it suit N?

130. If he showed the ability, how far would you like him to go with his education?

131. Have you any ideas now about what you would like him to do when he's grown up?

132. Has N any ideas about that?

133. Do you pay for any extra lessons for N – music or dancing or anything else at all? (*specify, and how often*)
Does anybody give him any special lessons that you *don't* pay for?

134. Does he do any drawing or painting at home?
Most days/sometimes/not much

135. What happens to his drawings when he's finished them? (*prompt if necessary*): Do you ever keep any of them yourself?

136. Does he do any writing for his own pleasure? (*If YES*): What does he write?

137. Does he ever write letters to people?   *YES/NO*
(*If YES*): What sort of letters does he write – what about?
(*If 'thank-you' letters only specified*): Does he ever write any other letters?
None/'thank-you' or Santa Claus only/occasional others/many
(*If any*): Does he like writing letters, or do you have to go on at him to get them done?

138. Does anyone play a musical instrument in your family? (*any degree of skill counts – specify who and what*)
(*If YES*): Has N learned to play it at all?

139. Do you ever take him to the pictures? (*Daddy counts, but specify*)

140. Have you ever taken him to a theatre or a concert? (*specify*)

141. What about museums and art galleries – has he been to any with you or his Daddy? (*specify*)

142. Is there any other exhibition or show or anything like that which you've taken him to? (*Prompt if necessary*): Has he ever been to a zoo or a circus with you?

143. Does he ever go to a football match, or any other sporting event?

144. Does he ever go to a church service with you or his Daddy?
Regularly.................per month/sometimes/NO

145. Does he go to Sunday School?
Regularly/sometimes/used to, not now/NO

146. Do you ever talk to him about religion? *YES/NO*   (*specify*)
If NO: What do you tell him if he asks about that sort of thing?
(*Prompt if necessary*): Does he say prayers at home at all?
YES/NO

147. Is there any special interest which you and N share – something which you both follow together?

148. Is there anything which he and his Daddy are both specially interested in?

149. Would you say he is closer now to you or to his Daddy
Mother/father/equally

150. Does your husband like doing things with him?
YES/NO/sometimes
Does he give N a lot of attention?
Very high/average/not much/ignores

151. Is there any outing that N particularly enjoys? (*Prompt*): If you were planning a treat specially for N, what do you think he would choose to do?
About how often do you do that?

152. When you're deciding what to do during the holidays, does N have any say in what you choose?

G. DISCIPLINE, ETC.

153. Now that N is seven, what is it about him that gives you most pleasure?

154. Is he a child who shows a lot of affection? (*If not to mother, prompt whether to anyone, including animals if any, and specify*)

155. Do you ever give him a cuddle nowadays, or do you think he's too old for that now?
(*If too old*): Do you kiss him at all now?   *No kissing or cuddling/ formal kissing only/frequent informal hugs or cuddling*

156. What about disagreements? What sort of things make you get on each other's nerves now, you and N?

157. Do you find that N takes a long time over doing as you ask him?
Often/sometimes/usually quick

158. What do you do if he is being very slow over this sort of thing?

159. (*If not smack*): What happens if he simply refuses to do something you want him to do? (*or what would*..................?)

160. How do you feel about smacking children of this age?

161. Do you think parents should try to do without smacking altogether, or do you think smacking is a good way of training children?

162. In general, do you think smacking has good results with children of this age? (*specify*)

163. Any bad results?

164. What effect does smacking have on N? (*Prompt if necessary*): Does he behave better? For how long? Does it upset him?

165. What effect does it have on you? Do you feel relieved or upset in

any way, (or is it just a part of the routine?) (*Omit last part if M clearly doesn't smack routinely*)

166. How often does N in fact get smacked?
1 per day +/1 per week +/1 per month +/less

167. (*If any smacking*): Is it just with your hand, or do you use a slipper or a cane or anything like that?
(*If hand only, prompt*): Do you ever *threaten* to use something more? (*specify*)

168. Do you ever $\begin{cases} \text{take his trousers down} \\ \text{turn her skirt up} \end{cases}$ to smack him/her?
YES/NO

169. (*If any smacking*): Who smacks most, your husband or yourself? (*ref. to N*) *Mother/father/equal*
(*If any difference*): Is that because you disagree about smacking, or is it just that you are/he is more often there when it's needed?

170. What sort of thing is N most often smacked for?

171. Of course, there are lots of other ways of dealing with naughtiness, besides smacking; for instance:
Do you ever promise N a reward for being good?
YES/NO/special circumstances........................

172. Do you ever say that if he's naughty he can't have something he likes – icecream or television, something like that? *YES/NO*

173. Do you carry out a threat if you've warned him, or do you usually let it go? *Mostly carries out/sometimes does/lets it go*

174. (*If ch. has pocket money*): Do you ever keep back some of his pocket money? *YES/NO*

175. Do you ever send him out of the room or put him in a room by himself for a bit? *YES/NO*

176. Do you ever threaten him with someone else – his teacher or the doctor or a policeman – someone like that? *YES...............(/NO*
(*If YES*): What do you say?

177. Do you ever say he will make you ill if he behaves badly? *YES/NO*

178. Do you ever threaten to leave him or send him away from home? *YES/NO*
(*If YES*): What do you say?

179. Do you tell him you won't love him if he's naughty? *YES/NO*
(*If YES*): When do you say that?

180. Do you ever hold up another child as an example? What do you say?

(*Prompt either way if necessary*): What about the other way round? Do you ever say: 'Look how nicely so-and-so behaves!' *or* 'You don't want to be like so-and-so, do you?'
Positive example/negative example/both/neither

181. Is there anything else you say to him which stops him being naughty, or which makes him sorry when he *has* been naughty?

182. Is there any other punishment which you use, or threaten to use, with N?

183. Some parents find that rudeness and cheekiness are a problem at this age. Does that happen with N? *A lot/some/very little*

184. What do you do when he is rude to you? (*specify rudeness*)
Smack/other punishment/rebuke/nothing

185. Has he ever picked up any bad language? (*If YES*): Can you tell me what it was? What did you do?
(*If NO*): What do you think you should do when that happens?

186. Does he ever try to smack you, now he's seven?
Often/sometimes/never

187. What do you do? (What would you do?)
(*If disapproved*): Is that because you don't like him striking anyone, or because you don't like him being disrespectful to his mother?
Striking/disrespect/ignored anyway

188. Suppose he tells you he hasn't done something naughty, and you know quite well that he has. What do you do then?

189. If he tells you something, can you usually take his word for it, or does he make things up a bit?

190. Does he ever come and tell you he's been naughty, before you actually find out? *YES/NO*

191. Does he ever seem to get a kick out of smashing something up?
YES, destructive/only expendables/NO
How do you feel about children doing that sort of thing?

192. Sometimes it's quite easy for high-spirited children to get themselves into trouble with neighbours or school or the police. Has N ever got into that sort of trouble? (*specify*)
(*If YES*): What did you say to N about it?

193. Does N ever get into a real rage – shouting and stamping and banging doors? (*Prompt if necessary*): About how often does it happen? What usually starts it off?
Do you do anything about it?

194. Do you expect him to say he's sorry to you when he's been naughty or rude?

(*If YES*): Would you make him do that, even if he didn't want to?
Makes/wouldn't force

195. Do you ever say sorry to *him* for being cross with him?   *YES/NO*

196. Do you find that how strict you are depends a great deal on your own mood at the time?

197. When do you most approve of yourself – when you're being strict with N, or when you're being easy-going?
Strict/easy-going/other (*specify*)

198. I think everyone agrees that temperamentally some children are much easier than others. Compared with other children, would you say that N is very easy, or fairly easy, or fairly difficult, or very difficult?   *Very easy/fairly easy/fairly difficult/very difficult*

199. Are there any problems which you've had with N since he was four, which are now over? (*specify, including age and how coped with*)

200. Have you any problems with him now, which you hope to see your way through in the next year or two?

H. PROSPECT
201. One last question: suppose you think ahead a bit, to when N is about sixteen; do you look forward to that time, or do you think they're nicest when they're this sort of age?

HOUSING   *Modern detached/modern semi/Victorian detached/Victorian semi/Victorian terraced/terraced with bays/terraced without bays/ self-contained flat/rooms/council house on estate/council (not estate?/council flat/other........................*
Dirty?........................

Appendix II

Sampling

1 Constitution

Altogether 697 mothers were interviewed at the seven-year-old stage. Table 64 shows the actual composition of this sample as a function of sex and social class, with, for comparison, the number that would have been expected in a fully random (unstratified) sample of approximately the same size.

Table 64 *Class/sex composition of interviewed sample: compared with (bracketed) expected composition of unstratified sample*

	social class					summary		
	I&II	*IIIwc*	*III man*	*IV*	*V*	*I&II, IIIwc*	*IIIman, IV,V*	*Total*
	N	N	N	N	N	N	N	N
boys	69	58	105	81	57	127	243	370
	(49)	(45)	(175)	(52)	(27)	(94)	(254)	(348)
girls	65	49	99	75	39	114	213	327
	(49)	(45)	(175)	(52)	(27)	(94)	(254)	(348)
both	134	107	204	156	96	241	456	697
	(98)	(90)	(350)	(104)	(54)	(188)	(508)	(696)
	14%	13%	50%	15%	8%	27%	73%	100%

The discrepancies are partly intentional and partly due to adventitious factors to do with the way the sample was originally drawn and then augmented to replace losses from the four-year-old sample (see section on losses below). As in our previous studies, the avowed aim was to arrive at a stratified random sample using occupational social class as the basis for the stratification. The strategy was to include at least 100 cases in each of the numerically smaller class groups, and as can be seen we fell short of this objective only in as much as we finally saw only 96 families in Class v. The practical problem, both in choosing the sample originally and in making up for losses later, was that the records that we used for our sampling frame did not provide sufficiently accurate or up-to-date information about the father's occupation. In fact they could not have been expected to do so, since from time to time people change their jobs, and sometimes their occupational status in consequence. The final confirmation of occupational social class could therefore only be obtained at the time of the interview itself.

The information contained in Table 64 does, however, enable us to calculate corrected proportions for the sample as a whole and for various sub-groups (such as all the middle-class children) by adopting an appropriate weighting procedure. Given that $x\%$ of actual respondents answer 'No' to Question Y in specified proportions according to social class, this procedure yields an estimate of what proportions would answer 'No' in a non-stratified random sample. The weighting was undertaken routinely, and thus the data tables throughout include totals in terms of proportions to be expected in a non-stratified sample with equal numbers of boys and girls, as shown in brackets in Table 64.

A further consequence of using a stratified sample obtained in this way is that the tests of significance (using chi-squared) applied to the summary tables could not easily be based upon actual numbers of cases. Instead, therefore, the weighted proportions were referred to a slightly smaller notional sample comprising 600 cases distributed as in Table 65.

Table 65 *Breakdown of the notional sample of 600 cases used as a basis for calculating chi-squared in the summary tables*

(the numbers in brackets indicate the total numbers of children interviewed in fact)

	Middle class I&II, IIIwc	Working class IIIman, IV,V	Both
boys	100 (127)	200 (254)	300 (370)
girls	100 (114)	200 (213)	300 (327)
both sexes	200 (241)	400 (456)	600 (697)

The implication of adopting this procedure is that our conclusions concerning the statistical significances of differences in the summary tables err on the side of caution. Thus the middle class/working class differences and the overall sex differences, while correctly represented, tend to be judged slightly less significant than they would have been had we adopted a more sophisticated but less convenient computation procedure which took into account the full number of cases interviewed.

2 *Losses*

Of the 700 children whose mothers we interviewed at four years, we lost 83 cases in the follow-up at seven. This represents an overall loss rate of just under 12%. In Table 66 below, these losses are analysed as a function both of social class and of reason for loss.

Table 66   *Losses in sample between four years and seven years*

	I&II N	IIIwc N	IIIman N	IV N	V N	Total N
			social class			
Outright or implied refusal	6	4	12	14	12	48
Moved away and untraceable (or abroad)	6	2	1	2	1	12
Non-contact, death, protracted illness	2	5	10	5	1	23
Total:	14	11	23	21	14	83
As percentage of interviews attempted	11%	10%	10%	15%	14%	12%

It is clear that more than half the losses were due to refusal or to mothers failing to keep appointments or finding it inconvenient on so many repeated occasions that it seemed obvious that they did not wish to co-operate. At the same time, by no means all these refusals resulted from unco-operative attitudes on the mothers' part. Some were going through genuine family crises at the time, while others were finding their commitments very heavy (sometimes starting new jobs) which made it difficult to find time for a protracted interview during this particular period. Two children were diagnosed as severely handicapped between four and seven, and although the interviews took place, the questions were much less appropriate than they had been for these children at four, and the children were dropped from the sample. One child died, and another was very severely injured and therefore omitted.

Losses were fairly evenly spread across the class spectrum; there were slightly greater losses at the lower end of the scale, but hardly enough to produce any systematic bias in the sample as a whole. The reason for analysing losses must always be to trace any systematic distortion effects, and the losses shown would be unlikely to distort overall results in any very serious way.

References

ALCOTT, Louisa M., 1867. *Little Women.*

ARMITAGE, P., 1955. 'Tests for linear trends in proportions and frequencies', *Biometrics, 11.*

BARNES, Peter, 1974. 'Some factors associated with reading disability' (unpublished thesis), University of Nottingham Library.

BENEDICT, Ruth, 1935. *Patterns of Culture,* Routledge & Kegan Paul, London.

CANNING, Frances, 1974. 'The socialisation of the child in the fatherless family' (unpublished thesis), University of Nottingham Library.

CHILDREN'S EMPLOYMENT COMMISSION, 1843. *Second report of the Commissioners on Trades and Manufactures,* Irish University Press series of British Parliamentary Papers, facsimile reproduction, IUP, Shannon, 1968.

CROXEN, Mary, 1966. 'Social adjustment of children' (unpublished thesis), University of Nottingham Library.

DICKENS, Charles, 1839. *Nicholas Nickleby.*

DOLTO, Françoise, 1955. 'French and American children as seen by a French child analyst', in M. Mead and M. Wolfenstein, *Childhood in Contemporary Cultures,* University of Chicago Press.

ERIKSON, Erik, 1955. 'Sex differences in play construction of twelve-year-old children', in J. M. Tanner and B. Inhelder, *Discussions on Child Development,* vol. III, Tavistock, London.

FESSLER, Audrey, 1974. 'The development of linguistic skills in primary school children' (unpublished thesis), University of Nottingham Library.

FREUD, Anna, with DANN, Sophie, 1951. 'An experiment in group upbringing', in *Psychoanalytic Study of the Child,* VI, Imago, London.

GENERAL REGISTER OFFICE, 1968. *Classification of Occupations,* HMSO, London.

GIBBENS, T. C. N. and PRINCE, Joyce, 1963. 'Child victims of sex offences', paper published by the Institute for the Study and Treatment of Delinquency, London.

GIBBENS, T. C. N., 1972. Review of *The Case of Mary Bell, New Society,* vol. 22, no. 522.

GOULART, R., 1970. *The Assault on Childhood,* Gollancz, London.

GREGORY, Susan. *The Deaf Child and his Family,* George Allen & Unwin, in press.

HEWETT, Sheila, with NEWSON, J. and E., 1970. *The Family and the Handicapped Child,* Allen & Unwin, London.

HOGGART, Richard, 1957. *The Uses of Literacy*, Chatto & Windus, London.

HOWARTH, C. I., ROUTLEDGE, D. A. and REPETTO-WRIGHT, R., 1974. 'An analysis of road accidents involving child pedestrians', *Ergonomics*.

1975. 'The exposure of young children to accident risk as pedestrians', *Ergonomics*.

1975. 'A comparison of interviews and observation to obtain measures of children's exposure to risk as pedestrians', *Ergonomics*.

HURLOCK, E. B. and BURSTEIN, W., 1932. 'The imaginary playmate', *J. Genet. Psychol.*, *41*.

JACKSON, Brian, 1968. Review of Ronald Goldman, *Breakthrough*, *Guardian*, 20 December.

JOHNSON, R. C. and MEDINNUS, G. R., 1965. *Child Psychology: Behaviour and Development*, Wiley, New York.

KORNER, A., 1971. 'Individual differences at birth: implications for early experience and later development', *Amer. J. Orthopsychiat.*, *41* (4).

LEES, J. P. and NEWSON, John, 1954. 'Family or sibship position and some aspects of juvenile delinquency', *Br. J. Delinquency*, *5*.

MACCOBY, Eleanor (ed.), 1967. *The Development of Sex Differences*, Tavistock, London.

MCGREW, W. C., 1972. 'Aspects of social development in nursery school children with emphasis on introduction to the group', in N. Blurton Jones (ed.), *Ethological Studies of Child Behaviour*, Cambridge University Press.

MCKELLAR, Peter, 1965. 'Thinking, remembering and imagining', in J. G. Howells (ed.), *Modern Perspectives in Child Psychiatry*, Oliver & Boyd, London.

MEAD, G. H., 1934. *Mind, Self and Society*, University of Chicago Press.

MEAD, Margaret, 1928. *Coming of Age in Samoa*, Penguin Books, Harmondsworth.

MEYER, J. W. and SOBIESZEK, B. I., 1972. 'Effect of a child's sex on adult interpretations of its behaviour', *Devel. Psychol.*, *6*.

MINARIK, Else H. and SENDAK, Maurice, 1958. *Little Bear*, World's Work, Kingswood, Surrey.

NEWSON, John and Elizabeth, 1963. *Infant Care in an Urban Community*, Allen & Unwin, London (published by Penguin Books as *Patterns of Infant Care in an Urban Community*.)

1966. Notes to exhibition, *The Innocent Eye*, British Association for the Advancement of Science Annual Meeting, Nottingham.

1968. *Four Years Old in an Urban Community*, Allen & Unwin, London.

1972. *The Innocent Eye*, illustrated audiotape, Medical Recording Service Foundation.

1974. 'Cultural aspects of child rearing in the English-speaking world', in M. P. M. Richards (ed.), *The Integration of a Child into a Social World*, Cambridge University Press.

1976. 'Parental roles and social context', in Marten Shipman (ed.), *The Organisation and Impact of Social Research: six original case studies in education and behavioural science*, Routledge & Kegan Paul, London.

NEWSON, John and Elizabeth, and BARNES, Peter, 1974. 'Longitudinal studies of children', in D. Pidgeon and D. Allen, *Measurement in Education*, BBC Publications, London.

in press. *Perspectives on School at Seven Years Old*, Allen & Unwin, London.

OPIE, Iona and Peter, 1959. *The Lore and Language of Schoolchildren*, Oxford University Press.

1969. *Children's Games in Street and Playground*, Oxford U. Press.

PIAGET, Jean, 1948. *The Language and Thought of the Child*, Routledge & Kegan Paul, London.

1968. *Six Psychological Studies*, University of London Press.

RITTER, Paul, 1964. *Planning for Man and Motor*, Pergamon, London.

RUTTER, M., TIZARD, J. and WHITMORE, K., 1970. *Education, Health and Behaviour*, Longman, London.

SEARS, R. R., MACCOBY, E. and LEVIN, H., 1957. *Patterns of Child Rearing*, Row, Peterson & Co., New York.

SILLITOE, Alan, 1959. *The Loneliness of the Long-Distance Runner*, W. H. Allen, London.

SMITH, M., 1962. *Vocabulary in Young Children*, Iowa Studies in Child Welfare, Iowa.

SVENDSEN, M., 1934. 'Children's imaginary companions', *Arch. Neurol. and Psychiat., 32.*

TANNER, J. M., WHITEHOUSE, R. H. and TAKAISHI, M., 1966. 'Standards from birth to maturity for height, weight, height velocity and weight velocity: British children, 1965', *Arch. Dis. in Childhood, 41.*

TERMAN, L. and MERRILL, M. A., 1961. *Stanford-Binet Intelligence Scale*, 3rd revision, Harrap, London.

THOMPSON, Denys (ed.), 1972. *Children as Poets*, Heinemann, London.

VYGOTSKY, L. S., 1962. *Thought and Language*, Wiley, New York.

WINNICOTT, D. W., 1971. *Playing and Reality*, Tavistock, London.

WOLFENSTEIN, Martha, 1955. Introduction to section on 'Child-rearing literature', in M. Mead and M. Wolfenstein, *Childhood in Contemporary Cultures*, University of Chicago Press.

1955. 'Implications of insight – I', in Mead and Wolfenstein, *op. cit.*

1955. 'Fun morality', in Mead and Wolfenstein, *op. cit.*

WOOD, Heather, 1970. 'Problems in the development and home-care of pre-school blind children' (unpublished thesis), University of Nottingham Library.

WRIGHT, Derek, 1971. 'A sociological portrait: sex differences', in *New Society*, vol. 18, no. 474.

Index

Fantasy 140f, 403; group 141f; solitary 148f; mothers' attitudes to 160f
Fantasy companions 153–7
Farrington, C. 67n
Fatalism 217–19, 399
Father 263f, 327–9
Fear, *see* Anxiety
Fighting 50–3, 194–207, 403
Four-year-olds 29–31, 47, 89, 105, 148–9, 152–7, 205–6, 221, 257, 273, 287, 292n, 306, 363, 400
Freud, A. 190, 220n
Friction 296–8
Friendships 50, 177f, 384; classroom sociogram of 219n; control of by mother 207f

Games 117f
Gibbens, T. C. N. 66n, 103n
Goulart, R. 138
Grace, A. 27n
Grainger, R. D. 220–4
Gregory, S. 27n
Growth, physical 30

Habits: 'nervous' 380, 384–7; 'comfort' 384–5, 403
Hewett, S. 27n
Hidden behaviour 198–9
Hoggart, R. 244, 247, 253n
Housing 74
Howarth, C. I. 105n
Hurlock, E. B. 175n
Hypotheses 20

Identification, child's 54, 258–9, 264f, 406
Identity 291–2, 404–5
Independence, child's 47–9, 102, 259–62, 301, 365, *see also* Employment, Work
Indices 24–6, 396; of child's amenability 378–80, 394–6; of mother's acceptance of punishment principle, 331–5; of 'bamboozlement' 361–3; of chaperonage 99–102; of child-centredness 286–92; of child's emotional stability 380–7, 394–6; of father's participation 273–6; of mother's reliance on corporal

punishment 326–8; of child's temperamental aggression 392–6
Individual differences, *see* personality
'Indoor children' 70–4, 387
Intellectual skills 30–1, 62–4, 301
Intentions, parental 18–20, 314–19, 329–30
Interests, child's 107f, 301; shared with parents 259, 263f
Interviewing methodology 20, 145, 254, 270, 274–5, 292n, 304, 409f

Jackson, B. 244, 253n
Jealousy 189–91, 220n
Johnson, R. C. 399, 407n
Jokes 156–7, 169–70, 175n

Korner, A. 66n

Language, development of 31–2, 53–4, 148, 220n; in socialisation 340f, 382; 'bad language' 211, 333, 366–70
Leadership 191–4
Lees, J. P. 219n
Levin, H. 358, 360
Lies/truth 161f, 350, 403, *see also* 'Bamboozlement'
Life-styles 243–4, 251, 252n, 277, 371n
Longitudinal approach 20–1, 394
Love 254f, 370; withdrawal of 358–61
Loyalties, child's 54–5, 194

Maccoby, E. 104n, 220n, 358, 360
McGrew, W. C. 104n
McKellar, P. 162, 175n
Mead, G. H. 175n
Mead, M. 27n, 371n
Medinnus, G. R. 399, 407n
Meyer, J. W. 220n
Mobility: of child 49–50, 68f; social 371n
Models, *see* Examples
Mood-dependence, mother's 310–14, 333–4
Motivation, parental 19, 29, 329–30, 399–401